Get Programming with JavaScript

MAR 1 3 2017

D1573215

Get Programming
with JavaScript

JOHN R. LARSEN

MANNING

SHELTER ISLAND

For online information and ordering of this and other Manning books, please visit
www.manning.com. The publisher offers discounts on this book when ordered in quantity.
For more information, please contact

> Special Sales Department
> Manning Publications Co.
> 20 Baldwin Road
> PO Box 761
> Shelter Island, NY 11964
> Email: orders@manning.com

Manning Publications Co.
20 Baldwin Road
PO Box 761
Shelter Island, NY 11964

Development editor:	Helen Stergius
Technical development editors:	Chuck Henderson, Ozren Harlovic
Review editor:	Ozren Harlovic
Project editor:	Tiffany Taylor
Copyeditor:	Linda Recktenwald
Proofreaders:	Elizabeth Martin
	Bonnie Culverhouse
Technical proofreader:	Romin Irani
Typesetter:	Dennis Dalinnik
Cover designer:	Leslie Haimes

ISBN: 9781617293108
Printed in the United States of America
1 2 3 4 5 6 7 8 9 10 – EBM – 21 20 19 18 17 16

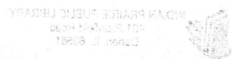

brief contents

v

contents

foreword

When John emailed me to ask if I would write a foreword for *Get Programming with JavaScript*, I have to admit the main thing that got me on the hook was that he had used JS Bin throughout the book to let readers try out live demos. JS Bin was created in 2008 as a place for programmers to collaborate, test, debug, experiment, and share. Education is close to JS Bin's heart, so John's background as a teacher and his practical approach seemed like a great fit with its ethos and purpose. I'm a firm believer that getting your hands dirty with real code is a great way to learn, and being encouraged to create, extend, play, and rewrite, all in a safe, no-mistakes-barred space, looked like a good idea for a beginners' programming book.

As the developer of JS Bin, an application created with JavaScript, I'm always excited to see JS Bin being used to teach beginners, and that's exactly what John does with this book. It goes without saying that different people in different contexts take different lengths of time to learn programming. But they all benefit from a practical approach. JS Bin, as a free resource requiring no installation, provides an instantly accessible environment in which to learn, and this book provides the guidance to get started, the support to keep practicing, and the encouragement to enjoy the adventure.

I remember seeing object dot notation well over 10 years ago and wondering how I was supposed to Google "What does . mean?" If I'd had John's gentle and thorough introduction to JavaScript back then, I would have saved myself a lot of pain wading through many failed search attempts! He doesn't cover everything, but he takes his time with key concepts, showing patience and consideration for readers and encouraging them to stretch their knowledge and build their skills. The variety of examples really helps; there's lots to get your teeth into, but also plenty of support and suggestions for further practice. Don't get lost in *The Crypt*—trust your guide. It builds into a substantial project and should help you see how little pieces can make big apps.

I've had the privilege of creating a number of tools for the programmer community, and a number of JavaScript tools in particular. Programming lets us make things for fun, for profit, and for others, and it's wonderful to welcome newcomers to the fold; who knows what great ideas they'll have as they build the next big thing (or the next small thing!)? I'm thrilled that their first steps on such an exciting path will be on JS Bin. Welcome! Create bins for your code, tinker, share, and build up your bank of modules. *Get Programming with JavaScript* shows you how to manage your code bins and combine them into bigger projects. (You even get to play with the HTML and CSS panels on JS Bin!)

Enjoy the book, dear reader. I expect that by the end of it, you'll have a firm grasp of how to write JavaScript.

REMY SHARP
FOUNDER OF JS BIN

preface

I started programming using the BASIC language on a Commodore VIC-20 in 1982. It had 3.5 KB of RAM, and programming involved me copying a program from a magazine, instruction by instruction and line by line. The process was time-consuming and error-prone, but it certainly built focus and attention to detail! Rather than cut-and-paste, it was read-and-type; but eventually, the program was transferred from the printed page to the computer's memory. Then the moment of truth ... and alas, it never worked the first time. And that's where my learning really began.

Staring at the code, trying to make sense of the instructions and follow the flow of the program as it jumped from line to line, I had to think carefully and patiently about what was going on. Not everything made sense—sometimes squeezing a program into 3.5 KB required some seriously supple code gymnastics—but, bit by bit, the program's secrets would start to reveal themselves. Sometimes my typos stopped the program from running; sometimes there were mistakes in the code itself. Most of the time, but not always, I eventually got the program to run.

Half the time, the program would turn out to be rubbish! I'd reach out and hit the VIC-20's off switch, and the program would be gone forever. (It took five minutes and a cassette-tape recorder to save, and some programs just weren't worth it.) I wasn't usually upset, and I didn't see it as a waste of time; from the start, I was amazed by the transformation of text into a working program (even a rubbish one) on the computer screen.

Today, in 2016, with our smartphones, tablets, drones, and AI Go champions, that sense of wonder has grown even stronger. Programming is magical and transformative.

Even knowing how it works, I still love how my typed instructions turn into a working website, a fun game, or a useful utility.

As a teacher in the United Kingdom, I'm privileged to be able to teach 16- and 17-year-olds programming. My philosophy is to let them get programming from lesson one: to enter code and see the result as soon as possible. I want them to be curious and experiment at all times. It's great to see their eyes widen and their smiles grow as they start their adventures in code and realize they can convert imagination into reality. Online code-editing environments such as JS Bin allow them to quickly try out ideas and build projects piece by piece. They don't learn a long list of language features before beginning; they learn a few concepts at a time, often in response to getting stuck but also directly from me (they don't know what they don't know), and they practice and experiment before moving on. Their skills build day by day and week by week, and code that might have seemed like cryptic hieroglyphs at the start of the course becomes second nature by the end. It's great to be a part of that learning process.

In addition to being a teacher, I'm also a programmer and develop education applications, including ones for organizing, sharing, and booking resources; creating online handbooks; planning lessons; managing timetables; and generating quizzes. It's great to see people using the applications as part of their day-to-day work; I'm lucky to understand the target audience, being one of them myself, and to see first-hand my applications used over an extended period—that's great feedback!

I've reviewed a number of book manuscripts for Manning. Having seen my bio describing me as a programmer and a teacher, Manning suggested that I write a book of my own. *Get Programming with JavaScript* is my attempt at translating my approach to teaching programming into book form. It's packed with code listings to get you thinking about the concepts as you progress, and there are plenty of exercises and supplementary materials online, as detailed shortly. I hope it fires your imagination and gets you started on your own programming adventures. Good luck, and have fun!

acknowledgments

Thank you to Robin de Jongh at Manning for suggesting I write a book and to my editor Helen Stergius for her patience, advice, and support throughout the writing process. Thanks also to all of the people who reviewed the book and provided excellent feedback to make it better, including Philip Arny, Dr. Markus Beckmann, Rocio Chongtay, Sonya Corcoran, Philip Cusack, Alvin Raj, Conor Redmond, Ivan Rubelj, Craig Sharkie, and Giselle Stidston; in particular, thanks to Ozren Harlovic, Chuck Henderson, Al Sherer, Brian Hanafee, and Romin Irani for their attention to detail, honest reactions, and constructive suggestions.

I'd also like to thank Remy Sharp, the creator of JS Bin, for responding to my questions and requests quickly and positively, for being kind enough to agree to write the foreword for this book, and for creating JS Bin!

Finally, I want to thank the people at Manning who made this book possible: publisher Marjan Bace and everyone on the editorial and production teams, including Janet Vail, Mary Piergies, Tiffany Taylor, Linda Recktenwald, Dennis Dalinnik, Elizabeth Martin, Bonnie Culverhouse, and many others who worked behind the scenes.

about this book

Get Programming with JavaScript is a book for beginners, for those with no programming experience. It makes extensive use of online code listings on the JS Bin website, a sandbox where you can experiment with the code and see the results instantly. There's no setup or installation required; if you've got internet access, you can just get programming straight away. If you don't have internet access, don't worry, the printed listings include helpful annotations, and all the ideas are explained in the text.

In addition to shorter examples to illustrate the concepts covered, there is an ongoing example—a text-based adventure game called *The Crypt*—that you build as you progress through the book.

Who should read this book

If you are happy working with computers, using a variety of applications, and saving and organizing your files but haven't written programs before and would like to learn how, then this book is for you. It doesn't try to cover all of JavaScript, or even all parts of JavaScript; it helps you to get programming with lots of practical examples and exercises that encourage you to think and explore. If you're already a programmer and are looking for a complete JavaScript reference, then move along. But if you want a patient introduction to the language, then it's worth sticking around; a strong understanding of the basics will make it much easier to access some of the other excellent books for programmers.

Roadmap

Get Programming with JavaScript has 21 printed chapters; an additional four chapters are available online only from the publisher's website at www.manning.com/books/get-programming-with-javascript. The book makes extensive use of code listings and exercises, with successive examples building on previous work. I recommend you read it in order, trying out the examples and exercises online and taking time to understand the ideas presented.

Part 1 covers some of the core concepts of programming with JavaScript. It sticks to using the text-based Console panel on JS Bin, letting you focus on the JavaScript and not worry about web pages and HTML:

- Chapter 1 looks at *programming* and programming with *JavaScript* in particular before introducing *JS Bin*, a website where you can get programming right away, and *The Crypt*, a text-based adventure game that you build as you progress through the book.

- Chapter 2 describes *variables*, a way of labeling and using values in your programs. Your variables can hold different types of values, like numbers or text, but their names must follow certain rules.

- In chapter 3 you learn how to group values into *objects*. Just like a first-aid kit can be passed around as a single object and its contents accessed only when needed, JavaScript objects can be treated as a single item and their properties accessed when required.

- *Functions* are central to JavaScript, helping you to organize your code and execute sets of instructions on-demand and multiple times. They are introduced over four chapters, chapters 4 to 7, so that you get a firm grasp of how to define them and use them, how to pass data to them and from them, and how they work beautifully with objects.

- Chapter 8 shows you how to create ordered lists, or *arrays*, of values. Whether they hold blog posts, calendar events, users, functions, or movie reviews, lists are very common in programming, and you learn how to create them and access, manipulate, and remove their items.

- Objects are at the heart of JavaScript, and programs often create many objects; a calendar could have thousands of events and an adventure game dozens of locations, for example. *Constructor functions* are a way of streamlining the creation of many similar objects, and chapter 9 investigates why they're useful and how you define them and use them.

- In chapter 10 you meet *square bracket notation*, an alternate method of accessing the values stored in JavaScript objects. Armed with this more flexible way of getting and setting object properties, you write some example programs that can cope with unpredictable values that may appear in external data or user input.

Having covered some key, core concepts in part 1, you learn how to better organize your code in part 2:

- Chapter 11 discusses the dangers of *global variables*, variables that can be seen throughout a program, and the benefits of *local variables*, variables defined inside functions. Along the way, you consider who might use your code and the difference between an *interface* and an *implementation*.

- If you want to find out about *conditions*, then chapter 12 is the place to go. Only executing code if a condition is met adds flexibility to your programs and lets you check input from users before using it.

- As your programs grow, it usually makes sense to organize the pieces that make them up into *modules*, separate files that can be combined and swapped to improve versatility, focus, portability, and maintainability. Chapter 13 considers ways of modularizing your code, including *namespaces* and the snappily titled *immediately invoked function expressions*.

- Having learned techniques for creating modules, in chapters 14, 15, and 16 you see three different roles that modules might play. *Models* help you work with data (calendar events, blog posts, or movie reviews, for example); *views* present that data to the user (as text, HTML, or a graph, for example); and *controllers* work with the models and views, responding to user actions and updating the models before passing them to the views for display.

Part 3 covers using JavaScript to update web pages and respond to user input via buttons, drop-down lists, and text boxes. It also introduces templates for displaying repetitive, dynamic data, and techniques for loading that data into an existing page:

- Chapter 17 has a brief introduction to *HyperText Markup Language* (HTML), a way of specifying the structure of your content in a web page (headings, paragraphs, or list items, for example) and of loading further resources like images, videos, scripts, and style sheets. It then shows how you can use JavaScript to access and update a page's content.

- In order to capture user input, you need to use HTML *controls*, like buttons, drop-down lists, and text boxes. Chapter 18 demonstrates how to set up code that can work with user input and that the program executes when a user clicks a button.

- *Templates* offer a way to design the presentation of data by using *placeholders*. In chapter 19 you learn how to include HTML templates in a page and replace their placeholders with data. You avoid the confusing mess of JavaScript, HTML, and data all mixed together and create a neat, clear way of populating a web page with nicely formatted information.

- Chapter 20 explains how to load further data into a web page by using `XMLHttpRequest` objects. Commonly referred to as *Ajax*, the techniques let you update parts of a page with fresh data in response to user actions, leading to more responsive applications.

- Chapter 21 wraps up everything in the printed book, discussing text editors and integrated development environments and how to organize your own files when creating projects away from JS Bin. It also suggests sources of further learning about JavaScript and wishes you well on your programming adventures.

Chapters 22–25 are available online only, at www.manning.com/books/get-programming-with-javascript. They're more advanced and cover programming on the server with Node.js and Express.js, polling the server with XHR, and real-time communication with Socket.IO.

About the code

This book contains many examples of source code both in numbered listings and in line with normal text. In both cases, source code is formatted in a `fixed-width font like this` to separate it from ordinary text. Sometimes code is also **in bold** to highlight code that has changed from previous steps in the chapter, such as when a new feature adds to an existing line of code.

In many cases, the original source code has been reformatted; we've added line breaks and reworked indentation to accommodate the available page space in the book. In rare cases, even this was not enough, and listings include line-continuation markers (↪). Additionally, comments in the source code have often been removed from the listings when the code is described in the text. Code annotations accompany many of the listings, highlighting important concepts.

Most of the code listings in the book include a link to the same code on the JS Bin website, where you can run the code and experiment with it. The code is also available on GitHub at https://github.com/jrlarsen/getprogramming and on the book's Manning.com page at www.manning.com/books/get-programming-with-javascript.

Other online resources

The book's website at www.room51.co.uk/books/getprogramming/index.html includes answers to many of the book's exercises as well as video tutorials, further articles and guides for learning JavaScript, and links to other resources on the Internet.

About the author

John Larsen is a mathematics and computing teacher with an interest in educational research. He has an MA in mathematics and an MSc in information technology. He started programming in 1982, writing simple programs for teaching mathematics in 1993, building websites in 2001, and developing data-driven web-based applications for education in 2006.

Author Online

Purchase of *Get Programming with JavaScript* includes free access to a private web forum run by Manning Publications where you can make comments about the book, ask technical questions, and receive help from the author and from other users. To access the forum and subscribe to it, point your web browser to www.manning.com/books/ get-programming-with-javascript. This page provides information on how to get on the forum once you are registered, what kind of help is available, and the rules of conduct on the forum.

Manning's commitment to our readers is to provide a venue where a meaningful dialog between individual readers and between readers and the author can take place. It is not a commitment to any specific amount of participation on the part of the author, whose contribution to the Author Online remains voluntary (and unpaid). We suggest you try asking the author some challenging questions lest his interest stray! The Author Online forum and the archives of previous discussions will be accessible from the publisher's website as long as the book is in print.

Part 1

Core concepts on the console

*G*et *Programming with JavaScript* starts by introducing the key concepts you use in every program. The ideas presented form the foundation for all the subsequent code you write. The discussion starts gently and takes its time, with plenty of examples. There is an overarching theme of organization, which runs throughout the book; you see how to store and retrieve values with variables, group values with objects and arrays, and group instructions with functions.

By the end of part 1, you'll have built a working version of an adventure game called *The Crypt*. Players will be able to explore a map of locations and move from room to room and tomb to tomb, collecting treasure. Chapter 1 sets the scene, introducing programming, JavaScript, and JS Bin, the online code environment in which your adventures take place. Let the games begin!

Programming, JavaScript, and JS Bin

This chapter covers

- Programming
- JavaScript
- JS Bin
- Our ongoing example: *The Crypt*

Get Programming with JavaScript is a practical introduction to programming. Through hands-on code samples coupled with carefully paced explanations, supporting video tutorials, and a variety of examples, this book will help you build knowledge and skills and get you on your way to coding expertise.

This chapter sets the scene with a brief overview of programming and programming with JavaScript and then an introduction to JS Bin, the online programming sandbox you'll be making full use of while you learn. Finally, you'll meet *The Crypt*, our ongoing context for the concepts covered in the book.

1.1 Programming

Programming is about giving the computer a series of instructions in a format it understands. Programs are everywhere, running Mars rovers, the Large Hadron Collider, engine management systems, financial markets, drones, phones, tablets,

3

TVs, and medical equipment. The power and versatility of programs are astonishing. Programs can be a few lines long or millions of lines long, with complex solutions built from simple building blocks.

Deep down in a computer's electronics is a land of binary, counters, registers, busses, and memory allocation. There are low-level programming languages that let us work in that land, known as machine code and assembly language. Luckily for us, high-level languages have been created that are much easier to read, follow, and use. We can write code that's almost understandable by anyone; here's some pretend code (pseudocode) that's close to what high-level languages allow:

```
increase score by 100
if score is greater than 5000 print "Congratulations! You win!"
otherwise load new level
```

Different languages set out how you might write such code; some use more symbols than others, some more natural words. Here's how it might look in JavaScript:

```
score = score + 100;
if (score > 5000) {
    alert("Congratulations! You win!");
} else {
    loadNewLevel();
}
```

The parentheses and curly braces and semicolons are all part of the language's *syntax*, its rules for setting out the code so it can be understood by the computer. The code you write will be automatically translated into low-level code for the computer to execute.

In the previous JavaScript snippet is the instruction `loadNewLevel();`, to load a new level in the game, presumably. Somewhere else in the program will be more code with instructions outlining, step-by-step, how to load a new level. Part of the art of programming is breaking larger programs into smaller pieces that perform specific jobs. The smaller pieces are then combined to fulfill the purpose of the main program.

There are many, many programming languages. Some you may have heard of are Java, C, PHP, Python, and Swift. Let's take a look at why you might choose JavaScript.

1.2   *JavaScript*

JavaScript is an incredibly popular programming language, mostly seen in web browsers but gaining popularity in other contexts. On web pages it adds interactivity, from simple animation effects to form validation to full-blown single-page applications. Servers—programs that make files, web pages, and other resources available on the internet—are now written using JavaScript with Node.js. Other programs can be scripted with JavaScript, like Photoshop and Minecraft, and some databases store JavaScript and let you query data with JavaScript. And as more and more network-enabled objects are added to the Internet of Things, JavaScript is becoming more popular for programming sensors, robots, drones, and Arduino-style electronics.

Learning to program gives you a great skill that's versatile, useful, stimulating, creative, fun, rewarding, and in demand. Learning to program with JavaScript puts one of the world's most widely used languages at your fingertips, letting you develop applications for all manner of uses, devices, platforms, and OSes.

1.3 *Learning by doing and thinking*

Learning follows thinking. The philosophy of *Get Programming with JavaScript* is that by experimenting with programs in an online sandbox, finding out firsthand what works and what doesn't, and by attempting challenges, you'll have to think carefully about the concepts in each chapter. That thinking will lead to understanding and learning.

The sandbox lets you run programs and get instant feedback. Sometimes the feedback will be unexpected and force you to question what you thought you knew. Some ideas may click into place quickly whereas others could take longer; careful consideration and further experimentation may be needed. Curiosity, commitment, and resilience are key attitudes when learning anything, and they'll certainly help you to be a better programmer.

That's not to say learning to program will be a chore! Far from it. Even after more than 30 years of programming, I still find the transformation of code into a useful and/or fun application to be almost magical. That lines of simple statements, when combined, can accomplish such a variety of outcomes is astonishing. And seeing others use something you've created to be more productive or more organized or just to have more fun is a privilege and a pleasure.

So be prepared for an adventure of discovery, and don't be disheartened if you find some concepts tricky at first. Take your time, do the exercises, and don't forget the resources on the *Get Programming with JavaScript* website; it has links to listings, solutions, videos, and further reading at www.room51.co.uk/books/getProgramming/index.html. Learning to program is worth the effort.

1.4 *JS Bin*

JavaScript is most commonly run by a web browser. The browser loads a web page from a server, and that page may include JavaScript code or a link to code the browser then fetches. The browser steps through the code, executing the instructions. For part 1 of *Get Programming with JavaScript*, you avoid the extra considerations of writing and loading web pages and linking to code files. You keep your focus on the JavaScript language itself. To do that, you make use of JS Bin, a free online service.

JS Bin is an online sandbox for developing and sharing web pages and JavaScript programs. All of the code listings in this book are available on JS Bin (www.jsbin.com) to give you hands-on practice with the code and to let you experiment and learn.

When you first visit the site, you'll see a header section with a picture of Dave the BinBot and some helpful links to get you started, as shown in figure 1.1. Feel free to explore, but don't be put off by any complicated information you might find. Once

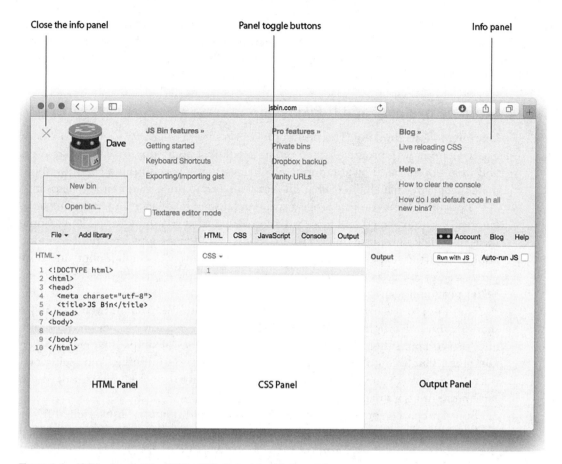

Figure 1.1   JS Bin showing the HTML, CSS, Output, and Info panels

you've finished exploring, close the header by clicking the X to the left of Dave. (You can close any welcome messages or other messages that JS Bin sometimes shows as well.)

1.4.1   JS Bin panels

JS Bin is a tool for developing web pages and applications. In addition to the Info panel at the top, it has five panels available for display: HTML, CSS, JavaScript, Console, and Output. Clicking a panel's name on the JS Bin toolbar toggles the panel on or off. In part 1 you work with just the JavaScript and Console panels, part 2 will use the HTML panel, and part 3 will add the CSS and Output panels. You'll be using only the JavaScript and Console panels to begin with, so toggle those two panels on and the others off; see figure 1.2.

HTML

HTML is used to structure the content of web pages. Text, images, video, and forms are examples of content.

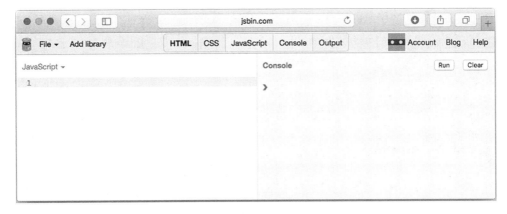

Figure 1.2   JS Bin showing the JavaScript and Console panels.

CSS

Cascading Style Sheets let you specify how your content should be presented. You can define background color, font details, margins, sizes, and so on.

JAVASCRIPT

JavaScript lets you add behavior and interactivity to your web pages. Or you can use it to write programs not in the context of a web page.

CONSOLE

The console can be used by a program to display information for users and developers. Warnings and errors about a program may be shown here. The console is interactive; you can type into it to find out about the state of a program. It's not normally used in finished applications, but you'll make good use of it as a quick and simple way of interacting with your programs as you learn.

OUTPUT

The Output panel shows a preview of the web page defined in the HTML, CSS, and JavaScript panels. It shows what a visitor to a page would normally see in a browser.

1.4.2   *Following the code listings on JS Bin*

You'll write programs by adding lines of code to the JavaScript panel on JS Bin. The programs will start simply and slowly increase in complexity as you cover more features of the language. For most of the code listings in part 1 of the book, you can test the code on JS Bin by following these steps:

1 Select New on the File menu on JS Bin.
2 Toggle the panels so that the JavaScript and Console panels are visible.
3 Enter code in the JavaScript panel.
4 Click Run.
5 Check the result on the Console panel.

1. Select New from the File menu   2. Toggle the JavaScript and Console panels   4. Click Run

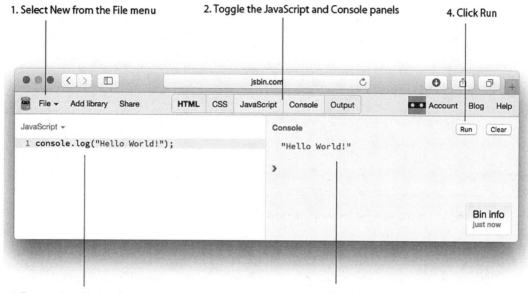

3. Enter code in the JavaScript panel   5. Check the result on the Console panel

Figure 1.3   The steps for running JavaScript on JS Bin

Figure 1.3 shows the steps on a screenshot from JS Bin.

Most of the listings in the book also have a link to the same code on JS Bin. The listings on JS Bin include extra information and exercises related to the code, discussed further in sections 1.4.4 and 1.4.5.

1.4.3   Logging to the console

At various points you want programs to output information by displaying it on the Console panel. To display information on the console, use the `console.log` command. Running the program in this listing displays the following on the console:

```
> Hello World!
```

> **Listing 1.1   Using `console.log` to display information**
> **(http://jsbin.com/mujepu/edit?js,console)**

```
console.log("Hello World!");
```

You place the message to be displayed between quotation marks, within the parentheses.

Notice that the listing title contains a JS Bin link. Click the link to see the live code on JS Bin. To execute the code in the JavaScript panel, click the Run button at the top of the Console panel. You'll see your message, "Hello World!", appear on the console.

Try clicking Run a few more times. Every time it's clicked, your code is executed and "Hello World!" is logged to the console. You can click Clear to clear all the messages from the console.

When following links to code on JS Bin, the program may run automatically. You can switch off auto-run in your preferences on JS Bin if you sign up for an account.

1.4.4 Code comments

Along with the code statements, the JS Bin listings for this book include *comments*, text that's not part of the program but is useful for explaining what the code does. Here's the first block comment from listing 1.1 on JS Bin:

```
/* Get Programming with JavaScript
 * Listing 1.1
 * Using console.log
 */
```

As well as block comments, which can span multiple lines, you'll sometimes see single-line comments:

```
// This is a single-line comment
```

On JS Bin, the comments are usually shown in green. Programmers add comments to their code if they feel it needs some explanation to be understood by other programmers. When a program is executed, the computer ignores the comments.

1.4.5 Further Adventures

Most code listings for *Get Programming with JavaScript* on JS Bin come with a small set of exercises, called *Further Adventures*, included as comments after the code. Some are easy, some are repetitive, and some are challenging. The best way to learn programming is to program, so I urge you to jump in and try the challenges. You can get help on the Manning Forums, and solutions to many of the tasks are given on the book's websites at www.manning.com/books/get-programming-with-javascript and www.room51.co.uk/books/getProgramming/index.html.

1.4.6 Error messages

As you add code to the JavaScript panel, JS Bin is continuously checking for errors. You'll see a red error section appear at the bottom of the JavaScript panel. Don't worry about it until you've finished adding a line of code. If the error section is still there, click it to see the error messages.

For example, try deleting the semicolon from the end of the line of code in listing 1.1. Figure 1.4 shows the error that JS Bin displays in response to the deleted semicolon.

Figure 1.4   The JS Bin error section (closed and then open)

The semicolon signals the end of a line of code. Each line of code, ending with a semi-colon, is called a *statement*. If you stop typing but the line does not end with a semico-lon, JS Bin will complain. The program may still run, and JavaScript will try to insert semicolons where it thinks they should go, but it's much better practice to put the semicolons in yourself; the errors in JS Bin are encouraging good practice.

JS Bin does its best to give error messages that help you fix any problems. Delete more characters, one by one, from the end of your line of code and watch as the error messages update.

1.4.7   *Line numbers*

The error message in figure 1.4 told you the line number where the error occurred. You had only one line of code, so the error was on line 1. Programs can get quite long, so it's helpful to have line numbers you can see. You don't add line numbers by hand; your text editor, in this case JS Bin, does that automatically. They're not part of the program; they help you while writing and testing the code. Figure 1.5 shows a longer program with a couple of errors. Don't worry about understanding the code for now, but see if you can spot the errors reported by JS Bin in the figure. Without the line numbers it would be much harder, especially if the program were longer.

To toggle the display of line numbers on JS Bin, double-click the word *JavaScript* at the top left of the JavaScript panel (see figure 1.5). A menu will open and close as you double-click, but the line numbers should switch from hidden to visible (or vice versa) as well. You can also switch on line numbers in your JS Bin profile, if you've registered.

1.4.8   *Get an account*

It's worth signing up for a free account on JS Bin. Your work will be saved and you'll be able to set a lot more preferences. As you start to write your own programs, it's a great place to try out your ideas and get immediate previews and feedback.

Double click to toggle line numbers

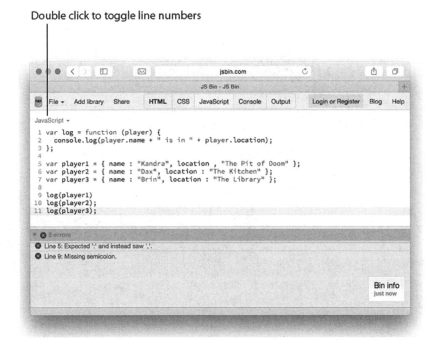

```
 1 var log = function (player) {
 2   console.log(player.name + " is in " + player.location);
 3 };
 4
 5 var player1 = { name : "Kandra", location , "The Pit of Doom" };
 6 var player2 = { name : "Dax", location : "The Kitchen" };
 7 var player3 = { name : "Brin", location : "The Library" };
 8
 9 log(player1)
10 log(player2);
11 log(player3);
```

Line 5: Expected ':' and instead saw ','.
Line 9: Missing semicolon.

Figure 1.5 Line numbers are helpful when finding errors.

1.5 The Crypt—our running example

Throughout the book, you're developing a text-based adventure game called *The Crypt*. Players will be able to explore locations on a map, moving from place to place, picking up items to help them solve challenges and get past obstacles. The last section of each chapter will use what you covered in the chapter to develop the game further. You're able to see how the programming concepts help you build the pieces that are then combined to produce a large program.

1.5.1 Playing The Crypt

The game will display a description of a player's current location along with any items that are found there and any exits, as shown in figure 1.6.

Players can type in commands to move from place to place, pick up items they discover, and use the items to overcome challenges.

You need to write code for all of the different elements within the game. But don't worry—you take it step by step, and I'll introduce what you need to know as you progress. You can play the game on JS Bin at http://output.jsbin.com/yapiyic.

The Crypt

The Kitchen

You are in a kitchen. There is a disturbing smell.

Items

a piece of cheese

Exits

south

west

east

north

Jahver

30

The Sword of Doom

holy water

*** A zombie sinks its teeth into your neck. ***

use holy water south   Make it so

Figure 1.6   Playing *The Crypt*

1.5.2   *Steps for building The Crypt*

In part 1, while learning some of the core concepts in JavaScript, you write code to represent the players and the places in the game and to let players move from place to place and pick up items they find. Figure 1.7 shows the components that you'll create for Players, Places, Maps, and the Game as a whole. Don't worry about all of the terms in the figure—you'll cover them in detail as you progress through the book.

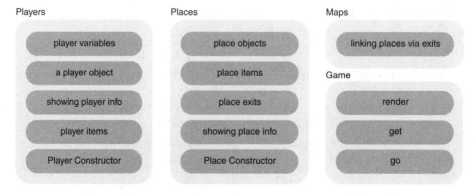

Players
- player variables
- a player object
- showing player info
- player items
- Player Constructor

Places
- place objects
- place items
- place exits
- showing place info
- Place Constructor

Maps
- linking places via exits

Game
- render
- get
- go

Figure 1.7   Game elements in *The Crypt* for part 1

A similar figure will be used in each chapter to highlight the ideas being discussed in the context of the whole game.

Both parts 1 and 2 will use the console on JS Bin to display game information and to accept input from users. Table 1.1 shows how the game elements correspond to the JavaScript being covered in part 1.

Table 1.1   Game elements and JavaScript in part 1 of *The Crypt*

Game element	Task	JavaScript	Chapter
Players	Deciding on the information we need to know about each player	Variables	Chapter 2
	Collecting player information in one place	Objects	Chapter 3
	Displaying information about players on the console	Functions	Chapters 4–7
	Creating a list of items collected by each player	Arrays	Chapter 8
	Organizing player creation code	Constructors	Chapter 9
Places	Creating lots of places to explore, all with a similar structure	Constructors	Chapter 9
	Joining places with exits	Square bracket notation	Chapter 10
Game	Adding simple functions for movement, collecting items, and displaying information	Square bracket notation	Chapter 10
Maps	Joining places with exits	Square bracket notation	Chapter 10

Part 2 adds challenges for players, blocking exits until the players use appropriate items to solve the puzzles. The programming focus is more about organizing your code, hiding how it works, checking user input, and building modules that you can reuse and swap to make the project more flexible.

Figure 1.8 shows how the game is split into modules for map data, constructors that you use to create players and places, views for displaying information on the console, and a controller for running the game and linking all of the pieces. Again, the figures are presented here to give a sense of what to expect and how the full game is

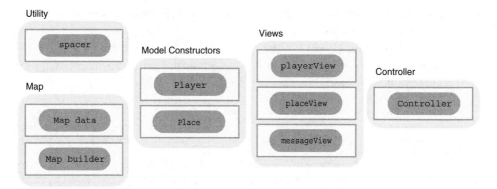

Figure 1.8 Game elements in *The Crypt* for part 2

made up of smaller building blocks—you're not expected to understand all of the terms at this point. You are allowed to be curious and excited! Each building block will be fully explained over the next 400 pages; take your time to explore the concepts and play with the code.

Part 3 updates the display to use HTML templates, modifies the game to load data while it's running, filling the templates with player and place information, and introduces text boxes and buttons so that players can enter commands via a web page (figure 1.9).

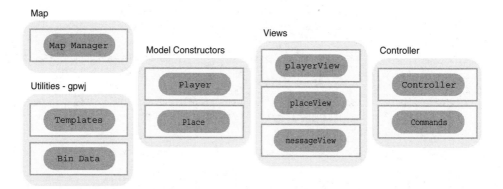

Figure 1.9 Game elements in *The Crypt* for part 3

Part 4, available online, shows how game data can be stored on a server using Node.js.

1.6   *Further examples and practice*

Although *The Crypt* is our ongoing context for learning JavaScript, each chapter includes other examples to show you concepts at work in a variety of situations. Some of the smaller examples will also be developed as you progress, letting you see how the new concepts help to improve the examples. In particular, you'll look at a quiz app, a fitness-tracking app, a movie ratings web page, and a news headlines page.

1.7 *Browser support*

Browsers are evolving all of the time. Some of the JavaScript listings in *Get Programming with JavaScript* may not work in older browsers (Internet Explorer 8 and earlier, for example). The discussions on the book's website will provide alternative methods to get code working for browsers that aren't happy with the main methods shown in the listings.

1.8 *Summary*

- Programs are sets of instructions for computers to follow.
- High-level languages let us write instructions that are easier to read and understand.
- JavaScript is one of the most widely used programming languages in the world. Associated most strongly with adding interactivity to web pages, it's also used in server-side programming, as a scripting language for applications, and as a way of programming robots and other devices.
- Learning follows from thinking. So, get involved in the practical examples in the book and be curious, committed, and resilient.
- JS Bin, an online code sandbox, will help you to focus on the JavaScript and give quick feedback as you experiment and practice.
- Our main running example is *The Crypt*. It gives you a context for learning programming concepts and for building a relatively complicated program from simple elements.
- Further examples will help you to gain depth through breadth and to appreciate how the concepts you learn are applied in a wider variety of situations.

Variables: storing data in your program

2

This chapter covers

- Storing and using information with variables
- Declaring variables
- Assigning values to variables
- Displaying variable values on the console

Get Programming with JavaScript has been written as a gentle introduction to programming. This chapter, then, is a gentle introduction to a gentle introduction. As far as adventures go, you hardly leave the house. You can think of it as the packing stage for your journey, vitally important—you don't want to get to the airport without your passport or to the Oscars without your selfie stick—but not the main event.

Almost without exception, programs store, manipulate, and display data. Whether you're writing a system for blogging, analyzing engine performance, predicting the weather, or sending a probe to land on a comet in 10 years' time, you need to consider the data you'll use and what kinds of values that data might take. To work with data in your programs, you use variables.

2.1   What is a variable?

A *variable* is a named value in your program. Whenever you use the name in the program, it's replaced with the value. You could create a variable called `score` and give it the value `100`. Then, if you tell the computer to "display the score," it will display `100`. Now, variables can change, hence the name, so later in the program, maybe in response to some action a player takes, you can update the score. If you add `50` to `score` and tell the computer to "display the score," it will now display `150`.

So how can you use JavaScript to make this magic happen?

2.2   Declaring variables and assigning values

Letting the computer know about information you'd like to store requires two steps:

1 You need to *set a name* you can use to refer to your data in the program, like *score* or *playerName* or *taxRate*.
2 You need to *link the name with the value* you want to store: something like *set score equal to 100* or *make 'George' the playerName* or *let the tax rate be 12%*.

In section 2.2.3, you'll see how both steps, giving a variable a name and giving it a value, can be completed in a single JavaScript statement. For now, you take things slowly and use a separate statement for each step.

2.2.1   Declaring variables

You've been dreaming of making it big with your design for the next mobile app craze, *The Fruitinator!* Players are sent back in time to splat fruit with their *Smoothie 9mm*, racking up record scores as they go. Your program needs to track those scores. That means setting up a variable.

Registering a name to represent a value is called *variable declaration*. You declare a variable by using the `var` keyword. The following listing shows the code statement needed to declare a variable called `score`.

> **Listing 2.1   Declaring a variable**
> **(http://jsbin.com/potazo/edit?js,console)**

```
var score;
```

The `var` keyword tells the computer to take the next word in the statement and turn it into a variable. Figure 2.1 annotates the code statement from listing 2.1.

The `var` keyword

```
var score;
```
End each statement with a semicolon

You choose the variable name

Figure 2.1   Declaring a variable

That's it! You've declared a variable called score ready for some splatted fruit action. It's the very first line of a fruit-based system that might just destroy humanity. Let's start scoring points.

2.2.2   Assigning values to variables

Your program now knows about the variable score. But how do you assign it a value? You use the humble equals symbol, =. (Actually, in JavaScript, it's not so humble. It turns up all over the place, performing a number of important jobs. A smooth operator.) Figure 2.2 illustrates the equals symbol at work, with listing 2.2 showing its use in context.

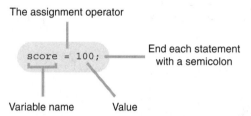

Figure 2.2   Assigning a value to a variable

Listing 2.2   Assigning a value to a variable (http://jsbin.com/yuvoju/edit?js,console)

```
var score;                    ⟵——  Declare a variable called score
score = 100;                  ⟵⏋ Assign the value 100 to score
```

You assign the variable score the value 100. In general, you assign the value on the right of the equals sign to the variable on the left of the equals sign (figure 2.3). When you use the equals sign to assign a value, JavaScript gives it a special name, the *assignment operator.*

You have declared a variable and assigned it a value. It's time to display it on the console. The output of the following listing should look something like this:

```
> 100
```

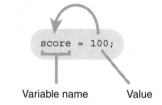

Figure 2.3   The equals sign is called the assignment operator.

Listing 2.3   Using a variable (http://jsbin.com/huvime/edit?js,console)

```
var score;
score = 100;
console.log(score);
```

Using the `console.log` function, introduced in chapter 1, you tell the computer to display the value of the `score` variable, whatever it happens to be. You've just assigned it a value of `100`, so that value appears on the console.

Why didn't you just print out `100` directly, using `console.log(100)`? Well, the values of variables usually change during the course of a program. By using a variable rather than a *literal* value, your programs can use current values, whatever they happen to be at the time. The next listing displays the value of `score` on the console, changes the value, and displays the new value, like this:

```
> 100
> 150
```

**Listing 2.4   Variables vary
(http://jsbin.com/jasafa/edit?js,console)**

```
var score;
score = 100;
console.log(score);

score = 150;
console.log(score);
```

You used the same instruction, `console.log(score)`, twice but the program printed two different values on the console. Your instruction used the variable `score`. Because its value had changed, so did the output.

You assigned the `score` variable numbers, `100` and then `150`, as values. Text is easy too; just wrap the text you want to assign in quotation marks. The next listing displays two messages on the console:

```
> Hello World!
> Congratulations! Your tweet has won a prize ...
```

**Listing 2.5   Assigning text to variables
(http://jsbin.com/hobiqo/edit?js,console)**

```
var message;
```
⟵ **Declare the message variable**

```
message = "Hello World!";
console.log(message);
```
⟵ **Assign the message variable a piece of text, using double quotation marks**

```
message = 'Congratulations! Your tweet has won a prize...';
console.log(message);
```
⟵ **Assign a new piece of text to message, using single quotation marks**

Programmers call sections of text *strings* because they're strings, or sequences, of characters. As you saw in listing 2.5, to denote a string you place the text inside quotation marks. The marks can be double, `"Hello World!"`, or single, `'Congratulations!'`, as long as they match. Without the quotation marks, JavaScript would try to interpret the text as instructions or variables.

2.2.3   One-step declaration and assignment

You've seen how to declare variables and then assign them values in two steps. It's also possible to declare a variable and assign it a value in a single statement, as illustrated in figure 2.4.

Declare a variable

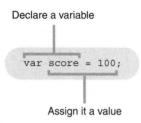

Assign it a value

Figure 2.4   You declare a variable and assign it a value in a single statement.

Listings 2.6 and 2.7 achieve exactly the same outcome, declaring variables and assigning them values before displaying the following message:

```
> Kandra is in The Dungeon of Doom
```

Listing 2.6   Declaring and assigning in two steps
(http://jsbin.com/vegoja/edit?js,console)

```
var playerName;
var locationName;

playerName = "Kandra";
locationName = "The Dungeon of Doom";

console.log(playerName + " is in " + locationName);
```
Use the + symbol to join strings

Listing 2.7   Declaring and assigning in one step
(http://jsbin.com/dorane/edit?js,console)

```
var playerName = "Kandra";
var locationName = "The Dungeon of Doom";

console.log(playerName + " is in " + locationName);
```
Declare a variable and assign a value to it in a single step

In listing 2.7, you assign the value on the right side of each equals symbol to the newly declared variable on the left. In both programs, you create the message displayed on the console by joining pieces of text using the addition symbol, +. Joining pieces of text is called *string concatenation* and + is the *string concatenation operator*.

If you know the value of a variable at the time you declare it, then this single-step approach can be a neat way of assigning the value to the variable. Sometimes, the value won't be known at the time of declaration; maybe some calculations need to be performed, user input is required, or you're waiting for a network response. In that case, declaration and assignment would be separate. It's common for programmers to declare their variables at the top of a program, even if they won't assign them values until later.

2.2.4 Using a variable in its own assignment

When you assign a value to a variable, JavaScript evaluates the *expression* to the right of the assignment operator and assigns the result to the variable.

```
var score;
score = 100 + 50;
```

JavaScript evaluates the expression, 100 + 50, and assigns the result, 150, to the variable score.

The values in the expression probably won't be hard-coded literals like 100 and 50; they're more likely to be variables. Here's an example, using the variables callOut-Charge, costPerHour, and numberOfHours, to calculate the total cost when hiring a plumber to do some work:

```
total = callOutCharge + costPerHour * numberOfHours;
```

The * symbol is used for multiplication; it is the *multiplication operator*. You can also use – for subtraction and / for division.

Because JavaScript evaluates the expression on the right first, before assigning its value to the variable on the left, you can even use the current value of a variable to set its new value. Say a player in your app sensation *The Fruitinator!* has just splatted a strawberry; that's 50 points! The player needs an update.

```
> Your score was 100
> Great splat!!!
> New score: 150
> Way to go!
```

Figure 2.5 shows a statement using the current score when assigning the updated score, and listing 2.8 is your score-updating program.

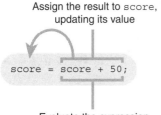

Assign the result to `score`,
updating its value

```
score = score + 50;
```

Evaluate the expression
using the current value of `score`

Figure 2.5 Updating a variable with the result of a calculation involving itself

Listing 2.8 Using a variable's current value to set its new value
(http://jsbin.com/kijuce/edit?js,console)

```
var score;
score = 100;
console.log("Your score was " + score);
```

```
console.log("Great splat!!!");
score = score + 50;                          Add 50 to the current score
console.log("New score: " + score);          and assign the result back
                                             to the score variable
console.log("Way to go!");
```

In the code, you evaluate the expression, score + 50, using the current value of score, 100, to give the result 150. This value, 150, is then assigned to score. Next up for *The Fruitinator!* … kumquats. Worth a cool 100 points! Kumquats are tricky. Never trust a kumquat.

2.3 *Choosing good variable names*

In all the code listings so far, there was nothing forcing you to give the variables the names you did. You tried to choose names that would help anyone reading the code understand the purpose of the variables. You almost have a free choice but must be careful not to tread on JavaScript's toes; there are names that JavaScript has set aside for its own use and further rules governing valid variable names.

2.3.1 *Keywords and reserved words*

JavaScript has a set of *keywords*, like var and function, that are part of the language itself and govern the actions and properties available in every program. It also sets aside some *reserved words* that may turn up as keywords in the language in the future. You can't use those keywords or reserved words as variable names. Other examples of keywords are if, switch, do, and yield, and a full list can be found on the Mozilla Developer Network (http://mng.bz/28d9). But don't take my word for it. Head over to JS Bin and try using one of those words as a variable name, as shown in figure 2.6.

Figure 2.6   JavaScript has some words that can't be used as variable names.

You don't have to learn the lists of keywords and reserved words; you'll pick up most of them as you do more programming, and they usually throw errors when you try to use them. But do bear them in mind if your program isn't working and you're not sure why.

2.3.2 *Rules for naming variables*

So now that keywords and reserved words are out, is everything else in? Not quite—there are a few further rules. Variable names can start with any letter, a dollar sign, $, or an underscore, _. Subsequent characters can be any of those or numbers. Spaces are not allowed. Listing 2.9 includes one block of valid names and one block of invalid names. If you visit the code on JS Bin, you'll see it reports a long list of errors. Take a look and try to make sense of them, but don't worry if you don't understand them all; the listing includes invalid names on purpose and JavaScript isn't happy about it.

> ### Listing 2.9 Valid and invalid variable names
> ### (http://jsbin.com/biqawu/edit?js,console)

```
var thisIsFine;
var $noProblemHere;
var _underscore56;          These variable
var StartWithCapital;       names are valid.
var z5;


var 999;
var 39Steps;                These variable
var &nope;                  names are not
var single words only;      allowed.
var yield;
```

JavaScript is case sensitive. Changing the case of characters in a variable name will give a different variable. score, Score, and SCORE are three different names. These differences can be hard to spot, so it's worth trying to be consistent, as discussed in the next section.

2.3.3 *camelCase*

You may have noticed the capitalization of letters in the variable names you've been using. Where names like costPerHour, playerName, and selfieStickActivated are made up of multiple words joined together, the first word is lowercase and the following words start with an uppercase character. This is called *camel casing* and is an extremely widespread convention that can help to make the names more readable.

Some programmers choose to separate words within variable names with underscores instead, like cost_per_hour, player_name, and selfie_stick_activated. How you name variables is up to you; it's part of your programming *style*. I'll be sticking with camel case throughout *Get Programming with JavaScript*.

2.3.4   Use descriptive variable names

Try to give your variables names that describe what they're for or what they do. You're free to choose the names but `costPerHour` is much easier to understand than `cph`. Other programmers may need to read and update your code in the future, and you'll thank yourself when you return to it at some point down the line. As your programs grow and involve more and more variables, objects, and functions, good variable names can really help you follow the flow of the program and understand its purpose. So keep those variable names simple, direct, and descriptive.

You've seen what variables are for, how to declare and assign them, and what makes for a good name. But how do you know what variables you need in a program? Analyzing the problem you're trying to solve and planning out a solution that fits your users is an important part of program design. In the next section, you take a little time to consider the information you need to represent the players in your ongoing example, *The Crypt*.

2.4   The Crypt—player variables

As discussed in chapter 1, *The Crypt* includes a number of elements: players, places, game, maps, and challenges. You need to consider the properties of all of those elements as you design and build the game. For now, you focus on the players, as shown in figure 2.7.

Figure 2.7   Elements in *The Crypt*

As players move from place to place, what does the program need to know to create fun and challenging adventures? You may want to keep track of names, health, items carried, or location. Or maybe hairiness of feet or color of lightsaber. Some of that information may stay the same during a game and some may change.

Part of the art of programming is *abstraction*, knowing what information to include and what to leave out. It might be that just how hairy a player's feet are has a role to play in the game, but it's likely to be more than you need to know. You should think carefully about what data you'll use as the player completes their quest.

Table 2.1 shows some possible properties that you may want to include when representing each player in your program.

Table 2.1 Possible player properties

Property	What's it for?	Example values
Name	Used when displaying player information and when interacting with other players.	`"Kandra"`, `"Dax"`
Health	Decreased by monsters and poison. Increased by food and potions.	`68`
Place	Where is the player on the map?	`"The Old Library"`
Hairiness of feet	A measure of how well the player copes in cold conditions, without boots.	`94`
Items	Keeping track of the items a player has picked up.	`"A rusty key"`, `"A purple potion"`, `"Cheese"`

You may well need other properties, and you can add and remove properties if necessary. Declaring player properties could go something like this:

```
var playerName = "Kandra";
var playerHealth = 50;
```

Part of a programmer's expertise is being able to model situations and predict which variables will be needed to complete a program. The more you get right ahead of time, the less chance there'll be a need for a big rewrite of your program—nobody wants that. Just as you don't want to realize you've forgotten your passport at the airport, you don't want to find you've overlooked a crucial part of a program when you've written lots of code.

2.5   *Summary*

- Variables let you store data for your program to use while it's running.
- Declare a variable by following the `var` keyword with a name:

  ```
  var costPerHour;
  ```

- Choose simple, descriptive names for your variables, avoiding JavaScript's keywords and reserved words.

- Assign values to variables with the assignment operator, the equals symbol =:

```
costPerHour = 40;
```

You assign the value on the right of the equals sign to the variable on the left.
- Use variables in expressions:

```
total = callOutCharge + costPerHour * numberOfHours;
```

- As part of the planning for your programs, consider what variables you'll need and what kinds of data they'll hold.

Objects: grouping your data

This chapter covers

- Organizing information with JavaScript objects
- Creating objects
- Adding properties to objects
- Accessing properties using dot notation
- Examples of objects

In chapter 2 you saw how to declare variables and assign them values, and you considered the variables you could use to model a player in *The Crypt*. As your programs grow, so does the number of variables you use; you need ways to organize all this data, to make your programs easier to understand and easier to update and add to in the future.

Sometimes it makes sense to group items and see them as a whole. Consider a first-aid kit; we happily treat it as a single item—"Have you packed the first-aid kit?" "Pass the first-aid kit." "We need the first-aid kit, *now!*"—but will quickly switch focus to its contents when the need arises—"Pass the antiseptic and the bandages from the first-aid kit, please." A number of items is neatly encapsulated by a single object.

This chapter introduces JavaScript objects, a simple and efficient way to collect variables together so that you can pass them around as a group rather than individually.

3.1 A need for organization

Your library of adventure stories is growing, and you decide to write a program to keep track of your precious collection. The following listing shows variables you use to generate this test output on the console:

```
> The Hobbit by J. R. R. Tolkien
```

**Listing 3.1 Using variables to represent a book
(http://jsbin.com/fucuxah/edit?js,console)**

```
var bookTitle;                              Declare the variables you'll
var bookAuthor;                             use in the program

bookTitle = "The Hobbit";                   Assign values to
bookAuthor = "J. R. R. Tolkien";            the variables

console.log(bookTitle + " by " + bookAuthor);    ◁──  Use the variables to display
                                                       information about the book
```

First, you declare two variables, bookTitle and bookAuthor, using the var keyword. You're going to use those two names to store and access values in the program. You then assign strings (text) to your freshly created variables. You wrap the strings in quotation marks so JavaScript doesn't try to interpret them as keywords or variable names. Finally, you log a message to the console. You build the message by using the concatenation operator (the + symbol) to join three strings.

It may be early days but you certainly have more than one book. How can you cope with the variables needed as you buy more? You could have a different prefix for each book. The next listing ups the number of books to three, printing these messages to the console:

```
> There are three books so far ...
> The Hobbit by J. R. R. Tolkien
> Northern Lights by Philip Pullman
> The Adventures of Tom Sawyer by Mark Twain
```

**Listing 3.2 Using prefixes to tell book variables apart
(http://jsbin.com/qowagi/edit?js,console)**

```
var book1Title = "The Hobbit";              Declare variables and assign
var book1Author = "J. R. R. Tolkien";       them values in one step

var book2Title = "Northern Lights";
var book2Author = "Philip Pullman";

var book3Title = "The Adventures of Tom Sawyer";
var book3Author = "Mark Twain";
```

```
console.log("There are three books so far...");
console.log(book1Title + " by " + book1Author);
console.log(book2Title + " by " + book2Author);
console.log(book3Title + " by " + book3Author);
```

This works up to a point. But as the number of books and the number of facts about each book increase, the number of variables is harder to manage. It would be helpful to be able to group all of the information about a book together, using a single variable.

3.2 *Creating objects*

In the same way as it is easier to ask for a first-aid kit rather than for the scissors, antiseptic, bandages, and sticking plasters separately, it can be easier to ask for `book1` rather than `book1Title`, `book1Author`, `book1ISBN`, and so on separately. JavaScript provides us with the ability to create *objects* to group variables. Very specific notation, or *syntax*, is used to define a new object. Let's look at a full example and then break it down into stages.

Listing 3.3 shows how to create a book as an object rather than as separate variables. Figure 3.1 shows the output on JS Bin when you log the `book` object to the console.

> **Listing 3.3   A book as an object**
> **(http://jsbin.com/ruruko/edit?js,console)**

```
var book;

book = {
    title : "The Hobbit",
    author : "J. R. R. Tolkien",
    published : 1937
};

console.log(book);
```

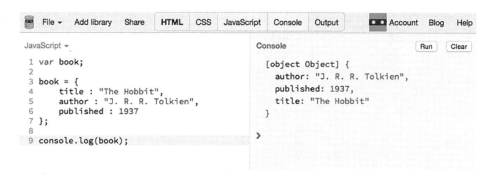

Figure 3.1   You log an object to the console on JS Bin.

When you run listing 3.3 on JS Bin, the console displays all the properties of your new book object, as well as telling you it's an object. Notice that it displays the properties in alphabetical order. The object itself doesn't order the properties; JS Bin has chosen an ordering purely for display.

Let's break down the object creation to get a clearer idea of what's going on and what all the different bits of notation represent.

3.2.1   Creating an empty object

In chapter 2 you saw that variables can be declared but not assigned a value until later in a program. You might have to wait for some user input or a response from a server or a reading from a sensor before you know the value you want to assign to the variable. In the same way, you can create an object with no properties, knowing that properties will be added at some point in the future.

To create an object, use curly braces, as in the following listing.

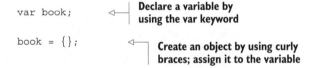

Listing 3.4   Creating an empty object
(http://jsbin.com/kaqatu/edit?js,console)

```
var book;        ⟵┤ Declare a variable by
                    using the var keyword

book = {};       ⟵┐ Create an object by using curly
                    braces; assign it to the variable
```

You create an empty object, one with no properties, and assign it to the variable book. It's not much use without any properties, and you'll see how to add new properties to an existing object in section 3.4. But how would you create your book object with properties in place?

3.2.2   Properties as key-value pairs

The book in listing 3.3 includes three properties: its title, its author, and its year of publication. The values of those properties are "The Hobbit", "J. R. R. Tolkien", and 1937. In a JavaScript object, the names of the properties are called *keys*. For book the keys are title, author, and published. When creating an object, you add a property by including its key and value, separated by a colon, between the curly braces. Figure 3.2 shows a property definition.

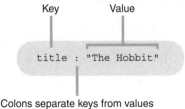

Key   Value

title : "The Hobbit"

Colons separate keys from values   **Figure 3.2 Set properties by using key-value pairs.**

Another name for a key-value pair is a name-value pair, but we'll stick with keys and values in this book.

In the next listing you create an object with a single property.

> **Listing 3.5 An object with a single property**
> **(http://jsbin.com/robupi/edit?js,console)**

```
var book;

book = {
    title : "The Hobbit"
};
```

You declare a variable and then create an object and assign it to the variable. The object has a single property. The key of the property is `title` and its value is `"The Hobbit"`. We usually simply say that the `title` property of `book` is `"The Hobbit"`.

Property values aren't restricted to number and string literals, like `50` or `"The Hobbit"`. You can also use previously declared variables as values. The following listing assigns the name of a book to a variable and then uses that variable as the value of an object's property.

> **Listing 3.6 Using a variable as a property value**
> **(http://jsbin.com/bafige/edit?js,console)**

```
var book;
var bookName;

bookName = "The Adventures of Tom Sawyer";      ⟵  Assign the name of
                                                    the book to a variable
book = {
    title : bookName                   ⟵  Use the variable as the
};                                         value of the title property
```

Having an object with a single property is a little extravagant; you might as well stick with a variable. Let's see how to create an object with more than one property.

When you need multiple properties, commas separate the key-value pairs. Figure 3.3 shows two properties as part of an object definition, and listing 3.7 creates two objects, each with two properties.

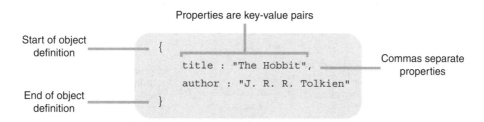

Figure 3.3 An object definition with two properties

Listing 3.7   Objects with multiple properties
(http://jsbin.com/bawiqev/edit?js,console)

```
var book1;
var book2;

book1 = {
    title : "The Hobbit",
    author : "J. R. R. Tolkien"
};

book2 = {
    title : "Northern Lights",
    author : "Philip Pullman"
};
```

Separate the properties
with a comma

Use key-value pairs to
set each property

Now that you've created an object, you need to be able to access its properties.

3.3   *Accessing object properties*

We're comfortable with the concept of a first-aid kit as a single object we can pass around from person to person and take from place to place. It's only when we need to use the kit that we consider what's inside: antiseptic, scissors, bandages, and so on.

For JavaScript objects, to access the values of an object's properties you can use *dot notation*. Join the name of the variable to the name of the property, its key, with a period or dot. For a first-aid kit as an object you might use `kit.antiseptic` or `kit.scissors` or `kit.bandages`. And for books, to access the `author` property of the object assigned to the variable called `book`, you write `book.author` (figure 3.4).

Variable name   Key

`book.author`

Dot operator

Figure 3.4   Accessing object properties using dot notation

In the next listing, you print the `title` and `author` properties of the book object to the console to give the following output:

```
> The Hobbit
> J. R. R. Tolkien
```

Listing 3.8   Using dot notation to access property values
(http://jsbin.com/funiyu/edit?js,console)

```
var book;

book = {
    title     : "The Hobbit",
    author    : "J. R. R. Tolkien",
    published : 1937
};

console.log(book.title);
console.log(book.author);
```

Set properties using
key-value pairs

Access property values
using dot notation

You line up the colons in the object properties in listing 3.8 to aid readability. Although JavaScript will ignore the extra spaces, indenting blocks of code and lining up values can make your programs easier to read and follow, especially as they grow in size. And the easier your code is to read, the easier it is to maintain and update, both for you and for other programmers.

Replacing a bunch of separate variables with a single object helps you manage the complexity of your programs. You can think more clearly about how programs work when details are hidden until you need them. You consider a book a single entity in your program until you need to access the book's title or author or publication date. It may seem that replacing three variables with one variable and three properties isn't an improvement, but when you start to use objects with functions in chapter 7 and arrays in chapter 8, their economy and clarity will be more obvious.

You use property values just like variables. The code in the following listing concatenates each book's title with the string " by " and its author to give this output:

```
> The Hobbit by J. R. R. Tolkien
> Northern Lights by Philip Pullman
```

Listing 3.9 Concatenating string properties (http://jsbin.com/yoweti/edit?js,console)

```
var book1;
var book2;

book1 = {
    title: "The Hobbit",
    author: "J. R. R. Tolkien"
};

book2 = {
    title: "Northern Lights",
    author: "Philip Pullman"
};

console.log(book1.title + " by " + book1.author);
console.log(book2.title + " by " + book2.author);
```

3.4 Updating object properties

In a quiz app, players attempt questions one after another. The number of questions attempted, number of questions correct, and score will change over time. You can create a player object with initial values set and then update them whenever a question is attempted. Use dot notation to change a property that already exists or to add a new property to an object, as in the following listing.

Listing 3.10   Using dot notation to update a property
(http://jsbin.com/mulimi/edit?js,console)

```
var player1;

player1 = {
    name: "Max",              Set initial properties when
    attempted: 0,             creating the object
    correct: 0,
};

player1.attempted = 1;        Update the property
player1.correct = 1;          using dot notation
player1.score = 50;
                              Add a new property
                              and assign it a value
```

Your code in listing 3.10 sets the `attempted` and `correct` properties to an initial value when the object is created but then updates them to a new value. It uses the assignment operator, `=`, to assign the value, 1, on the right of the operator, to the property, `player1.attempted`, on its left. You set the `attempted` and `correct` properties and then immediately update them; in the actual quiz app, the change would be in response to the player answering a question.

You can add new properties to an object after creating it. In listing 3.10, you assign the value 50 to the `score` property of the `player1` object.

```
player1.score = 50;
```

You didn't set the `score` property when creating the object; assigning a value automatically creates the property if it does not yet exist.

Just like using variables, you can use properties in a calculation and assign the result back to the property. The next listing shows code updating a player's properties:

```
> Max has scored 0
> Max has scored 50
```

Listing 3.11   Using a property in a calculation
(http://jsbin.com/cuboko/edit?js,console)

```
var player1;

player1 = {
    name: "Max",
    score: 0                          Evaluate the
};                                    expression on the
                                      right and assign
console.log(player1.name + " has scored " + player1.score);
                                      the result to the
player1.score = player1.score + 50;   property

console.log(player1.name + " has scored " + player1.score);
```

When you update the `score` property (in bold in the listing), JavaScript evaluates the right side of the assignment first. Because `player1.score` is 0, the expression becomes 0 + 50, which is 50. JavaScript then assigns that value to the left side, that is, back to the `score` property. So, you update `player1.score` from 0 to 50.

3.5 *Further examples*

Although developing *The Crypt* program gives you an ongoing context for introducing and discussing new concepts, a broader range of examples will help to deepen your understanding of the different ideas presented. You can also revisit some of these examples throughout the book to apply fresh techniques as you master them.

The examples all use curly braces to create an object and then assign the object to a variable created with the `var` keyword, in a single step.

3.5.1 *Writing a blog*

A blog is made up of blog posts. It would be good to have more information about each author, to be able to tag posts with keywords, and to add comments to each post. For now, here's a minimal object to represent a single post.

Listing 3.12 A blog post
(http://jsbin.com/jiculu/edit?js,console)

```
var post = {
    id : 1,
    title : "My Crazy Space Adventure",
    author : "Philae",
    created : "2015-06-21",
    body : "You will not believe where I just woke up!! Only on a comet..."
};
```

3.5.2 *Creating a calendar*

Calendar events clearly involve dates. JavaScript does have a `Date` object, but you won't be using it in the book. The next listing represents dates as strings in a specific format.

Listing 3.13 A calendar event
(http://jsbin.com/viroho/edit?js,console)

```
var event = {
    title : "Appraisal Meeting",
    startDate : "2016-10-04 16:00:00",
    endDate : "2016-10-04 17:00:00",
    location : "Martha's office",
    importance: 1,
    notes : 'Don\'t forget the portfolio!'
};
```

Include an apostrophe in the string when the string is delimited by double quotes

Use an escaped apostrophe when the string is delimited by single quotes

Notice how to cope with the apostrophe in the `notes` property. A backslash character before the apostrophe stops JavaScript from seeing it as the end of the string. The backslash is called an escape character and won't be shown.

```
event.notes = 'Don\'t forget the portfolio!';
```

Use the escape character to display double quotes when a string is already wrapped in double quotes.

```
var story = "She looked at me. \"What did you say?\" she asked.";
```

JavaScript also uses the backslash escape character to specify special characters like tabs and new lines. You'll see it in action throughout the book.

   A calendar contains lots of event objects. In chapter 9, you'll see how to streamline the process of creating objects that all have a similar structure when you investigate constructor functions.

3.5.3 *What's the weather like?*

Online weather information services provide weather data you can use in your programs. The data is often formatted using JSON (JavaScript Object Notation—see chapter 20) that's very similar to the objects you've been learning about in this chapter. The data can be quite detailed with many properties. The next listing shows a cutdown version of location data supplied by one of these services.

> **Listing 3.14 Location for a weather app**
> **(http://jsbin.com/diguhe/edit?js,console)**

```
var location = {
    "city"      : "San Francisco",
    "state"     : "CA",
    "country"   : "US",
    "zip"       : "94101",
    "latitude"  : 37.775,
    "longitude" : -122.418,
    "elevation" : 47.000
};
```

The property keys are within double quotation marks. JavaScript is happy for you to wrap keys, the property names, in quotation marks, single or double, although you haven't been doing that in the examples so far. In fact, quotation marks are required if the property name doesn't satisfy the rules for valid variable names discussed in chapter 2. You'll take a more detailed look at working with such property names in chapter 10. The JSON specification, which sets out how programs should transmit JavaScript object data as text across the internet, requires all keys to be in double quotation marks. Because it's sometimes required, many programmers recommend that property names always be placed within quotation marks to avoid inconsistency and potential errors.

This example also lines up the colons in the key-value pairs. Do you think that helps? Compare it to the other examples in this section. Are they easy to read and follow? You don't have to rigidly stick to one style or the other, although it's quite common for programmers to adopt particular stylistic habits over time.

3.5.4 *The testing effect*

A great way to learn is to test yourself often. A quiz app could represent its questions and answers as properties of objects like the one in the next listing.

> **Listing 3.15 A question and answer for a quiz app**
> **(http://jsbin.com/damoto/edit?js,console)**

```
var questionAndAnswer = {
    question: "What is the capital of France?",
    answer1: "Bordeaux",
    answer2: "F",
    answer3: "Paris",
    answer4: "Brussels",
    correctAnswer: "Paris",
    marksForQuestion: 2
};
```

A quiz app is likely to include a small set of question types. Listing 3.15 is an example of a multiple-choice question type. Each type of question would have a fixed form of presentation. Templates are a great way of presenting copies of similarly structured data, and we'll look at them in more detail in chapter 19.

3.5.5 *Create your own*

Think of some programs you'd like to create. What kinds of objects could you design to represent entities in the program? Head to JS Bin and have a go at building objects and displaying properties on the console. Maybe share your creations or ask any questions they inspire over on the *Get Programming with JavaScript* forum at https://forums.manning.com/forums/get-programming-with-javascript.

3.6 *The Crypt—a player object*

You'll now apply your knowledge of JavaScript objects to *The Crypt*. Figure 3.5 shows where the focus of this section, a player object, fits into the overall structure of our ongoing game example.

In chapter 2, you considered the kind of information you need to store for players in *The Crypt*. For a single player, you start off with variables like these:

```
playerName = "Kandra";
playerHealth = 50;
playerPlace = "The Dungeon of Doom";
playerItems = "a rusty key, The Sword of Destiny, a piece of cheese";
```

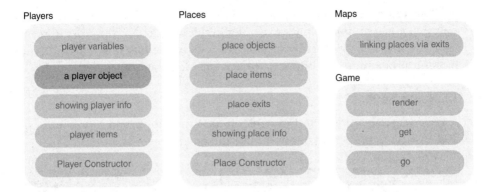

Figure 3.5 Elements in *The Crypt*

You then need to replicate those variables for each player in the game, maybe by using variable prefixes like `player1Name`, `player2Name`, and so on.

Clearly, it's much neater to use JavaScript objects as a way of grouping all of the information about a single player. Listing 3.16 shows how you can represent a player as an object and display some of their properties on the console. The output is as follows:

```
> Kandra
> Kandra is in The Dungeon of Doom
> Kandra has health 50
> Items: a rusty key, The Sword of Destiny, a piece of cheese
```

**Listing 3.16   A player object
              (http://jsbin.com/qelene/edit?js,console)**

```
var player;

player = {
    name: "Kandra",
    health: 50,
    place: "The Dungeon of Doom",
    items: "a rusty key, The Sword of Destiny, a piece of cheese"
};

console.log(player.name);
console.log(player.name + " is in " + player.place);
console.log(player.name + " has health " + player.health);
console.log("Items: " + player.items);
```

The last four lines of the listing are just for displaying player information. Having to repeat those lines of code every time you want to display a player's information seems a little tedious. It would be great to be able to write the lines of code once and then call them up on demand.

You're in luck! JavaScript lets you define *functions* to execute blocks of code whenever you need them. Functions are very powerful and will help streamline the display of player properties and the creation of multiple player objects. You'll take a really detailed look at functions over the next four chapters.

3.7   *Summary*

- Group related variables as properties of an object.
- Define objects as collections of comma-separated properties between curly braces:

```
var player = { name : "Hadfield", location : "The ISS" };
```

- For each property use a key-value pair, with key and value separated by a colon:

```
name : "Hadfield"
```

- Access property values by using dot notation. If the object is assigned to a variable, join the property name to the variable name with a dot:

```
player.name
```

- Use properties in expressions just as you would variables:

```
console.log(player.name + " is in " + player.location);
```

- Assign values to properties using the assignment operator, =:

```
player.location = "On a space walk";
```

- Add new properties to existing objects whenever you want:

```
player.oxygen = 96;
```

Functions: code on demand

4

This chapter covers

- Organizing instructions with functions
- Defining a function—specifying code to be executed on demand
- Calling a function—executing code on demand
- Reducing repetition in code
- Making programs easier to read and update

One of the main themes of *Get Programming with JavaScript* is managing complexity through good organization. In chapter 2, you stored information in variables and saw how choosing good names for those variables helps you understand their purpose in a program. In chapter 3, you grouped variables as properties of objects. You can focus on objects as a whole or drill down into the details when needed. In this chapter you take a look at another important method for organizing code and avoiding repetition, the function.

4.1 Noticing repetition

As the programs you write become longer and more complex, you find yourself repeating similar sections of code with only slight differences. Common tasks, like displaying text, animating an image, or saving to a database, may need to be performed often. You need to notice these recurring bits of code; they're prime function fodder.

A *function* is a way of writing code once but using it many times. Section 4.2 looks at how to create functions. This section explores a couple of examples of JavaScript repeated.

4.1.1 Displaying object properties as text

Programs use objects and variables to store all kinds of information—profiles, posts, documents, and photos—you name it and someone has stored it on a computer somewhere. A common task is to display that information to the user. Say you have some objects representing movies and need to display the information about each movie on the console. The kind of output expected is shown in figure 4.1.

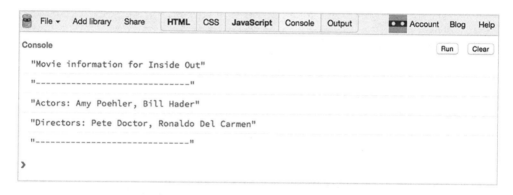

Figure 4.1   Movie information shown on the console in JS Bin

As you can see in the following listing, the code required to create the output in figure 4.1 includes five calls to `console.log`. And that's just for one movie.

**Listing 4.1   Displaying an object's properties on the console
(http://jsbin.com/besudi/edit?js, console)**

```
var movie1;

movie1 = {
    title: "Inside Out",
    actors: "Amy Poehler, Bill Hader",
    directors: "Pete Doctor, Ronaldo Del Carmen"
};

console.log("Movie information for " + movie1.title);
console.log("---------------------------");
console.log("Actors: " + movie1.actors);
console.log("Directors: " + movie1.directors);
console.log("---------------------------");
```

Create a movie object

Use five calls to console.log to display the values of various movie properties

If you have to write those five lines of code every time you want to display movie information and for every movie, that's going to get pretty repetitive. And if you then decide to change the information displayed, you'll have to go through all the places where it appears in the code and make sure it's changed consistently.

The next listing shows the code repeated for three different movies.

> **Listing 4.2   Displaying information from similar objects**
> **(http://jsbin.com/gewegi/edit?js,console)**

```
console.log("Movie information for " + movie1.title);
console.log("----------------------------");
console.log("Actors: " + movie1.actors);
console.log("Directors: " + movie1.directors);
console.log("----------------------------");

console.log("Movie information for " + movie2.title);
console.log("----------------------------");
console.log("Actors: " + movie2.actors);
console.log("Directors: " + movie2.directors);
console.log("----------------------------");

console.log("Movie information for " + movie3.title);
console.log("----------------------------");
console.log("Actors: " + movie3.actors);
console.log("Directors: " + movie3.directors);
console.log("----------------------------");
```

There could be many more than three movies and a number of places where the information needs to be displayed. If you later need to change the word *information* to *info*, you'll have to make sure you find all the places it's used.

The three blocks of five statements are almost identical. All that varies is which movie's properties are being displayed. It would be great to be able to define one block of statements and ask JavaScript to use that block whenever needed. That's what functions are for!

The next section has one more example of repetitive code. (Don't worry, we'll get to functions before the examples get too repetitive!)

4.1.2   *Adding tax and displaying a summary*

A simple task like adding tax to a price is the kind of thing that happens again and again. You calculate the tax and add it to the price to give a total cost.

```
> price = $140
> tax @ 15% = $21
> total cost = $161
```

The following listing shows a program to add tax for three different transactions. The two operators, * and /, perform multiplication and division, respectively.

Listing 4.3   Adding tax to find the total cost
(http://jsbin.com/kawocu/edit?js,console)

```
var sale1;
var sale2;
var sale3;

sale1 = { price: 140, taxRate: 15 };
sale2 = { price: 40, taxRate: 10 };
sale3 = { price: 120, taxRate: 20 };

sale1.tax = sale1.price * sale1.taxRate / 100;
sale2.tax = sale2.price * sale2.taxRate / 100;
sale3.tax = sale3.price * sale3.taxRate / 100;

sale1.total = sale1.price + sale1.tax;
sale2.total = sale2.price + sale2.tax;
sale3.total = sale3.price + sale3.tax;

console.log("price = $" + sale1.price);
console.log("tax @ " + sale1.taxRate + "% = $" + sale1.tax);
console.log("total cost = $" + sale1.total);

console.log("price = $" + sale2.price);
console.log("tax @ " + sale2.taxRate + "% = $" + sale2.tax);
console.log("total cost = $" + sale2.total);

console.log("price = $" + sale3.price);
console.log("tax @ " + sale3.taxRate + "% = $" + sale3.tax);
console.log("total cost = $" + sale3.total);
```

> **All three calculations have the same structure, using * and / to multiply and divide.**

> **Again, all three calculations have the same structure.**

Wow! That's a riot of repetition. As well as the blocks of `console.log` lines, you repeat the structure of the calculations. It's essentially the same code every time you want to perform the calculation. Rest assured, you'll learn a much better way to write this program. Enter the function!

4.2   *Defining and calling functions*

Just as an object is a collection of properties, a function is a collection of statements or instructions. Functions help you avoid repetition and make your code more organized and easier to update and maintain. Well-named functions should also make your programs easier to follow. If you find your functions are used a lot in a program and would be useful in other programs too, you can create libraries of helpful functions to include in other projects.

In the previous section you saw two examples of programs where blocks of code with the same structure were repeated. To reduce the code bloat you want to replace those blocks with something like the following:

```
showMovieInfo();
showCostBreakdown();
```

The two functions, showMovieInfo and showCostBreakdown, should produce the same output as the code blocks in listings 4.2 and 4.3, and you should be able to use them again and again, whenever you want. Let's see how such code-on-demand magic is conjured.

4.2.1   Defining new functions

Define a function by using the following pieces, as shown in figure 4.2:

- The function keyword
- Parentheses, ()
- A code block between curly braces, {}

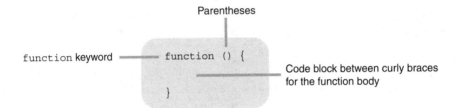

Figure 4.2   The pieces of a function definition

The code block contains the list of instructions you'd like to execute whenever you use the function. The list of instructions is also called the *function body*.

It's common to see function definitions set out like this:

```
function () {
    // Lines of code to be executed go here
}
```

Once you've defined a function, you can assign it to a variable, just like any value. The next listing defines a function to display "Hello World!" on the console and assigns the function to the variable sayHello.

Listing 4.4   A simple function definition and assignment
(http://jsbin.com/tehixo/edit?js,console)

```
var sayHello;                    ⟵——— Declare a variable

sayHello = function () {                ⟵┐   Define a function and assign
    console.log("Hello World!");  ⟵┘       it to the sayHello variable
};

                                 Include code between the curly
                                 braces, to be executed whenever
                                 you run the function
```

It's easy to see the different pieces that make up the function definition in listing 4.4: the function keyword, the empty parentheses, and the code block for the function body. The function body has only a single statement, console.log("Hello World!");. At this point, you have only *defined* the function, ready for use later. The code in the function body won't be executed until you run the function—you'll see how to do that in section 4.2.3.

The following listing shows a couple more examples of defining functions and then assigning them to variables.

Listing 4.5 Two more function definitions and assignments (http://jsbin.com/xezani/edit?js,console)

```
var findTotal;
var displayMenu;

findTotal = function () {
    result = number1 + number2;
};

displayMenu = function () {
    console.log("Please choose an option:");
    console.log("(1) Print log");
    console.log("(2) Upload file");
    console.log("(9) Quit");
};
```

The variables result, number1 and number2, would have to have been declared elsewhere.

4.2.2 Function expressions and function declarations

In the previous examples you've been using *function expressions* to define functions and assign them to variables with the assignment operator.

```
var findTotal = function () { … };    // The function expression is in bold.
```

You can also use an alternative syntax, called a *function declaration*. Rather than defining the function and then assigning it to a variable, you can declare a name for the function as part of the definition.

```
function findTotal () { … }  // Declare a name with the function
```

You can treat the two ways of defining functions as equivalent; there are some subtle differences but we won't go into them here. *Get Programming with JavaScript* uses function expressions throughout parts 1 and 2 to highlight the similarities between creating and assigning different values, including objects, functions, and arrays.

```
var numOfDays = 7;                       // Assign a number
var player = { … };                      // Create and assign an object
var findTotal = function () { … };       // Define and assign a function
var items = [];                          // Create and assign an array (ch8)
```

Don't worry about the function declaration syntax for now or even about the difference between declarations and expressions. You'll be much more comfortable with functions when you meet the declaration syntax again in part 3.

Just defining the functions isn't enough to make "Hello World!" appear on the console, calculate the total, or display the menu. You need a way to tell the function to execute its list of instructions.

4.2.3   Using functions

Once you've assigned a function to a variable, whenever you want to execute the statements in the function body, you write the variable name followed by parentheses, ().

```
sayHello();
findTotal();
displayMenu();
```

Other names for running the function are *calling* the function or *invoking* the function.

In listing 4.6, you call the sayHello function three times. It displays the string "Hello World!" three times, like this:

```
> Hello World!
> Hello World!
> Hello World!
```

**Listing 4.6   Calling the sayHello function three times
(http://jsbin.com/vozuxa/edit?js,console)**

```
var sayHello;

sayHello = function () {                    Define the function and
    console.log("Hello World!");           assign it to a variable
};

sayHello();                                 Call the function by
sayHello();      Call the function         adding parentheses
sayHello();      again and again           after the variable name
```

The next listing uses the findTotal function to update the result variable. It then displays the whole calculation on the console:

```
> 1000 + 66 = 1066
```

**Listing 4.7   Using the findTotal function to display a calculation
(http://jsbin.com/hefuwa/edit?js,console)**

```
var number1 = 1000;
var number2 = 66;
var result;
var findTotal;
```

```
findTotal = function () {
    result = number1 + number2;
};

findTotal();

console.log(number1 + " + " + number2 + " = " + result);
```

Listing 4.8 calls the `displayMenu` function to, well, display a menu. (These functions do exactly what they say on the tin!)

```
> Please choose an option:
> (1) Print log
> (2) Upload file
> (9) Quit
```

Listing 4.8 Displaying a menu
(http://jsbin.com/cujozo/edit?js,console)

```
var displayMenu;

displayMenu = function () {
    console.log("Please choose an option:");
    console.log("(1) Print log");
    console.log("(2) Upload file");
    console.log("(9) Quit");
};

displayMenu();
```

It may seem strange to use empty parentheses as the notation for calling a function. But, as you'll see in chapter 5, they're not always empty … *[cue mysterious music].*

> **DEFINITION** For those who like their terminology, the parentheses, `()`, added to the end of a variable when calling a function are called the *function invocation operator* or the *function call operator.*

4.2.4 *Functions step by step*

Table 4.1 summarizes the steps used to define and call a function.

Table 4.1 Steps used to define and call a function

Action	Code	Comments
Declare a variable	`var sayHello;`	Sets aside the name for your use in the program.

Define a function	`function () {`
	`    console.log("Hello World!");`
	`}`
		The code in the function body is not executed at this point.

Table 4.1   Steps used to define and call a function *(continued)*

Action	Code	Comments
Assign to a variable	```sayHello = function () { console.log("Hello World!"); };```	Assigning the function to a variable gives you a label you can use to call the function.
Call the function	```sayHello();```	The code in the function body is executed.
Call the function again and again as needed	```sayHello(); sayHello(); sayHello();```	The code in the function body is executed every time the function is called.

The second row in the table, Define a function, doesn't usually occur on its own; you're much more likely to define a function and assign it to a variable, as seen on the third row, Assign to a variable. (You'll see in later chapters that you can assign function definitions as elements in arrays [lists] and pass them to and from other functions—they're not always assigned to variables.)

4.3   *Reducing repetition*

In listings 4.2 and 4.3 you saw the repeated blocks of code needed when you didn't have functions at your disposal. It's time to rein in those runaways, cut back those fast-growing weeds, put the kids on a diet, cap the spending—you get the picture; let's reduce the repetition!

4.3.1   *A function for displaying object properties as text*

Returning to the code from listing 4.2, you streamline the display of movie information. Write the movie display code once, in a function, and simply call the function whenever it's needed.

> **Listing 4.9   Using a function to display object properties**
> **(http://jsbin.com/toqopo/edit?js,console)**

```
var showMovieInfo;

showMovieInfo = function () {
    console.log("Movie information for " + movie.title);
    console.log("---------------------------");
    console.log("Actors: " + movie.actors);
    console.log("Directors: " + movie.directors);
    console.log("---------------------------");
};
```

The code assigns the new function to the showMovieInfo variable. Call the function by writing the variable name followed by parentheses, showMovieInfo(), as shown in the next listing. You should end up with the following output on the console, matching the aim seen way back in figure 4.1.

```
> Movie information for Inside Out
> ----------------------------
> Actors: Amy Poehler, Bill Hader
> Directors: Pete Doctor, Ronaldo Del Carmen
> ----------------------------
```

Listing 4.10   Calling the showMovieInfo function
(http://jsbin.com/menebu/edit?js,console)

```
var movie1;
var showPlayerInfo;
var movie;

movie1 = {
    title: "Inside Out",
    actors: "Amy Poehler, Bill Hader",
    directors: "Pete Doctor, Ronaldo Del Carmen"
};

showMovieInfo = function () {                                          Define the function.
    console.log("Movie information for " + movie.title);              The code in the
    console.log("----------------------------");                     function body is not
    console.log("Actors: " + movie.actors);                          executed at this point.
    console.log("Directors: " + movie.directors);
    console.log("----------------------------");
};

movie = movie1;              Call the function. Now
                            the code is executed.
showMovieInfo();        ◁─
```

With the `movie` variable, used by the `showMovieInfo` function, you can switch which movie's information the function will use. Listing 4.11 shows how to switch between movies. Information for three different movies is printed to the console.

```
> Movie information for Inside Out
> ----------------------------
> Actors: Amy Poehler, Bill Hader
> Directors: Pete Doctor, Ronaldo Del Carmen
> ----------------------------
> Movie information for Spectre
> ----------------------------
> Actors: Daniel Craig, Christoph Waltz
> Directors: Sam Mendes
> ----------------------------
> Movie information for Star Wars: Episode VII - The Force Awakens
> ----------------------------
> Actors: Harrison Ford, Mark Hamill, Carrie Fisher
> Directors: J.J.Abrams
> ----------------------------
```

Listing 4.11 Using the same function with multiple objects (http://jsbin.com/mavutu/edit?js,console)

```
var movie1;
var movie2;
var movie3;
var movie;              ◁─┐  Declare a movie variable
var showMovieInfo;        └─ to hold the current
                             movie for display

movie1 = {
    title: "Inside Out",
    actors: "Amy Poehler, Bill Hader",
    directors: "Pete Doctor, Ronaldo Del Carmen"
};

movie2 = {
    title: "Spectre",
    actors: "Daniel Craig, Christoph Waltz",
    directors: "Sam Mendes"
};

movie3 = {
    title: "Star Wars: Episode VII - The Force Awakens",
    actors: "Harrison Ford, Mark Hamill, Carrie Fisher",
    directors: "J.J.Abrams"
};

showMovieInfo = function () {
    console.log("Movie information for " + movie.title);
    console.log("---------------------------");
    console.log("Actors: " + movie.actors);
    console.log("Directors: " + movie.directors);
    console.log("---------------------------");
};
```

The movie variable is used in the showMovieInfo function.

```
movie = movie1;       ◁─┐  Assign movie1 to the movie
showMovieInfo();        └─ variable, ready for display

movie = movie2;       ◁─┐
showMovieInfo();        │  Switch the movie
                        │  to be displayed
movie = movie3;       ◁─┘
showMovieInfo();
```

4.3.2 *Functions for adding tax and displaying a summary*

Listing 4.12 shows a function to add tax for sales and display a summary of each transaction. Most of the code that you need to repeat is in the two functions, calculateTax and displaySale. You call them for each sale object in turn. The output is shown here.

```
price = $140
tax @ 15% = $21
total cost = $161
price = $40
tax @ 10% = $4
```

```
total cost = $44
price = $120
tax @ 20% = $24
total cost = $144
```

As with all of the listings on JS Bin, there are "Further Adventures" below the program that suggest ways of exploring the code and building your understanding. In this case, one challenge is to reduce the repetition of the function calls; calculateTax and displaySale are always called together. Although it's good to have two different functions—they do different jobs—can you avoid having to call them both for each sale object? If you're connected, click the link above listing 4.12 to head to JS Bin now and embrace the adventure. If you're reading a print copy of the book, away from technology, it's paper and pencil for you! Solutions to most problems are on the *Get Programming with JavaScript* website at www.room51.co.uk/books/getProgramming/listings.html.

**Listing 4.12   Using functions to add and display tax
(http://jsbin.com/raqiri/edit?js,console)**

```
var sale1;
var sale2;                          Declare a sale
var sale3;                          variable to be used
var sale;                     ◁──┘  by the functions
var calculateTax;
var displaySale;

sale1 = { price: 140, taxRate: 15 };
sale2 = { price: 40, taxRate: 10 };
sale3 = { price: 120, taxRate: 20 };
                                                    Use the sale variable
calculateTax = function () {                        here and in the
    sale.tax = sale.price * sale.taxRate / 100;  ◁─┘ displaySale function
    sale.total = sale.price + sale.tax;
};

var displaySale = function () {
    console.log("price = $" + sale.price);
    console.log("tax @ " + sale.taxRate + "% = $" + sale.tax);
    console.log("total cost = $" + sale.total);
};

sale = sale1;              ◁──   Assign sale1 to sale before
calculateTax();                  calling the two functions to
displaySale();                   update and display it

sale = sale2;
calculateTax();
displaySale();

sale = sale3;
calculateTax();
displaySale();
```

The two functions use the sale variable in their definitions, accessing properties on the object, sale.price, sale.taxRate, and so on. The code in the function bodies won't run until the program calls the two functions, by which time the program will have assigned one of the sale objects to the `sale` variable.

The function names `calculateTax` and `displaySale` help to make the program in listing 4.12 easier to follow and understand. Section 4.4 investigates these ideas in more detail.

4.4   *Making code easier to read and update*

As your programs get longer and more complicated, you manage that complexity by breaking them into well-named objects and functions. Anyone reading your code can follow its flow and understand the purpose of the pieces and of the whole.

Take a look at the following code snippet; you should get a sense of what's happening even if you don't know the details of how the functions work.

```
...
var balance = getAccountBalance();

displayBalance();

addInterest()
addBonus();
setAccountBalance();

displayBalance();
...
```

Each function should have a single, clear purpose. If you need to investigate what a function does, you should be able to find it defined in one place. Let's look at an example of updating a function.

4.4.1   *Updating the showMovieInfo function*

In listing 4.11, you created a `showMovieInfo` function to display information about a movie object. It was great to be able to encapsulate the blocks of display code into a single function. But having the information for multiple movies squashed together on the console makes it hard to pick out individual facts about particular movies. It would be useful to add blank lines, making it easier to see each movie.

```
> Movie information for Inside Out
> -----------------------------
> Actors: Amy Poehler, Bill Hader
> Directors: Pete Doctor, Ronaldo Del Carmen
> -----------------------------
>
> Movie information for Spectre
> -----------------------------
> Actors: Daniel Craig, Christoph Waltz
> Directors: Sam Mendes
> -----------------------------
>
> Movie information for Star Wars: Episode VII - The Force Awakens
> -----------------------------
> Actors: Harrison Ford, Mark Hamill, Carrie Fisher
```

```
> Directors: J.J.Abrams
> -----------------------------
>
```

Because you have all of the display code inside your showMovieInfo function, you can head right there and add an extra call to console.log to create the blank line, as shown in the next listing. Your organization is already paying off!

> **Listing 4.13 Updating your display function to add a blank line
> (http://jsbin.com/cijini/edit?js,console)**

```
showMovieInfo = function () {
    console.log("Movie information for " + movie.title);
    console.log("----------------------------");
    console.log("Actors: " + movie.actors);
    console.log("Directors: " + movie.directors);
    console.log("----------------------------");
    console.log("");
};
```

Add an extra call to console.log to give you the blank line you want

So close! Because the JS Bin console wraps strings in speech marks, you don't quite get your blank lines. You get empty quotation marks instead. But if you check the browser's own console (see the online guide at www.room51.co.uk/guides/browser-consoles.html), you should see the blank lines expected, as shown in figure 4.3.

Figure 4.3   JS Bin displays empty strings in quotation marks but the Safari browser doesn't.

If this example were part of a larger (maybe much larger) program and you didn't have the player display logic safely nestled in a single function, you'd have to inspect all the code to find the lines where changes should be made. Text editors and development environments should have tools to help, but they're not foolproof and your program could end up with coy corners of uncorrected code. You try it out and, to begin with, everything seems fine. Then later there's running and, um, screaming. Avoid the nightmare—use functions.

4.5   *The Crypt—displaying player information*

You'll now apply your knowledge of JavaScript functions to *The Crypt*. Figure 4.4 shows where the focus of this section, showing player information by using functions, fits into the overall structure of our ongoing game example.

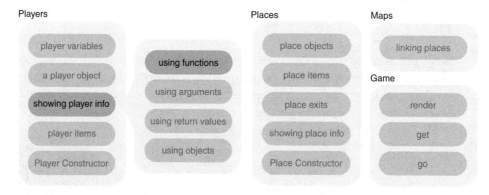

Figure 4.4   Elements of *The Crypt*

In chapter 3 you saw how to group information about a player into a single JavaScript object. You create the object using curly braces and set the properties using key-value pairs, like this:

```
var player;

player = {
    name: "Kandra",
    health: 50,
    place: "The Dungeon of Doom"
};
```

Once you assign the new object to the `player` variable, you can get the property values by using dot notation. Displaying information about the player involves logging properties to the console.

```
console.log(player.name + " is in " + player.place);
```

In the game, you may have to display player info a number of times and for a number of players. You should use your new knowledge of functions to make the display of information more efficient; make it *code on demand*—code you can execute by calling a function.

4.5.1 *A function to display player information*

The `showMovieInfo` function from listing 4.13 looks like exactly the kind of function you need. Whereas `showMovieInfo` displays information about movies, listing 4.14 shows a `showPlayerInfo` function doing a very similar job for players, producing the following output:

```
> Kandra
> ----------------------------
> Kandra is in The Dungeon of Doom
> Kandra has health 50
> ----------------------------
>
> Dax
> ----------------------------
> Dax is in The Old Library
> Dax has health 40
> ----------------------------
>
```

**Listing 4.14 A function to display player information
(http://jsbin.com/mafade/edit?js,console)**

```
var player1;
var player2;                    Declare the variables
var player;                     you'll be using
var showPlayerInfo;

player1 = {
    name: "Kandra",
    place: "The Dungeon of Doom",
    health: 50
};                              Create objects using curly
                                braces and key-value pairs.
player2 = {                     Assign them to variables.
    name: "Dax",
    place: "The Old Library",
    health: 40
};

showPlayerInfo = function () {
    console.log(player.name);                                              Define a function
    console.log("----------------------------");                          to display player
    console.log(player.name + " is in " + player.place);                  properties. The
    console.log(player.name + " has health " + player.health);            code will run
    console.log("----------------------------");                          when the
    console.log("");                                                      function is called.
};
```

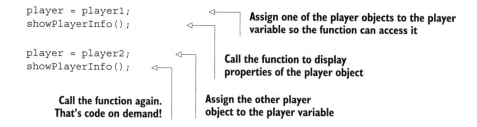

```
player = player1;
showPlayerInfo();
```
◁———— **Assign one of the player objects to the player variable so the function can access it**

```
player = player2;
showPlayerInfo();
```
◁———— **Call the function to display properties of the player object**

Call the function again. That's code on demand!   **Assign the other player object to the player variable**

Excellent! That does the job. A single call to a function now displays player information. It's a shame you have to keep assigning different players to the `player` variable to make it work; it would be better if you could somehow say to the function, "Show info for player1" or "Show info for player2." Well, passing information to and from functions will be investigated in detail over the next three chapters. Flexibility, reusability, efficiency, here we come!

4.6   Summary

- A function is a block of code that you write once but use many times. It should have a clear, single purpose.

- You *define* a function by using the function keyword, parentheses, and a function body in a code block between curly braces:

```
function () {
    // Statements go here in the function body
};
```

- You *assign* the function to a variable with the equals symbol, = , also known as the assignment operator:

```
showPlayerInfo = function () { … };
```

- Once a function is assigned to a variable, you *call* or *invoke* the function by adding parentheses to the end of the variable name:

```
addTax();
showPlayerInfo();
evadeRaptor();
```

- Be on the lookout for repetition; sections of code with the same structure and only slight changes in values or variables used. Move repeated code into a function.

- Give functions clear names that communicate their purpose. Use the functions to organize your code, making your programs easier to follow and maintain.

5

Arguments:
passing data to functions

This chapter covers

- Defining functions with parameters, ready to accept data
- Calling functions, passing in data with arguments

Functions are an essential means of organization; you write them once and use them many times. But so far, your functions have been tied to the values of variables around them. It's time to set your functions free, letting them name their own variables and passing them the data they need.

5.1 Function reuse and versatility

The functions you've used up to now have relied on variables declared and assigned values elsewhere in the program. In the following listing, the showMessage function relies on a variable called message, declared outside the function definition.

**Listing 5.1   Relying on a variable outside the function
(http://jsbin.com/taqusi/edit?js,console)**

```
var message;
var showMessage;

message = "It's full of stars!";

showMessage = function () {
    console.log(message);
};

showMessage();
```

**Assign the string to be displayed
to the message variable**

**Use the message variable,
defined outside the showMessage
function, in the function body**

**Call the showMessage function. It uses the
current value of the message variable.**

In the `showMessage` function definition, you use a variable called `message`. The `message` variable has to exist for the function to do its job. If you change the name of the variable, the function breaks. If `message` is renamed `msg`, as shown in the next listing, and the program is run on JS Bin, you should get an error something like this: "Reference error: Can't find variable: message." (Different browsers may give slightly different error messages.)

**Listing 5.2   Breaking a function by changing a variable name
(http://jsbin.com/yaresa/edit?js,console)**

```
var msg;
var showMessage;

msg = "It's full of stars!";

showMessage = function () {
    console.log(message);
};

showMessage();
```

**Assign the string to be
displayed to the msg variable**

**Use a variable called message
in the function body**

**Produce an error by trying to
call the showMessage function**

The instructions in the function body *can* use variables defined elsewhere in your program but that couples the function with the external variable; a better practice is to pass the information a function needs to the function when it's called. This helps avoid the variables a function needs being misnamed, missing, deleted, or changed by other parts of your program and makes it easier to follow the flow of the program and spot mistakes if they occur.

We don't want arrogant Rock God functions demanding particular variables in their dressing rooms before they'll perform; we want easy-going functions that are reliable and happy to strut their stuff wherever they are in the world. By decoupling functions from variables, you make the functions more portable; the function definitions can be moved to other parts of your program or be reused in other programs or code libraries, without causing havoc and throwing errors.

So, how is this decoupling achieved?

5.2 *Passing information to functions*

Passing information to functions is achieved in two stages: when you define the function and when you call the function:

1 When you *define* the function, you set up variable names, called *parameters*, ready for when you call the function.

2 When you *call* the function, you include data to assign to the variables you named in step 1.

You'll look at a number of examples over the course of this chapter (and there are plenty more throughout the rest of the book), but there's nothing like practice to make permanent. The *Further Adventures* section for each code listing on JS Bin should get you started.

5.2.1 *Passing one argument to a function*

It's time to make use of those empty parentheses in your function definitions! To pass information to functions when you call them, include it between the parentheses, like this:

```
showMessage("It's full of stars!");
showPlayerInfo("Kandra");
getMovieActors("The Hobbit");
square(12);
```

You pass each of the four functions some information for their code to use. Each value included in the parentheses is called an *argument*. Each of the four functions shown here includes a single argument. The arguments are "It's full of stars!", "Kandra", "The Hobbit", and 12.

To use the information in the parentheses, you need to make the functions ready to accept it. You add a *parameter* when you define the function. The parameter shows that the function expects you to give it some information when you call it, as shown in figure 5.1.

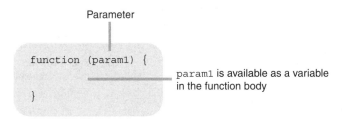

Figure 5.1   Including a parameter in the parentheses when defining a function

For the four functions in the previous example, the function definitions could be something like this:

```
showMessage = function (message) { … };
showPlayerInfo = function (playerName) { … };
getMovieActors = function (movieTitle) { … };
square = function (numberToSquare) { … };
```

Each function definition includes a parameter, shown in bold. The parameter is a variable that you can use only inside the function body.

Let's update the `showMessage` function from listing 5.1 to accept a message, rather than relying on an external variable. When defining the function, include a `message` parameter. The `message` parameter is available as a variable in the function body. Now when you call the function, you pass the message to display in parentheses, `showMessage("It's full of stars!")`. The function adds extra text and displays the following:

```
> The message is: It's full of stars!
```

**Listing 5.3   Passing information to a function
(http://jsbin.com/xucemu/edit?js,console)**

```
var showMessage;

showMessage = function (message) {        ⟵┐ Include a parameter, message,
    console.log("The message is: " + message);   when defining the function
};                                        ⟵┐ Use message anywhere
                                             inside the function body
showMessage("It's full of stars!");       ⟵┐ When the function "It's full of stars!" is
                                             assigned to message and the statements
                                             in the function body are executed
```

When you call the `showMessage` function at the end of listing 5.3, you include the string "It's full of stars!" in the parentheses. A value included in the function call parentheses like this is called an *argument*. The program assigns the argument to the variable named `message`. The function then uses the `message` variable to generate the string that's logged to the console, `"The message is: It's full of stars!"`

Table 5.1 lists the steps involved in declaring a function with parameters and then calling it with different arguments.

Table 5.1   Steps used to define and call a function, passing it data

Action	Code	Comments
Declare a variable	`var showMessage;`	Sets aside the name for use in the program.

Table 5.1 Steps used to define and call a function, passing it data

Action	Code	Comments
Define a function with a parameter	```function (message) {

}``` | Sets aside a variable name, message, for use in the function body. |
| Use the parameter | ```function (message) {
   console.log(message);
}``` | The parameter is available as a variable within the function body. |
| Assign the function to a variable | ```showMessage = function (message) {
   console.log(message);
};``` | Assigning the function to a variable gives you a label you can use to call the function. |
| Call the function with an argument | ```showMessage("It's full of stars!");``` | The code in the function body is executed with the argument in parentheses assigned to message. |
| Call the function again and again with different arguments | ```showMessage("It's full of stars!");
showMessage("Yippee!");
showMessage("Cowabunga!");``` | Every time you call the function, the argument is assigned to the message parameter. |

You can call the showMessage function with any text you choose. The text is assigned to the message variable and used as part of the full message logged to the console.

In listing 5.4 you call the showMessage function with three different arguments, leading to three different messages on the console:

```
> The message is: It's full of stars!
> The message is: Hello to Jason Isaacs
> The message is: Hello to Jason Isaacs and Stephen Fry
```

Listing 5.4   Calling the same function with different arguments
(http://jsbin.com/zavavo/edit?js,console)

```
var showMessage;                          Declare a        Define a function with a
                                          variable         message parameter; assign
                                                           the function to a variable
showMessage = function (message) {
    console.log("The message is: " + message);            Use the parameter in
};                                                         the function body

showMessage("It's full of stars!");                       Call the function,
showMessage("Hello to Jason Isaacs");                     passing a different
showMessage("Hello to Jason Isaacs and Stephen Fry");     argument each time
```

Because you declared the name of the parameter along with the function definition, the `showMessage` function no longer relies on variable names from elsewhere, making it less brittle. Decoupling complete.

Listing 5.5 shows the definition of a square function, including a `numberToSquare` parameter. The function squares the number you pass to it as an argument. You call the function four times to give the following output:

```
> 10 * 10 = 100
> -2 * -2 = 4
> 1111 * 1111 = 1234321
> 0.5 * 0.5 = 0.25
```

Listing 5.5   Using the square function
(http://jsbin.com/vequpi/edit?js,console)

```
var square;

square = function (numberToSquare) {
    var result;
    result = numberToSquare * numberToSquare;
    console.log(numberToSquare + " * " + numberToSquare + " = " + result);
};

square(10);
square(-2);
square(1111);
square(0.5);
```

> Square the number by multiplying it by itself; the * is the multiplication operator.

Parameters vs. arguments

You knew those parentheses would come in handy!

The names you include in the parentheses *when defining the function* are available as variables in the function body. They're called *parameters* and show that you expect information to be included when the function is called.

```
var myExample;
myExample = function (parameter) { … }
```

The values you include in the parentheses *when calling the function* are assigned to the parameter variables to be used in the function body. These values are called *arguments*.

```
myExample(argument);
```

Don't worry too much about the terminology; it can take a little while to get used to. After you've created and used a few functions, you'll pick up an intuitive sense of what's going on even if you mix up the terms *parameter* and *argument* from time to time.

5.2.2 *Passing multiple arguments to a function*

You can define functions with as many parameters as they need to complete their work. Simply separate the parameters with commas in the parentheses of the definition (figure 5.2).

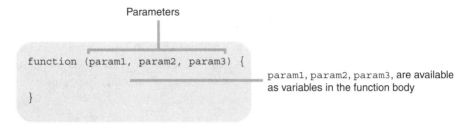

Parameters

```
function (param1, param2, param3) {


}
```

param1, param2, param3, are available as variables in the function body

Figure 5.2 Including multiple parameters in a function definition

Suppose you want a function to add two numbers together. If you have two pairs of numbers, 30 and 23, and 2.8 and -5, the correct output would be

```
> The sum is 53
> The sum is -2.2
```

How do you do this?

**Listing 5.6   A function with two arguments
(http://jsbin.com/siyelu/edit?js,console)**

```
var showSum;

showSum = function (number1, number2) {
    var total = number1 + number2;
    console.log("The sum is " + total);
};

showSum(30, 23);
showSum(2.8, -5);
```

You define the function with two parameters, number1 and number2.

You call the function with two arguments, 30 and 23.

When you call the showSum function, the program automatically assigns the two arguments you provide to the two parameters in the definition, number1 and number2. For the first call to showSum in listing 5.6, it's as if the function body becomes

```
var number1 = 30;
var number2 = 23;
var total = number1 + number2;
console.log("The sum is " + total);
```

You can define a function with as many parameters as you want. As the number of parameters increases, it becomes more likely for people (including you!) to make mistakes when using your function; they might miss an argument or put the arguments in the wrong order when calling the function. A neat way to overcome the problem is to pass an object to the function. The function definition needs only a single parameter and the function body can access whichever properties it needs. You'll take a look at using objects with functions in chapter 7.

5.3   *The Crypt—displaying player information*

You'll now apply your knowledge of JavaScript function arguments to *The Crypt*. Figure 5.3 shows where the focus of this section, showing player information by using functions with arguments, fits into the overall structure of our ongoing game example.

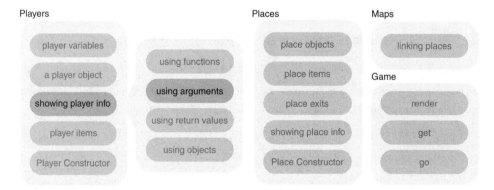

Figure 5.3   Elements of *The Crypt*

In chapter 4, you wrote a showPlayerInfo function as code on demand. You could display player information on the console whenever you wanted, just by calling the function. Unfortunately, it relied on a player variable being set elsewhere in the code. Let's update the showPlayerInfo function, setting parameters so you can pass it the information it needs directly.

In order to display information about each player, you break the job into subtasks and create functions for each piece of information. You then show information about a player like this:

```
showPlayerName("Kandra");
showPlayerHealth("Kandra", 50);
showPlayerPlace("Kandra", "The Dungeon of Doom");
```

Each function has a specific job to do. If you want to display all of the information at once, you wrap the individual functions inside one master function and pass it all the information it needs:

```
showPlayerInfo("Kandra", "The Dungeon of Doom", 50);
```

Over the next few sections, you define the four functions and see them working with player objects. The first three functions are very similar; pay attention to what changes and what stays the same. Notice how you use parameters when defining the functions and how you use arguments when calling them.

5.3.1 Displaying players' names

Your first function's job is to display the player's name. That's it. No bells or whistles. The next listing shows the showPlayerName function definition and calls the function with two different names to produce the following output:

```
> Kandra
> Dax
```

Listing 5.7   Displaying a player's name (http://jsbin.com/yubahi/edit?js,console)

```
var showPlayerName;

showPlayerName = function (playerName) {        ◁——  Include a playerName parameter
    console.log(playerName);          ◁——              when defining the function
};
                                                     Log the value assigned to
showPlayerName("Kandra");                            the parameter when the
showPlayerName("Dax");                               function is called
```

In the actual *The Crypt* program, you're not likely to call the showPlayerName function with literal values like "Kandra" and "Dax". You're much more likely to use variables. In particular, JavaScript objects will represent players. The next listing updates the code to use a couple of player objects instead.

Listing 5.8   Displaying a player's name via an object property (http://jsbin.com/juhewi/edit?js,console)

```
var player1;
var player2;
var showPlayerName;

showPlayerName = function (playerName) {
    console.log(playerName);
};

player1 = {
    name: "Kandra",
    place: "The Dungeon of Doom",
    health: 50
};

player2 = {
    name: "Dax",
    place: "The Old Library",
    health: 40
};
```

```
showPlayerName(player1.name);
showPlayerName(player2.name);
```
| **Pass the player's name to the**
| **showPlayerName function as an argument**

That's names covered. Next up, health.

5.3.2   *Displaying players' health*

The `showPlayerHealth` function definition in the following listing includes two parameters, `playerName` and `playerHealth`, to produce output like this:

```
> Kandra has health 50
> Dax has health 40
```

> Listing 5.9   **Displaying a player's health**
>   **(http://jsbin.com/nomija/edit?js,console)**

```
var showPlayerHealth;

showPlayerHealth = function (playerName, playerHealth) {
    console.log(playerName + " has health " + playerHealth);
};

showPlayerHealth("Kandra", 50);
showPlayerHealth("Dax", 40);
```

Include two parameters, playerName and playerHealth, in the definition

Use the values assigned to the parameters to produce a string for display

The call to `showPlayerHealth` in listing 5.9 used the literal values `"Kandra"` and `50`. In the final program, each player's information is assigned to the properties of a player object. Your calls to `showPlayerHealth` are much more likely to use those properties than hard-coded values. The next listing updates the code to include player objects.

> Listing 5.10   **Displaying a player's health via object properties**
>   **(http://jsbin.com/zufoxi/edit?js,console)**

```
var player1;
var player2;
var showPlayerHealth;

showPlayerHealth = function (playerName, playerHealth) {
    console.log(playerName + " has health " + playerHealth);
};

player1 = {
    name: "Kandra",
    place: "The Dungeon of Doom",
    health: 50
};

player2 = {
    name: "Dax",
    place: "The Old Library",
    health: 40
};
```

```
showPlayerHealth(player1.name, player1.health);
showPlayerHealth(player2.name, player2.health);
```

Pass each player's name
and health properties to the
showPlayerHealth function
as arguments

Name: check. Health: check. That just leaves location.

5.3.3 *Displaying players' locations*

The `showPlayerPlace` function definition in the following listing also includes two
parameters, this time `playerName` and `playerPlace`, and produces output like this:

```
> Kandra is in The Dungeon of Doom
> Dax is in The Old Library
```

> **Listing 5.11 Displaying a player's location**
> **(http://jsbin.com/yifahe/edit?js,console)**

```
var showPlayerPlace;

showPlayerPlace = function (playerName, playerPlace) {
    console.log(playerName + " is in " + playerPlace);
};

showPlayerPlace("Kandra", "The Dungeon of Doom");
showPlayerPlace("Dax", "The Old Library");
```

Once again, switching from the hard-coded literal values in listing 5.11 to object properties gives you an updated version in the next listing.

> **Listing 5.12 Displaying a player's location via object properties**
> **(http://jsbin.com/mejuki/edit?js,console)**

```
var player1;
var player2;
var showPlayerPlace;

showPlayerPlace = function (playerName, playerPlace) {
    console.log(playerName + " is in " + playerPlace);
};

player1 = {
    name: "Kandra",
    place: "The Dungeon of Doom",
    health: 50
};

player2 = {
    name: "Dax",
    place: "The Old Library",
    health: 40
};

showPlayerPlace(player1.name, player1.place);
showPlayerPlace(player2.name, player2.place);
```

You have the three functions you need to show individual pieces of information about players. Now it's time to use the functions together.

5.3.4 Putting it all together—displaying players' information

The `showPlayerInfo` function uses your three individual functions—`showPlayer-Name`, `showPlayerHealth`, and `showPlayerPlace`—and adds a touch of formatting to produce a display of each player's properties. The output for one player looks like this:

```
>
> Kandra
> --------------------------
> Kandra is in The Dungeon of Doom
> Kandra has health 50
> --------------------------
>
```

The next listing leaves out the three component functions to focus on the new function. They're included on JS Bin.

> **Listing 5.13   Displaying a player's information
>   (http://jsbin.com/likafe/edit?js,console)**

```
var showPlayerInfo;

showPlayerInfo = function (playerName, playerPlace, playerHealth) {
    console.log("");

    showPlayerName(playerName);

    console.log("--------------------------");

    showPlayerPlace(playerName, playerPlace);
    showPlayerHealth(playerName, playerHealth);

    console.log("--------------------------");
    console.log("");
};

showPlayerInfo("Kandra", "The Dungeon of Doom", 50);
showPlayerInfo("Dax", "The Old Library", 40);
```

You call the `showPlayerInfo` function with three arguments each time. It, in turn, passes the required arguments on to the `showPlayerName`, `showPlayerHealth`, and `showPlayerPlace` functions.

You end with all the pieces put together in a single listing, shown next. It includes each variable declaration and assignment as a single step and uses player object properties, like `player1.name`, rather than literal values, like `"Kandra"`, when calling `show-PlayerInfo`.

Listing 5.14 Displaying a player's information using properties (http://jsbin.com/loteti/edit?js,console)

```js
var showPlayerName = function (playerName) {
    console.log(playerName);
};

var showPlayerHealth = function (playerName, playerHealth) {
    console.log(playerName + " has health " + playerHealth);
};

var showPlayerPlace = function (playerName, playerPlace) {
    console.log(playerName + " is in " + playerPlace);
};

var showPlayerInfo = function (playerName, playerPlace, playerHealth) {
    console.log("");
    showPlayerName(playerName);
    console.log("--------------------------");
    showPlayerPlace(playerName, playerPlace);
    showPlayerHealth(playerName, playerHealth);
    console.log("--------------------------");
    console.log("");
};

var player1 = {
    name: "Kandra",
    place: "The Dungeon of Doom",
    health: 50
};

var player2 = {
    name: "Dax",
    place: "The Old Library",
    health: 40
};

showPlayerInfo(player1.name, player1.place, player1.health);
showPlayerInfo(player2.name, player2.place, player2.health);
```

5.4 Summary

- Define a function with named *parameters* to show that you expect to pass data to the function when you call it. Commas separate the parameters inside the parentheses of the definition:

```js
function (param1, param2) { … }
```

- Use the parameters inside the function body as if they are variables.
- Call the function with *arguments*. When you run the program, the arguments are automatically assigned to the parameters for use in the function body:

```js
myFunction(arg1, arg2)
```

Return values: getting data from functions

In chapter 4 you discovered how functions can increase your efficiency by allowing you to write code once but use it many times. In chapter 5, you made functions much more flexible by passing them information with each call; a function can act in different ways and produce different outputs depending on the arguments you give it. In this chapter you give functions the chance to talk back by returning the results of their work. You also call functions directly at the console prompt to investigate the values they return.

6.1 Returning data from functions

It's often useful to have a function do some work for you and give you back the result of that work. You can then use the result however you want. In listing 5.6 you saw a showSum function that displays the sum of two numbers on the console. It may be better to have an add function that simply adds the numbers and returns the result. Whereas showSum always displays the result on the console, with add you can display the result the function returns if you choose, use it in further calculations, send it across a network, or save it to a database.

6.1.1 *The return value replaces the function call*

Most of the functions you've written so far have executed code for you on demand and then logged something to the console. They've helped you to break up programs into understandable chunks. By assigning the functions to well-named variables, you've made the programs easier to follow. For an example of well-named variables, here's a snippet of code for displaying player information in *The Crypt*:

```
showPlayerName("Kandra");
showLine();
showPlayerPlace("Kandra", "The Dungeon of Doom");
showPlayerHealth("Kandra", 50);
showLine();
```

Even if you don't know how the functions perform their jobs, their names give you a good idea of the intentions of the code.

Functions can also return information: the result of a calculation, a constructed piece of text, or data from a database. You can assign the returned value to a variable or use it as an argument with other functions. The following examples show, in bold, calls to the four functions add, getPlayerPlace, findPlanetPosition, and getMessage:

```
var sum = add(50, 23);
var placeInfo = getPlayerPlace("Kandra", "The Dungeon of Doom");
console.log(findPlanetPosition("Jupiter"));
console.log(getMessage());
```

Each function returns a value and the returned value replaces the function call. Assuming the functions return the following values in bold, the previous four statements become

```
var sum = 73;
var placeInfo = "Kandra is in The Dungeon of Doom";
console.log("Jupiter: planet number 5");
console.log("I'm going on an adventure!");
```

Figure 6.1 shows what happens when you call the add function.

To return a value from a function, use the return keyword.

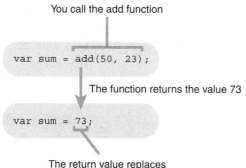

You call the add function

```
var sum = add(50, 23);
```

The function returns the value 73

```
var sum = 73;
```

The return value replaces the function call

Figure 6.1 You call the add function and it returns the value 73.

6.1.2 *The return keyword*

Return a value from a function by using the `return` keyword. Whatever follows `return` in a statement is the value that replaces the function call.

Listing 6.1 shows the definition of a `getMessage` function. It includes a *return statement*, a statement that starts with the `return` keyword:

```
return "I'm going on an adventure!";
```

The function returns the string `"I'm going on an adventure!"` because the string follows the `return` keyword. The program assigns the string to the `response` variable and logs it to the console to show

```
> I'm going on an adventure!
```

**Listing 6.1   Returning a value from a function
(http://jsbin.com/yucate/edit?js,console)**

```
var getMessage;
var response;

getMessage = function () {
    return "I'm going on an adventure!";
};

response = getMessage();

console.log(response);
```

Return the message from the function by using the return keyword

Call the getMessage function and assign the returned value to the response variable

The `getMessage` function always returns the same value. It's common to determine the return value by using information you pass in as arguments when you call the function.

6.1.3 *Using arguments to determine the return value*

In chapter 5, you passed information into a function by including parameters in the function definition and arguments in the function call. You can use that information in the function body to determine the value the function returns and so call the function again and again with different arguments to produce different return values.

The following listing shows a `getHelloTo` function that returns a string including a name passed in as an argument. The program assigns the return value to a variable and logs it to the console.

```
> Hello to Kandra
```

**Listing 6.2   Using an argument to determine the return value
(http://jsbin.com/nijijo/edit?js,console)**

```
var getHelloTo;
var fullMessage;
```

```
getHelloTo = function (name) {
    return "Hello to " + name;
};

fullMessage = getHelloTo("Kandra");

console.log(fullMessage);
```

Include a parameter in the function definition

Use the value assigned to the parameter to build the return value

In listing 6.2, you assign the return value to a variable, `fullMessage`, and log it to the console. The variable is redundant; you could just log the return value directly, as shown in the next listing, in which you call the `getHelloTo` function twice to give the following output:

```
> Hello to Kandra
> Hello to Dax
```

<table>
<tr><td>Listing 6.3　Using the return value as an argument
(http://jsbin.com/yapic/edit?js,console)</td></tr>
</table>

```
var getHelloTo;

getHelloTo = function (name) {
    return "Hello to " + name;
};

console.log(getHelloTo("Kandra"));
console.log(getHelloTo("Dax"));
```

Call the getHelloTo function and use the return value as an argument for console.log

Functions can return any type of value: strings, numbers, objects, and even other functions. Let's look at an example that returns a number.

Figure 6.2 shows a call to the `add` function, `add(50, 23)`. The figure shows how the arguments passed to `add` are used to calculate the return value.

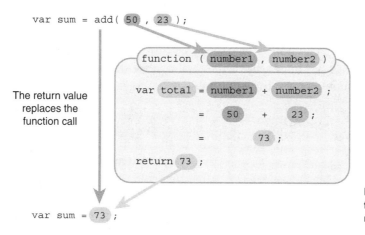

Figure 6.2　The add function calculates the return value.

The next listing shows the code to make the add function do its thing. Notice, in particular, the return keyword.

```
var add;

add = function (number1, number2) {              Assign the result of the
    var total = number1 + number2;               calculation to the total variable

    return total;                    Use the return keyword to pass the result
};                                   back to where the function is called

var sum = add(50, 23);               Call the add function and assign the
                                     value returned to the sum variable
console.log(sum);
```

add(50, 23) calls the add function, assigning 50 to number1 and 23 to number2. The value of number1 is then added to the value of number2 and the result assigned to the total variable. The return keyword then ends the function and replaces the call to the function with the value of total.

```
var sum = add(50, 23);
```

becomes

```
var sum = 73;
```

because add(50, 23) returns 73.

Remember, the assignment operator, =, works by assigning the value on its right to the variable on its left. If a function call is on its right, then it assigns the function's return value.

The total variable in the add function in listing 6.4 isn't really needed; it's assigned a value and then immediately returned. You could have returned the result of the calculation directly, as the totalCost function does in listing 6.5. Given the call-out charge and hourly rate charged by a plumber, totalCost calculates the total cost for a certain number of hours of work. So, say the call-out charge is $30 and the plumber charges $40 per hour, what is the total cost for three hours of work? total-Cost(30, 40, 3) should return the result $150.

```
var totalCost;                                    Evaluate the total cost and return the value

totalCost = function (callOutCharge, costPerHour, numberOfHours) {
    return callOutCharge + costPerHour * numberOfHours;
};
                                                  The call to totalCost is replaced
console.log("$" + totalCost(30, 40, 3));          by the value returned.
```

When you call the `totalCost` function, it evaluates the calculation to the right of the `return` keyword and returns the value. It follows the usual rules of arithmetic: it performs the multiplication first and then the addition: 30 + 40 * 3 = 30 + 120 = 150.

6.2 Experimenting at the console prompt

Programmers don't generally use the console in production, that is, in published programs and websites. They use it in development, when designing and writing programs. It provides a convenient way for programmers (that's you) to log values and errors and investigate the state of their programs while they're running. That interactivity, the chance to get immediate feedback, makes the console really useful for learning—particularly for learning through experimentation. It's time to go on an adventure of discovery with the functions you've seen so far in this chapter.

6.2.1 Calling functions

The next listing includes four functions from earlier listings. If you run the program, it won't produce any output on the console; it doesn't include any calls to `console.log`.

> **Listing 6.6 A collection of functions that return values**
> **(http://jsbin.com/lijufo/edit?js,console)**

```
var getMessage;
var getHelloTo;
var add;
var totalCost;

getMessage = function () {
    return "I'm going on an adventure!";
};

getHelloTo = function (name) {
    return "Hello to " + name;
};

add = function (number1, number2) {
    return number1 + number2;
};

totalCost = function (callOutCharge, costPerHour, numberOfHours) {
    return callOutCharge + costPerHour * numberOfHours;
};
```

Running the program assigns the four functions to the four variables declared at the top of the program. You can then access the variables from the console prompt. You can call the functions assigned to the variables to investigate their return values.

Follow the link to the listing on JS Bin and make sure you run the program. At the console prompt type

```
> getMessage()
```

and press Enter. The getMessage function runs and displays its return value:

```
"I'm going on an adventure!"
```

At the prompt, press the up arrow on your keyboard. It should bring up the last line you typed. (You can navigate through your previous entries at the console with the up and down arrows.) Press Enter to resubmit a command. The getMessage function always returns the same string. If you look at its function body, you can see it returns a string literal, a hard-coded value.

```
return "I'm going on an adventure!";
```

The next function in the program, getHelloTo, includes a name parameter in its definition. The name parameter allows the return value to vary in response to the argument you pass to the function when you call it.

```
getHelloTo = function (name) {
    return "Hello to " + name;
};
```

Have a go at calling the function at the console with different arguments each time:

```
> getHelloTo("Jason")
  "Hello to Jason"
> getHelloTo("Rosemary")
  "Hello to Rosemary"
```

You can immediately see how changing the argument affects the return value.

6.2.2   Declaring new variables

As well as giving you access to variables declared in your programs, the console allows you to declare new variables and assign them values.

Carrying straight on from the previous section, at the console type

```
> var friend
```

and press Enter. The console displays the value of your previous entry. Because you didn't assign a value to the friend variable, undefined is logged to the console.

```
undefined
```

Give it a value. Type

```
> friend = "Amber"
```

and press Enter. The console displays the new value.

```
"Amber"
```

Finally, use your new `friend` variable as an argument for the `getHelloTo` function.

```
> getHelloTo(friend)
  "Hello to Amber"
```

Have a play with the `add` and `totalCost` functions, passing them different arguments and checking the return values displayed on the console, for example:

```
> add(30, 12)
  42
> totalCost(10, 20, 3)
  70
```

The console is more than a place to log messages from your programs. You can really dig into your programs and check that they behave as expected. Don't wait for permission; jump in and test all the listings.

Now let's use your new knowledge of return values to improve how *The Crypt* displays player information.

6.3   *The Crypt—building player information strings*

Figure 6.3 shows where the focus of this section, showing player information by using return values, fits into the overall structure of our ongoing game example.

Figure 6.3   Elements of *The Crypt*

In chapter 5, you divided the work of displaying player information among a number of functions, with each function having a specific job to do.

```
showPlayerName("Kandra");
showPlayerPlace("Kandra", "The Dungeon of Doom");
showPlayerHealth("Kandra", 50);
```

The functions each logged a string of information to the console. But what if you don't want the information on the console? You might want to send it in an email, serve it as a response to a web request, or append it to an existing element on a web page. It would be more flexible if the functions built the information strings and returned them for the program to use as required.

6.3.1 Building strings for a player's name, health, and location

You pass your new functions the information they need as arguments and they return a string containing that information. The kind of return values you expect are shown here:

```
getPlayerName("Kandra");                  // --> "Kandra"
getPlayerHealth("Kandra", 50);            // --> "Kadra has health 50"
getPlayerPlace("Kandra", "The Dungeon");  // --> "Kandra is in The Dungeon"
```

First up is getPlayerName. At the moment it just returns the name it's given, which seems like a waste of time. But defining a function allows you to make all the player information accessible in the same way; getting the name is similar to getting the health or the location. It also makes it easier to update the code later if you decide to change how the name is displayed. The following listing shows the getPlayerName function definition and an example call to it, producing the output

```
> Kandra
```

Listing 6.7 Getting a string for a player's name
(http://jsbin.com/hijeli/edit?js,console)

```
var getPlayerName;

getPlayerName = function (playerName) {
    return playerName;
};

console.log(getPlayerName("Kandra"));
```

The next two functions, getPlayerHealth and getPlayerPlace, are very similar, both building a simple string from the information passed in. The next listing includes the definitions of both functions along with some usage examples, producing the following on the console:

```
> Kandra has health 50
> Kandra is in The Dungeon of Doom
```

Listing 6.8 Getting strings for a player's health and location
(http://jsbin.com/pemore/edit?js,console)

```
var getPlayerHealth;
var getPlayerPlace;

getPlayerHealth = function (playerName, playerHealth) {
    return playerName + " has health " + playerHealth;
};
```

```
getPlayerPlace = function (playerName, playerPlace) {
    return playerName + " is in " + playerPlace;
};

console.log(getPlayerHealth("Kandra", 50));
console.log(getPlayerPlace("Kandra", "The Dungeon of Doom"));
```

Calling the three functions from one main `getPlayerInfo` function will give you the display string you want. The next section shows how the pieces are assembled.

6.3.2 *A function for player information—putting the pieces together*

With the pieces in place you can now build the main function to produce a string of information about a player. You want the output to look something like this:

```
>
> Kandra
> ********************
> Kandra is in The Dungeon of Doom
> Kandra has health 50
> ********************
>
```

To construct the lines of characters separating the player information, you make use of a `getBorder` function that returns a line of asterisk symbols. The listing that follows shows the `getPlayerInfo` definition. It includes calls to other functions not shown in the printed listing but included in the JS Bin version.

> **Listing 6.9   Getting a string for a player's information**
> **(http://jsbin.com/javuxe/edit?js,console)**

```
var getPlayerInfo;

getPlayerInfo = function (playerName, playerPlace, playerHealth) {
    var playerInfo;

    playerInfo = "\n" + getPlayerName(playerName);        ◁──┐ Build up the info string by
    playerInfo += "\n" + getBorder();                        │ using the other functions
    playerInfo += "\n" + getPlayerPlace(                     │ to create the pieces
                        playerName, playerPlace);
    playerInfo += "\n" + getPlayerHealth(
                        playerName, playerHealth);
    playerInfo += "\n" + getBorder();                     ◁──┐ Use += to
    playerInfo += "\n";                                      │ append a string to
                                                             │ an existing string
    return playerInfo;          ◁──┐ Return the completed
};                                 │ info string
```

```
console.log(getPlayerInfo("Kandra", "The Dungeon of Doom", 50));
```

The `getPlayerInfo` function builds up the player information string piece by piece, appending the strings returned by the functions called to the `playerInfo` variable. The extra string, `\n`, appended at each stage is a new-line character; text following the new-line character will appear on a new line on the console. You use the += operator to append a string to the end of an existing string.

The final example for this chapter gathers all of the code into a single listing, listing 6.10, along with two player objects used to test the getPlayerInfo function. It also uses a different separator character in the getBorder function, producing output for both players like this:

```
>
> Kandra
> ==============================
> Kandra is in The Dungeon of Doom
> Kandra has health 50
> ==============================
>
>
> Dax
> ==============================
> Dax is in The Old Library
> Dax has health 40
> ==============================
>
```

> **Listing 6.10   Displaying player information using objects**
> **(http://jsbin.com/puteki/edit?js,console)**

```
var getPlayerName = function (playerName) {                    ◁─┐
    return playerName;                                            │
};                                                                │
                                                                  │
var getPlayerHealth = function (                               ◁──┤  Define functions to
                    playerName, playerHealth) {                   │  return strings of
    return playerName + " has health " + playerHealth;            │  specific player info
};                                                                │
                                                                  │
var getPlayerPlace = function (                                ◁──┘
                    playerName, playerPlace) {
    return playerName + " is in " + playerPlace;
};

var getBorder = function () {                                  ◁─┐  Define a function to return
    return "==============================";                      │  a string used as a border
};

var getPlayerInfo = function (                                 ◁─┐  Define a function that calls
        playerName, playerPlace, playerHealth) {                  │  previous functions to build
                                                                  │  a player info string
    var playerInfo;

    playerInfo = "\n" + getPlayerName(playerName);
    playerInfo += "\n" + getBorder();
    playerInfo += "\n" + getPlayerPlace(playerName, playerPlace);
    playerInfo += "\n" + getPlayerHealth(playerName, playerHealth);
```

```
        playerInfo += "\n" + getBorder();
        playerInfo += "\n";

        return playerInfo;
};

var player1 = {
        name: "Kandra",
        place: "The Dungeon of Doom",
        health: 50
};

var player2 = {
        name: "Dax",
        place: "The Old Library",
        health: 40
};

console.log(
        getPlayerInfo(
                player1.name, player1.place, player1.health));
console.log(
        getPlayerInfo(
                player2.name, player2.place, player2.health));
```

Create two
player objects

Test the functions,
displaying the
returned strings
on the console

You've successfully switched from functions that always print the output on the console to ones that return player information as strings. You then choose what to do with the strings.

Having to pass individual bits of information about the players to the functions is a bit of a drag. The different functions require different bits of info and you have to make sure to put the arguments in the right order. It would be easier if you could just pass the whole player object as an argument and let the functions access whichever properties they need. In chapter 7 you'll see how useful it is to use JavaScript objects both as arguments and as return values.

6.4   Summary

- Pass information out of functions by using the return keyword:

```
return "Pentaquark!";
return 42;
return true;
```

- Use a function call as a value to assign to a variable or use as an argument. The value the function returns replaces the function call:

```
var particle = getDiscovery();
console.log(getPlayerPlace("Kandra"));
```

- Include parameters in the function definition and use the arguments passed in to the function to determine the value returned:

```
var sum = add(28, 14);
```

- Use the console to explore and test programs.
- Call functions at the console prompt and see their return values displayed.
- Declare variables at the console, assign them values, and use them as arguments for functions.

7

Object arguments: functions working with objects

This is the last of the run of four chapters introducing functions. By now, you know about using functions to execute code on demand and passing information to and from functions using parameters, arguments, and the return keyword. You've also seen how to use objects to collect values together as named properties. Well, it's time to combine functions and objects to turbocharge productivity, efficiency, and readability.

Remember the first-aid kit from chapter 3? We consider the kit to be a single object that we can pass around, pack in a rucksack, and speak about. Such encapsulation, or chunking, where we treat a collection as singular, is an important part of how we as humans cope with complex information, both in language and in memory.

When the need arises, we can consider the elements that make up the kit: antiseptic, plasters, bandages, and so on.

You use the same concept of encapsulation throughout this chapter as you pass objects to and from functions as arguments and return values.

7.1 Using objects as arguments

Being able to pass an object to a function is really useful, especially if the function needs to access lots of the object's properties. You need only a single parameter in the function definition and you don't need a long list of arguments when calling the function. showPlayerInfo(player1) is neater, more easily understood, and less prone to error than showPlayerInfo(player1.name, player1.location, player1.health).

You can pass the same information to the function but wrapped into a single object rather than as separate values (figure 7.1).

An object as a single argument

```
showPlayerInfo( player1 );

showPlayerInfo( player1.name , player1.location , player1.health );
```

Multiple arguments can be harder to work with

Figure 7.1 A single object as an argument is neater than multiple arguments.

7.1.1 Accessing properties of an object argument

Inspired by the space adventures of New Horizons, Curiosity, Rosetta, and Philae, you decide to write a quick app for displaying information about the solar system. One feature of the app is to display information about planets.

Your first listing shows the getPlanetInfo function with a planet parameter. When you call the function using a planet object as an argument, the function body returns a string built using some of the planet's properties. The code produces the following output:

```
> Jupiter: planet number 5
```

Listing 7.1 Passing a function an object as an argument
(http://jsbin.com/tafopo/edit?js,console)

```
var planet1;
var getPlanetInfo;

planet1 = {
    name: "Jupiter",
```

```
    position: 5,
    type: "Gas Giant",
    radius: 69911,
    sizeRank: 1
};

getPlanetInfo = function (planet) {
    return planet.name + ": planet number " + planet.position;
};

console.log(getPlanetInfo(planet1));
```

Include a planet parameter, expecting a planet object to be passed in

Access properties of the planet object

Call the getPlanetInfo function, passing in a planet as an argument

Passing an object to a function as a single argument is neat and tidy. There's no need to make sure you've included all the required arguments in the right order—a single argument does the job.

Once you've passed an object to a function, JavaScript automatically assigns it to the parameter included in the function's definition.

You access the properties of the object through the parameter, as shown in figure 7.2. The function has full control of the object via the parameter; it can even add new properties.

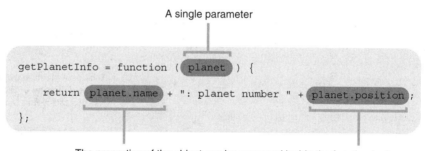

A single parameter

The properties of the object can be accessed inside the function body

Figure 7.2   Object properties can be accessed inside the function body.

7.1.2   *Adding properties to an object argument*

When you pass an object to a function as an argument, the code in the function body has access to the object's properties. It can read them, change them, and delete them and can add new properties too.

Listing 7.2 shows two functions with `planet` parameters. When you pass a planet object, encapsulating a name and a radius, to the `calculateSizes` function, the function adds two new properties, `area` and `volume`, to the object (figure 7.3).

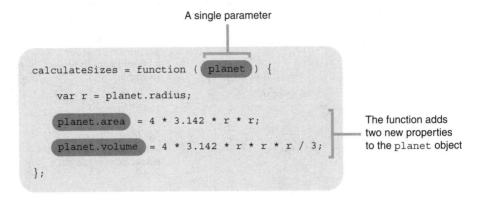

Figure 7.3 The calculateSizes **function adds new properties to the** planet **object.**

The displaySizes function uses the two new properties to print information about the planet on the console:

```
> Jupiter
> surface area = 61426702271.128 square km
> volume = 1431467394158943.2 cubic km
```

Listing 7.2   A function that adds properties to an object
                (http://jsbin.com/qevodu/edit?js,console)

```
var planet1 = { name: "Jupiter", radius: 69911 };

var calculateSizes = function (planet) {
    var r = planet.radius;
    planet.area = 4 * 3.142 * r * r;
    planet.volume = 4 * 3.142 * r * r * r / 3;
};

var displaySizes = function (planet) {
    console.log(planet.name);
    console.log("surface area = " + planet.area + " square km");
    console.log("volume = " + planet.volume + " cubic km");
};

calculateSizes(planet1);
displaySizes(planet1);
```

Include a planet parameter in the definition of the calculateSizes function

Add an area property to the planet object passed to the function when it's called

Add a volume property

Include a planet parameter in the definition of the displaySizes function

Pass the planet1 object as an argument to both functions

You create the planet object and assign it to the planet1 variable:

```
planet1 = { name: "Jupiter", radius: 69911 };
```

When you call the `calculateSizes` function, you pass `planet1` to it as an argument:

```
calculateSizes(planet1);
```

JavaScript assigns the object referred to by `planet1` to the `planet` parameter for use within the function. The function uses the `planet` parameter to add two new properties to the object, `planet.area` and `planet.volume`. By the time you call the `display-Sizes` function, the object has the two new properties needed to display all the required information:

```
displaySizes(planet1);
```

As well as passing objects *to* functions, you can return objects *from* functions.

7.2 *Returning objects from functions*

Just as passing objects to functions as arguments is an efficient way of moving information to where it's needed, so is using objects as return values. Functions can either manipulate objects that you pass to them and then return them, or they can return brand-new objects that they create in the function body.

This section explores two examples: the first uses a number of parameters to build a new planet object and the second uses two object parameters to create a point in 2D space.

7.2.1 *Building planets—an object creation function*

Back with your solar system app, you decide to streamline the creation of planets. You write a function to which you pass the key facts, and it returns a `planet` object with properties set accordingly. Your `buildPlanet` function lets you create planets like this:

```
planet1 = buildPlanet("Jupiter", 5, "Gas Giant", 69911, 1);
```

Figure 7.4 shows how JavaScript assigns the arguments to parameters when you call `buildPlanet`. You use the parameters to create a new object.

Listing 7.3 shows the definition of the `buildPlanet` function. It also has a `get-PlanetInfo` function that it uses to get planet information for display. Once displayed, the information looks like this:

```
JUPITER: planet 5
NEPTUNE: planet 8
```

Notice here how the planet names are in uppercase. The `getPlanetInfo` function makes use of a built-in JavaScript function, `toUpperCase`, that converts strings to uppercase. `toUpperCase` and some other JavaScript functions will be discussed in section 7.3.

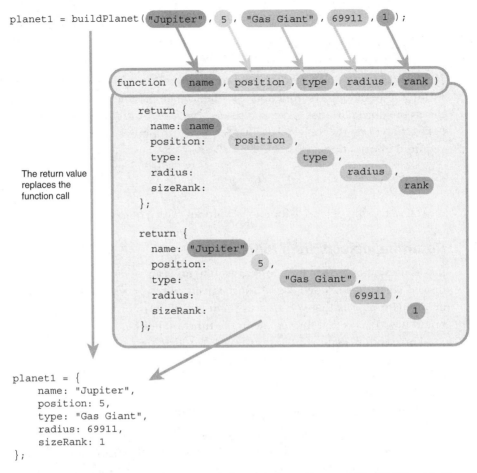

```
planet1 = buildPlanet("Jupiter", 5, "Gas Giant", 69911, 1);
```

```
function ( name, position, type, radius, rank )
    return {
        name: name
        position:    position ,
        type:                      type ,
        radius:                          radius ,
        sizeRank:                              rank
    };

    return {
        name: "Jupiter" ,
        position:        5 ,
        type:                "Gas Giant" ,
        radius:                        69911 ,
        sizeRank:                          1
    };
```

The return value replaces the function call

```
planet1 = {
    name: "Jupiter",
    position: 5,
    type: "Gas Giant",
    radius: 69911,
    sizeRank: 1
};
```

Figure 7.4 JavaScript assigns the arguments to parameters when you call `buildPlanet`. The function uses the parameters to create an object.

Listing 7.3 A function to create planets
          (http://jsbin.com/coyeta/edit?js,console)

```
var buildPlanet;
var getPlanetInfo;
var planet1;
var planet2;

buildPlanet = function (name, position, type, radius, rank) {
    return {
        name: name,
        position: position,
        type: type,
        radius: radius,
        sizeRank: rank
```

Create an object using curly braces and immediately return it from the function

Create a name property and assign it the value of the name parameter

```
        };
    };

    getPlanetInfo = function (planet) {
        return planet.name.toUpperCase() + ": planet " + planet.position;
    };

    planet1 = buildPlanet("Jupiter", 5, "Gas Giant", 69911, 1);
    planet2 = buildPlanet("Neptune", 8, "Ice Giant", 24622, 4);

    console.log(getPlanetInfo(planet1));
    console.log(getPlanetInfo(planet2));
```

The key-value pairs inside the object created by the `buildPlanet` function look a little strange at first:

`name: name, position: position`, and so on.

For each key-value pair, the key is to the left of the colon and the value is to the right. You use the parameters as values, so for the function call

```
planet1 = buildPlanet("Jupiter", 5, "Gas Giant", 69911, 1);
```

the object-creation code becomes

```
name: "Jupiter",
position: 5,
type: "Gas Giant",
radius: 69911,
sizeRank: 1
```

7.2.2   Points in 2D space

Keen to create an animation showing the planets in the solar system, you start to investigate coordinates in two dimensions. All of the coordinates have two values associated with them, x and y. This seems like an obvious place to use objects. Each point is an object with x and y properties:

```
point1 = { x : 3 , y : 4 };
point2 = { x : 0 , y : -2 };
```

You can access individual values using dot notation: `point1.x`, `point2.y`, and so on.

As an initial experiment, you write a program to move a point a certain amount in the x direction and a certain amount in the y direction. Because the change in position also has x and y components, you use an object for that too. For example, to represent a movement of four across and two down you use the object `{ x : 4, y : -2 }`.

Listing 7.4 includes a `move` function that takes two arguments, an initial point object and a change object. It returns a new point representing the final position if you started from the first point and moved by the change specified.

The program uses a `showPoint` function to produce the following output:

```
( 2 , 5 )
Move 4 across and 2 down
( 6 , 3 )
```

Listing 7.4   Moving a point in 2D
                (http://jsbin.com/baxuvi/edit?js,console)

```
var point1;
var point2;
var move;
var showPoint;

move = function (point, change) {
    return {
        x: point.x + change.x,
        y: point.y + change.y
    };
};

showPoint = function (point) {
    console.log("( " + point.x + " , " + point.y + " )");
};

point1 = { x : 2, y : 5 };

point2 = move(point1, { x : 4, y : -2 });

showPoint(point1);
console.log("Move 4 across and 2 down");
showPoint(point2);
```

Create an object using curly braces and immediately return it

Set the new coordinates by applying the change to the original point

Pass in the original point as a variable and the change as an object literal

The second argument you pass to the `move` function in listing 7.4 is written using an object literal, `{ x : 4, y : -2 }`. You could assign it to a variable first but, because you use it only once, a literal value is okay too. The two points are plotted and their coordinates shown in figure 7.5.

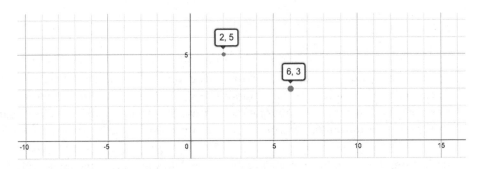

Figure 7.5   The points before and after the move of 4 across and 2 down (plotted using desmos.com—an application written in JavaScript)

You've seen objects being passed to functions and objects being returned from functions and, in listing 7.4, a function that uses objects as arguments and returns an object. That's functions using objects. You can also set functions as properties of objects.

7.3 Methods—setting functions as properties of objects

In JavaScript, you can use functions as values, just like numbers, strings, and objects. That means you can pass them as arguments, return them from other functions, and set them as properties of objects. In this section, continuing the theme of functions working with objects, you look at an example of setting functions as properties of an object.

7.3.1 Namespaces—organizing related functions

Let's write some functions to help format text displayed on the console. Displaying text is a big part of your interactive console applications, so the number of helper functions you create will expand. For now, you start with two really simple functions: blank returns an empty string and newLine returns a new-line character.

Because all of the functions are related to the same job, it's good to collect them together. You can do just that by setting each function as the property of a single object. Call it spacer:

```
var spacer = {};
```

Once you have an object, you can set functions as properties. First, here's a function to return an empty string:

```
spacer.blank = function () {
    return "";
};
```

Figure 7.6 illustrates how you create the function and then assign it to the blank property of the spacer object.

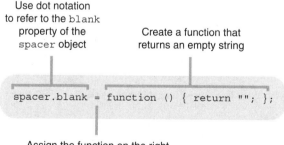

Use dot notation to refer to the blank property of the spacer object

Create a function that returns an empty string

```
spacer.blank = function () { return ""; };
```

Assign the function on the right to the property on the left

Figure 7.6 Create a function and assign it to an object property

Sometimes it's useful to include line breaks in a string, to space it over multiple lines. The special *escape sequence*, `"\n"`, is called the new-line character. Add a function to return the new-line character:

```
spacer.newLine = function () {
    return "\n";
};
```

Now you have two functions set as properties of the `spacer` object. When we use an object to collect functions together in this way, we call it a *namespace*. The `newLine` and `blank` functions belong to the `spacer` namespace. You can call the functions by adding parentheses as normal:

```
console.log(spacer.blank());
console.log("Line 1" + spacer.newLine() + "Line 2");
console.log(spacer.blank());
```

That code snippet produces this output:

```
>
> Line 1
> Line 2
>
```

The individual functions don't have to be added to the namespace one at a time. You can use the object literal syntax, curly braces with comma-separated key-value pairs, to set up the namespace with properties in place:

```
spacer = {
    blank: function () {
        return "";
    },
    newLine: function () {
        return "\n";
    }
};
```

Functions set as properties of an object are called *methods*. Currently, the `spacer` object has two methods, `blank` and `newLine`. You'll return to `spacer` in sections 7.3.4 and 7.3.5, where you'll add more methods and have a play with it on JS Bin.

JavaScript includes a number of useful objects and methods. Before you expand your `spacer` object, let's investigate `Math` and `String` methods.

7.3.2   *Math methods*

`Math` is a namespace built into JavaScript that provides properties and functions all related to mathematical calculations. Listing 7.5 shows the `Math.min` and `Math.max` methods in action. They return the smaller of two numbers and the larger of two numbers, respectively. The program produces the following output:

```
3 is smaller than 12
-10 is smaller than 3
```

```
var showSmaller = function (num1, num2) {
    var smaller = Math.min(num1, num2);
    var larger = Math.max(num1, num2);

    console.log(smaller + " is smaller than " + larger);
};

showSmaller(12, 3);
showSmaller(-10, 3);
```

Assign the smaller of the two numbers to smaller

Assign the larger of the two numbers to larger

`Math.min` and `Math.max`, when used together, are useful for making sure a value is in a specified range. Say a `lineLength` variable has to be between 0 and 40 inclusive. To force `lineLength` to be at least zero you can use

```
lineLength = Math.max(0, lineLength);
```

If `lineLength` is greater than zero, it will be the biggest and its value won't change. But, if `lineLength` is less than zero, zero will be the biggest and `lineLength` will be assigned zero.

Similarly, you can force `lineLength` to be less than or equal to 40:

```
lineLength = Math.min(40, lineLength);
```

Listing 7.6 shows such constraints in action. `line` is a function that returns a separator line of a specified length. The length must be between 0 and 40. Trying to display lines of length 30, 40, and 50 produces the following output:

```
> ==============================
> ========================================
> ========================================
```

Notice, the last two lines are both of length 40. Although 50 is specified as the length of the last line, the `line` function constrains the length to 40.

```
var line = function (lineLength) {
    var line = "========================================";
    lineLength = Math.max(0, lineLength);
```

Make sure lineLength is at least 0

```
        lineLength = Math.min(40, lineLength);
        return line.substr(0, lineLength);
}

console.log(line(30));
console.log(line(40));
console.log(line(50));
```

Make sure lineLength is at most 40

Use the substr string method to return a line of the right length

The `substr` method returns part of a string and is discussed in the next section.

There are a large number of `Math` methods for all kinds of mathematical tasks, many of which are used often. You can investigate some of them at www.room51.co.uk/js/math.html.

7.3.3   String methods

For every string you create, JavaScript makes available a number of methods. These functions help you manipulate the strings in a variety of ways. The next listing uses the `toUpperCase` method to convert a string to uppercase, like this:

```
> Jupiter becomes JUPITER
```

Listing 7.7   Converting a string to uppercase
(http://jsbin.com/jizaqu/edit?js,console)

```
var planet = "Jupiter";
var bigPlanet = planet.toUpperCase();

console.log(planet + " becomes " + bigPlanet);
```

Use dot notation to call the toUpperCase method on the planet string

You use dot notation to call the method on the `planet` string. As a method, `toUpperCase` is able to use the value of the `planet` variable to which it's attached; you don't need to pass `planet` to the function as an argument in parentheses.

Although string methods can act on the variables to which they are attached, they're still functions and you can also pass them arguments. Figure 7.7 shows how the `substr` method uses the value of `message` and two arguments.

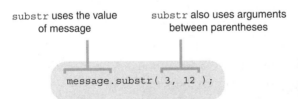

substr uses the value of message

substr also uses arguments between parentheses

`message.substr( 3, 12 );`

Figure 7.7   Methods can use arguments as well as the value of the object to which they're attached.

The following listing shows an example of using the `substr` method, displaying a substring on the console.

```
> choose to go
```

**Listing 7.8   Finding substrings
             (http://jsbin.com/mesisi/edit?js,console)**

```
var message = "We choose to go to the Moon!";

console.log(message.substr(3, 12));
```

The substr method accepts two arguments: the starting position in the original string and the number of characters to return. When specifying the position of a character in a string, counting is zero based: the first character is position 0, the second position 1, the third position 2, and so on. (I know starting at zero seems a bit odd at first; it's actually very common in programming languages.)

0	1	2	3	4	5	6	7	8	9	10	11	12	13	14
W	e		c	h	o	o	s	e		t	o		g	o

substr(3, 12) starts with the character at position 3, *c*, and returns a string of length 12, from position 3 to position 14.

But you don't have to spend all your time counting the positions of characters in strings, however exciting that sounds; you can use the indexOf method instead. The indexOf method returns the position, or *index*, of the first occurrence of a specified search string within a string.

The next listing uses indexOf to find the position of the *M* character in a string. It then passes the position to substr to grab a substring of length 3, producing the bovine pronouncement Moo on the console.

**Listing 7.9   Finding a character with indexOf
             (http://jsbin.com/bidabi/edit?js,console)**

```
var message = "The cow jumped over the Moon!";

var charIndex = message.indexOf("M");

console.log(message.substr(charIndex, 3));
```

You can use indexOf to find search strings longer than a single character. Here's an example using message from listing 7.9:

```
message.indexOf("cow");    // Returns 4
message.indexOf("the");    // Returns 20
message.indexOf("not");    // Returns -1
```

Notice that indexOf is case sensitive, so *the* and *The* are different, and it returns -1 if a string is not found.

Just like for Math, there are a lot of String methods available in JavaScript. Once again, the book's website has you covered: www.room51.co.uk/js/string-methods.html.

"So, are strings objects now?"

In listing 7.7, the string `"Jupiter"` is assigned to the `planet` variable. The `toUpperCase` method is then called: `planet.toUpperCase();`.

If methods are functions set as properties of objects, how is it we can call methods on strings?

Well, behind the scenes, whenever we access a string value, JavaScript creates a special `String` object that wraps the value. That object includes all the handy string methods. Once the statement has finished executing, the object is destroyed.

So, no, *strings are not objects*, but JavaScript provides a useful way to give us properties and methods for working with them.

7.3.4   *spacer—more methods for your namespace*

In section 7.3.1 you created a `spacer` object with a couple of functions attached, `blank` and `newLine`. You now add a few more interesting functions to help format your output nicely.

- `line` is your line separator function, upgraded! It returns a line of a given length between 0 and 40 characters long, now with a choice of five gorgeous characters! (`"*"`, `"+"`, `"="`, `"-"`, or `" "`).

```
spacer.line(10, "*");
spacer.line(6, "+");

> **********
> ++++++
```

- `wrap` returns text padded to a given length with added prefix and suffix characters.

```
spacer.wrap("Saturn", 10, "=");
spacer.wrap("Venus", 12, "-");
spacer.wrap("Mercury", 14, "+");

> = Saturn =
> - Venus    -
> + Mercury    +
```

- `box` returns text padded to a given length, with a line of characters above and below.

```
spacer.box("Saturn", 10, "=");
spacer.box("Venus", 12, "-");

==========
= Saturn =
==========

------------
- Venus    -
------------
```

The following listing shows the code for your new methods. Notice that `spacer.wrap` uses `spacer.line` to pad the text with space characters and `spacer.box` uses both `spacer.line` and `spacer.wrap` to generate its box outline. You'll look in detail at how the new methods work after the listing.

> **Listing 7.10 Organizing functions as object properties**
> **(http://jsbin.com/kayono/edit?js,console)**

```
var spacer = {
  blank: function () {                          Return an
    return "";                                  empty string
  },

  newLine: function () {                        Return a new
    return "\n";                                line character
  },

  line: function (length, character) {          Return a line of
    var longString =                            characters of a
          "******************************************";    given length
    longString += "----------------------------------------";
    longString += "========================================";
    longString += "++++++++++++++++++++++++++++++++++++++++";
    longString += "                                        ";
    length = Math.max(0, length);
    length = Math.min(40, length);
    return longString.substr(longString.indexOf(character), length);
  },

  wrap : function (text, length, character) {   Pad the text with
    var padLength = length - text.length - 3;   spaces and add a prefix
    var wrapText = character + " " + text;      and suffix character
    wrapText += spacer.line(padLength, " ");
    wrapText += character;
    return wrapText;
  },
                                                Surround the text in a box
  box: function (text, length, character) {     of a specified character
    var boxText = spacer.newLine();
    boxText += spacer.line(length, character) + spacer.newLine();
    boxText += spacer.wrap(text, length, character) + spacer.newLine();
    boxText += spacer.line(length, character) + spacer.newLine();
    return boxText;
  }
};

console.log(spacer.box("Mercury", 11, "="));    Test the box
console.log(spacer.box("Mars", 11, "*"));       method
```

TIP Notice how the wrap and box methods use the same parameters in the same order: text, length, and character. The line method has only two of those three parameters but is also consistent with the ordering: length and character. Such a conscious choice of parameter order reduces the chance of errors when calling the methods.

7.3.5   *Deep namespace exploration*

So how do your wonderful new methods work? Be brave and curious as you indulge in some deep namespace exploration. And remember, you can try code out on JS Bin, both in the JavaScript panel and at the prompt. For example, for the line method explanation that follows, declare and assign the longString variable at the console prompt:

```
> var longString = "**********------------===========+++++++++           "
```

Then you can try out the indexOf method:

```
> longString.indexOf("*")
  0
> longString.indexOf("=")
  20
```

Be playful and take your time. But don't worry if you don't follow everything the first time; the methods use a lot of ideas you've only just met. Stick with it; learning follows thinking.

THE LINE METHOD

Both the wrap and box methods use the trusty line method. It returns a string of a given length made up of one of five repeated characters:

```
line: function (length, character) {
    var longString = "****************************************";
    longString += "----------------------------------------";
    longString += "========================================";
    longString += "++++++++++++++++++++++++++++++++++++++++";
    longString += "                                        ";
    length = Math.max(0, length);
    length = Math.min(40, length);
    return longString.substr(longString.indexOf(character), length);
},
```

The method starts by creating one long string made up of all of the characters to be made available. It uses the += operator to append new strings to an existing string. The variable longString ends up as a string of the following form:

```
longString = "**********------------===========+++++++++           ";
```

This snippet has 10 of each character, whereas the actual method has 40 of each. The code uses the string method indexOf to find the position of the first character that matches the one specified when you call line. Here's an example, using the shorter snippet shown previously:

```
longString.indexOf("*");  // 0
longString.indexOf("-");  // 10
```

```
longString.indexOf("=");   // 20
longString.indexOf("+");   // 30
longString.indexOf(" ");   // 40
```

Having found where the requested character first appears, the code then uses `substr` to grab a substring of the specified length:

```
longString.substr(10, 6);   // ------
longString.substr(30, 3);   // +++
```

But the `line` method doesn't use hard-coded values; it uses parameters, `length` and `character`, to hold the arguments passed in when you call it:

```
// Get the index of the first matching character
var firstChar = longString.indexOf(character);

// Get a string of the requested length, starting at the first matching
// character
var requestedLine = longString.substr(firstChar, length);
```

The extra variables aren't really needed, although they could be used to make the method easier to follow. `line` finds the substring and returns it in one go:

```
return longString.substr(longString.indexOf(character), length);
```

Notice that a space is one of the available characters. Strings of spaces can be used to pad titles and boxes on the console. The `wrap` method uses `line` to do just that.

THE WRAP METHOD

To form the middle line of some boxed text, the `wrap` method returns a string of a specified length. The `character` argument specifies the first and last characters of the string:

```
wrap : function (text, length, character) {
  var padLength = length - text.length - 3;
  var wrapText = character + " " + text;
  wrapText += spacer.line(padLength, " ");
  wrapText += character;
  return wrapText;
},
```

Here are some strings of increasing length returned by `wrap`:

```
spacer.wrap("Neptune", 11, "=");   // = Neptune =
spacer.wrap("Neptune", 12, "=");   // = Neptune  =
spacer.wrap("Neptune", 13, "=");   // = Neptune   =
```

The method pads the last character with spaces on its left to make the whole string the correct length (figure 7.8).

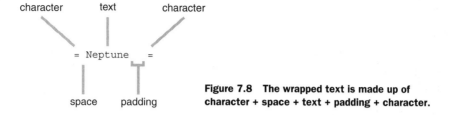

Figure 7.8   The wrapped text is made up of character + space + text + padding + character.

To find the length of the padding, start with the desired length of the whole string and subtract the length of the text you're wrapping and then three more to account for the first character, the leading space, and the last character:

```
var padLength = length - text.length - 3;
```

JavaScript makes the `length` property available on all strings:

```
var text = "Neptune";
text.length; // 7
```

Having calculated the required length of the padding, `wrap` then enlists the help of the `line` method to grab a string of spaces of that length:

```
spacer.line(padLength, " ");
```

The `wrap` method builds the string to be returned by concatenating all the pieces: character, space, text, padding, character.

THE BOX METHOD

And finally, the `box` method uses `line` and `wrap` to surround a string in a box of a specified length:

```
spacer.line(11, "*");                   //   ***********
spacer.wrap("Neptune", 11, "*");        //   * Neptune *
spacer.line(11, "*");                   //   ***********
```

The method uses `newLine` so that the single returned string can span multiple lines on the console:

```
box: function (text, length, character) {
  var boxText = spacer.newLine();
  boxText += spacer.line(length, character) + spacer.newLine();
  boxText += spacer.wrap(text, length, character) + spacer.newLine();
  boxText += spacer.line(length, character) + spacer.newLine();
  return boxText;
}
```

Excellent! The spacer namespace now has a number of useful methods to format the display of information on the console. They'll be really handy in *The Crypt*. So, let's mix them in!

7.4   *The Crypt–player objects as arguments*

You'll now apply your knowledge of JavaScript objects as arguments, return values, and namespaces to *The Crypt*. Figure 7.9 shows where the focus of this section, showing player information by using functions with objects, fits into the overall structure of our ongoing game example.

Figure 7.9   Elements in *The Crypt*

In chapter 6 you built up a number of functions to help display information about players in the game. The functions rely on separate arguments for different player properties. Here's the `getPlayerInfo` function being called:

```
getPlayerInfo(player1.name, player1.place, player1.health);
```

You've seen in this chapter that you can simply pass a player object as an argument and let the function pick out the properties it needs. The `getPlayerInfo` function call should become

```
getPlayerInfo(player1);
```

Much neater!

You can use the helper methods in your `spacer` namespace to format the text—`box` and `wrap` will do the trick. But how can you find the right box length to snugly wrap the information? The `place` string will probably be the longest, but might the `health` string sometimes stretch farther?

```
> ==================================        > ++++++++++++++++++++
> = Kandra is in The Dungeon of Doom =       > + Dax is in Limbo    +
> = Kandra has health 50            =        > + Dax has health 40 +
> ==================================        > ++++++++++++++++++++
```

You have to check which is the longest. The `Math.max` method has you covered:

```
var longest = Math.max(place.length, health.length);
```

Don't forget the border and single space at either end:

```
var longest = Math.max(place.length, health.length) + 4;
```

The following listing uses the `spacer` namespace methods, so the live example includes that code on JS Bin.

> **Listing 7.11   Displaying player information using objects**
> **(http://jsbin.com/beqabe/edit?js,console)**

```
var getPlayerName = function (player) {
    return player.name;
};

var getPlayerHealth = function (player) {
    return player.name + " has health " + player.health;
};

var getPlayerPlace = function (player) {
    return player.name + " is in " + player.place;
};

var getPlayerInfo = function (player, character) {
    var place = getPlayerPlace(player);            Find the longer
    var health = getPlayerHealth(player);          of the place and
    var longest = Math.max(place.length, health.length) + 4;   health strings

    var info = spacer.box(getPlayerName(player), longest, character);
    info += spacer.wrap(place, longest, character);
    info += spacer.newLine() + spacer.wrap(health, longest, character);
    info += spacer.newLine() + spacer.line(longest, character);
    info += spacer.newLine();

    return info;
};

var player1 = { name: "Kandra", place: "The Dungeon of Doom", health: 50 };
var player2 = { name: "Dax", place: "Limbo", health: 40 };

console.log(getPlayerInfo(player1, "="));      Specify the character to be used
console.log(getPlayerInfo(player2, "+"));      when displaying player info
```

7.5   *Summary*

- Use objects as arguments and access their properties from within the function body:

```
var getPlayerHealth = function (player) {
    return player.name + " has health " + player.health;
};
getPlayerHealth(player1);
```

- Update objects and add new properties from within the function body:

```
var calculateSizes = function (rectangle) {
    rectangle.area = rectangle.width * rectangle.height;
    rectangle.perimeter = 2 * (rectangle.width + rectangle.height);
};
```

- Return new or existing objects from functions, using the `return` keyword:

```
var getRectangle = function (width, height) {
    return {
        width: width,
        height: height,
        area: width * height
    };
};
```

- Create *methods* by setting functions as properties of objects.
- Use objects as *namespaces* to collect related functions and properties:

```
var spacer = {};
spacer.newLine = function () {
    return "\n";
};
```

- Make use of the `Math` object and its methods, like `Math.max` and `Math.min`.
- Use the `length` property of strings and string methods like `indexOf` and `substr`.

Arrays: putting data into lists

This chapter covers

- Grouping values as lists
- Creating an array
- Accessing elements in an array
- Manipulating the elements in an array
- Using `forEach` to visit each element

Almost everything you've covered so far has been about organizing your data or organizing your code. This chapter continues that theme but with a twist: it's not just about grouping items; now you can put them in order.

In *The Crypt*, you'll finally have the ability for players to collect items they find on the journey; with arrays they can start on their very own treasure hoards.

8.1 Creating arrays and accessing elements

Working with lists is an essential part of programming. Blog posts, quiz questions, stock prices, emails, files, tweets, and bank transactions all turn up as lists. In fact, you've just read a list of lists! Sometimes the order doesn't matter and sometimes it does. A list of names could represent the members of a team, with no order, or it could represent places in a race—I'm sure Usain Bolt thinks the order is important there! An ordered list is called an *array* in JavaScript, as it is in many programming languages.

The items in an array are called its *elements* and you usually want to work on the elements in some way. You might want to

- Perform some action with each element, say display it on the console or increase it by 20%
- Find only certain elements that match a condition, say all tweets by Lady Gaga, blog posts in a given month, or questions answered correctly
- Combine all the elements into a single value, say to find the total of a list of prices or the average number of points scored per game

The array object in JavaScript provides functions to help you perform all of these actions and more. But, we're getting ahead of ourselves. Let's go back to the start and find out how to create an array.

8.1.1 Creating an array

To create an array, use square brackets. Once it's created, you can assign the array to a variable so you can refer to it in your code. Figure 8.1 illustrates the process.

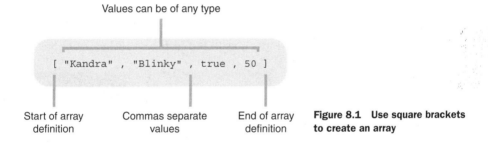

Values can be of any type

`[ "Kandra" , "Blinky" , true , 50 ]`

Start of array definition   Commas separate values   End of array definition

Figure 8.1   Use square brackets to create an array

The following listing creates two arrays and displays them on the console to give this output:

```
> [3, 1, 8, 2]
> ["Kandra", "Dax", "Blinky"]
```

Listing 8.1   Creating arrays
(http://jsbin.com/cevodu/edit?js,console)

```
var scores;
var names;

scores = [ 3, 1, 8, 2 ];
names = [ "Kandra", "Dax", "Blinky" ];

console.log(scores);
console.log(names);
```

Create an array of numbers and assign it to the scores variable

Create an array of strings and assign it to the names variable

Figure 8.2   JS Bin displays each of the two arrays in listing 8.2 between square brackets.

Commas separate the elements, which can be numbers, strings, objects, functions, or any data type or mix of types—you can even have arrays of arrays. Like the curly braces for objects and the function keyword for functions, the square brackets tell JavaScript to create an array. Once it's created, you can assign the array to a variable, set it as a property, include it in another array, or pass it to a function.

Listing 8.2 creates a couple of arrays of objects representing places to visit, this-Year and nextYear. Figure 8.2 shows how JS Bin displays the arrays of objects.

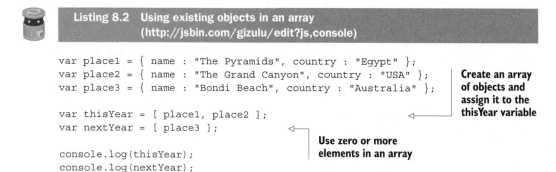

Listing 8.2   Using existing objects in an array
(http://jsbin.com/gizulu/edit?js,console)

```
var place1 = { name : "The Pyramids", country : "Egypt" };
var place2 = { name : "The Grand Canyon", country : "USA" };          Create an array
var place3 = { name : "Bondi Beach", country : "Australia" };         of objects and
                                                                      assign it to the
var thisYear = [ place1, place2 ];                                    thisYear variable
var nextYear = [ place3 ];
                                        Use zero or more
console.log(thisYear);                  elements in an array
console.log(nextYear);
```

8.1.2   Accessing array elements

You've created an array and assigned it to a variable, so now you can pass that variable to functions, like console.log. At some point you'll want to access the elements that make up the array, to peel away the skin to get at the juicy goodness inside. Well, those square brackets do double duty; they enclose the list when you define the array, and you use them to access individual elements.

As shown in figure 8.3, you specify each element with an index, a whole number marking where in the list the element occurs. The first element in an array has an

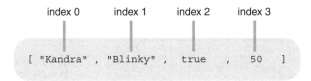

Figure 8.3 **Each element of an array has an index, starting at 0.**

index of 0, the second an index of 1, and so on. You can think of the index as an offset from the start of the array; the first element is zero away from the start, the second is one away from the start, and so on.

To retrieve the value of an element at a given index, put the index inside square brackets after the name of a variable to which the array has been assigned, as shown in figure 8.4.

Figure 8.4 **Use square brackets and an index to access elements of an array assigned to a variable**

Here, you create an array and assign it to a variable:

```
var scores;
scores = [ 3, 1, 8, 2 ];
```

To get the value of the third item in the array, 8, place the index, 2 (because you start with 0), in square brackets after the name of the variable:

```
scores[2];
```

You can assign `scores[2]` to another variable, set it as a property on an object, use it in an expression, or pass it as an argument to a function. Listing 8.3 creates strings using the values of elements in the `scores` array and displays them on the console to give the following:

```
> There are 4 scores:
> The first score is 3
> The second score is 1
> The third score is 8
> The fourth score is 2
```

It also makes use of the array's `length` property that simply gives the number of elements in the array.

Listing 8.3   Accessing array elements
(http://jsbin.com/qemufe/edit?js,console)

```
var scores = [ 3, 1, 8, 2 ];

console.log("There are " + scores.length + " scores:");
console.log("The first score is " + scores[0]);
console.log("The second score is " + scores[1]);
console.log("The third score is " + scores[2]);
console.log("The fourth score is " + scores[3]);
```

Use the length property to show how many elements are in the array

The first element in the array has an index of 0.

The last element in the array has an index one less than the number of elements.

Now, say you have a days array, holding the names of the weekdays, and you want to get the name of a particular day in the week, maybe the fourth day.

```
var days = ["Monday", "Tuesday", "Wednesday", "Thursday", "Friday"];
```

There's a mismatch between the index in JavaScript and the words used to describe a particular element. The first day of the week has index 0. The fourth day of the week has index 3. You might want to access a different day at different times, so you could use a variable, dayInWeek, to hold the day in the week you want.

```
// I want the fourth day of the week
dayInWeek = 4;
```

But using dayInWeek as the index for the array will give you the wrong day. An index of 4 will give you the fifth day in the week.

The next listing shows code for this scenario. It displays two days on the console: the wrong one (that is, not the fourth day of the week) and then the right one:

```
> Friday
> Thursday
```

Listing 8.4   Using a variable as an index
(http://jsbin.com/veyexa/edit?js,console)

```
var days = ["Monday", "Tuesday", "Wednesday", "Thursday", "Friday"];
var dayInWeek = 4;

console.log( days[dayInWeek] );
console.log( days[dayInWeek - 1] );
```

Use the value of the dayinWeek variable as an index

Subtract 1 from dayInWeek to access the correct element for the day wanted

The first call to console.log displays the wrong day because the dayInWeek variable doesn't take into account that arrays are zero-based; they start with an index of 0, not 1. The second call to `console.log` fixes the problem by subtracting one from `dayInWeek`; the fourth day of the week has an index of 3.

Okay. It's time to hold onto your hat. In listing 8.5 you'll define a function and add it to the mix. The local pencil museum records the number of visitors through its doors each day. The owners ask you to create a program that, when given a week's worth of visitor numbers as an array, will display how many visitors there were on a given day:

```
> There were 132 visitors on Tuesday
```

You decide to write a function, `getVisitorReport`, to generate the report and return it. You then would have the option of displaying the report on the console, on a web page, or in an email. In the next listing you generate a report for a Tuesday and display it on the console.

> ### Listing 8.5 Passing an array to a function
> (http://jsbin.com/bewebi/edit?js,console

```
var getVisitorReport = function (visitorArray, dayInWeek) {      ⟵
    var days = [
        "Monday",                              Include parameters for an
        "Tuesday",                             array of visitor numbers and
        "Wednesday",                           the day in week of the report
        "Thursday",
        "Friday"
    ];
    var index = dayInWeek - 1;
    var visitorReport;

    visitorReport = "There were ";
    visitorReport += visitorArray[index];         Use the += operator to update
    visitorReport += " visitors ";                visitorReport, concatenating more
    visitorReport += "on " + days[index];         text to its current value

    return visitorReport;                    ⟵   Return the report
};                                               from the function

var visitors = [ 354, 132, 210, 221, 481 ];

var report = getVisitorReport(visitors, 2);    ⟵   Get the report for
                                                   Tuesday and assign it to
console.log(report);                               the report variable
```

You create an array of visitor numbers, assign it to the `visitors` variable, and pass it to the `getVisitorReport` function as an argument. Within the function, the array is assigned to the `visitorArray` variable and used to generate the report. The report is returned from the function, assigned to the `report` variable, and displayed on the console. The += operator in the function adds the value on its right to the variable on its left. Because a string has been assigned to the `visitorReport` variable, += concatenates the value on its right to the variable on its left.

So, you can create an array and access its elements. But, once you have data in an array, there's a whole host of ways you can manipulate it. Let's get started with a few of the most common ways to work with arrays.

8.2   Array methods

Arrays are a type of object provided by the JavaScript language to help you manage lists. JavaScript also provides you with a number of functions you can use to work with arrays. When we assign functions to properties of an object, we call the functions *methods* of the object; arrays are a type of object, so their functions are also called methods.

In this section you look at just a few of the many methods available when working with arrays: `push` and `pop` and `splice` let you add and remove elements, `slice` lets you grab consecutive elements, `join` lets you concatenate the array elements to form a string, and `forEach` allows you to pass each element as an argument to a specified function. These methods are summarized in table 8.1. Further array methods and examples can be found on the book's website at www.room51.co.uk/js/array-methods.html.

Table 8.1   Array methods

Method	What's it for?	Example
push	Appending an element to the end of an array.	`items.push("Put me last");`
pop	Removing an item from the end of an array.	`wasLast = items.pop();`
join	Concatenating all of the elements in the array, inserting an optional string between each pair of elements.	`allItems = items.join(",");`
slice	Creating an array from a range of elements in an existing array. Passing in the indexes at which to start and stop the range.	`section = items.slice(2, 5);`
splice	Changing an array by adding and/or removing consecutive elements. Passing in the index at which to start removing elements, the number of elements to remove, and any elements to add.	`out = items.splice(1,2,"new");`

forEach	Passing each element in turn to a specified function.	`items.forEach(function (item){`
		`    console.log(item);`
		`}`

Let's begin with `push`, `pop`, and `join`.

8.2.1 Adding and removing elements

In listing 8.6, you create an empty array and assign it to the `items` variable. The `push` method is used to append three elements to the array. Once you've added the three elements, you log the whole array to the console:

```
> ["The Pyramids", "The Grand Canyon", "Bondi Beach"]
```

You then use the `pop` method to remove the last item and display it. Finally, you log the whole array to the console again, this time with the elements joined to make a single string.

```
> Bondi Beach was removed
> The Pyramids and The Grand Canyon
```

Listing 8.6   Manipulating arrays with push, pop, and join (http://jsbin.com/faqabu/edit?js,console)

```
var items = [];                          ⟵⎯  Create an empty array and
var item = "The Pyramids";                     assign it to the items variable
var removed;

                                               Add the value of item to
                                               the end of the array
items.push(item);                        ⟵⎯
items.push("The Grand Canyon");          ⟵⎯
items.push("Bondi Beach");                     Add a string to the
                                               end of the array

console.log(items);

                                               Remove the last item and assign
removed = items.pop();                    ⟵⎯  it to the removed variable

console.log(removed + " was removed");         Use the join method to concatenate
console.log(items.join(" and "));        ⟵⎯  the array items, inserting " and "
                                               between each pair
```

JavaScript makes the `push`, `pop`, and `join` functions available as properties on every array. Because they're properties of the array, you can use dot notation to call the functions, `items.push(itemToAdd)`, just as you can to access any object property.

8.2.2 Slicing and splicing arrays

To demonstrate the two array methods, `slice` and `splice`, you continue with your array of holiday destinations. Play along on the JS Bin console. Commands can span multiple lines on the console; press Shift-Enter to move to a new line without executing a statement. If you press Enter by mistake and execute an unfinished statement, you may be able to retrieve your previous entry by pressing the up arrow on your keyboard. The statements that you type are shown starting with >. The console automatically shows the return value of each function called. I show those values in bold.

```
> var items = [
    "The Pyramids",
    "The Grand Canyon",
    "Bondi Beach",
    "Lake Garda"]
  undefined

> items
  ["The Pyramids", "The Grand Canyon", "Bondi Beach", "Lake Garda"]
```

SLICE

The slice method returns a new array made up of part of the original array. It doesn't change the original array. The arguments are the index of the first element you want and the index of the first subsequent element you don't want. Remember, the first element has index 0.

```
> items.slice(0, 2)
  ["The Pyramids", "The Grand Canyon"]

> items.slice(2, 3)
  ["Bondi Beach"]
```

items.slice(2, 3) says you want the items from index 2 onward but not the items from index 3 onward. In other words, you just want the item with index 2.

Omit the second argument if you want all elements after the one specified by the first argument. Omit both arguments if you want the whole array.

```
> items.slice(2)
  ["Bondi Beach", "Lake Garda"]

> items.slice()
  ["The Pyramids", "The Grand Canyon", "Bondi Beach", "Lake Garda"]
```

SPLICE

The splice method does change the original array. It lets you remove items from an array and, optionally, insert new items. To remove items, specify the index of the first element to remove and the number of elements to remove. The method returns the removed elements as an array.

```
> items.splice(2, 1)
  ["Bondi Beach"]

> items
  ["The Pyramids", "The Grand Canyon", "Lake Garda"]

> items.splice(0, 2)
  ["The Pyramids", "The Grand Canyon"]

> items
  ["Lake Garda"]
```

To insert new elements into the array, add them as arguments after the start index and the number of items to remove. In this example, no items are removed:

```
> items.splice(0, 0, "The Great Wall", "St Basil's")
  []

> items
  ["The Great Wall", "St Basil's", "Lake Garda"]
```

In this example, one item is removed:

```
> items.splice(1, 1, "Bondi Beach", "The Grand Canyon")
  ["St Basil's"]

> items
  ["The Great Wall", "Bondi Beach", "The Grand Canyon", "Lake Garda"]
```

You'll use both `slice` and `splice` when working with player and place items in *The Crypt*.

8.2.3 *Visiting each element with forEach*

If you have a list of items that you want to display on the console, you could manually call a function for each one:

```
showInfo(items[0]);
showInfo(items[1]);
showInfo(items[2]);
```

Unfortunately, it's common not to know in advance how many items will be in the list, so you can't hard-code the right number of `showInfo` calls ahead of time. Also, as the number of elements increases, you don't want to be manually calling a function for each one.

What you need is a way to make JavaScript call a given function for every element in the list, however many there are. That's exactly what the `forEach` method does. To call `showInfo` for each element in the `items` array, replace the individual calls with

```
items.forEach(showInfo);
```

The `forEach` method *iterates* over the array, passing each element in turn as an argument to the function specified in parentheses, as shown in figure 8.5.

Listing 8.7 shows `forEach` in action, displaying the elements of an `items` array on the console:

```
> The Pyramids
> The Grand Canyon
> Bondi Beach
```

```
items.forEach( showInfo );
```

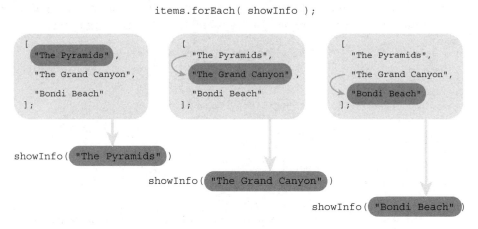

Figure 8.5   `items.forEach` **passes each item in the** `items` **array to the** `showInfo` **function.**

| Listing 8.7   Iterating over an array with forEach (http://jsbin.com/sokosi/edit?js,console) |

```
var items;                              Use the var keyword to
var showInfo;                           declare two variables

items = [                               Use square brackets to
    "The Pyramids",                     create an array. Assign the
    "The Grand Canyon",                 array to the items variable.
    "Bondi Beach"
];

showInfo = function (itemToShow) {      Use the function keyword to
    console.log(itemToShow);           create a function. Assign it to
};                                      the showInfo variable.

items.forEach(showInfo);                Call the showInfo function for
                                        each element in the array
```

In listing 8.7, your function to display each item was assigned to the `showInfo` variable. You then passed the `showInfo` variable to `forEach` as an argument.

  If you're going to use a function only once, as the argument for `forEach`, you can create the function and pass it to `forEach` inline, without the need for an extra variable. The code in listing 8.8 passes the function definition directly to `forEach`. You also add extra information to set the scene and improve the output:

```
> Dream destinations:
> - The Pyramids
> - The Grand Canyon
> - Bondi Beach
```

**Listing 8.8   Calling forEach with an inline function
(http://jsbin.com/yapecu/edit?js,console)**

```
var items = [ "The Pyramids", "The Grand Canyon", "Bondi Beach" ];

console.log("Dream destinations:");

items.forEach(function (item) {
    console.log(" - " + item);
});
```
⟵ **Use the forEach method,
passing it an inline function**

The forEach method actually passes three arguments to the specified function: the element, the index of the current element, and the whole array. You can capture the extra arguments by including extra parameters in the definition of the function you pass to forEach.

```
items.forEach(function (item, index, wholeArray) {
    // item is the current item being passed to the function
    // index is the index of the current item
    // wholeArray is the same as 'items'
});
```

Listing 8.9 shows all three arguments in action. It uses forEach to pass each player in the players array to the showArguments function, producing the following output:

```
> Item: Dax
> Index: 0
> Array: Dax,Jahver,Kandra
> Item: Jahver
> Index: 1
> Array: Dax,Jahver,Kandra
> Item: Kandra
> Index: 2
> Array: Dax,Jahver,Kandra
```

**Listing 8.9   Using the arguments passed by forEach
(http://jsbin.com/suvegi/edit?js,console)**

```
var players;
var showArguments;

players = [ "Dax", "Jahver", "Kandra" ];

showArguments = function (item, index, wholeArray) {
  console.log("Item: " + item);
  console.log("Index: " + index);
  console.log("Array: " + wholeArray);
};

players.forEach(showArguments);
```
⟵ **Include extra
parameters to capture
all the arguments
passed by forEach**

The `forEach` method does the job of calling a function for you. In listing 8.9, it calls the `showArguments` function. It calls the function for each element in the `players` array. It always passes the three arguments to the function it calls, although you don't have to use all three.

You can call array methods like `forEach` directly on arrays without the need for variables. Listing 8.10 rewrites listing 8.9 without assigning the array or the function to variables.

```
["Dax", "Jahver", "Kandra"].forEach(function (item, index, wholeArray) {
    console.log("Item: " + item);
    console.log("Index: " + index);
    console.log("Array: " + wholeArray);
});
```

If you're using the array and function only once, the compact syntax in listing 8.10 can be appropriate. But the longer form in listing 8.9 is more readable, so if the meaning of the code isn't obvious in context, it might be better to opt for the longer version. Being able to write something like

```
players.forEach(showScore);
```

can help you and other programmers make better sense of your code.

To further demonstrate using the index argument, you're off to the shops in listing 8.11. (If you have your adventure head on, then maybe you're buying equipment for your travels.) You buy four types of items but different amounts of each. The program calculates the total cost and displays it, like this:

```
> The total cost is $41.17
```

It uses two arrays, one for the numbers of each item bought and one for their costs.

```
var getTotalBill = function (itemCosts, itemCounts) {
    var total = 0;

    itemCosts.forEach(function (cost, i) {          ⟵      Include an extra parameter,
        total += cost * itemCounts[i];              ⟵      i, in the function definition
    });                                                    to be assigned the index

    return total;
};                                                         Use the += operator to add
                                                           the result of the calculation
var costs = [ 1.99, 4.95, 2.50, 9.87 ];                    to the total variable's value
var numOfEach = [ 2, 1, 5, 2 ];

console.log("The total cost is $" + getTotalBill(costs, numOfEach));
```

Listing 8.11 uses the index to match the current item cost with the correct number of items. For this to work, the arrays have to be in the same order. I hope you noticed that i isn't a very descriptive variable name! It is so common to need index variables that most programmers are happy to use short names—i, j, and k—for them. They're quicker to type and it's such a well-established convention that most people reading your code will expect them to be used as a counter or index. If you'd rather call the variable index or itemIndex or something similar, that's fine.

As one last example, let's return to your quiz questions. A multiple-choice question has a list of possible answers that need to be displayed to whomever is taking the quiz. Sounds like a good fit for an array and forEach; see listing 8.12. You could even have an array of question-and-answer objects. For now, stick with a single question, displayed like this:

```
> What is the capital of France?
> A - Bordeaux
> B - F
> C - Paris
> D - Brussels
```

**Listing 8.12   Displaying a multiple choice question
              (http://jsbin.com/lobahu/edit?js,console)**

```
var displayQuestion = function (questionAndAnswer) {        Include a parameter
    var options = [ "A", "B", "C", "D", "E" ];              to which the question-
                                                            and-answer object can
    console.log(questionAndAnswer.question);                be assigned

    questionAndAnswer.answers.forEach(                      Access properties of
        function (answer, i) {                              the question-and-
            console.log(options[i] + " - " + answer);       answer object via
        }                                                   the parameter
    );
};                                                          Use forEach to visit
                                                            each element of the
var question1 = {                                           array assigned to the
    question : "What is the capital of France?",            answers property
    answers : [
        "Bordeaux",              Assign an array
        "F",                     to the answers
        "Paris",                 property
        "Brussels"
    ],
    correctAnswer : "Paris"
};

displayQuestion(question1);
```

You'll look at actually answering questions when you investigate user interaction in part 2.

8.3   *The Crypt—a player items array*

You'll now apply your knowledge of JavaScript arrays to *The Crypt*. Figure 8.6 shows where the focus of this section, displaying a list of player items by using arrays, fits into the overall structure of our ongoing game example.

Figure 8.6   Elements of *The Crypt*

In part 1 of *Get Programming with JavaScript*, we've covered some core concepts to help you model and use players in *The Crypt*. You have variables to store and retrieve player information, objects to collect player properties together, arrays so you can list the items a player collects, array methods to add and remove items in the collection, and functions to display information about each player.

Listing 8.13 brings all of these concepts together: creating a player, displaying information about them, picking up a new item, and displaying the updated info. You format the output using the spacer namespace developed in chapter 7. The elements that make up the output are highlighted in figure 8.7.

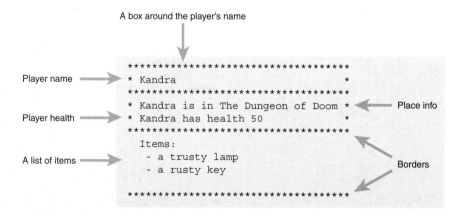

Figure 8.7   The elements shown when a Player object is displayed on the console

To save space, spacer isn't shown in the listing (it hasn't changed) but it is on JS Bin. The code in this listing builds on the player display code from chapter 7, adding the ability to list a player's items.

Listing 8.13   Displaying player items
(http://jsbin.com/mecude/edit?js,console)

```js
var getPlayerName = function (player) {
    return player.name;
};

var getPlayerHealth = function (player) {
    return player.name + " has health " + player.health;
};

var getPlayerPlace = function (player) {
    return player.name + " is in " + player.place;
};

var getPlayerItems = function (player) {
    var itemsString = "Items:" + spacer.newLine();

    player.items.forEach(function (item) {
      itemsString += "   - " + item + spacer.newLine();
    });

    return itemsString;
};

var getPlayerInfo = function (player, character) {
    var place = getPlayerPlace(player);
    var health = getPlayerHealth(player);
    var longest = Math.max(place.length, health.length) + 4;

    var info = spacer.box(getPlayerName(player), longest, character);
    info += spacer.wrap(place, longest, character);
    info += spacer.newLine() + spacer.wrap(health, longest, character);
    info += spacer.newLine() + spacer.line(longest, character);

    info += spacer.newLine();
    info += "  " + getPlayerItems(player);
    info += spacer.newLine();
    info += spacer.line(longest, character);

    info += spacer.newLine();

    return info;
};

var showPlayerInfo = function (player, character) {
    console.log(getPlayerInfo(player, character));
};

var player1 = {
    name: "Kandra",
    place: "The Dungeon of Doom",
    health: 50,
    items : ["a trusty lamp"]
};
```

- Define a function to build a string for the display of player items
- Use forEach to append each element of the items array to the string
- Call getPlayerItems to include the items string in the player info
- Create a showPlayerInfo function to display the info string on the console
- Give the player an item

```
showPlayerInfo(player1, "=");

player1.items.push("a rusty key");

showPlayerInfo(player1, "*");
```

> Call showPlayerInfo, passing the player and a border character
>
> Use push to add an extra item to the items array

The `Player` object now includes an `items` array:

```
var player1 = {
    name: "Kandra",
    place: "The Dungeon of Doom",
    health: 50,
    items: ["a trusty lamp"]
};
```

It starts with only one element, but you add another by using the `push` array method:

```
player1.items.push("a rusty key");
```

`getPlayerItems` uses `forEach` to pass each item in the `items` array to a function. The function appends the item to a string using `+=`, building a list of all of the player's items:

```
player.items.forEach(function (item) {
    itemString += "   - " + item + spacer.newLine();
});
```

The `showPlayerInfo` function calls `getPlayerInfo` to retrieve the player information string and then displays the information on the console.

You're starting to build up quite a collection of functions to help with the display of players; you should really organize them. You could collect them into a namespace or, seeing as they all relate to players, include them as part of each `Player` object. JavaScript provides a way to streamline the creation of many similar objects, incorporating the methods that work with them: *constructor functions*. That's what you investigate in chapter 9, where you also build the places the players will explore in *The Crypt*.

8.4   Summary

- Create an array with a comma-separated list of values between square brackets:

  ```
  [ "Kandra", "Dax", true, 50 ]
  ```

- Assign the array to a variable and then access its elements by adding an index in square brackets to the variable name. The following code displays `"Dax"`:

  ```
  var items = [ "Kandra", "Dax", true, 50 ]
  console.log(items[1]);
  ```

- Remember to use a zero-based index for array elements. `items[1]` refers to the second element in the `items` array. You can think of the index as an offset from the start of the array: the first element is zero away from the start, the second is one away from the start, and so on.
- Use array methods, functions provided by JavaScript, to add, remove, join, and iterate over array elements. The methods covered in this chapter are `push`, `pop`, `join`, `slice`, `splice`, and `forEach`.

Constructors: building objects with functions

9

This chapter covers

- Using functions to create objects
- The keyword `new`
- Using constructor functions to create objects
- The special variable `this`
- Defining constructor functions for players and places

It's common for programs to create many similar objects—a blog post could have hundreds of posts and a calendar thousands of events—and to include functions for working on those objects. Rather than building each object by hand using curly braces, you can use functions to streamline the process. You want to change

```
planet1 = {
    name: "Jupiter",
    position: 8,
    type: "Gas Giant"
};
```

```
showPlanet = function (planet) {
    var info = planet.name + ": planet " + planet.position;
    info += " - " + planet.type;
    console.log(info);
};

showPlanet(planet1);
```

into

```
planet1 = buildPlanet("Jupiter", 8, "Gas Giant");
planet1.show();
```

where the `buildPlanet` function creates the planet object for you and adds the `show` method automatically. You define a blueprint for your object in the function body of `buildPlanet` and then use that blueprint to generate new objects whenever you need them. That keeps your object-creation code in one place; you've seen throughout the book how such organization makes it easier to understand, maintain, and use your programs.

You can do even better than a simple function to create many similar objects; you can use a *constructor function*. Writing functions to generate objects is so common that JavaScript includes a built-in way of streamlining the process. With a constructor function, creating and displaying a planet looks like this:

```
planet1 = new Planet("Jupiter", 8, "Gas Giant");
planet1.show();
```

Constructor functions standardize object creation—standardizing code is generally a good thing—and provide a way of identifying objects, making it easier to differentiate among planets, players, posts, and positions, for example. They also provide a way of sharing a single function among many objects by using *prototypes*, covered in part 4.

In section 9.1 you write your own functions to make it easier to build objects with properties and methods in place. In section 9.2, you investigate constructor functions and see how they simplify the process. It's time to get the production line rolling.

9.1   *Using functions to build objects*

Rather than using curly braces to manually construct each object, create a function to do the heavy lifting. Just pass the function the information it needs and it will return a shiny new object for you. In larger programs, you may well want to create similar objects in a number of places in the code. Having a single function you can call on saves you from repeating yourself and makes it easy to make changes if what you need your object to do develops over time.

Section 9.1.1 shows a simple object-creation function, and section 9.1.2 builds on it to add a method to your created objects.

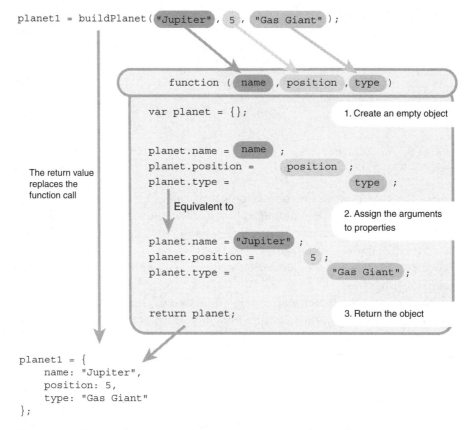

Figure 9.1 The `buildPlanet` function creates and returns an object.

9.1.1   Adding properties

Figure 9.1 shows a `buildPlanet` function to help you create each planet object. You pass the function the planet data as arguments and it returns an object with those arguments set as properties. You've only just started learning JavaScript and you're already building planets!

The first listing shows the code for the `buildPlanet` function. Notice how it starts by creating an object and ends by returning the object.

Listing 9.1   Using a function to create an object
(http://jsbin.com/jiroyo/edit?js,console)

```
var buildPlanet = function (name, position, type) {
    var planet = {};

    planet.name = name;
    planet.position = position;
    planet.type = type;
```

Create an empty object for the new planet being constructed

Set properties on the planet object using the arguments passed in

```
        return planet;
};
```
← Return the new planet object you've created

```
var planet1 = buildPlanet(
    "Jupiter",
    5,
    "Gas Giant"
);
```
Call the buildPlanet function and assign the object returned to the planet1 variable

```
console.log(planet1.name);
console.log(planet1.position);
console.log(planet1.type);
```

The steps the buildPlanet function takes are important for understanding how JavaScript's constructor functions streamline the process of object creation. You take a look at constructor functions in section 9.2. But first, you enhance what your created objects can do, with methods.

9.1.2 Adding methods

As well as setting some initial properties, you can make buildPlanet add methods into the mix. Remember, a *method* is a just function you assign to an object property. Rather than defining an external function to display information about each planet object, bake it into the object itself.

In the next listing, you add a showPlanet method to each planet object before returning the object. The output looks like this:

```
> Jupiter: planet 5 - Gas Giant
```

Listing 9.2 Adding methods to your constructed object
(http://jsbin.com/zogure/edit?js,console)

```
var buildPlanet = function (name, position, type) {
    var planet = {};
```
← Create an empty object for the new planet being constructed

```
    planet.name = name;
    planet.position = position;
    planet.type = type;
```
Set properties on the planet object using the arguments passed in

```
    planet.showPlanet = function () {
        var info = planet.name;
        info += ": planet " + planet.position;
        info += " - " + planet.type;
        console.log(info);
    };
```
Define a display function and assign it to the showPlanet property

```
    return planet;
};
```
← Return the new planet object you have created

```
var planet1 = buildPlanet(
    "Jupiter",
    5,
    "Gas Giant"
);

planet1.showPlanet();
```

> **Use dot notation and parentheses to call the showPlanet method**

In the `showPlanet` method you build up an information string including the planet's properties (`name`, `position`, and `type`) before logging the string to the console. You use the `+=` operator to append strings to the `info` variable.

You can include as many methods as you need to give your objects the functionality required. Every time you call `buildPlanet`, it returns an object with the properties and methods required to do its job in your program. You can put the function to work, churning out as many planet objects as you want. You can't have too many planets, am I right?

Listing 9.3 uses the `buildPlanet` function to construct three planets (okay, not quite a production line, but you get the idea!) and display their details on the console:

```
> Jupiter: planet 5 - Gas Giant
> Neptune: planet 8 - Ice Giant
> Mercury: planet 1 - Terrestrial
```

Listing 9.3   An array of constructed objects
(http://jsbin.com/jiweze/edit?js,console)

```
var buildPlanet = function (name, position, type) {
    var planet = {};

    planet.name = name;
    planet.position = position;
    planet.type = type;

    planet.showPlanet = function () {
        var info = planet.name;
        info += ": planet " + planet.position;
        info += " - " + planet.type;
        console.log(info);
    };

    return planet;
};

var planets = [
    buildPlanet( "Jupiter", 5, "Gas Giant" ),
    buildPlanet( "Neptune", 8, "Ice Giant" ),
    buildPlanet( "Mercury", 1, "Terrestrial" )
];

planets.forEach(function (planet) {
    planet.showPlanet();
});
```

> **Define the same buildPlanet function as in listing 9.2**

> **Create an array of planet objects and assign it to the planets variable**

> **Use forEach to pass each planet object to a function that calls showPlanet**

In listing 9.3 you create an array with three elements, the objects that each call to buildPlanet returns. You assign the array to the planets variable and then iterate over the array using forEach. You don't need to assign the three planets to individual variables; the objects are accessible via an array index, with the first planet at index 0:

```
planets[0].name    // "Jupiter"
planets[2].type    // "Terrestrial"
```

In defining buildPlanet, you moved object creation into a function, returning the nascent planet once you had set its properties. But JavaScript can create and return objects for you. Let's see how.

9.2 *Using constructor functions to build objects*

Creating your own function to build objects and attach methods should have given you an insight into the steps involved in an object production line. It's such a common way to build objects that JavaScript provides its own standard mechanism—the *constructor function*.

In the buildPlanet function, *you* created an empty object and set its properties, and *you* returned the object.

```
var buildPlanet = function (name, position, type) {
    var planet = {};               // You create an empty object

    planet.name = name;            //
    planet.position = position;    // Assign properties
    planet.type = type;            //

    return planet;                 // You return the object
};
```

Well, JavaScript has you covered; with constructor functions it will create the empty object and return it for you free of charge. You still get to set the properties, but the rest is automagical. And what mystic invocations transform an ordinary function into a constructor function? Two keywords: this and new.

9.2.1 *Constructor functions*

In JavaScript, you define a *constructor function* just like any other function but call it after the new keyword. If you have a Planet function, you could create new planet objects like this:

```
planet1 = new Planet("Jupiter", 5, "Gas Giant");
planet2 = new Planet("Neptune", 8, "Ice Giant");
```

To use the Planet function as a constructor function you simply add the new keyword before the call to Planet. It's a convention to start the names of constructor functions with capital letters so programmers know to use the new keyword when calling them. Figure 9.2 shows how the constructor function automatically creates and returns an object.

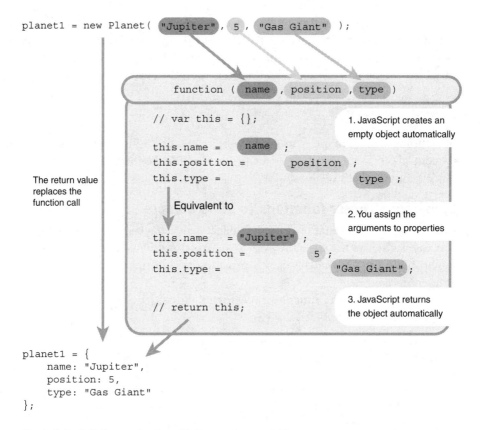

```
planet1 = new Planet( "Jupiter" , 5 , "Gas Giant" );
```

function (name , position , type)

// var this = {};

1. JavaScript creates an empty object automatically

this.name = name ;
this.position = position ;
this.type = type ;

The return value replaces the function call

Equivalent to

2. You assign the arguments to properties

this.name = "Jupiter" ;
this.position = 5 ;
this.type = "Gas Giant" ;

// return this;

3. JavaScript returns the object automatically

```
planet1 = {
    name: "Jupiter",
    position: 5,
    type: "Gas Giant"
};
```

Figure 9.2   Call the constructor with the new keyword. The constructor automatically creates and returns an object.

The following listing shows the full Planet constructor along with an example of calling Planet with new.

Listing 9.4   The Planet constructor
(http://jsbin.com/bixico/edit?js,console)

```
var Planet = function (name, position, type) {
    this.name = name;
    this.position = position;
    this.type = type;

    this.showPlanet = function () {
        var info = this.name + ": planet " + this.position;
        info += " - " + this.type;
        console.log(info);
    };
};
```

Assign to a variable that begins with a capital letter

Set properties on this, which has been assigned an empty object automatically

```
var planet = new Planet(
    "Jupiter",
    5,
    "Gas Giant"
);
```

←┐ **Call the function with the new
keyword to tell JavaScript to
assign an empty object to this**

```
planet.showPlanet();
```

Within the function body, but only when you call the function with new, JavaScript creates an empty object for you and assigns it to the special variable this. You can imagine the hidden first line of the Planet function being

```
var this = {};
```

You can then set properties on this just as you did with planet in the buildPlanet function earlier. The function automatically returns the object assigned to this, so there's no need to add a return statement. You can imagine the hidden last line of the Planet function being

```
return this;
```

When you execute the code in listing 9.4, the newly created object replaces the call to the Planet constructor and is assigned to the planet variable. The following

```
var planet = new Planet( "Jupiter", 5, "Gas Giant" );
```

becomes

```
var planet = {
    name: "Jupiter",
    position: 5,
    type: "Gas Giant",
    showPlanet: function () {
        var info = this.name + ": planet " + this.position;
        info += " - " + this.type;
        console.log(info);
    }
};
```

You can add as many properties and methods to the this object as you need. Listing 9.5 extends the Planet constructor to add a moons property and an addMoon method to the generated objects:

```
> Jupiter: planet 5 - Gas Giant
> Moons: Io, Europa.
```

```
var Planet = function (name, position, type) {
    this.name = name;
    this.position = position;              Create an empty array
    this.type = type;                      and assign it to the
    this.moons = [];                 ◁──── moons property

    this.showPlanet = function () {
        var info = this.name + ": planet " + this.position;
        info +=  " - " + this.type;
        console.log(info);                            Join the elements of
        console.log(                                  the moons array to
            "Moons: " + this.moons.join(', ') + ".");  ◁── form a string
    };

    this.addMoon = function (moon) {       Add the new moon to
        this.moons.push(moon);       ◁──── the moons array using
    };                                     the push method
};

var planet = new Planet( "Jupiter", 5, "Gas Giant" );

planet.addMoon("Io");
planet.addMoon("Europa");

planet.showPlanet();
```

Remember from chapter 8, the push method adds a new element to the end of an array and the join method joins all of the elements of an array to form a single string, with an optional separator string between each pair of elements.

Planets *and* moons! Your industriousness knows no bounds. Io, Io, it's off to work we go ….

9.2.2   *World building—making use of the Planet constructor*

Listing 9.6 uses an updated implementation of the Planet constructor. When you call addMoon, it now prepends new moons at the beginning of the moons array using an array method you haven't seen before: unshift. You create three planet objects and assign them to variables planet1, planet2, and planet3 before calling show-Planet on each one. In the partial output shown here, pay close attention to the order of the moons:

```
> Jupiter
> Planet 5 - Gas Giant
> Moons: Europa, Io.
```

> **Listing 9.6 Creating multiple planets with our constructor**
> **(http://jsbin.com/wewewe/edit?js,console)**

```
var Planet = function (name, position, type) {
    this.name = name;
    this.position = position;
    this.type = type;
    this.moons = [];

    this.showPlanet = function () {
        console.log(this.name);
        console.log("Planet " + this.position + " - " + this.type);
        console.log("Moons: " + this.moons.join(', ') + ".");
    };

    this.addMoon = function (moon) {            Use unshift to prepend
        this.moons.unshift(moon);            ⟵  elements at the start of
    };                                           the array
};

var planet1 = new Planet("Jupiter", 5, "Gas Giant");
planet1.addMoon("Io");                         First add "Io" and
planet1.addMoon("Europa");                     then add "Europa"

var planet2 = new Planet("Neptune", 8, "Ice Giant");
planet2.addMoon("Triton");

var planet3 = new Planet("Mercury", 1, "Terrestrial");
                                                        Use square brackets
[ planet1, planet2, planet3 ].forEach(function (planet) {  ⟵  to create an array and
    planet.showPlanet();                                        immediately iterate
});                                                             over it with forEach
```

In the code for `planet1`, you added Io first, then Europa. But in the output the order is reversed. That's because you now use `unshift` to add items at the start of the `moons` array rather than `push` to add items at the end.

9.2.3   Telling objects apart with the instanceof operator

When working with many different objects in a program, objects that you may have created with a number of different constructor functions, it's sometimes useful to be able to tell one type of object from another: is `item1` a planet, a player, a post, or a position? The JavaScript `instanceof` operator lets you check if a particular constructor function was involved in the creation of an object. Assuming you've defined the Planet constructor, the following code snippet logs `true` to the console:

```
var item1 = new Planet("Jupiter", 5, "Gas Giant");

console.log(item1 instanceof Planet);
```

The `instanceof` operator returns either `true` or `false`. The values `true` and `false` are called *boolean* values. In fact, they're the only two boolean values. You won't be using `instanceof` in the rest of *Get Programming with JavaScript*—I mention it here as another reason why a programmer may prefer constructor functions over their own object-creation functions. You'll see a lot more of `true` and `false` in parts 2 and 3 of the book; they're central to making decisions and running code only if certain conditions are met.

To get a better feel for constructors, it's worth looking at a few more examples. The next section does just that, with constructors for quiz questions and calendar events.

9.3   *Building mastery—two examples of constructors*

A quiz is likely to have tens of questions and a calendar hundreds or thousands of events. The questions will probably all have a similar structure and the events likewise. Both types of objects seem like prime candidates for constructor functions.

In listing 9.7, you use a `QuizQuestion` constructor to create a single question and display it on the console:

```
> What is the capital of France?
> (1) Bordeaux
> (2) F
> (3) Paris
> (4) Brussels
```

Listing 9.7   A quiz question constructor
(http://jsbin.com/vuyesi/edit?js,console)

```
var QuizQuestion = function (question, answer) {
    this.question = question;
    this.answer = answer;
    this.options = [];

    this.addOption = function (option) {
        this.options.push(option);
    };

    this.showQuestion = function () {
        console.log(this.question);
        this.options.forEach(function (option, i) {
            console.log("(" + (i + 1) + ") " + option);
        });
    };
};

var question1 = new QuizQuestion(
    "What is the capital of France?",
    "Paris"
);

question1.addOption("Bordeaux");
question1.addOption("F");
question1.addOption("Paris");
question1.addOption("Brussels");

question1.showQuestion();
```

Include a second parameter to catch the index argument

Use brackets to add 1 to the index and use the result in the string

In the showQuestion function in listing 9.7, you use the forEach method to iterate over the options array of possible answers. The forEach method passes each option and its index to a function that displays the option along with an option number.

```
function (option, i) {
    console.log("(" + (i + 1) + ") " + option);
}
```

The index of the first option is 0 but you want the displayed numbers to start at (1). You use (i + 1) rather than i to shift each index up by one for display.

```
> (1) Bordeaux
> (2) F
> (3) Paris
> (4) Brussels
```

The next listing is a simple constructor for calendar events. The showEvent method produces the following output:

```
> Annual Review
> 3/5/16, from 4.00pm to 5.00pm
```

 Listing 9.8   A calendar event constructor
(http://jsbin.com/gemiyu/edit?js,console)

```
var CalendarEvent = function (title, startDate, startTime, endTime) {
    this.title = title;
    this.startDate = startDate;
    this.startTime = startTime;                          Define a method to display
    this.endTime = endTime;                              information about the current
                                                         calendar event
    this.showEvent = function () {
        var dateString = [
            this.startDate,
            ", from ",                                   Build up the pieces of the
            this.startTime,                              date string as elements
            " to ",                                      in an array
            this.endTime
        ].join("");
                                                         Join the elements of
        console.log(this.title);                         the array to form the
        console.log(dateString);                         full date string
    };
};

var calEvent = new CalendarEvent(
    "Annual Review",
    "3/5/16",
    "4.00pm",
    "5.00pm"
);

calEvent.showEvent();
```

In the `showEvent` method, you create and immediately `join` an array to form a string for the date information. You met the `join` method in chapter 8. This is quite a neat way of building a string from multiple pieces. JavaScript programmers used to see string concatenation, for example, using +=, as a relatively slow way of building strings from substrings. Joining the elements of an array was a common alternative. These following two ways of building `dateString` give the same result:

```
var dateString = [
    this.startDate,
    ", from ",
    this.startTime,
    " to ",
    this.endTime
].join("");

var dateString = this.startDate;
dateString += ", from ";
dateString += this.startTime;
dateString += " to ";
dateString += this.endTime;
```

These days, in modern browsers, string concatenation is much faster than it was. I've included an example of using `join` because you may well come across it in the wild.

Constructor functions provide a standardized, streamlined way of creating multiple objects using a single template. A great adventure will involve many locations; let's revisit *The Crypt* and use constructors to give your players plenty of places to plunder.

9.4   *The Crypt—providing places to plunder*

You'll now apply your knowledge of constructor functions to *The Crypt*. Figure 9.3 shows where the focus of this section, creating `Place` objects by using constructor functions, fits into the overall structure of our ongoing game example.

Up until now, you've been focusing on the players in *The Crypt*. It's time to build some *places* to explore. Each place needs a title and description, a collection of items,

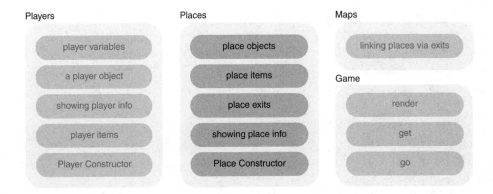

Figure 9.3   Elements of *The Crypt*

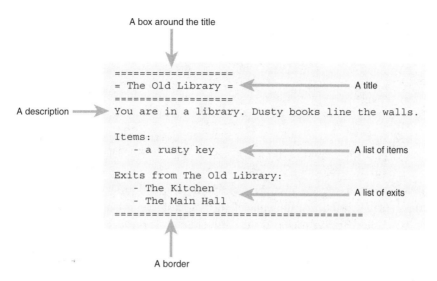

Figure 9.4 The elements shown when a `Place` object is displayed on the console.

and a collection of exits to other places. It also needs methods for adding items and exits and for displaying its information. Figure 9.4 highlights the elements you want to see when you display a `Place` object on the console.

Managing all of those elements will require quite a lot of code. As you've seen, a constructor function is a good way to organize all that code and streamline the creation of multiple `Place` objects. This will be your most complicated constructor yet, so let's build it in stages.

9.4.1 Building the Place constructor—title and description

Okay, here's a nice bare-bones constructor to get you started. It simply sets up the `title` and `description` properties and a basic `getInfo` method that you can develop as you add more properties. The initial output looks like this:

```
> The Old Library
> You are in a library. Dusty books line the walls.
```

Listing 9.9 A Place constructor, part 1
(http://jsbin.com/pogive/edit?js,console)

```
var Place = function (title, description) {
    this.title = title;
    this.description = description;

    this.getInfo = function () {
        var infoString = this.title + "\n";
```

Assign the constructor function to a variable that begins with a capital letter

Assign values to properties of the automatically created this object

Create a method by assigning a function to a property

```
        infoString += this.description + "\n";
        return infoString;
    };
};

var library = new Place(
    "The Old Library",
    "You are in a library. Dusty books line the walls."
);

console.log(library.getInfo());
```

> Call the constructor function with the new keyword

> Call the getInfo method and log the return value to the console

No boxes or borders yet—just the bare bones. You define a `getInfo` method that returns a string containing the place's title and description. Remember, `"\n"` is an escape sequence used to specify a new-line character; the title will be on one line and the description on the next.

Okay, so you can create places. But how can players plunder those places? You need some treasure!

9.4.2 *Building the Place constructor—items for your hoard*

As players explore their environment they expect to come across items that will help them solve puzzles and overcome obstacles like locked doors, putrid zombies, snarling leopards, and over-friendly tentacles. You need a way to add items to the places you create and to include the items in the information displayed about each location.

Listing 9.10 extends your bare-bones constructor to include the item functionality needed. You've upgraded the display of information by using the `spacer` namespace from chapter 7; it now looks like this:

```
====================
= The Old Library =
====================
You are in a library. Dusty books line the walls.
Items:
   - a rusty key
==========================================
```

That's more like your target output from figure 9.4! The `spacer` code isn't shown in the listing but is on JS Bin.

> **Listing 9.10   A Place constructor, part 2**
>   **(http://jsbin.com/qemica/edit?js,console)**

```
var Place = function (title, description) {
    this.title = title;
    this.description = description;
    this.items = [];
```

> Create an empty array and assign it to the items property

```
    this.getItems = function () {
        var itemsString = "Items: " + spacer.newLine();
        this.items.forEach(function (item) {
            itemsString += "   - " + item;
            itemsString += spacer.newLine();
        });

        return itemsString;
    };
```
> Define a getItems method to build a string of the items

```
    this.getInfo = function () {
        var infoString = spacer.box(
            this.title,
            this.title.length + 4,
            "="
        );

        infoString += this.description;
        infoString += spacer.newLine();
        infoString += this.getItems();
        infoString += spacer.line(40, "=") + spacer.newLine();
        return infoString;
    };
```
> Include a call to getItems when building info about a place

```
    this.addItem = function (item) {
        this.items.push(item);
    };
};
```
> Define an addItem method to add a new item to the items array

```
var library = new Place(
    "The Old Library",
    "You are in a library. Dusty books line the walls."
);

library.addItem("a rusty key");

console.log(library.getInfo());
```
> Use the addItem method to add an item

You use the spacer namespace to add new-line characters, put a box around the title, and end the information string with a border. There's a detailed description of how the spacer methods work in chapter 7, so check back there if you need a reminder.

You could have included an items parameter as part of the Place constructor function. But you want to be able to add items to a place while the game is running—when a player drops an item, for example—so you've kept the constructor function simple and included an addItem method instead.

What's that down that dark passageway? A dragon's lair? The bridge of a starship? A lost valley of dinosaurs?

9.4.3   *Building the Place constructor—exits to explore*

One location does not an adventure make; players want to wander vast worlds of wonder. The last addition to your Place constructor is a way to add exits leading to other

locations. You include an array of exits for each place and a method for adding destinations to the array. You need to display the exits, leading to your target output:

```
====================
= The Old Library =
====================
You are in a library. Dusty books line the walls.

Items:
   - a rusty key

Exits from The Old Library:
   - The Kitchen
   - The Main Hall
==========================================
```

Once again, the spacer code has been omitted from the printed listing.

> **Listing 9.11   A Place constructor, part 3**
> **(http://jsbin.com/parale/edit?js,console)**

```
var Place = function (title, description) {
    var newLine = spacer.newLine();              ◁──┐  Assign the new-line character
                                                      │  returned by spacer.newLine()
    this.title = title;                               │  to the newLine variable
    this.description = description;
    this.items = [];
    this.exits = [];                                ◁──┐  Create an empty
                                                        │  array and assign it
    this.getItems = function () { /* see listing 9.10 */ };  │  to the exits property

    this.getExits = function () {                   ◁──┐
        var exitsString = "Exits from " + this.title;   │  Define a getExits
        exitsString += ":" + newLine;                   │  method to build
                                                        │  an exit info string
        this.exits.forEach(function (exit) {
            exitsString += "   - " + exit.title;
            exitsString += newLine;
        });

        return exitsString;
    };

    this.getTitle = function () {                   ◁──┐  Move the title
        return spacer.box(                             │  boxing code to its
            this.title,                                │  own method
            this.title.length + 4,
            "="
        );
    };

    this.getInfo = function () {
        var infoString = this.getTitle();          ◁──┐
        infoString += this.description;               │  Use the new
        infoString += newLine + newLine;              │  methods to help
        infoString += this.getItems() + newLine;      │  build the info string
        infoString += this.getExits();             ◁──┘
```

```
        infoString += spacer.line(40, "=") + newLine;
        return infoString;
    };

    this.showInfo = function () {
        console.log(this.getInfo());
    };

    this.addItem = function (item) {
        this.items.push(item);
    };

    this.addExit = function (exit) {              Define an addExit
        this.exits.push(exit);                    method to add a new
    };                                            place to the exits array
};

var library = new Place(
    "The Old Library",
    "You are in a library. Dusty books line the walls."
);

var kitchen = new Place(
    "The Kitchen",
    "You are in the kitchen. There is a disturbing smell."
);

var hall = new Place(
    "The Main Hall",
    "You are in a large hall. It is strangely empty."
);

library.addItem("a rusty key");
library.addExit(kitchen);                    Join the library to the
library.addExit(hall);                       kitchen and to the hall

library.showInfo();
```

The listing is quite long, but you've seen all of the techniques before and there's some repetition. Focus on the methods one by one and take your time to follow the code.

You start by setting up a quick shortcut. The `spacer.newLine` method always returns the new-line escape sequence, `"\n"`, so you call it once and assign the return value to the `newLine` variable. You then use `newLine` instead of `spacer.newLine()`. That saves you some typing without impacting the readability of the code. You also add `getExits` and `getTitle` methods that build their part of the place information string. And the `addExits` method is just like the `addItems` method but—you guessed it—for adding exits instead of items.

The `exits` property holds an array of `Place` objects. In other words, each `Place` object contains a collection of `Place` objects. This ability to nest objects inside objects can lead to sophisticated models of real-world situations. Although a full model can be quite complicated, each component should be relatively easy to understand. Your game, *The Crypt*, provides you with enough moving parts to appreciate how complicated programs can be constructed from simple pieces. Let's revisit a piece you know well and define a constructor function for player objects.

9.5   *The Crypt—streamlining player creation*

Figure 9.5 shows where a `Player` constructor function fits into the overall structure of our ongoing game example.

Figure 9.5   Elements of *The Crypt*

In chapter 8 you added an array of items to `Player` objects and defined functions to include the items when displaying player information. You still created the players manually:

```
var player1 = {
    name: "Kandra",
    place: "The Dungeon of Doom",
    health: 50,
    items : ["a trusty lamp"]
};
```

You assigned the player display functions to their own variables—you collected quite a bunch!

```
var getPlayerName = function (player) { … };
var getPlayerHealth = function (player) { … };
var getPlayerPlace = function (player) { … };
var getPlayerItems = function (player) { … };
var getPlayerInfo = function (player, character) { … };
var showPlayerInfo = function (player, character) { … };
```

The display functions combined to show information on the console, as shown in figure 9.6.

To add an item to the player's collection, you pushed it directly to the items array:

```
player1.items.push("a rusty key");
```

A box around the player's name

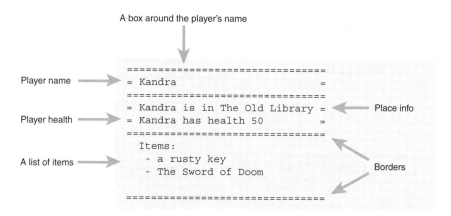

Player name

Place info

Player health

A list of items

Borders

Figure 9.6 The elements shown when a `Player` object is displayed on the console.

9.5.1 Organizing player properties

It's time to wrangle all those pieces; you use your mastery of constructor functions to streamline player creation, make the functions into methods, and do away with the growing number of variables. The `Player` constructor will let you create `Player` objects like this:

```
var player1 = new Player("Kandra", 50);
```

The constructor will also add a method you can call to add items, for example:

```
player1.addItem("a rusty key");
```

Listing 9.12 shows the code for the `Player` constructor function. It uses methods from the `spacer` namespace introduced in chapter 7. The `spacer` code is included on JS Bin but is not shown in the listing. To test a `Player` object created by the `Player` constructor, the listing also uses the `Place` constructor from section 9.4. Again, that code is omitted here but included on JS Bin. And there's a new type of value, `null`, that's explained in the sections after the listing.

Once again, there's quite a lot of code here (and even more on JS Bin), but don't worry; you've seen similar code before. Check the annotations, read the explanations below the listing, and try the *Further Adventures* on JS Bin. It might be worth having a quick look at *The Crypt* section from chapter 8 too; this builds on that.

**Listing 9.12 A Player constructor function
(http://jsbin.com/leqahi/edit?js,console)**

```
var Player = function (name, health) {
  var newLine = spacer.newLine();

  this.name = name;
  this.health = health;
```

```
  this.items = [];
  this.place = null;
```
◄—┤ **Assign null to the place property until you create a place to assign it**

```
  this.addItem = function (item) {
    this.items.push(item);
  };
```
Define a method to add items to the items array

```
  this.getName = function () {
    return this.name;
  };

  this.getHealth = function () {
    return this.name + " has health " + this.health;
  };
```
◄—┐ **Return strings of player information from the 'get' functions**

```
  this.getPlace = function () {
    return this.name + " is in " + this.place.title;
  };
```
◄—┐ **Use the title property of the Place object assigned to this.place**

```
  this.getItems = function () {
    var itemsString = "Items:" + newLine;

    this.items.forEach(function (item, i) {
      itemsString += "    - " + item + newLine;
    });

    return itemsString;
  };

  this.getInfo = function (character) {
    var place = this.getPlace();
    var health = this.getHealth();
    var longest = Math.max(place.length, health.length) + 4;

    var info = spacer.box(this.getName(), longest, character);
    info += spacer.wrap(place, longest, character);
    info += newLine + spacer.wrap(health, longest, character);
    info += newLine + spacer.line(longest, character);

    info += newLine;
    info += "  " + this.getItems();
    info += newLine;
    info += spacer.line(longest, character);
    info += newLine;

    return info;
  };
```
◄—┐ **Use the spacer methods to format player information**

```
  this.showInfo = function (character) {
    console.log(this.getInfo(character));
  };
};
```
Define a method to get a player information string and display it on the console

```
// Test the Player constructor

var library = new Place(
    "The Old Library",
    "You are in a library. Dusty books line the walls."
);
```
Create a Place object

```
var player1 = new Player("Kandra", 50);          ◁──┐   Create a
                                                     │   Player object
player1.place = library;                         ◁───┘

player1.addItem("a rusty key");                      │   Assign the Place
player1.addItem("The Sword of Doom");                │   object to the player

player1.showInfo("=");
```

Phew! That's another long listing. Let's break it down.

9.5.2   *Turning functions into methods*

In chapters 7 and 8, you defined a number of functions to build up a string of player information and display it, for example,

```
var getPlayerHealth = function (player) {
    return player.name + " has health " + player.health;
};
```

You pass a Player object to the function as an argument:

```
getPlayerHealth(player1);
```

The function then uses properties of the Player object to build up and return an information string.

You've now moved the functions into the Player constructor and assigned them to properties of the special this object.

```
this.getHealth = function () {
    return this.name + " has health " + this.health;
};
```

When we assign functions as properties of objects, we call them *methods*. You invoke the methods by using dot notation and parentheses:

```
player1.getHealth();
```

You no longer need to pass the Player object as an argument to the function. Where this has been used in the function body, player1 will take its place.

```
return this.name + " has health " + this.health;
```

becomes

```
return player1.name + " has health " + player1.health;
```

Converting all of the functions into methods of the Player object does away with the need for a separate variable for each function. It also keeps the function definitions with the object on which they act. Neat!

9.5.3   *Assigning places to players*

You need to know where players are in *The Crypt*. In earlier chapters, you assigned a string to each player's place property:

```
player1.place = "The Old Library";
```

But places are more than titles; Place objects created with the Place constructor have titles, descriptions, arrays of items, exits, and methods. From now on, you'll assign players full Place objects:

```
var library = new Place(
    "The Old Library",
    "You are in a library. Dusty books line the walls."
);

var player1 = new Player("Kandra", 50);

player1.place = library;
```

As players explore their environment, you're able to update the place property, assigning a previously built Place object for each new location.

Now that you're assigning full Place objects to a player's place property, the get-Place method has to do a little extra work to build its information string:

```
this.getPlace = function () {
    return this.name + " is in " + this.place.title;
};
```

Previously, this.place held the title of the player's current location; it now holds a Place object. The title is now accessed via this.place.title.

9.5.4   *Using null as a placeholder for objects*

Notice, in listing 9.12, that you assign the special value null to the place property in the constructor function. This shows that you intend to use a place property in your program but you don't have a value for it yet; you'll only be able to assign a player's place property when you've created some places.

```
player.place = null;      // You expect an object to be assigned later
/* other code */

player.place = library;   // An object is assigned, as expected
```

> **DEFINITION**   null is its own type of value. It's not a string, number, boolean (true or false), or undefined. And it's not an object. Programmers often use it, as you have, to show that they haven't yet assigned an object to a variable or property but expect to assign one at some point.

Now that you have an efficient way of creating many objects, you can build all of the places in *The Crypt* using a constructor function. You can add items and link the places together into a map. You can assign places to players. You still need to find a way for players to move from place to place. Once you've done that, you'll have a game environment you can explore!

9.6 *Summary*

- Use constructor functions to create objects with similar structures.
- Assign constructor functions to variables starting with a capital letter. Naming constructor functions this way is a widely followed convention:

```
var Person = function (name) { … };
```

- Call constructor functions with the new keyword. Assign the object returned to a variable:

```
var person = new Person("Jahver");
```

- Use the special this variable to set properties within the constructor function. this is automatically returned from the constructor:

```
var Person = function (name) {
    this.name = name;
};

var person = new Person("Jahver");
```

- Access properties of the returned object just like any other object:

```
person.name; // Jahver
```

- Assign functions to properties to create methods. Call the methods using dot notation and parentheses:

```
var Person = function (name) {
    this.name = name;
    this.sayHello = function () {
        return this.name + " says hi.";
    };
};

var person = new Person("Jahver");
person.sayHello();  // Jahver says hi.
```

- Assign the value null to variables or properties if you expect to assign an object at some point but the object is not yet available:

```
player1.place = null;

/* other code */

player1.place = library;
```

- Use the `instanceof` operator to check if a constructor function was involved in creating an object. The operator returns a boolean value, `true` or `false`:

```
var person = new Person("Jahver");

person instanceof Person;    // true

person instanceof Planet;    // false
```

Bracket notation: flexible property names

10

This chapter covers

- Square brackets as an alternative to dot notation
- The use of square brackets to set and get properties
- The flexibility of square bracket notation
- How to build a working game in *The Crypt*

In chapter 3 you saw how to create objects with curly braces and get and set properties with dot notation. You've used objects to model players, places, planets, and posts as well as quizzes and calendar events. You've added functions as properties to make methods and passed your objects to and from functions as arguments and return values. Objects are the center of the JavaScript universe!

In this chapter you take a look at a new way of working with object properties that gives you more flexibility with the property names, lets you use variables as keys, and gives you the ability to generate new properties from data while programs are running.

We also bring part 1 of *Get Programming with JavaScript* to a close with a working version of *The Crypt*, finally giving players the chance to explore a map and collect treasure! Square bracket notation provides a better way for you to manage the links between locations in the game, create a web of `Place` objects, and add a touch of mystery to the adventure. Ooooo, mystery …

10.1 Using square brackets instead of dots

Up until now you've used dot notation to set and get object properties.

```
question1.question = "What is the capital of France?";

console.log(player1.name);

this.title = title;
```

The property name, its *key*, is joined to a variable name with a period, or dot. JavaScript also offers an alternative approach: you can set and get properties by including a property's key as a string between square brackets.

```
question1["question"] = "What is the capital of France?";

console.log(player1["name"]);

this["title"] = title;
```

This new approach gives you more flexibility in the strings you can use as keys and lets you add dynamic properties while your programs are running. Say you had a `states` object that held the abbreviations of U.S. states as values, using the full names of states as keys. You could use dot notation to find the abbreviation for Ohio

```
console.log(states.ohio);    // OH
```

but, because of that pesky space, not for New Hampshire

```
console.log(states.new hampshire);    // ERROR!
```

Square brackets solve the problem (figure 10.1):

```
console.log(states["new hampshire"]);    // NH
```

Wrap the key in quotation marks

```
states [ "new hampshire" ] = "NH";
```

Use square brackets to specify a property

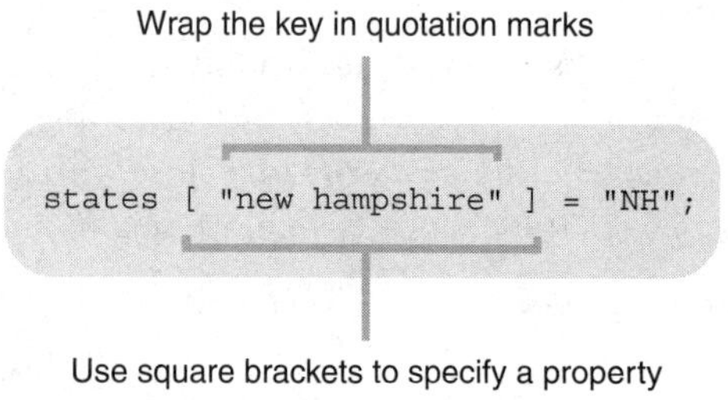

Figure 10.1   Using square bracket notation to set a property

And if you had a `getStateCode` function that used the `states` object, square bracket notation would let you use a parameter as a key:

```
var getStateCode = function (stateName) {
    var stateCode = states[stateName];
    return stateCode;
};
```

Using a parameter to provide the key isn't possible with dot notation. Table 10.1 shows more situations in which square bracket notation is needed.

Table 10.1 Situations in which certain keys do and don't work

I want to	I try	Success?

Use `ohio` as a key in an object literal	`states = {`
	`  ohio : "OH"`
	`};`
		Yes

Use `new hampshire` as a key in an object literal	`states = {`
	`  new hampshire : "NH"`
	`};`
		No

Use `"new hampshire"` as a key in an object literal	`states = {`
	`  "new hampshire" : "NH"`
	`};`
		Yes

Use `maryland` as a key with dot notation	`states.maryland = "MD";`	Yes
Use `south carolina` as a key with dot notation	`states.south carolina = ".SC";`	No
Use `south carolina` as a key with square bracket notation	`states["south carolina"] = "SC";`	Yes

Use a parameter as a key with dot notation	`function (stateName) {`
	`  return states.stateName;`
	`}`
		No

Use a parameter as a key with square bracket notation	`function (stateName) {`
	`  return states[stateName];`
	`}`
		Yes

Let's investigate these ideas with a few more examples.

10.1.1 Brackets in action—people's names as keys

Say you need to keep a simple record of people's ages. You could use an `ages` object where each person's name is a key and their age is the corresponding value. Listings 10.1, 10.2, and 10.3 develop this approach, logging two ages to the console:

```
> 56
> 21
```

In the first listing, you set the properties using bracket notation and get them using dot notation.

Listing 10.1   Bracket notation for object properties
                 (http://jsbin.com/kipedu/edit?js,console)

```
var ages = {};

ages["Kandra"] = 56;          Set the properties using bracket
ages["Dax"] = 21;             notation and the names as keys

console.log(ages.Kandra);     Get the properties using dot
console.log(ages.Dax);        notation and the names as keys
```

The two methods are equivalent for the keys used in listing 10.1. If you want to include spaces in the property names, you *must* use bracket notation. The next listing shows a similar example using full names.

Listing 10.2   Longer strings as keys
                 (http://jsbin.com/toviya/edit?js,console)

```
var ages = {};

ages["Kandra Smith"] = 56;
ages["Dax Aniaku"] = 21;

console.log(ages["Kandra Smith"]);
console.log(ages["Dax Aniaku"]);
```

Trying to use dot notation with property names that include spaces will confuse JavaScript: `ages.Kandra Smith` will be interpreted as `ages.Kandra` and `Smith` will be seen as a separate variable name, as shown in figure 10.2.

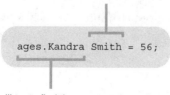

JavaScript will look for the `Smith` variable or keyword

`ages.Kandra Smith = 56;`

JavaScript will try to find the `Kandra` property

Figure 10.2   Spaces in property names don't work with dot notation.

The bracket notation immediately gives you the flexibility to use property names that may make more sense in context, like people's names, rather than being restricted to the single words of dot notation.

Bracket notation also allows you to add properties on the fly, when you may not know the keys in advance. Maybe a user is entering the information or it's being fetched from a file or database. In the next listing, you include an addAge function for adding new people to the ages object. If you run this listing you'll be able to use the function to add new people via the console.

Listing 10.3 Using a function to add ages
(http://jsbin.com/pipuva/edit?js,console)

```
var ages = {};

var addAge = function (name, age) {        Include a name parameter; you
    ages[name] = age;                       expect a name to be passed to the
};                                          function as an argument
addAge("Kandra Smith", 56);                 Use the name passed to
addAge("Dax Aniaku", 21);                   the function as the key

console.log(ages["Kandra Smith"]);
console.log(ages["Dax Aniaku"]);
```

In listing 10.3 you use the name parameter in the addAge function as the key for the ages object. When you call addAge, the first argument you include in the call is assigned to the name parameter. For example,

```
addAge("Kandra Smith", 56);
```

assigns "Kandra Smith" to name and 56 to age, so that

```
ages[name] = age;
```

becomes

```
ages["Kandra Smith"] = 56
```

This ability to use a variable between the square brackets for setting a property gives you great versatility to dynamically create and mutate objects in your programs. You make further use of the technique in sections 10.1.2 and 10.2.

If you want to create an object with properties already in place, then you use the curly braces syntax, with commas separating the key-value pairs. You can include spaces in the keys if you wrap the keys in quotation marks. The following listing shows the idea. It also introduces the Object.keys method that returns an array containing all of the keys set on an object. In the listing, you print the keys array to the console.

```
> ["Kandra Smith", "Dax Aniaku", "Blinky"]
```

Listing 10.4   Using Object.keys
(http://jsbin.com/mehuno/edit?js,console)

```
var ages = {
    "Kandra Smith" : 56,
    "Dax Aniaku"   : 21,
    "Blinky"       : 36
};

var keys = Object.keys(ages);

console.log(keys);
```

Blinky doesn't need the
quotation marks; include
them for consistency.

Use Object.keys to obtain an
array of the property names
set on the ages object

Object is a built-in JavaScript object. It provides a number of methods, one of which is called keys. Because Object.keys returns an array, you can use forEach to pass each key to a function. Listing 10.5 passes each key in turn to the console.log function that simply logs the key to the console.

```
> Kandra Smith
> Dax Aniaku
> Blinky
```

Listing 10.5   Iterating over Object.keys with forEach
(http://jsbin.com/seteco/edit?js,console)

```
var ages = {
    "Kandra Smith" : 56,
    "Dax Aniaku"   : 21,
    "Blinky"       : 36
};

var keys = Object.keys(ages);

keys.forEach(function (key) {
    console.log(key);
});
```

Obtain an array of the
property names used
with the ages object

Log each property
name to the console

Let's check out another example of using square bracket notation's ability to include complicated property names.

10.1.2   Making the most of square bracket notation—word counts

As the social media expert at your workplace, you've been tasked with analyzing tweets. Your first job is to count the number of times each word is used in a batch of tweets. Figure 10.3 shows parts of the console output of a tweet-analyzing program.

The program is shown in the following listing (with only three tweets to save space) and uses an object, words, to record the word counts.

```
#ESERO: 1,          is: 4,             subscribers!: 1,
#pet: 1,            is_a: 1,           sure,: 1,
#STEMeducation: 1,  it: 3,             technology: 1,
&: 1,               It: 1,             test: 1,
-: 1,               just: 1,           that: 2,
a: 3,               learn: 1,          the: 4,
A: 1,               LIVE: 1,           This: 1,
about: 1,           look: 1,           time: 1,
across: 1,          loyalty: 1,        to: 8,          Figure 10.3  Counting
age: 1,             M:I5: 1,           Trying: 1,      words used in tweets
```

**Listing 10.6   Counting words from tweets
(http://jsbin.com/figati/edit?js,console)**

```
var tweets = [
  "Education is showing business the way by using technology to share
⇥ information. How do we do so safely?",
  "Enjoy a free muffin & coffee with Post Plus, our new loyalty club
⇥ exclusive to subscribers!",
  "We're LIVE on Periscope right now answering all your #pet questions
⇥  - tweet us yours now!"
];

var words = {};
var tweetText = tweets.join(" ");         ⟵  Join all the tweets to
var tweetWords = tweetText.split(" ");         make one long string

                                          ⟵  Create an array of words
tweetWords.forEach(function (word) {          using the split method
    words[word] = 0;
});                                       ⟵  Create a property for each
                                              word, setting its value to 0

tweetWords.forEach(function (word) {
    words[word] = words[word] + 1;        ⟵  Add one to the value every
});                                           time the word appears

console.log(words);
```

The program does quite a lot in a few lines of code. First, it uses the `join` array method (introduced in chapter 8) to join all of the tweets to form one long string with a space between each pair of tweets. Next, it uses the `split` method to create an array of all of the words. `split` is a built-in string method. You can use it to break a string into pieces, with each piece as an element of an array. If you assign a string to the `message` variable

```
var message = "I love donuts";
```

you can break the string into an array with three elements by calling the `split` method on the variable.

```
console.log(message.split(" "));

> ["I", "love", "donuts"]
```

The argument you pass to the split method is a string the function uses to decide where to split the text. The previous example uses a space as the separator, but any string will work. Here's an example using commas:

```
var csv = "Kandra Smith,50,The Dungeon of Doom";
var details = csv.split(",");
console.log(details);

> ["Kandra Smith", "50", "The Dungeon of Doom"]
```

If you pass the empty string, "", as the argument to split, it creates an array of all of the individual characters used in the text:

```
var message = "I love donuts";
console.log(message.split(""));

> ["I", " ", "l", "o", "v", "e", " ", "d", "o", "n", "u", "t", "s"]
```

Back to your tweet analyzer. Once it generates the array of words with split, listing 10.6 iterates over the array of words twice. The first time, it creates properties with the words as keys and zero as the values. ["I", "love", "donuts"] leads to

```
words["I"] = 0;
words["love"] = 0;
words["donuts"] = 0;
```

If a word appears more than once, its property will be assigned zero each time—a little redundancy but not a problem. On the second iteration, the code adds one to a property's value every time the word appears.

```
words["I"] = words["I"] + 1;
words["love"] = words["love"] + 1;
words["donuts"] = words["donuts"] + 1;
```

Alternatively, you could use the += operator to add one to the count for each word. You've seen += used to concatenate strings but it also works with numbers, adding a new number to an existing number. The following two statements are equivalent:

```
words[word] = words[word] + 1;
words[word] += 1;
```

In fact, if you just want to add one each time, there's an operator for exactly that purpose, ++. The following two statements are equivalent:

```
words[word] += 1;
words[word]++;
```

But you want your code to be easy to follow and ++ is a bit terse (as well as having some other complications we won't go into). You'll probably bump into it out and about in codeland, but you won't use it in this book until part 4.

You've iterated over all of the words twice. By the end of the second iteration, each property has a word as a key and the word's count as its value. Well done; have a pay raise! Do check out the working example on JS Bin and add more tweets or text from other sources for analysis.

With a simple tweak, you can perform a letter count instead of a word count. The next listing shows how.

Listing 10.7   Counting letters from tweets (http://jsbin.com/rusufi/edit?js,console)

```
var tweets = [ /* unchanged from listing 10.6 */ ];

var letters = {};                              Pass the empty string to
var tweetText = tweets.join("");               split to create an array of
var tweetLetters = tweetText.split("");        individual characters

tweetLetters.forEach(function (letter) {
    letters[letter.toLowerCase()] = 0;         Convert all letters to lowercase
});                                            and use them as keys

tweetLetters.forEach(function (letter) {
    letters[letter.toLowerCase()] += 1;        Use the += operator to add 1
});                                            for each occurrence of a letter

console.log(letters);
```

Listing 10.7 works in the same way as listing 10.6, using `join` and `split` to create an array and then iterating over the array twice to perform the count.

In the next section, you put square bracket notation's ability to work with arbitrary strings to good use managing exits in *The Crypt*.

10.2   *The Crypt—enhancing exit excitement*

You'll now apply your knowledge of square bracket notation to *The Crypt*. Figure 10.4 shows where the focus of this section, linking places via exits, fits into the overall structure of our ongoing game example.

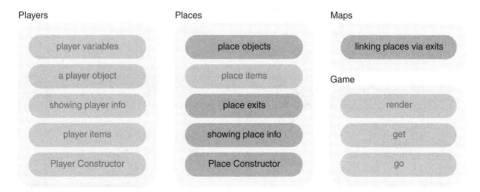

Figure 10.4   Elements of *The Crypt*

As it stands, the `Place` constructor you defined for *The Crypt* in chapter 9 gives away a little too much when it lists the exits for the current place in a game:

```
===============
= The Kitchen =
===============
You are in a kitchen. There is a disturbing smell.

Items:
    - a piece of cheese

Exits from The Kitchen:
    - The Kitchen Garden
    - The Kitchen Cupboard
    - The Old Library
=========================================
```

It lists what players will find when they leave the current location. By the end of this section, you inject a bit more mystery by simply listing the directions available rather than the destinations.

```
Exits from The Kitchen:
    - west
    - east
    - south
```

Players will find out what's around the corner only when they get there. Feel the tension!

To help you focus on using objects with square bracket notation to enhance the exits—that's what this chapter is all about after all—you create a new, simplified `Place` constructor on which to experiment. Then, in section 10.2.4, you use your burgeoning square bracket skills to update your constructor from chapter 9.

10.2.1 *Using an object to hold the exits*

To add that extra layer of the unknown, you use an exits *object* rather than an exits *array*. The object keys are directions, like `"north"` or `"the trapdoor"`, and the values are the destinations. Listing 10.8 displays the directions and destinations on the console. You hide the destinations later.

```
> north goes to The Kitchen
> the trapdoor goes to The Dungeon
```

Listing 10.8   An exits object
(http://jsbin.com/daqato/edit?js,console)

```
var Place = function (title) {          Define a simple Place
    this.title = title;                 constructor function
};

var kitchen = new Place("The Kitchen");     Use the Place constructor function
var dungeon = new Place("The Dungeon");     to create two Place objects
```

<table>
<tr>
<td>

Create an empty object and assign it to the exits variable

</td>
<td>

```
var exits = {};

exits["north"] = kitchen;
exits["the trapdoor"] = dungeon;

var keys = Object.keys(exits);

keys.forEach(function (key) {
    console.log(key + " goes to " + exits[key].title);
});
```

</td>
</tr>
</table>

Assign the Place objects to properties of the exits object, using directions as keys

Use the title property of each Place to show the destination

In listing 10.8, you begin by defining a very simple `Place` constructor function. Remember from chapter 9 that when you call a constructor function with the `new` keyword, JavaScript automatically creates an empty object and assigns it to the special `this` variable. You set the `title` property of `this` to the value of the `title` parameter.

```
var Place = function (title) {
    this.title = title;
};
```

You immediately use the constructor function to create two `Place` objects:

```
var kitchen = new Place("The Kitchen");
var dungeon = new Place("The Dungeon");
```

To keep things simple, you use a single `exits` variable for now. Later, you include it as part of the `Place` constructor function. So, you create an empty object and assign it to the `exits` variable:

```
var exits = {};
```

You have two `Place` objects, `kitchen` and `dungeon`, and you want to set them as destinations for different directions. You create corresponding properties on the `exits` object, using the directions as keys and the destinations as values:

```
exits["north"] = kitchen;
exits["the trapdoor"] = dungeon;
```

Finally, you use the `forEach` method to pass each key (in other words, each direction) in turn to the function specified.

```
console.log(key + " goes to " + exits[key].title);
```

The keys are `"north"` and `"the trapdoor"`, so the code is the same as

```
console.log("north" + " goes to " + exits["north"].title);
console.log("the trapdoor" + " goes to " + exits["the trapdoor"].title);
```

But exits["north"] is the kitchen object and exits["the trapdoor"] is the dungeon object, so the code becomes

```
console.log("north" + " goes to " + kitchen.title);
console.log("the trapdoor" + " goes to " + dungeon.title);
```

leading to the output shown before the listing.

10.2.2 Creating functions to add and display exits

Okay, so you successfully used square bracket notation to associate directions and destinations. In listing 10.9 you add a couple of helper functions to the code, addExit and showExits, to simplify the adding and displaying of exits. The output is the same as for listing 10.8:

```
> north goes to The Kitchen
> the trapdoor goes to The Dungeon
```

> **Listing 10.9   Functions to add and show exits**
> **(http://jsbin.com/mibube/edit?js,console)**

```
var Place = function (title) {
    this.title = title;
};

var kitchen = new Place("The Kitchen");
var dungeon = new Place("The Dungeon");

var exits = {};

var addExit = function (direction, place) {        Define an addExit
    exits[direction] = place;                      function to add a Place
};                                                 for a given direction

var showExits = function () {                       Define a showExits function
    var keys = Object.keys(exits);                  to display the destinations
                                                    for each exit
    keys.forEach(function (key) {
        console.log(key + " goes to " + exits[key].title);
    });
};

addExit("north", kitchen);          Call addExit twice
addExit("the trapdoor", dungeon);   to add two exits

showExits();              Call showExits to display
                         information about all the exits
```

The addExit function takes two arguments: a direction string and a Place object. The direction string becomes a new key on the exits object; the Place object becomes the corresponding value.

```
addExit("north", kitchen);
```

executes the code

```
exits["north"] = kitchen;
```

The `showExits` function iterates over the keys of the `exits` object (in other words, it iterates over the directions) and displays the destination for each direction.

10.2.3 *Giving each place object its own set of exits*

You've seen how you can use an `exits` object to model directions and destinations. But each place object needs its own set of exits. You don't want to mix up the exits from The Fairy Fun Park with the exits from The Dungeon of Doom. In listing 10.10, you move the `exits` object into the `Place` constructor. To test the functionality of the new `Place` constructor, you create three places, `library`, `kitchen`, and `garden`, and add a couple of exits to `kitchen`. The `kitchen` exits are then displayed:

```
> Exits from The Kitchen:
> south
> west
```

 Listing 10.10   An exits object in the Place constructor
(http://jsbin.com/foboka/edit?js,console)

```
var Place = function (title, description) {          Add an exits object to the
    this.title = title;                             constructor so that each place
    this.exits = {};                            ◁─  created gets a set of exits

    this.addExit = function (direction, exit) {  ◁─
        this.exits[direction] = exit;              Set the addExit
    };                                             function as a method
                                                   of each Place object
    this.showExits = function () {             ◁─
        console.log("Exits from " + this.title + ":");   Set the showExits
                                                          function as a method
        Object.keys(this.exits).forEach(function (key) {  of each Place object
            console.log(key);
        });
    };
};

var library = new Place("The Old Library");        Use the Place constructor
var kitchen = new Place("The Kitchen");            to create Place objects
var garden = new Place("The Kitchen Garden");

kitchen.addExit("south", library);     Use dot notation to call the addExit method
kitchen.addExit("west", garden);       and link the kitchen to the library and garden

kitchen.showExits();          ◁──   Use dot notation to call
                                    the showExits method
```

The addExit and showExits functions are designed to work with Place and exits objects, so it makes sense to bundle them with the other place code inside the constructor. You can then use dot notation and parentheses to call the functions:

```
kitchen.addExit("south", library);
kitchen.showExits();
```

Listing 10.11 uses the same Place code to build a slightly bigger map, linking four locations, as shown in figure 10.5.

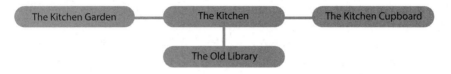

Figure 10.5   A map with four locations

The output from two locations is shown on the console:

```
> Exits from The Old Library:
> north
> Exits from The Kitchen:
> south
> west
> east
```

**Listing 10.11   A map with four locations
            (http://jsbin.com/bufico/edit?js,console)**

```
var Place = function (title, description) {          ◁───┐  Use the same Place
    this.title = title;                                  │  constructor as listing 10.10
    this.exits = {};

    this.addExit = function (direction, exit) {
        this.exits[direction] = exit;
    };

    this.showExits = function () {
        console.log("Exits from " + this.title + ":");

        Object.keys(this.exits).forEach(function (key) {
            console.log(key);
        });
    };
};

var library = new Place("The Old Library");             Use the constructor
var kitchen = new Place("The Kitchen");                 to create four Place
var garden = new Place("The Kitchen Garden");           objects
var cupboard = new Place("The Kitchen Cupboard");
```

```
library.addExit("north", kitchen);
garden.addExit("east", kitchen);
cupboard.addExit("west", kitchen);
```
**Add exits to
the kitchen**

```
kitchen.addExit("south", library);
kitchen.addExit("west", garden);
kitchen.addExit("east", cupboard);
```
**Add exits from
the kitchen**

```
library.showExits();
kitchen.showExits();
```
**Show the exits for the
library and kitchen**

Notice how, once you've defined a `Place` constructor, you can use it to create and link as many places as you need. The constructor code can stay the same—you can move it from one adventure into another—all you need to change are the places you create, the map data.

10.2.4 Adding the exits object to the full Place constructor

So far in section 10.2, you've seen how to combine an `exits` object with square bracket notation to manage the links between `Place` objects in *The Crypt*. To keep the focus on the square brackets, you built up the code starting with a new, simple `Place` constructor. It's time to combine the enhanced exits with the great work you did building constructors in chapter 9, to produce the format of output for each place shown in figure 10.6.

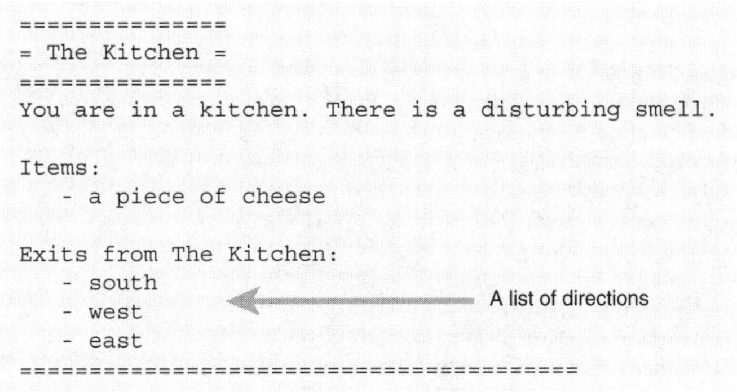

```
================
= The Kitchen =
================
You are in a kitchen. There is a disturbing smell.

Items:
    - a piece of cheese

Exits from The Kitchen:
    - south
    - west                          A list of directions
    - east
==========================================
```

**Figure 10.6 The console
output for a `Place` object
when you call `showInfo`**

Listing 10.12 shows the complete `Place` constructor function code. Most of it was discussed in chapter 9, so head back there if you need to refresh your memory. The new exits code is shown in bold and is annotated. The listing on JS Bin includes map info that is discussed in the next section.

Listing 10.12   A Place constructor function
(http://jsbin.com/zozule/edit?js,console)

```
var Place = function (title, description) {
    var newLine = spacer.newLine();

    this.title = title;
    this.description = description;           Change the exits
    this.items = [];                         property from an
    this.exits = {};                 ◁────── array to an object

    this.getItems = function () {
        var itemsString = "Items: " + newLine;
        this.items.forEach(function (item) {
            itemsString += "   - " + item;
            itemsString += newLine;
        });
        return itemsString;
    };

    this.getExits = function () {
        var exitsString = "Exits from " + this.title;
        exitsString += ":" + newLine;

        Object.keys(this.exits).forEach(function (key) {      Update the getExits
            exitsString += "   - " + key;                     method to show
            exitsString += newLine;                           directions rather
        });                                                   than destinations

        return exitsString;
    };

    this.getTitle = function () {
        return spacer.box(
            this.title,
            this.title.length + 4,
            "="
        );
    };

    this.getInfo = function () {
        var infoString = this.getTitle();
        infoString += this.description;
        infoString += newLine + newLine;
        infoString += this.getItems() + newLine;
        infoString += this.getExits();
        infoString += spacer.line(40, "=") + newLine;
        return infoString;
    };

    this.showInfo = function () {
        console.log(this.getInfo());
    };

    this.addItem = function (item) {
        this.items.push(item);
    };
```

```
    this.addExit = function (direction, exit) {
        this.exits[direction] = exit;
    };
};
```

Update the addExit function to work with the exits object

With this latest version of the `Place` constructor, you can create place objects, manage their items and exits, and display formatted information (courtesy of `spacer`) on the console. Let's take it for a spin.

10.2.5 *Testing the Place constructor*

To test the `Place` constructor, you re-create the map from listing 10.11 that links four locations: `kitchen`, `library`, `garden`, and `cupboard`. The next listing shows the map-creation code. The output is shown in figure 10.6.

> **Listing 10.13   Testing the Place constructor**
> **(http://jsbin.com/zozule/edit?js,console)**

```
var kitchen = new Place(
    "The Kitchen",
    "You are in a kitchen. There is a disturbing smell."
);
var library = new Place(
    "The Old Library",
    "You are in a library. Dusty books line the walls."
);
var garden = new Place(
    "The Kitchen Garden",
    "You are in a small, walled garden."
);
var cupboard = new Place(
    "The Kitchen Cupboard",
    "You are in a cupboard. It's surprisingly roomy."
);

kitchen.addItem("a piece of cheese");
library.addItem("a rusty key");
cupboard.addItem("a tin of spam");

kitchen.addExit("south", library);
kitchen.addExit("west", garden);
kitchen.addExit("east", cupboard);

library.addExit("north", kitchen);
garden.addExit("east", kitchen);
cupboard.addExit("west", kitchen);

kitchen.showInfo();
```

Call the Place constructor with the new keyword to create place objects

Add items to each place

Add exits from the kitchen

Add exits to the kitchen

Show the information for the kitchen on the console

You follow the map-creation code with a call to `kitchen.showInfo` to test that the `kitchen` object and its items and exits have been created as expected.

10.3   The Crypt—let the games begin!

You're so close! You have everything you need to build and display a universe of worlds for players to explore:

- The spacer namespace
- The Player constructor
- The Place constructor
- The map-creation code

There's one more piece to be added before players can be set free on their adventures:

- Game controls

Figure 10.7 shows the three game functions you'll create in this section and how they fit into the overall structure of our ongoing example.

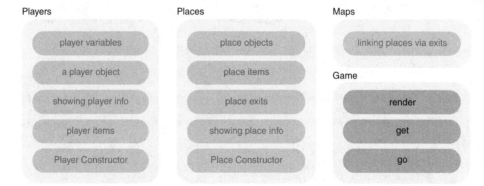

Figure 10.7   Elements of *The Crypt*

You want players to be able to issue commands at the console prompt, commands to move from place to place and to pick up items that they find. For example, to move north and pick up an item, a player would type

```
> go("north")
> get()
```

Luckily, because of the work you put into the constructors, the game control code is actually quite short. It's shown here.

Listing 10.14   Playing the game
        (http://jsbin.com/sezayo/edit?js,console)

```
var render = function () {
    console.clear();
    player.place.showInfo();
    player.showInfo("*");
};
```

Define a render function to clear the console and display player and place info

```
var go = function (direction) {
    player.place = player.place.exits[direction];
    render();
    return "";
};
```

Define a go function that moves a player to the place in the specified direction

```
var get = function () {
    var item = player.place.items.pop();
    player.addItem(item);
    render();
    return "";
};
```

Define a get function that lets a player pick up items

```
var player = new Player("Kandra", 50);
player.addItem("The Sword of Doom");
player.place = kitchen;
```

Create a player, give them a sword, and put them in the kitchen

```
render();
```

Call render to display initial info about the player and place

You create three functions: render, go, and get. Each function is discussed in its own section next. Both go and get end by returning an empty string, "". When you call functions at the console, it automatically displays their return values. Returning an empty string prevents the console from displaying the return value undefined.

10.3.1 *Updating the display—render*

At the start of each game and each time a player takes an action, you want to update the display on the console. Both Place objects and Player objects have showInfo methods to display their current state; for example,

```
player.showInfo("*");
kitchen.showInfo();
```

The program assigns the player's current location to their place property. To display information about the current place, you therefore include the code

```
player.place.showInfo();
```

You could keep appending text to the console, but it's neater to clear it and start from a blank slate after each player action. The clear method removes the text from the console.

```
console.clear();
```

You update the console after a player moves and after they pick up an item. Rather than repeating the display code, you wrap it inside the render function and call it on demand.

10.3.2 Exploring the map—go

To move to a new location, a player calls the go function, specifying the direction in which they want to move:

```
go("south");
```

You need to find the destination for the direction the player specifies and assign it as the player's new location:

```
player.place = player.place.exits[direction];
```

In the expression on the right side of the assignment, you use square bracket notation to retrieve the Place object for the direction specified, exits[direction]. You use dot notation to access the exits object:

```
player;     // The Player object

player.place;    // The player's current location
                 // A Place object

player.place.exits;    // The exits from the current location.
                       // An object with directions as keys and
                       // destinations as values.

player.place.exits[direction];    // The place is the specified direction.
                                   // A Place object.
```

The Place object for the destination is assigned to the player's place property, replacing their old location. They've moved.

10.3.3 Collecting all the things—get

To pick up an item, the player calls the get function:

```
get();
```

You remove the item from the current location and add it to the player's array of items. The current location is player.place. The items at the current location are held in the player.place.items array. To remove and return the last item in the items array, you use the pop method:

```
var item = player.place.items.pop();
```

You then add it to the player's collection:

```
player.addItem(item);
```

And that's it! You've given players the ability to boldly go from place to place, picking up any treasure they might find.

10.3.4 *Designing a bigger adventure—Jahver's ship*

Four locations based around a kitchen may not be the world of adventure you were hoping for. To conjure mystical realms, replicate dystopian futures, and weave webs of intrigue, all you need to do is change the map section of the code. Have a go at building your own locations, linking them via exits, and stocking them with interesting artifacts.

To get you started, there's a brief adventure you can explore and extend on JS Bin, at http://jsbin.com/yadabo/edit?console. You may need to click Run to start the game. It's set on a small space-freighter called *The Sparrow.* There are six items to collect, not including your blaster. Once you've collected all of the items, open up the JavaScript panel and try adding a few more locations. Happy hunting!

10.4 What's next?

While it's great to have a working game, the code for *The Crypt* isn't very robust. A player can easily break it, by trying to go in a nonexistent direction, for example. They can also access all the game objects at the console—it's easy to award themselves extra treasure or teleport to a new location:

```
> player.addItem("riches beyond my wildest dreams")
> player.place = treasureRoom
```

And the game could certainly do with more challenge. There should be puzzles that can be overcome only with certain items.

In part 2 of *Get Programming with JavaScript*, you'll address those issues by splitting your code into modules, preventing access to objects, setting conditions for when code runs, and separating data from the display of data. Such organization will help you design and manage programs as they get larger and more complicated and set you up nicely for working with web pages in part 3.

10.5 Summary

- Use a string between square brackets to specify property names:

```
player["Kandra"] = 56;
exits["north"] = kitchen;
words["to"] = words["to"] + 1;
```

- In particular, use square brackets when the property names include spaces or other characters not allowed with dot notation:

```
player["Kandra Smith"] = 56;
exits["a gloomy tunnel"] = dungeon;
words["!"] = 0;
```

- Use function parameters to dynamically assign property names when the function is called:

```
var scores = {};
var updateScore = function (playerName, score) {
    scores[playerName] = score;
};
updateScore("Dax", 2000);
console.log(scores["Dax"]);
```

- Pass an object as an argument to the `Object.keys` method to create an array of the object's keys:

```
var scores = {
    Kandra : 100,
    Dax : 60,
    Blinky : 30000
};
var keys = Object.keys(scores);     // ["Kandra", "Dax", "Blinky"]
```

- Break a string into an array with the `split` method. Pass as an argument the string used to determine where to make the breaks:

```
var query = "page=5&items=10&tag=pluto";
var options = query.split("&");     // ["page=5", "items=10", "tag=pluto"]
```

Part 2

Organizing your programs

Sharing code is common among programmers; many problems have been solved by others already, and your solutions could prove useful in your own future projects, to your team, or to the wider developer community. When code modules are shared, it's important to make clear how others should use them by defining a clear *interface*, or set of properties and functions you expect users to utilize. The internals of a module—how you make it do its job—should be protected. Part 2 looks at ways of using local rather than global variables to hide a module's implementation from other code.

As your programs grow, the need for organization increases, and you'll start to notice patterns and procedures you use again and again. Part 2 also looks at ways of using *modules* in your code to improve flexibility, reuse, and maintainability. Your code's flexibility may be improved by executing parts of it only if certain conditions are met, and you'll see how to specify those conditions with if statements.

The modules you create will usually perform specific, well-defined tasks within a project. Three common types of module are *models*, for representing and working with data, *views* for presenting the data in models, and *controllers* for updating models and views in response to user or system actions.

By the end of part 2, you'll have broken *The Crypt* into modules and updated the game to include challenges: puzzles for players to overcome.

Scope: hiding information

11

You want the user to be able to interact with your console-based programs. But you don't want to give them too much control! This chapter explores ways of hiding parts of your program from the user at the console and clearly defining the properties and methods you expect them to use. For example, for a quiz program the user should be able to submit an answer but not change their score:

```
> quiz.submit("Ben Nevis")    // OK

> quiz.score = 1000000        // Don't let the user do this!
```

By separating the public interface from the private variables and functions that make the program work, you declare your intentions, setting out what a user *can* do and what other programmers using your code *should* do, and reduce the risk of code being misused. That's good for the program, for the players, and for other programmers.

Functions are the key. Whereas variables declared outside functions are accessible everywhere in the program, those declared inside functions are accessible only within the function. This chapter will show you how to return objects from functions with only those properties and methods you want to be accessible to users. Constructors are functions too, and you'll see how to use their special `this` object to set up public properties and methods.

Finally, you'll apply what you've learned to *The Crypt*, removing user access to constructors, places, and player properties and providing methods to display player and place information and to navigate the map. Users will be able to do this:

```
> game.go("north")     // Move from place to place
> game.get()           // Pick up an item
```

Users won't be able to cheat the game by doing this:

```
> player.health = 1000000
> player.place = exit
> player.items.push("The Mega-Sword of Ultimate Annihilation")
```

Let's start by highlighting the pitfalls of variables you can see anywhere in the program; they seem like such a good idea! *[Spoiler: they're not.]*

11.1   *The dangers of global variables*

Way back in chapter 2, at the start of your adventures in JavaScript, you discovered how to declare, assign, and use variables. The following listing shows a really simple example of the process that displays the name of a mountain on the console:

```
> Ben Nevis
```

**Listing 11.1   Declare, assign, and use a variable
(http://jsbin.com/gujacum/edit?js,console)**

```
var mountain;

mountain = "Ben Nevis";

console.log(mountain);
```

You declare the variable, `mountain`, on the first line of the program. You can then use the variable throughout the code; you assign it a value and pass it to `console.log` as an argument.

Functions in the program can also access the `mountain` variable (figure 11.1).

functions can see out
and use variables declared
outside of them

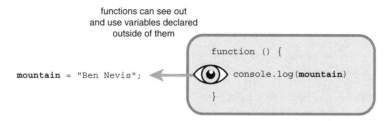

```
                                    function () {

mountain = "Ben Nevis";  ◄─────       console.log(mountain)

                                    }
```

Figure 11.1 **The function can see the `mountain` variable that's outside the function body.**

The next listing shows a `showMountain` function using `mountain`, leading to the same output as listing 11.1.

Listing 11.2 **Accessing a variable from within a function**
(http://jsbin.com/zojida/edit?js,console)

```
var mountain = "Ben Nevis";                    ◄─┐  Declare the mountain variable,
                                                  │  outside any function
var showMountain = function () {
    console.log(mountain);                     ◄─┐  Use the variable, even
};                                                │  inside a function

showMountain();
```

Variables like `mountain`, declared outside any function and so accessible everywhere, are called *global variables*. You may think these global variables sound really useful: declare them once and then use them freely from anywhere in your code. Unfortunately, they have some serious downsides and are generally considered to be *a bad thing*. Let's investigate reasons for avoiding these naughty globals.

11.1.1 *Access all areas—peeking and tweaking*

You want users to be able to interact with your programs at the console. You don't want them to have a sneaky peek at all the geeky variables. The next listing shows a tiny quiz.

Listing 11.3 **A tiny quiz**
(http://jsbin.com/nubipi/edit?js,console)

```
var question = "What is the highest mountain in Wales?";
var answer = "Snowdon";

console.log(question);
```

Because `question` and `answer` are global variables, they're accessible throughout the program and via the console. At the console prompt, once users run the program, they can type answer and press Enter and display the value of the answer variable. A sneaky peek at our geeky peak!

```
> answer
Snowdon
```

It's not just sneaky peeks that are a problem; it's sneaky tweaks too! Users can change the value of global variables at will, updating scores, bank balances, velocities, prices, and answers.

```
> answer = "Tryfan"
```

11.1.2 *Access all areas—relying on an implementation*

The idea of not relying on an implementation is important but might require time to appreciate fully. Don't worry if not everything clicks the first time through—you can always return to it after reading the other examples in the chapter.

Sneaky peeks and tweaks can be a problem for programmers too (see the sidebar "Who's using your code?"). If you've written code that is then used by other programmers, you probably don't want them to be tinkering under the hood, writing their own code that relies on the internals of yours. When you release a new version of your code that uses a more efficient algorithm internally, other code that has been relying on some of your variables may break.

Who's using your code?

Consider the spacer functions you created in chapter 7. You've been using them in your code for *The Crypt* ever since. That's an example of *you* using your own code.

It's common for programmers to be part of a *team*, small or large. The team could be working on different aspects of the same program. There's no need for each programmer to create their own formatting functions, so they all use your spacer namespace.

Your team members are so impressed by your formatting prowess that they encourage you to share the spacer namespace more widely. You upload your code to a *community* repository like Github.com (https://github.com) or npmjs.com (https://www.npmjs.com). Other programmers can then download and use your code and even contribute improvements and extensions.

The spacer code catches on and is developed further by a team of dedicated enthusiasts. It even gets its own website! It's so popular that *everyone* is using the spacer.js library.

Users should be able to rely on your *interface*—the functionality you make public—and not be concerned with your *implementation*—how you program that functionality.

> **DEFINITION** An *interface* is a set of properties and functions that you want users to access. It's how they interact with your application. For example, the screen, buttons, and cash dispenser on an ATM.

DEFINITION An *implementation* is the code you use to make an application do its job behind the scenes. It isn't usually visible to users. For example, the code that makes an ATM work, how it communicates with your bank, and how it counts the cash.

For example, to implement links between places in *The Crypt* you might use an `exits` array for exit directions and a `destinations` array for the places to which the exits lead.

```
var exits = [];
var destinations = [];
```

Then, to manage adding new exits you write an `addExit` function.

```
var addExit = function (direction, destination) {
    exits.push(direction);
    destination.push(destination);
};
```

You expect other programmers working with your `Place` objects to use the `addExit` function (figure 11.2).

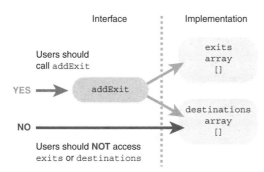

Figure 11.2 **Users should use the interface, not the implementation.**

You document the fact that `addExit` is part of the *interface*, the set of properties and functions that users—in this case programmers—should work with.

```
addExit("north", kitchen);      // Good—using function
```

But if they have access to the `exits` and `destinations` variables, they might choose to use those variables directly, bypassing the function.

```
exits.push("north");             // Bad—accessing variables directly
destinations.push(kitchen);
```

Everything seems fine and the other programmers' programs are working well. Then, after reviewing your code, you decide you can improve on having two separate arrays by using a single object.

```
var exits = {};
// No destinations array. No longer needed in new implementation.
```

To use the new way you've implemented `exits`, you update the `addExit` function.

```
var addExit = function (direction, destination) {
    exits[direction] = destination;
};
```

Programmers who were using the interface will see no change in their programs. But programmers who bypassed the interface and accessed the variables directly will see their programs break! (See figure 11.3.)

```
addExit("north", kitchen);      // Good. Works just the same.

exits.push("north");            // ERROR! exits is not an array.
destinations.push(kitchen);     // ERROR! destinations doesn't exist.
```

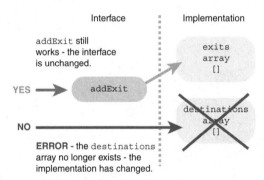

Figure 11.3   Relying on the implementation can lead to errors if it changes.

Allowing access to all areas of our programs by using global variables blurs the line between implementation and interface, giving users freedom to peek and tweak and setting up programs to fail when implementation details change.

11.1.3   Naming collisions

Because our programs can be made up from lots of pieces of code written by different teams or programmers, it's quite possible that the same variable names will be used in multiple places. If one programmer declares a variable name, say `spacer` (a name-space of formatting functions), and then later in the program another programmer declares the same variable name, `spacer` (a canine character in a console-based space-adventure game), the second will overwrite the first—a collision! We really need a way to protect our variables from such collisions. (Chapter 13 looks at collisions in more detail.)

11.1.4 Crazy bugs

Programs can be thousands of lines long. Relying on global variables that may be declared a long way away in the code and that may be peeked at and tweaked by functions and instructions throughout the program leads to a fragile program. If anything goes wrong with the program (and it probably will), it could be difficult to follow the flow of the code and pin down the location of the problems.

11.2 The benefits of local variables

Variables declared inside the body of a function can't be accessed outside the function. They're called *local variables*; they are local to the function in which they're declared (figure 11.4).

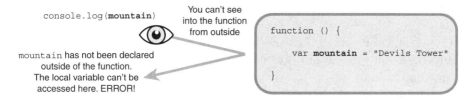

Figure 11.4 Variables declared inside a function are local to the function.

Trying to access a local variable outside its function will cause an error. Listing 11.4 tries to log the value of the mountain variable to the console but produces a message like this:

```
> ReferenceError: Can't find variable: mountain
```

(The error you get might look slightly different. Different browsers may format the error messages in different ways.)

 **Listing 11.4   A variable hidden from the console
(http://jsbin.com/bobilu/edit?js,console)**

```
var hide = function () {
    var mountain = "Devils Tower";          Declare the mountain
};                                          variable inside a function

console.log(mountain);          Try to access the mountain
                                variable outside its function
```

The collection of variables outside all functions is called the *global scope*. Each function creates its own *local scope*, its own collection of variables. In listing 11.4, the variable mountain is not in the global scope outside the function and so an error is reported when it's used in the console.log statement.

Using a variable from within the same scope causes no trouble, as shown in the following listing.

```
> Devils Tower
```

**Listing 11.5   The variable is visible from within the function
(http://jsbin.com/raluqu/edit?js,console)**

```
var show = function () {
    var mountain = "Devils Tower";          Within the function body, pass the
    console.log(mountain);          ◄───    mountain variable to console.log
};                                          as an argument.

show();
```

Listing 11.6 combines global and local variables. You can access the global variables anywhere, but you can only use the local variable, secretMountain, inside the show function.

Listing 11.6 produces the following output:

```
> Ben Nevis
> Devils Tower
> Ben Nevis
> ReferenceError: Can't find variable: secretMountain
```

**Listing 11.6   Global and local variables
(http://jsbin.com/riconi/edit?js,console)**

```
var mountain;           Declare global variables, mountain and
var show;               show, visible throughout the program

mountain = "Ben Nevis";
                                          Declare a local variable,
show = function () {                       secretMountain, visible only
    var secretMountain = "Devils Tower";  in the show function
                                   ◄───
                    console.log(mountain);          Use the secretMountain
Use the             console.log(secretMountain);    variable. No problem, it's in
mountain      ┌─►  };                        ◄───    the same local scope.
variable. No
problem,            show();                  ◄───
it's global.                                          Call the show function. No problem,
                    console.log(mountain);     ◄───   show is a global variable too.
                    console.log(secretMountain);  ◄──┐

                    Use the secretMountain variable.    Use the mountain variable.
                    Error! it's not in the global scope.  No problem, it's global.
```

11.3   Interfaces—controlling access and providing functionality

You want users to interact with your program on the console but you don't want them digging into its implementation to make changes you didn't intend. The set of properties and actions you make available to a user is called an *interface*. You need a way to provide a simple interface while hiding everything else.

In this section you use a very simple program, a counter, as an example. In section 11.4, you develop an interface for a quiz app and in sections 11.5, 11.6, and 11.7 you apply what you've learned to *The Crypt*.

The following listing shows the first version of the counter program, using a global variable to hold the current count.

> **Listing 11.7   A counter**
> **(http://jsbin.com/yagese/edit?js,console)**

```
var counter = 0;                          Declare a global variable,
                                          counter, and assign it a value
var count = function () {
    counter = counter + 1;                Access counter from
    return counter;                       within a function
};
```

Run the program and follow these steps at the console prompt. (Your actions show the prompt, >, but the responses do not.)

```
> count()
  1
> count()
  2
> count()
  3
```

It seems to be working, so what's the problem? Well, because counter is a global variable, the user can change it at any time.

```
> counter = 99
  99
> count()
  100
```

You probably don't want the user tweaking your counting variable like that. Next, you use what you learned about local variables in section 11.2 to hide the counter variable from the user.

11.3.1 *Using a function to hide variables*

You want to achieve two outcomes with your counting app:

- The counter variable is hidden from the user.
- The count function can be seen by the user.

Listing 11.8 shows a solution. Running the program enables the following console interaction, as required:

```
> count()
  1
> counter
  Can't find variable: counter
```

(Again, the error your browser displays may be slightly different.)

> ## Listing 11.8   Hiding the counter variable
> ## (http://jsbin.com/fuwuvi/edit?js,console)

```
var getCounter = function () {
  var counter = 0;                      ◁─┐  Declare counter as a local variable
                                            inside the getCounter function

  var countUpBy1 = function () {
    counter = counter + 1;                   Nest the definition of the
    return counter;                          counting function, countUpBy1,
  };                                         inside getCounter

  return countUpBy1;          ◁─┐  Return the counting function
};                               so it can be assigned

var count = getCounter();       ◁─┐  Assign the counting function
                                     returned by getCounter to the
                                     count variable, ready for use
```

Table 11.1 summarizes the key ideas as a series of problems and solutions; figure 11.5 illustrates how the returned counting function, assigned to count, still has access to the local counter variable.

Table 11.1   Problems and solutions for the counter app

Problem	Solution
I want the counter variable to be hidden from the user.	Declare the counter variable inside the getCounter function. As a local variable, counter won't be accessible by the user.
My function, countUpBy1, which increments the counter, needs access to the counter variable.	Define the countUpBy1 function inside the getCounter function as well. Because it's inside getCounter, it will have access to the counter variable.
I want the user to be able to call the counting function.	Return the counting function, countUpBy1, from the getCounter function. It can then be assigned to a global variable.

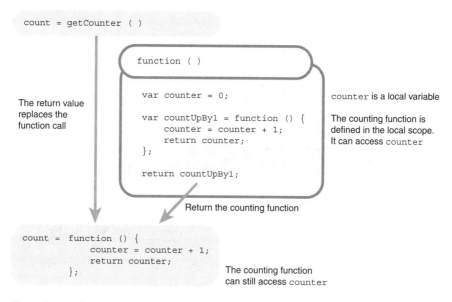

Figure 11.5   The returned function still has access to the local `counter` variable.

By returning a function and assigning it to the `count` variable (figure 11.5), you've given the user a way to use the program; you've given them an interface—they just call `get-Counter()` to obtain a counting function and then `count()` to increment the counter.

11.3.2   *Creating multiple independent counters with getCount*

In listing 11.8 you defined a function, `getCounter`, to create counters. Each time you call `getCounter` it executes the same three steps:

1   Declare a `counter` variable and assign it the value `0`.
2   Define a function to do the counting. The function uses the `counter` variable from step 1.
3   Return the function that does the counting.

Each time you call `getCounter`, it declares a `counter` variable and defines a counting function. If you call `getCounter` multiple times, don't the `counter` variables interfere with each other? No, because `getCounter` creates a fresh local scope each time it runs; you get multiple copies of the `counter` variable, each within its own isolated collection of variables, its own local scope.

Listing 11.9 updates the `getCounter` code to create two counters. You can then perform the following console interactions:

```
> climbCount()
  1
> climbCount()
  2
```

```
> climbCount()
  3
> peakCount()
  1
> climbCount()
  4
```

peakCount and climbCount do not interfere with each other.

Listing 11.9   Multiple counters
(http://jsbin.com/sicoce/edit?js,console)

```
var getCounter = function () {
  var counter = 0;                           Define the counting function
                                             and return it in one step;
  return function () {                        there's no need for a variable.
    counter = counter + 1;
    return counter;
  };
};

var peakCount = getCounter();                Call getCounter multiple times to
var climbCount = getCounter();               create independent counters
```

Having counter as a local variable allows you to have multiple independent counters.

11.3.3   *Creating multiple independent counters with a constructor function*

If you're going to be creating lots of counters, you could use a constructor function to define what a counter is and does. As detailed in chapter 9, a constructor function streamlines the common process of creating objects with similar properties and methods. You call a constructor by using the new keyword. For counters, you might have the following:

```
var peaks = new Counter();
var climbs = new Counter();
```

The constructor will automatically create an object assigned to the special this variable and return it. You can set the counting function as a property of this to make it available outside the constructor; see listing 11.10. On the console, you might call the counting function like this:

```
> peaks.count()
  1
> peaks.count();
  2
> climbs.count();
  1
```

Listing 11.10   A counter constructor
(http://jsbin.com/yidomap/edit?js,console)

```
var Counter = function () {
  var counter = 0;

  this.count = function () {          ⟵─┐  Assign the counting
    counter = counter + 1;                  function as a property of
    return counter;                         the special this object
  };
};

var peaks = new Counter();
var climbs = new Counter();
```

Compare listings 11.9 and 11.10. They're almost identical! The only difference is that in listing 11.10 you set the counting function as a property of this rather than returning it. The constructor function automatically returns the this object, so you don't need to. The constructor is still a function, so counter is still a local variable. Either approach, the plain function or the constructor function, is valid. They both let you return an interface while hiding the implementation details.

The counter was a nice, simple example. Let's look at something with a few more moving parts, the quiz app. No cheating!

11.4   Creating a quick quiz app

You want to create a simple quiz app. The app should be able to do three things:

1 Display a question on the console.
2 Display the answer to the current question on the console.
3 Move to the next question in the question bank.

The start of a typical interaction on the console might look like this:

```
> quiz.quizMe()
  What is the highest mountain in the world?
> quiz.showMe()
  Everest
> quiz.next()
  Ok
> quiz.quizMe()
  What is the highest mountain in Scotland?
```

As you can see, there are three functions, quizMe, showMe, and next, that satisfy the app's three requirements. You also need an array of questions and answers and a variable to keep track of which is the current question. Global variables, those declared outside any functions, are said to be in the *global namespace*. To avoid *polluting the global namespace* with all those quiz variables, you can set them as properties of a single object. As you saw in chapter 7, when a single object is used to collect related variables together in this way, it's often called a *namespace*.

11.4.1 *Using an object as a namespace*

The app will create a single global variable, `quiz`. All of your variables can then be set as properties of the `quiz` object, as shown in listing 11.11. The array of questions and answers starts like this:

```
var quiz = {
    questions: [
        {
            question: "What is the highest mountain in the world?",
            answer: "Everest"
        }
    ]
};
```

You then access the array via `quiz.questions`. Remember, array indexes start at 0, so to access the first question-and-answer object, use `quiz.questions[0]`. To get the first question and the first answer from the `questions` array, use the following:

```
quiz.questions[0].question;
quiz.questions[0].answer;
```

You keep track of the current question with the `qIndex` property.

Listing 11.11   Improving the quiz app
(http://jsbin.com/tupoto/edit?js,console)

```
var quiz = {                                    ← Create an object and assign
                                                   it to the quiz variable

    questions: [                                 ← Create an array and assign
                                                   it to the questions property
                                                   of the quiz object

        {
            question: "What is the highest mountain in the world?",     Use an object for
            answer: "Everest"                                           each question-and-
        },                                                              answer pair
        {
            question: "What is the highest mountain in Scotland?",
            answer: "Ben Nevis"
        },
        {                                        Set a question property
            question: "How many munros are in Scotland?",    and an answer property for
            answer: "284"                                    each object in the array
        }
    ],
                                                 Create a qIndex property
    qIndex: 0,                                 ← to keep track of the
                                                   current question

    quizMe: function () {
        return quiz.questions[quiz.qIndex].question;     Use quizMe to display
    },                                                   the current question

    showMe: function () {
        return quiz.questions[quiz.qIndex].answer;       Use showMe to display
    },                                                   the current answer
```

```
  next: function () {
    quiz.qIndex = quiz.qIndex + 1;          Use next to move to
    return "Ok";                            the next question
  }
};
```

Listing 11.11 satisfies the three requirements of your app and is polite enough to use only a single global variable, `quiz`. Everything it needs is within the `quiz` object. Because all of the properties are accessed as properties of `quiz`, we say they're in the `quiz` namespace.

Unfortunately, your app doesn't overcome the *access all areas* drawback of global variables seen in section 11.1.1. All of the properties of the `quiz` object are *public*—the user can still steal a peak and tweak all the values.

11.4.2 Hiding the questions array

In listing 11.11, players can access all of the `quiz` object's properties at the console. This allows them to cause mischief, changing properties on a whim:

```
> quiz.qIndex = 300
> quiz.questions[2].answer = "282"
```

But you want them to use only `quiz.quizMe`, `quiz.showMe`, and `quiz.next`. Let's make the `questions` array and the `qIndex` value *private* by using local variables, as shown in figure 11.6.

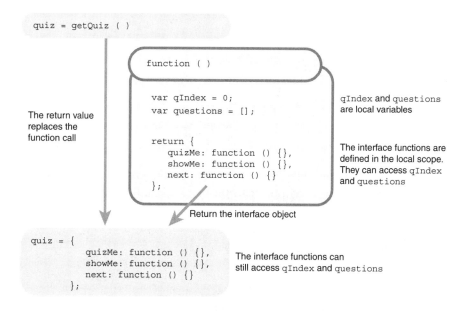

Figure 11.6   Use local variables to make `qIndex` and `questions` private

The next listing uses the getQuiz function to create a local scope in which to hide the questions array and the qIndex value.

Listing 11.12   Hiding the questions and answers
(http://jsbin.com/qahedu/edit?js,console)

```
                                          Use a function to
                                          create a local scope
var getQuiz = function () {        ◄──┘
    var qIndex = 0;                    Declare local variables
    var questions = [                  inside the function
        {
            question: "What is the highest mountain in the world?",
            answer: "Everest"
        },
        {
            question: "What is the highest mountain in Scotland?",
            answer: "Ben Nevis"
        },
        {
            question: "How many munros are in Scotland?",
            answer: "284"
        }
    ];                                 Return an object with properties
    return {                   ◄──┘    for the user to access
        quizMe : function () {
            return questions[qIndex].question;
        },
        showMe : function () {
            return questions[qIndex].answer;
        },
        next : function () {
            qIndex = qIndex + 1;
            return "Ok";
        }
    };                             Call the function, assigning
};                                 the object returned to the
                                   quiz variable
var quiz = getQuiz();      ◄──┘
```

The program returns an object with three properties: quizMe, showMe, and next. The last line assigns the returned object to the quiz variable. You can then use quiz to access the three functions:

```
> quiz.quizMe()
  What is the highest mountain in the world?
> quiz.answer()
  Everest
```

The code that makes the quiz app work is called its *implementation*. Some of the implementation is hidden in the getQuiz function by using local variables. The object returned by the function provides the user with an *interface*, a public way of interacting with the program. The user can call the quizMe, showMe, and next functions because they're methods of the interface object. The user can't access the qIndex and questions variables because they're local to the getQuiz function.

Figure 11.7 shows how errors are thrown when an attempt is made to access the variables qIndex and questions at the console prompt on JS Bin. (Your error messages may be slightly different.)

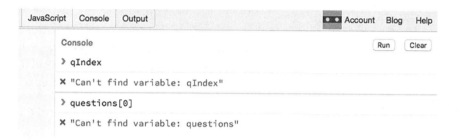

Figure 11.7 Trying to access qIndex and questions from the console now causes errors.

11.5 The Crypt—hiding player info

In this section, and in sections 11.6 and 11.7, you update your code for *The Crypt* to hide variables, properties, and functions that are part of the implementation and that should not be spied by outside eyes. At the same time, you consider what form your interfaces should take—what information and actions you'll make available to players and to programmers.

11.5.1 Our current Player constructor—everything is public

Up to this point, you haven't made any attempt to control a user's access to the data in a Player object. The following listing shows the current form of your Player constructor.

Listing 11.13 The Player constructor
(http://jsbin.com/dacedu/edit?js,console)

```
var spacer = { /* visible on JS Bin */ };

var Player = function (name, health) {
    var newLine = spacer.newLine();

    this.name = name;          Make all data available
    this.health = health;      by setting properties on
    this.items = [];           the this object
    this.place = null;
```

```
    this.addItem = function (item) { … };

    this.getNameInfo = function () { … };

    this.getHealthInfo = function () { … };

    this.getPlaceInfo = function () { … };

    this.getItemsInfo = function () { … };

    this.getInfo = function (character) { … };

    this.showInfo = function (character) { … };
};
```

Make all methods available by setting properties on the this object

You set all of the player data and all of the functions as properties of the special `this` object. The constructor creates the `this` object automatically when you call it with the new keyword. In the snippet that follows, you call the `Player` constructor to create a new player.

```
var player1 = new Player("Jahver", 80);
```

The constructor function automatically returns the `this` object, and you then assign the object to the `player1` variable. Because you attached everything to `this` within the constructor, and `this` was returned and assigned to `player1`, you can now use `player1` to access data and methods: `player1.name`, `player1.items`, `player1.addItem`, `player1.getInfo`, and `player1.showInfo` are all accessible, for example.

11.5.2 *An updated Player constructor—some variables are hidden*

To control users' access to player data you can use parameters and variables without assigning values to properties of the `this` object. Parameters, between the opening parentheses in a function definition, act just like variables declared within the function body. They're local to the function and can be used anywhere within the function but can't be accessed by code outside the function.

```
var Player = function (name, health) {

    // name and health are local variables.
    // They can be used here.

    this.getHealthInfo = function () {
        // name and health can be used here.
    };
};

// name and health can NOT be used here.
// This is outside the scope of the player function.
```

Figure 11.8 shows the change in visibility of variables and properties from the old `Player` constructor (listing 11.13) to the new (listing 11.14). The new constructor hides most of the functions in the local scope, assigning only four functions to the special `this` object as an interface.

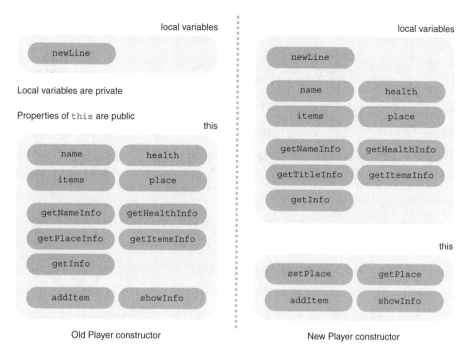

Figure 11.8 Hiding variables and functions in the local scope of the constructor function

The next listing shows the changes in code; local variables, declared with var, are used to prevent direct access to a player's data.

Listing 11.14 Hiding player info in the constructor
**   (http://jsbin.com/fuyaca/edit?js,console)**

```
var spacer = { /* visible on JS Bin */ };

var Player = function (name, health) {          Create private variables
    var newLine = spacer.newLine();            with parameters and
    var items = [];                            the var keyword
    var place = null;

    var getNameInfo = function () {
        return name;
    };

    var getHealthInfo = function () {          Make these
        return "(" + health + ")";             functions
    };                                         private—they're
                                               for internal use.
    var getItemsInfo = function () {
        var itemsString = "Items:" + newLine;

        items.forEach(function (item, i) {
            itemsString += "  - " + item + newLine;
        });
```

```
        return itemsString;
    };

    var getTitleInfo = function () {
        return getNameInfo() + " " + getHealthInfo();
    };

    var getInfo = function () {
        var info = spacer.box(getTitleInfo(), 40, "*");
        info += "   " + getItemsInfo();
        info += spacer.line(40, "*");
        info += newLine;

        return info;
    };

    this.addItem = function (item) {
        items.push(item);
    };

    this.setPlace = function (destination) {
        place = destination;
    };

    this.getPlace = function () {
        return place;
    };

    this.showInfo = function (character) {
        console.log(getInfo(character));
    };
};
```

> Make these functions private—they're for internal use.

> Add methods to manage access to the place variable

The properties and functions you don't want to be seen outside the constructor you assign to local variables. The methods you want to make visible you assign as properties of the this object.

```
var items = [];    // Keep private

this.showInfo = function () { };    // Make public
```

The setPlace and getPlace methods give users access to the place variable. Why bother using a variable to make place private if you're only going to provide methods to access it anyway? They provide an interface and allow you to hide the implementation and also let you mediate access. When the setPlace method is called, you can check that the destination argument is a valid place before assigning it to the place variable. When the getPlace method is called, you can check that the user is allowed to get access before returning the place. You haven't put those extra checks in place yet, but your two methods are ready for when you need to add any conditions.

You've also simplified the information displayed by showInfo so that it no longer includes the current place. Place objects have their own showInfo method, so there's no need to double up and display place details as part of a player's information. When you display player info on the console, it now looks like this:

```
*****************************************
* Kandra (50)                           *
*****************************************
  Items:
   - The Sword of Doom
*****************************************
```

The player's health is shown in parentheses after their name. To show information about a player's current location, you can call getPlace to retrieve the place object and then call the place object's showInfo method:

```
var place = player.getPlace();
place.showInfo();
```

11.6   *The Crypt—hiding place info*

You now do for the Place constructor what you did for the Player constructor. You hide the data and provide methods that access it as required. The next listing shows the structure of the previous Place constructor, from chapter 10, with data and methods set on the this object.

Listing 11.15   The Place constructor
(http://jsbin.com/kavane/edit?js,console)

```
var spacer = { /* visible on JS Bin */ };

var Place = function (title, description) {
    var newLine = spacer.newLine();

    this.title = title;                        ◁── Use properties to
    this.description = description;                 hold place data
    this.items = [];
    this.exits = {};

    this.getItemsInfo = function () { };       ◁── Create functions
    this.getExitsInfo = function () { };            that build strings
    this.getTitleInfo = function () { };            of information
    this.getInfo = function () { };

    this.showInfo = function () { };           ◁── Create functions
    this.addItem = function (item) { };             that update place
    this.addExit = function (direction, exit) { };  data and display it
};
```

The following listing shows your updated version of the Place constructor, using parameters and variables to hide data, a new getExit function to return the destination for a specified direction, and a new getLastItem method to return the last item from the items array.

```js
var spacer = { /* visible on JS Bin */ };

var Place = function (title, description) {        Create private variables
    var newLine = spacer.newLine();               with parameters and
    var items = [];                               the var keyword
    var exits = {};

    var getItemsInfo = function () {
        var itemsString = "Items: " + newLine;
        items.forEach(function (item) {
            itemsString += "   - " + item;
            itemsString += newLine;
        });
        return itemsString;
    };

    var getExitsInfo = function () {
        var exitsString = "Exits from " + title;
        exitsString += ":" + newLine;            Make these
                                                 functions private.
        Object.keys(exits).forEach(function (key) {  They're for
            exitsString += "   - " + key;        internal use.
            exitsString += newLine;
        });

        return exitsString;
    };

    var getTitleInfo = function () {
        return spacer.box(title, title.length + 4, "=");
    };

    var getInfo = function () {
        var infoString = getTitleInfo();
        infoString += description;
        infoString += newLine + newLine;
        infoString += getItemsInfo() + newLine;
        infoString += getExitsInfo();
        infoString += spacer.line(40, "=") + newLine;
        return infoString;
    };

    this.showInfo = function () {
        console.log(getInfo());
    };

    this.addItem = function (item) {
        items.push(item);
    };

    this.addExit = function (direction, exit) {
        exits[direction] = exit;
    };
```

```
    this.getExit = function (direction) {
        return exits[direction];
    };
```

Add a public method to give access to destinations

```
    this.getLastItem = function () {
        return items.pop();
    };
};
```

Add a public method to grab the last item from the items array

You've hidden certain properties and functions in the `Player` and `Place` constructors while making a small set of methods—your interface—visible via the `this` object. Other parts of your program that use the constructors (or programmers who may use your code in their own adventure game programs) can use only the methods in the interface.

For players typing commands at a console, you'll preserve their enjoyment of the game by preventing them from stumbling inadvertently over important game values they find they can change. (*Cheating* is such a nasty word.) You'll present the players with a small, simple set of actions they can take to explore, collect, smite, and destroy—whatever is appropriate as they journey through *The Crypt.*

11.7 *The Crypt—user interaction*

In chapter 10 you created a version of *The Crypt* that let the player move from place to place and pick up items they found. Unfortunately, you polluted the global namespace with all of your variables. Don't beat yourself up about it; you were young and naïve. Now you have a way to hide the implementation from the user.

Listing 11.17 shows an outline of the current implementation; the full version is on JS Bin. It's almost the same as the version from chapter 10 but uses the `getPlace` and `setPlace` player methods and the `getExit` and `getLastItem` place methods from this chapter's constructor updates. The code that uses them is shown in full.

Listing 11.17 Lots of global variables in the game (http://jsbin.com/dateqe/edit?js,console)

```
// The spacer namespace
var spacer = { /* formatting functions */ };

// Constructors
var Player = function (name, health) { … };
var Place = function (title, description) { … };

// Game controls
var render = function () {
    console.clear();
    player.getPlace().showInfo();
    player.showInfo();
};

var go = function (direction) {
    var place = player.getPlace();
    var destination = place.getExit(direction);
```

```
        player.setPlace(destination);
        render();
        return "";
};

var get = function () {
        var place = player.getPlace();
        var item = place.getLastItem();
        player.addItem(item);
        render();
        return "";
};

// Map
var kitchen = new Place("The Kitchen", "You are in a kitchen…");
var library = new Place("The Old Library", "You are in a library…");

kitchen.addItem("a piece of cheese");
library.addItem("a rusty key");

kitchen.addExit("south", library);
library.addExit("north", kitchen);

// Game initialization
var player = new Player("Kandra", 50);
player.addItem("The Sword of Doom");
player.setPlace(kitchen);

render();
```

Notice all the global variables—the spacer namespace, the Player and Place constructors, the game control functions, all the places, and the player—are assigned to variables outside any functions. Smelly pollution. Only the game control functions, go and get, need to be available to players. You can hide the rest.

11.7.1 *The interface—go and get*

There are only two actions you want the user to take for now:

```
game.go("north"); // Move; e.g. to the place north of the current location
game.get();       // Pick up an item from the current location
```

To hide the implementation, you wrap the game code inside a function. Then, to allow the user to take the two desired actions and no more, you return an interface object from the function, with the two methods:

```
return {
        go: function (direction) {
            // Move to a new place
        },

        get: function () {
            // Pick up an item
        }
};
```

The interface methods use the functionality of player and place objects to do their jobs, with those objects created by their respective constructor functions.

11.7.2 Hiding the implementation

To hide the rest of the code from the users, you wrap it in a function to create a local scope. Only your interface object is returned. The listing that follows shows highlights from the updated code. The full listing is available on JS Bin.

> **Listing 11.18 Letting users interact with the game via an interface object (http://jsbin.com/yuporu/edit?js,console)**

```
var getGame = function () {          ◁─── Wrap the implementation in a
                                          function to create a local scope

    var spacer = { … };                              ┐ Include spacer and
    var Player = function (name, health) { … };      │ the Player and Place
    var Place = function (title, description) { … };  ┘ constructor functions

    var render = function () { … };     ◁── Include a function for updating the console

    var kitchen = new Place("The Kitchen", "You are in a kitchen…");
    var library = new Place("The Old Library", "You are in a library…");
    kitchen.addItem("a piece of cheese");
    library.addItem("a rusty key");
    kitchen.addExit("south", library);
    library.addExit("north", kitchen);

    var player = new Player("Kandra", 50);      ┐ Create a player—yep,
    player.addItem("The Sword of Doom");        │ it's local—and give
    player.setPlace(kitchen);                   ┘ them a starting place.

    render();        ◁── Show initial info on the console

    return {                          ◁── Return an object to
        go: function (direction) {         act as the interface;
            var place = player.getPlace();  players can access
            var destination = place.getExit(direction);  its methods.
            player.setPlace(destination);
            render();
            return "";
        },

        get: function () {
            var place = player.getPlace();
            var item = place.getLastItem();
            player.addItem(item);
            render();
            return "";
        }
    };
};

var game = getGame();        ◁── Call the getGame function to
                                 return the interface object and
                                 assign it to the game variable
```

The last statement of the listing calls the `getGame` function. The function executes and then returns the interface object that has the `go` and `get` methods. The statement assigns the interface object to the `game` variable. The player can access the `go` and `get` methods via the `game` variable by using dot notation:

```
game.get();
game.go("east");
```

The player can't access any other variables or functions from the game. Your work is done! At least for this chapter.

The *wrap-and-return* process of wrapping code in a function from which you then return an interface object is called the *module pattern*. It's a common way of separating the interface from the implementation and helps package your code for portability and reuse. You'll see it a lot from now on, particularly in chapter 13 when you investigate importing modules by using HTML `script` tags. Before you get to that, you have some decisions to make in chapter 12. *If* you're ready, read on; *else* take a break, chill out, try the Further Adventures, and gird your loins.

11.8   Summary

- Reduce the number of global variables in your programs. Global variables are variables declared outside all functions. They can be accessed anywhere in the program but pollute the global namespace, expose your implementation, can create naming collisions, and can help introduce hard-to-find bugs:

```
var myGlobal = "Look at me";

var useGlobal = function () {
    console.log("I can see the global: " + myGlobal);
};

console.log("I too can see the global: " + myGlobal);
```

- Reduce the number of global variables by collecting related variables and functions as properties of a single object. Such an object is often called a namespace:

```
var singleGlobal = {
    method1 : function () { … },
    method2 : function () { … }
};
```

- Wrap code in functions to create local scopes, collections of local variables:

```
var getGame = function () {
    var myLocal = "A local scope, for local people.";
    console.log(myLocal);  // Displays message
};

console.log(myLocal);  // ERROR! myLocal is not declared here.
                       // It is not in the global scope.
```

- Wrap code in functions to make variables private, hide your implementation, avoid naming collisions, and reduce the risk of hard-to-find bugs.
- Return public interfaces from functions to clearly define the properties and methods you expect users to access (the module pattern).
- Return a single function:

```
var getCounter = function () {
    var counter = 0;      // Private

    return function () { … };
};

var count = getCounter();
```

- Return an object:

```
var getGame = function () {
    // Game implementation

    return {
        // Interface methods
    };
};

var game = getGame();
```

- Remember that constructor functions create a local scope, just like any other functions. The special `this` variable is automatically returned. It acts as the public interface:

```
var Counter = function () {
    var counter = 0;      // Private

    this.count = function () { … };
};
```

Conditions: choosing code to run

This chapter covers

- Comparing values with comparison operators
- Checking conditions that are `true` or `false`
- The `if` statement—running code only if a condition is met
- The `else` clause—running code when a condition is not met
- Making sure user input won't break your code
- Generating random numbers with `Math.random()`

So far, all of your code follows a single path. When you call a function, every statement in the function body is executed. You've managed to get a lot done and covered quite a few core ideas in JavaScript but your programs have lacked flexibility; they haven't been able to decide whether or not to execute blocks of code.

In this chapter you learn how to run code only when specified conditions are met. Suddenly, your programs can branch, providing options, flexibility, and richness. You can increase a player's score *if* they splat a kumquat, move to a new location *if* the user specifies a valid direction, or post a tweet *if* it's less than 141 characters long.

If you want to find out how your programs can make decisions, read on, else, … well, read on anyway. You really need to know this stuff!

12.1 Conditional execution of code

To start, create a simple program that asks the user to guess a secret number. If they guess correctly, the program says, "Well done!" An interaction at the console might look like this:

```
> guess(2)
  undefined
> guess(8)
  Well done!
  undefined
```

What's with the ugly appearances of `undefined`? When you call a function at the console, its code is executed and then its return value is displayed. The `guess` function in the following listing doesn't include a return statement so it automatically returns `undefined`.

Listing 12.1   Guess the number
http://jsbin.com/feholi/edit?js,console

```
var secret = 8;                              ◁─┤   Assign a number to
                                                   the secret variable

var guess = function (userNumber) {          ◁─┐  Define a function that accepts
  if (userNumber === secret) {          ◁──────┤  the user's number and assign
    console.log("Well done!");     ◁────────┐     it to the guess variable
  }
};                 Log "Well done!" to the      Check if the user's number
                   console if the numbers match   matches the secret number
```

The `guess` function checks to see if the user's number is equal to the secret number. It uses the *strict equality operator*, `===`, and an *if statement* so that you display the "Well done!" message only if the numbers match. The following sections look at the strict equality operator and the `if` statement in more detail and introduce the *else clause*.

12.1.1 The strict equality operator, ===

The strict equality operator compares two values. If they're equal it returns `true`; if they're not equal it returns `false`. You can test it at the console:

```
> 2 === 8
  false
> 8 === 8
  true
> 8 === "8"
  false
> "8" === "8"
  true
```

In the third example, you can see that the strict equality operator doesn't consider the number 8 and the string "8" to be equal. That's because numbers and strings are different types of data. The values true and false are a third type of data; they're called *boolean* values. In fact, true and false are the only possible boolean values. Boolean values are useful when deciding what a program should do next; for example, by using an if statement.

12.1.2   *The if statement*

To execute a block of code only when a specified condition is met, you use an if statement.

```
if (condition) {
    // Code to execute
}
```

If the condition in parentheses evaluates to true, then JavaScript executes the statements in the code block between the curly braces. If the condition evaluates to false, then JavaScript skips the code block. Notice there's no semicolon after the curly braces at the end of an if statement.

Listing 12.1 used the strict equality operator to return a true or false value for the condition.

```
if (userNumber === secret) {
    console.log("Well done!");
}
```

The code logs the "Well done!" message to the console only if the value of user-Number is equal to the value of secret. For example, say the secret is 8 and the user chooses 2:

```
if (2 === 8) {                        // The condition is false.
    console.log("Well done!");        // Not executed
}
```

If the user chooses 8, the if statement becomes

```
if (8 === 8) {                        // The condition is true.
    console.log("Well done!");        // This is executed.
}
```

12.1.3   *The else clause*

Sometimes we want different code to be executed if the condition in an if statement evaluates to false. We can make that happen by appending an else clause to the if statement (figure 12.1).

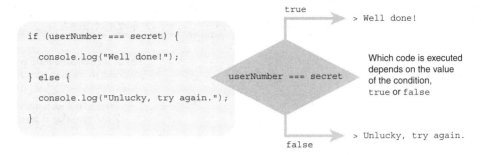

Figure 12.1 **Executing code depending on the value of a condition, with if and else**

From listing 12.2:

```
if (userNumber === secret) {
    console.log("Well done!");
} else {
    console.log("Unlucky, try again.");
}
```

If userNumber and secret are equal, JavaScript displays "Well done!" Otherwise, it displays "Unlucky, try again." Notice there's no semicolon after the curly braces at the end of an else clause. Once again, say the secret is 8 and the user chooses 2:

```
if (2 === 8) {                              // The condition is false.
    console.log("Well done!");              // Not executed.
} else {
    console.log("Unlucky, try again.");     // This is executed.
}
```

If the user chooses 8, the if statement becomes

```
if (8 === 8) {                              // The condition is true.
    console.log("Well done!");              // This is executed.
} else {
    console.log("Unlucky, try again.");     // Not executed.
}
```

A guessing game interaction at the console might now look something like this:

```
> guess(2)
  Unlucky, try again.
  undefined
> guess(8)
  Well done!
  undefined
```

```
var secret = 8;                              Add an if statement with the
                                             condition to check in parentheses
var guess = function (userNumber) {
    if (userNumber === secret) {             Execute this code only
                                             if the condition is true
        console.log("Well done!");

    } else {                                 Add an else clause for
                                             when the condition is false
        console.log("Unlucky, try again.");

    }                                        Execute this code only if
};                                           the condition is false
```

Next, you use local variables to make `secret` secret.

12.1.4   *Hide the secret number inside a function*

In listing 12.2, both the `secret` and the `guess` variables are declared outside any function. You saw in chapter 11 how that makes them global variables, accessible at the console and throughout the program. That's great for `guess`—you want users to be able to guess numbers—but it's a disaster for `secret`—users can peek and tweak its value at will. If you run the code in listing 12.2, you can then perform the following actions at the console:

```
> secret           // You can access secret. It's a global variable.
  8
> guess(8)
  Well done!
  undefined
> secret = 20      // You can reset secret to whatever you want.
  20
> guess(20)
  Well done!
  undefined
```

That's not much of a guessing game!

Chapter 11 also discussed how functions are used in JavaScript to create a local scope, a collection of variables accessible only within the function. Listing 12.3 uses the `getGuesser` function to hide the secret number. The function returned by `getGuesser` is assigned to the `guess` variable (figure 12.2).

`guess` is a global variable, available at the console:

```
> guess(2)
  Unlucky, try again
  undefined
```

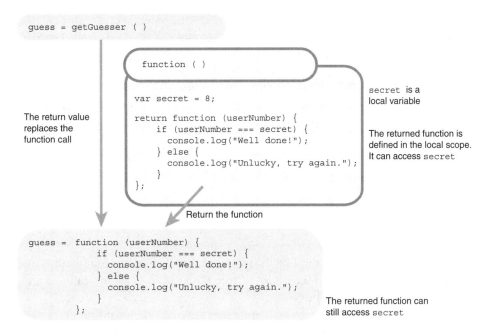

Figure 12.2   **The function returned by `getGuesser` is assigned to the `guess` variable.**

Listing 12.3   **Guess the number—using local scope**
(http://jsbin.com/hotife/edit?js,console)

```
                                              ⌐  Use a function to
var getGuesser = function () {      ◁─────┘     create a local scope
  var secret = 8;

Hide the                                           ⌐  Return a function the user
secret                                                can use to guess the number
number       return function (userNumber) {   ◁────┘
within         if (userNumber === secret) {      ◁────┐  Check to see if the user's guess
the local        console.log("Well done!");      ◁────┘  is equal to the secret number
scope          } else {
                 console.log("Unlucky, try again.");  ◁──┐  Log "Well done!" only if
               }                                          │  the numbers match
             };
};                                                ⌐  ... otherwise log
                                                     "Unlucky, try again"
var guess = getGuesser();              ◁────┐  Call getGuesser and assign the function
                                             it returns to the guess variable
```

The function assigned to `getGuesser` creates a local scope that lets you protect the secret variable from the user. It returns another function that lets the user guess a number. That function is assigned to the `guess` variable. Because the guess-checking function is defined in the local scope created by the `getGuesser` function, it has access to the `secret` variable and is able to do its checking.

You have a guessing game but it's always the same secret number. Really, it's a not-so-secret number! Let's make use of a couple of methods from JavaScript's `Math` namespace to inject some extra mystery into our guessing game.

12.2   *Generating random numbers with Math.random()*

The `Math` namespace provides you with a `random` method for generating random numbers. It always returns a number greater than or equal to 0 and less than 1. Give it a whirl at the console prompt:

```
> Math.random()
  0.7265986735001206
> Math.random()
  0.07281153951771557
> Math.random()
  0.552000432042405
```

Obviously, your numbers will be different because they're random! Unless you're really into guessing games and have a lot of free time, those random numbers are probably a bit too tricky for your purposes.

To tame the numbers, scale them up to fall in a range you want and then convert them to whole numbers (integers). Because they start off less than 1, multiplying by 10 will make them less than 10. Here's a series of assignments using `Math.random`:

```
var number = Math.random();          //  0 <= number < 1
```

To scale the possible numbers, multiply:

```
var number = Math.random() * 10;     //  0 <= number < 10
```

To shift the possible numbers up or down, add or subtract:

```
var number = Math.random() + 1;      //  1 <= number < 2
```

To scale and then shift, multiply and then add:

```
var number = Math.random() * 10 + 1; //  1 <= number < 11
```

Notice for the last assignment the numbers will be between 1 and 11; they can equal 1 but will be less than 11. The `<=` symbol means less than or equal to, whereas the `<` symbol means less than. The inequality `0 <= number < 1` means the number is between 0 and 1 and can equal 0 but not 1 (see section 12.3.1).

Okay, so you've scaled up the random numbers, but they're still a trifle tricky. At the console you can see the kind of numbers you're generating:

```
> Math.random() * 10 + 1
  3.2726867394521832
> Math.random() * 10 + 1
  9.840337357949466
```

The last step is to lose the decimal fraction part of each number, to round the numbers down to integers. For that you use the `floor` method of the `Math` namespace.

```
> Math.floor(3.2726867394521832)
  3
> Math.floor(9.840337357949466)
  9
```

The `floor` method *always rounds down*, whatever the decimals are: 10.00001, 10.2, 10.5, 10.8, and 10.99999 are all rounded down to 10, for example. You use `floor` to get an expression that returns a random integer between 1 and 10 inclusive:

```
var number = Math.random() * 10 + 1            // 1 <= number < 11
var number = Math.floor(Math.random() * 10 + 1)   // 1 <= number <= 10
```

There's also a `Math.ceil` method that always rounds up and a `Math.round` method that rounds up or down, following the usual rules for mathematical rounding. More information about JavaScript's `Math` object can be found on the *Get Programming with JavaScript* website: http://www.room51.co.uk/js/math.html.

Listing 12.4 puts the `Math` methods into practice. The `guess` function now *returns* strings rather than logging them; the console automatically displays the return values, tidying up the interactions:

```
> guess(2)
  Unlucky, try again.
> guess(8)
  Unlucky, try again.
> guess(7)
  Well done!
```

Listing 12.4   Guess the random number
(http://jsbin.com/mezowa/edit?js,console)

```
var getGuesser = function () {
    var secret = Math.floor(Math.random() * 10 + 1);    ◁——  Use Math.random and Math.floor
                                                              to generate a whole number
                                                              between 1 and 10 inclusive

    return function (userNumber) {
                                                    Use an if statement to execute commands
        if (userNumber === secret) {    ◁——        only if the condition evaluates to true

            return "Well done!";        ◁——
                                                   The return value will be displayed on
        } else {                        ◁——        the console when the function is called.

            return "Unlucky, try again.";
                                              Include an else clause with
        }                                     commands to be executed if
    };                                        the condition evaluates to false
};
var guess = getGuesser();       ◁——  Call getGuesser and assign the function
                                     that's returned to the guess variable
```

Using random numbers has made your guessing game more interesting. But there isn't a great deal of strategy involved; it's just straight guessing. The game could be improved by giving better feedback after each guess.

12.3 *Further conditions with else if*

By receiving better feedback for each guess, users can develop more efficient strategies when battling your guessing game. And strategy games are always more fun than guessing games. If a user's guess is incorrect, tell them if it's too high or too low.

```
> guess(2)
  Too low!
> guess(7)
  Too high!
> guess(5)
  Well done!
```

Figure 12.3 shows the conditions used to produce the three possible types of feedback for a user's guess.

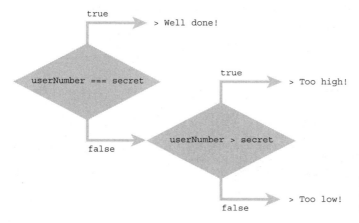

Figure 12.3   Nesting conditions can provide multiple options.

The following listing shows how an extra `if` statement can be used to differentiate between the two types of incorrect answer.

Listing 12.5   **Higher or lower**
              (http://jsbin.com/cixeju/edit?js,console)

```
var getGuesser = function () {
    var secret = Math.floor(Math.random() * 10 + 1);

    return function (userNumber) {
        if (userNumber === secret) {
            return "Well done!";
```

◁─┤ **Use a condition to check if the user has guessed the secret number**

```
        } else {
            if (userNumber > secret) {      ←────┐  Execute the first else clause
                return "Too high!";          ←───┐│  if the guess is incorrect
            } else {                        ←──┐  ││
                return "Too low!";                ││  Check if the user's guess is
            }                                  │  ││  greater than the secret number
        }                                     │  ││
    };                                        │  ││  Include code for when the
};                                            │  ││  incorrect guess is not greater
                                              │  ││  than the secret number
var guess = getGuesser();
```

If a code block contains a single statement, JavaScript lets us leave out the curly braces; the following three statements are equivalent:

```
if (userNumber === secret) {
    return "Well done!";
}

if (userNumber === secret)
    return "Well done!";

if (userName === secret) return "Well done!";
```

As `if` and `else` clauses get more complicated and when code gets updated over time, if you leave out the curly braces it can sometimes be hard to spot which statements go with which clauses. Many programmers (including me) recommend that you always use curly braces for the code blocks (apart from the case of nested `if` statements, as shown shortly). Others aren't so strict. Ultimately, it can come down to personal (or team) preferences. For now, I'd go with whatever you find easiest to understand.

An `if` statement, even with an `else` clause, counts as one statement. When an `else` clause contains a single `if` statement, it's common to leave out the curly braces. The following three code snippets are equivalent:

First, the code as shown in listing 12.5. The nested `if-else` statement is inside a pair of curly braces.

```
else {                               // Curly braces at start
    if (userNumber > secret) {
        return "Too high!";
    } else {
        return "Too low!";
    }
}                                    // Curly braces at end
```

The inner `if-else` is a single statement, so it doesn't need to be wrapped in curly braces.

```
else                                 // No curly braces
    if (userNumber > secret) {
        return "Too high!";
```

```
    } else {
        return "Too low!";
    }
                                    // No curly braces
```

And finally, because JavaScript mostly ignores spaces and tab characters, the inner if-else statement can be moved to follow on from the initial else.

```
else if (userNumber > secret) {     // if moved next to else
    return "Too high!";
} else {
    return "Too low!";
}
```

The last version is the format most commonly seen. The next listing shows the neater else-if block in context.

Listing 12.6　A neater else-if block
(http://jsbin.com/cidoru/edit?js,console)

```
var getGuesser = function () {
    var secret = Math.floor(Math.random() * 10 + 1);

    return function (userNumber) {
        if (userNumber === secret) {
            return "Well done!";
        } else if (userNumber > secret) {
            return "Too high!";
        } else {
            return "Too low!";
        }
    };
};

var guess = getGuesser();
```

The second if statement is shown in bold for comparison with listing 12.5. You've removed the curly braces for the first else block and moved the second if next to the first else. Listing 12.6 shows the most common way of writing else-if blocks. If you prefer the longer version in listing 12.5, feel free to stick with it; there are no *Block Judges* waiting to sentence you for syntax abuse. (*At this point the author is called away to deal with a ruckus—some very loud banging on the door to his apartment … it's The Law!*)

All possible outcomes are catered for in the guessing game; the guess could be correct or too high or too low. If the guess is not correct and it's not too high, then it must be too low.

12.3.1　*Comparison operators*

Listings 12.5 and 12.6 both make use of the *greater than operator,* >. It operates on two values and returns true or false. It's one of a family of operators that compare two values. Some of the operators are shown in table 12.1.

Table 12.1 Comparison operators

Operator	Name	Example	Evaluates to
>	Greater than	5 > 3 3 > 10 7 > 7	true false false
>=	Greater than or equal to	5 >= 3 3 >= 10 7 >= 7	true false true
<	Less than	5 < 3 3 < 10 7 < 7	false true false
<=	Less than or equal to	5 <= 3 3 <= 10 7 <= 7	false true true
===	Strictly equal to	5 === 3 7 === 7 7 === "7"	false true false
!==	Not strictly equal to	5 !== 3 7 !== 7 7 !== "7"	true false true

Because the operators in table 12.1 return `true` or `false`, they can be used in the condition for `if` statements. You may be wondering about the strict part of the strict equality operator—something we'll be sticking to throughout the book—and whether there's a non-strict version. Yes, there is. For non-strict equality you can use `==`. See the "Loose equality and coercion" sidebar.

> ## Loose equality and coercion
>
> The *loose equality operator*, `==`, is allowed to *coerce* values into different types in order to compare them for equality.
>
> *Coercion* is the process of converting a value from one type to another, for example, from a string to a number.
>
> So, whereas the strict comparison `7 === "7"` evaluates to `false`, because one value is a number and the other is a string, the loose comparison `7 == "7"` evaluates to `true`, because the string is first coerced to a number and `7 == 7` is `true`.
>
> The rules for coercion are beyond the scope of this book (although ignore people who say they're not worth learning), and we'll stick to strict equality comparisons.

Now, obviously, guessing numbers is great fun, but you can learn more from a fact-based quiz like the one you've considered a few times earlier in the book. Adding the ability to check your answers will help raise the quiz app above a mere trivial pursuit.

12.4   *Checking answers in the quiz app*

Now that you can check conditions in an `if` statement, you're finally able to keep a score for the number of questions a user gets right in the quiz program. A typical console interaction could be this:

```
> quiz.quizMe()
  What is the highest mountain in the world?
> quiz.submit("Everest")
  Correct!
  Your score is 1 out of 1
> quiz.quizMe()
  What is the highest mountain in Scotland?
> quiz.submit("Snowdon")
  No, the answer is Ben Nevis
  You have finished the quiz
  Your score is 1 out of 2
```

The code for the quiz program is shown in the next listing. The `getQuiz` function contains the implementation of the quiz and returns an interface object with only two methods, `quizMe` and `submit`. You take a good look at how the program works after the listing.

Listing 12.7   Checking quiz answers
(http://jsbin.com/hidogo/edit?js,console)

```
var getQuiz = function () {
  var score = 0,
      qIndex = 0,            Use a single var
      inPlay = true,         keyword to declare all
      questions,             the variables in the
      next,                  getQuiz function
      getQuestion,
      checkAnswer,
      submit;

  questions = [
    {
      question: "What is the highest mountain in the world?",
      answer: "Everest"
    },
    {
      question: "What is the highest mountain in Scotland?",
      answer: "Ben Nevis"
    }
  ];

  getQuestion = function () {
    if (inPlay) {
      return questions[qIndex].question;      Define the getQuestion
    } else {                                  method to return the
      return "You have finished the quiz.";   current question
    }
  };
```

```
next = function () {
  qIndex = qIndex + 1;

  if (qIndex >= questions.length) {
    inPlay = false;
    console.log("You have finished the quiz.");
  }
};
```

Define the next method to move to the next question and check if any questions remain

Define the checkAnswer method to check if the answer is correct and update the score

```
checkAnswer = function (userAnswer) {
  if (userAnswer === questions[qIndex].answer) {
    console.log("Correct!");
    score = score + 1;
  } else {
    console.log("No, the answer is " + questions[qIndex].answer);
  }
};
```

```
submit = function (userAnswer) {
  var message = "You have finished the quiz.";

  if (inPlay) {
    checkAnswer(userAnswer);
    next();
    message = "Your score is " + score + " out of " + qIndex;
  }

  return message;
};
```

Define the submit method to handle the user's submitted answer

```
return {
  quizMe: getQuestion,
  submit: submit
};
};
```

Return an interface object with two methods, quizMe and submit

```
var quiz = getQuiz();
```

Call the getQuiz function and assign the interface object it returns to the quiz variable

Your new quiz program has a number of moving parts; let's break it down into smaller pieces.

12.4.1 *Multiple declarations with a single var keyword*

Up until now you've been using a var keyword for each variable you've declared:

```
var score;
var getQuestion;
var next;
var submit;
```

JavaScript allows you to declare a list of variables with a single var keyword. Commas separate the variables, with a semicolon ending the list. The previous declarations can be rewritten in the following shorter form:

```
var score,
    getQuestion,
    next,
    submit;
```

You could even declare the variables on a single line:

```
var score, getQuestion, next, submit;
```

Most programmers prefer one variable per line. You can include assignments too:

```
var score = 0,
    getQuestion,
    next,
    submit = function (userAnswer) {
        // function body
    };
```

The aim is to make sure all variables are declared and the code is easy to read and understand. The style in listing 12.7 is what I tend to prefer; I find it slightly easier to read and it's slightly less typing. Some programmers declare each variable on its own line with a var keyword, just as we've been doing in our listings up until now; it's easier to cut and paste variables if each has its own var keyword. It's not worth worrying about—you'll probably settle on one style over time.

12.4.2   *Displaying a question*

The getQuestion function returns a question from the questions array. It uses the qIndex variable to pick the current question-and-answer object from the array. It returns the question property of the question-and-answer object.

```
return questions[qIndex].question;
```

But it returns the question only if the quiz is still in progress. Otherwise, it returns a string to say the quiz is finished:

```
return "You have finished the quiz.";
```

The program uses the inPlay variable to flag when the quiz is in progress and when it has finished. The inPlay variable has a value of true while the quiz is in progress and false when it has finished. The getQuestion function uses the inPlay variable as the condition in an if statement:

```
if (inPlay) {
  return questions[qIndex].question;
```

```
} else {
  return "You have finished the quiz.";
}
```

When inPlay is true, the question is returned. When inPlay is false, the message is returned. (Remember, when you call a function at the console prompt, the console automatically displays the return value.)

12.4.3 *Moving to the next question*

The program calls the next function to move from one question to the next. It moves by incrementing the qIndex variable.

```
qIndex = qIndex + 1;
```

The program stores the index of the current element in the questions array in qIndex. Remember that the array index is zero based, so for an array of length 4 the index could be 0, 1, 2, or 3. An index of 4 would be past the end of the array (3 is the last index). In general, if the index is greater than or equal to the length of the array, you're past the end of the array. All arrays have a length property. In the quiz, it represents the number of questions.

The next function checks the index to see if it is past the last question:

```
if (qIndex >= questions.length)
```

If the index is past the end of the array, then all the questions have been asked and the quiz is over, so inPlay is set to false.

```
if (qIndex >= questions.length) {
  inPlay = false;
  console.log("You have finished the quiz.");
}
```

12.4.4 *Checking the player's answer*

The checkAnswer function is straightforward. If the player's submitted answer is equal to the current answer from the questions array, the player's score is incremented. Otherwise, the correct answer is displayed.

```
if (userAnswer === questions[qIndex].answer) {
  console.log("Correct!");
  score = score + 1;
} else {
  console.log("No, the answer is " + questions[qIndex].answer);
}
```

12.4.5 *Handling a player's answer*

The submit function orchestrates what happens when a player submits an answer. It returns either a message with the player's score or a message to say the quiz is over.

```
Your score is 1 out of 2       // If inPlay is true

You have finished the quiz.    // If inPlay is false
```

If the quiz is still in progress, submit calls two other functions, checkAnswer and next. Each will execute its code in turn. You're using the functions to run code on demand.

```
if (inPlay) {
  checkAnswer(userAnswer);
  next();
  message = "Your score is " + score + " out of " + qIndex;
}
```

12.4.6 *Returning the interface object*

You've kept the interface object returned by getQuiz simple. It has no implementation code of its own. You assign its two properties functions from within the local scope of getQuiz.

```
return {
  quizMe: getQuestion,
  submit: submit
};
```

As discussed in chapter 11, the interface object allows you to maintain a consistent interface over time, even if the implementation within getQuiz is changed. The user will always call quiz.quizMe() and quiz.submit(). You can change which functions are assigned to those two properties of the interface object and how those functions work, but you never remove or rename those properties.

Notice how the program is made up of small pieces working together to build its functionality. As ever, your aim is to make the code readable, understandable, and easy to follow. The if statement and its else clause help you to direct the flow of the program to take the appropriate actions at each stage.

It's time to put these new ideas to work in *The Crypt*.

12.5 *The Crypt—checking user input*

In chapter 11, you created a getGame function that returns a public interface for *The Crypt*. Players can call a go method to move from place to place and a get method to pick up items:

```
return {
    go: function (direction) {
        var place = player.getPlace();
        var destination = place.getExit(direction);
        player.setPlace(destination);
```

```
            render();
            return "";
    },

    get: function () {
        var place = player.getPlace();
        var item = place.getLastItem();
        player.addItem(item);
        render();
        return "";
    }
};
```

12.5.1 *Step by step through the go method*

Let's step through the first three lines of the go method. See if you can spot where a problem could arise.

RETRIEVE THE PLAYER'S LOCATION

You start with the getPlace method. It returns the player's current location.

```
var place = player.getPlace();
```

You then assign the location to the place variable. If the player is currently in the kitchen, then the code is equivalent to

```
var place = kitchen;
```

The program assigned the player's starting location earlier, using the setPlace method:

```
player.setPlace(kitchen);
```

USE THE DIRECTION TO FIND THE DESTINATION

Now that you have the current place, you can call its getExit method to retrieve the destination for a given direction.

```
var destination = place.getExit(direction);
```

When the player calls the go method, the argument is assigned to the direction parameter.

```
> game.go("south")
```

The previous command will execute code equivalent to the following:

```
var destination = place.getExit("south");
```

If The Library is south of The Kitchen, then the code is equivalent to

```
var destination = library;
```

MOVE THE PLAYER TO THE DESTINATION

You have the destination; you only need to update the player's location.

```
player.setPlace(destination);
```

Fantastic! The user can decide where to go in the game. So, can you let them loose in your carefully crafted castles? Well, no. You see, users are evil. Pure evil!

12.5.2 *Never trust user input*

Sorry, I panicked. Of course users aren't evil. But they do make mistakes. And they sometimes own cats. And most cats can't type. Whenever a user is expected to provide input for a program, we must guard against mistakes, whether typos (possibly of cat origin), misunderstandings (which may be our fault), or curiosity-driven explorations of what the program can do.

The go method expects the user to enter a valid direction as a string. It uses that direction to find a destination, the place to which the player is to be moved. If the user enters a direction that doesn't exist, the whole game breaks!

```
> game.go("snarf")
```

Figure 12.4 shows what happened on JS Bin when I entered the previous command while playing the chapter 11 version of *The Crypt* at http://jsbin.com/yuporu/edit?js,console.

```
> game.go("snarf")
✗ "undefined is not an object (evaluating 'place.showInfo')"
> game.go("south")
✗ "undefined is not an object (evaluating 'place.getExit')"
>|
```

Figure 12.4 Specifying a direction that doesn't exist breaks *The Crypt*.

Error messages on your browser might be slightly different. Even entering a valid direction after the mistake doesn't fix things. From the errors in figure 12.4 it looks like there may be a problem with the place variable. The key statement in the go method is the one that uses the user input:

```
var destination = place.getExit(direction);
```

If the specified direction is not one of the place's exits, then the getExit function will return undefined. The program assigns undefined to the destination variable and sets that value as the new place for the player:

```
player.setPlace(destination);
```

So the player's location is now `undefined`, not a place constructed with the `Place` constructor. `undefined` has no `showInfo` or `getExit` methods; it has no methods at all! The errors in figure 12.4 should now make more sense.

So how can you guard against users (and their cats) making errors?

12.5.3 *Safe exploration—using the if statement to avoid problems*

You can use an `if` statement to check that you have a valid destination before updating the player's location:

```
go: function (direction) {
    var place = player.getPlace();
    var destination = place.getExit(direction);

    if (destination !== undefined) {
        player.setPlace(destination);
        render();
        return "";
    } else {
        return "*** There is no exit in that direction ***";
    }
}
```

The `getExit` method returns `undefined` if the current place doesn't have an exit for the specified direction. You just need to check that the destination is not `undefined` before calling `setPlace`.

```
if (destination !== undefined) {
    // There is a valid destination.
}
```

Remember from table 12.1 that the `!==` operator returns `true` when two values are *not* equal and `false` when they *are* equal. You can add an `else` clause to catch the cases where the destination *is* undefined.

```
if (destination !== undefined) {
    // There is a valid destination.
} else {
    // There is no exit in the direction specified.
}
```

Listing 12.8 shows an updated version of the `go` and `get` methods returned from the `getGame` function. Entering a nonexistent direction at the console now looks like this:

```
> game.go("snarf")
  *** You can't go in that direction ***
```

Calling `get` when there are no items to pick up looks like this:

```
> game.get()
  *** There is no item to get ***
```

Only partial code is shown in this listing. The full listing with `Player` and `Place` constructors and more places is on JS Bin.

Listing 12.8   Checking user input
              (http://jsbin.com/zoruxu/edit?js,console)

```
var getGame = function () {
  var spacer = { … };
  var Player = function (name, health) { … };
  var Place = function (title, description) { … };
  var render = function () { … };

  var kitchen = new Place("The Kitchen", "You are in a kitchen…");
  var library = new Place("The Old Library", "You are in a library…");

  kitchen.addExit("south", library);
  library.addExit("north", kitchen);

  // Game initialization
  var player = new Player("Kandra", 50);
  player.addItem("The Sword of Doom");
  player.setPlace(kitchen);

  render();

  return {
    go: function (direction) {
      var place = player.getPlace();
      var destination = place.getExit(direction);

      if (destination !== undefined) {

        player.setPlace(destination);
        render();
        return "";

      } else {

        return "*** You can't go in that direction ***";

      }
    },

    get: function () {
      var place = player.getPlace();
      var item = place.getLastItem();

      if (item !== undefined) {
        player.addItem(item);
        render();
        return "";
      } else {
        return "*** There is no item to get ***";
      }
    }
  };
};

var game = getGame();
```

Return an interface object with go and get methods

Use getExit to find the destination for the direction specified by the user

Check that the destination is not undefined; that is, check that it is valid

Only set and show the new place if the destination exists

Add an else clause to handle when the destination is undefined

Give the user feedback about the invalid direction specified

Update the get method to make similar checks to the go method

In the printed listing 12.8, the details of the `Player` and `Place` constructors were left out to make it easier to focus on the changes to the go and get methods. In chapter 13 you'll move each constructor function to its own file and see how to import the files in JS Bin. Such increased modularity can help you focus on one thing at a time and make it easier to reuse code across multiple projects.

12.6 Summary

- Use comparison operators to compare two values. The operators return `true` or `false`, boolean values:

```
>  5 === 5    // Strict equality
   true
>  10 > 13    // Greater than
   false
```

- Use an `if` statement to execute code only if a condition is met:

```
if (condition) {
    // Execute code if condition evaluates to true
}
```

- Set conditions using comparison operators and/or variables:

```
if (userNumber === secret) {
    // Execute code if userNumber and secret are equal
}

if (inPlay) {
    // Execute code if inPlay evaluates to true
}
```

- Add an `else` clause to execute code when a condition is not met:

```
if (condition) {
    // Execute code if condition evaluates to true
} else {
    // Execute code if condition evaluates to false
}
```

- Include extra `if` statements in the `else` clause to cover all possibilities:

```
if (userNumber === secret) {
   console.log("Well done!");
} else if (userNumber > secret) {
   console.log("Too high!");
} else {
   console.log("Too low!");
}
```

- Generate random numbers with `Math.random()`. The numbers generated are between 0 and 1. They can equal 0 but not 1:

```
> Math.random()
  0.552000432042405
```

- Scale up the random numbers to the range you want:

```
Math.random() * 10                    // 0 <= decimal < 10
Math.random() * 10 + 1                // 1 <= decimal < 11
```

- Round the random numbers to integers with `Math.floor()`:

```
Math.floor(Math.random() * 10 + 1)     // 1 <= integer <= 10
```

- Never trust user input. Put checks in place to make sure any input is valid.

Modules: breaking
a program into pieces

This chapter covers

- Importing code into JS Bin with script elements
- Avoiding repeated variable names
- Running functions without assigning them to variables
- Using modules to organize your (shared) codebase

As the applications you develop become larger, involving more and more variables, objects, arrays, and functions, it can become harder and harder to work efficiently within a single program file. Good text editors and development environments can help, but even with their tools, it quickly becomes a good idea to split the code across multiple files.

For example, in *The Crypt* you have spacer, players, places, maps, and the game logic itself. You've probably noticed how long the code listings have become on JS Bin when all of the elements are included. Putting the code for each element in its own file can help you to focus on one piece of the program at a time and make it easier for different programmers to develop and test different parts of applications. Figure 13.1 shows your aim of splitting one large program into modules.

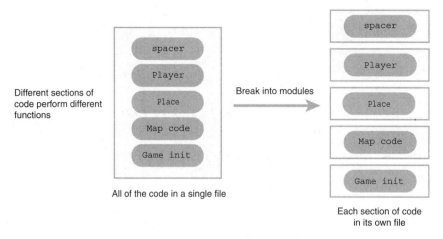

Figure 13.1   Breaking one large program into modules

Having discrete pieces of functionality and data in different files also promotes code reuse. Rather than cutting and pasting useful functions and snippets of JavaScript from one project into others, they can stay in a single library file that's imported into other projects when needed. For example, our trusty spacer namespace from chapter 7, for formatting text on the console, could be used in a quiz app and a blog app. Rather than repeating the spacer code in each app, you could place it in its own file and import it when needed (figure 13.2).

I'm going to loosely call such files *modules*. There are a number of published Java-Script projects and standards for managing modules that will have their own, stricter

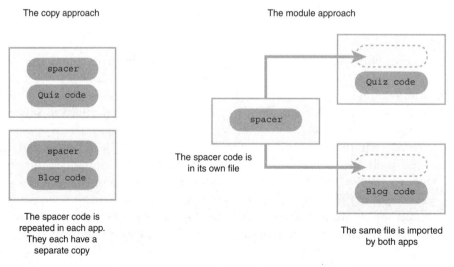

Figure 13.2   Moving spacer into a module allows the same single file to be used in many projects.

definitions for what form a module must take, and the latest versions of JavaScript itself are introducing a native module system, but I'm happy to keep things simple for now.

This chapter looks at how to import modules into JS Bin using HTML `script` elements. You'll see how a random number generator function and the text-formatting capabilities of the `spacer` namespace can be incorporated into other projects. When you start to include code from various modules into a single program, you have to keep a close eye on which variable names are being used; there's a danger that imported files could overwrite your variables. You also take a look at how to minimize such problems by using namespaces and by making use of immediately invoked function expressions, a way of running function code without assigning the functions to variables.

First up, let's look at how JS Bin works with files.

13.1 *Understanding bins and files on JS Bin*

In chapter 12 you created a simple game that challenged players to guess a number between 1 and 10. You generated the number using the `Math.random` method. In a similar way, you now want to update your quiz app to display a random question from its bank of questions. Both the guessing game and the quiz need to be able to generate a random whole number between two limits. They can both use a function like the following:

```
var between = function (lowest, highest) {
    // Return a whole number between lowest and highest inclusive
};
```

In this section, you create and save a JavaScript file on JS Bin that contains the Number Generator code. In section 13.2 you learn how to load the file, and in section 13.3 you load it into the guessing game and the quiz app, as illustrated in figure 13.3.

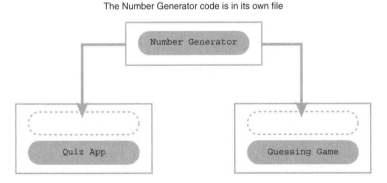

The Number Generator code is in its own file

Number Generator

Quiz App

Guessing Game

The same file is imported by both apps

Figure 13.3   The Number Generator code is imported by the quiz app and the guessing game.

Before you learn how to import files, we need to take a brief look at how JS Bin saves your work.

JS Bin is a simple development environment that lets you work on HTML, CSS, and JavaScript code in separate panels. Figure 13.4 shows those three panels open at the same time, all containing code.

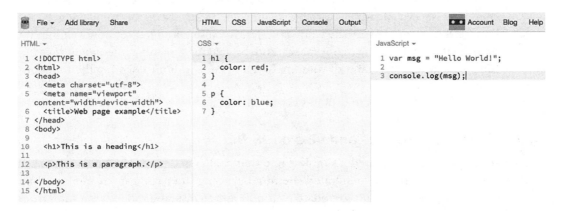

Figure 13.4 HTML, CSS, and JavaScript panels on JS Bin

JS Bin combines the code in the HTML, CSS, and JavaScript panels to produce your web page, which it shows in the Output panel (figure 13.5). You'll look at HTML (and a little CSS) in more detail in part 3.

Figure 13.5 The HTML, CSS, and JavaScript code are all used to produce the web page output.

Any errors or warnings that occur when you run your code appear in the Console panel. You can also log messages to the Console panel from within your JavaScript code—that's how you've been displaying your output so far. You're focusing on JavaScript, so you haven't been bothered about the web page generated in the Output panel. You can see the page from figures 13.4 and 13.5 on JS Bin at http://jsbin.com/jejunu/edit?output. Toggle the panels to see the code.

As well as providing a combined environment for you to edit the different types of code that make up a web page, JS Bin gives you access to the HTML, the CSS, and the JavaScript code as separate files. To create JavaScript code and see it as a separate file, follow these steps on JS Bin:

1. Create a bin
2. Write some code in the JavaScript panel
3. Make a note of the filename
4. View an individual code file

13.1.1 Creating a bin

On the File menu on JS Bin, click New. JS Bin will create HTML, CSS, and JavaScript files for you. It calls those three files together a *bin* and displays the contents of each file on its matching panel. The HTML file includes some boilerplate code that's common to most new web pages; the CSS and JavaScript files are blank.

13.1.2 Writing some code

Add the following code to the JavaScript panel.

```
var between = function (lowest, highest) {
    var range = highest - lowest + 1;
    return lowest + Math.floor(Math.random() * range);
};
```

The `between` function returns a random whole number between the values of `lowest` and `highest` inclusive. For example, `between(3, 5)` will return 3 or 4 or 5.

13.1.3 Making a note of the filename

JS Bin assigns each bin a code used to edit the bin's files and to access them individually. Take a look at the current URL in your browser's address bar. (You may have to click the address bar to see the full address.) Figure 13.6 shows the URL with the bin code and visible panels highlighted.

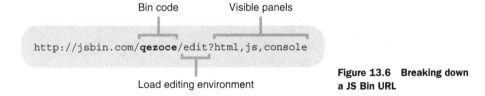

Figure 13.6   Breaking down a JS Bin URL

Make a note of the bin code for your current work on JS Bin—it will be different from figure 13.6. The bin code for my work is `qezoce`.

13.1.4   *Viewing an individual code file*

To access individual code files, you use a different format of URL, shown in figure 13.7. It has a prefix of `output` and ends with the bin code and a file extension. The file extension specifies what type of file you want to load. Use `js` for JavaScript.

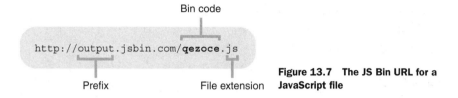

Figure 13.7   **The JS Bin URL for a JavaScript file**

Visiting http://output.jsbin.com/qezoce.js loads just the JavaScript file, as shown in figure 13.8. All the panels and menus and controls that are part of the JS Bin editing environment are not loaded; it's just the plain text of the JavaScript file.

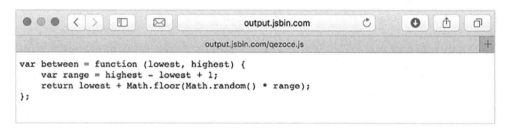

Figure 13.8   **A JavaScript file on JS Bin**

(The output isn't always formatted nicely for human readers; unnecessary spaces and line-breaks may have been removed.) Have a go at loading your version of the file, using your bin code from JS Bin.

Great! You can get your hands on your pure JavaScript. But how do you make it appear in another program?

13.2   *Importing files into other projects*

You're going to create a program that uses the number generation function, `between`, from the last section. You take these steps:

1   Create a bin
2   Write some code in the JavaScript panel
3   Add a `script` element to the HTML panel
4   Refresh the page
5   Run the program

13.2.1 Creating a bin

Create a bin on JS Bin by clicking New on the File menu. The HTML, CSS, and Java-Script panels are reset.

13.2.2 Writing some code

Enter the following code in the JavaScript panel:

```
// requires the Number Generator module
var num = between(3, 7);
console.log(num);
```

Running the program now will cause an error—there's no between variable declared or function defined. The between function is in a separate file. This brings up the issue of *dependencies*; when splitting code into modules, it's not uncommon for one module to depend on another in order to function. The previous code depends on the Number Generator module. More advanced module systems usually let you explicitly record and automatically load dependencies; for now, you can add comments to show any required modules.

13.2.3 Adding a script element

It's time to make use of the HTML panel on JS Bin. HTML is the code used for the structure and content of web pages; it's how you specify headings and paragraphs and lists and links and so on. You'll get a proper introduction in chapter 17 and make good use of it throughout part 3. For now, your focus is still very much on the JavaScript and using JS Bin to help you learn and explore. You're going to use only a tiny snippet of HTML to help you break up longer programs into separate files and load them as needed.

You use an HTML script element to specify the JavaScript file you want to load. Figure 13.9 shows the parts that make up the element.

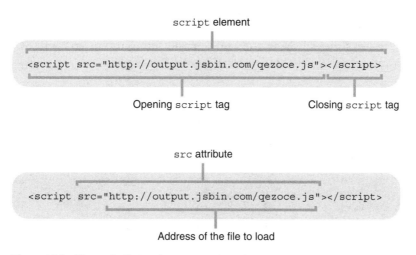

Figure 13.9 **The parts that make up a `script` element**

Don't worry too much for now about the names of all of the parts. You can use the `script` element to load files without a full understanding of HTML elements, tags, and attributes. You'll focus on those in chapter 17.

Show the HTML panel on JS Bin. You'll see some default HTML already in place. You don't need that for your purposes—you're not building a web page; you're just interested in loading a JavaScript file. Replace the default HTML with code to load the JavaScript, using the bin code of the file you created in the last section.

```
<script src="http://output.jsbin.com/qezoce.js"></script>
```

The HTML included is a single `script` element with an `src` attribute. You use the `script` element to load the JavaScript file specified by the `src` attribute. (`src` is short for *source*—the address of the file.) In general, to load a file, use the following format:

```
<script src="path/to/someFile.js"></script>
```

Modern browsers will assume the file contains JavaScript. For older browsers, you can include a `type` attribute as well.

```
<script src="path/to/someFile.js" type="text/javascript"></script>
```

13.2.4 Refreshing the page

JS Bin doesn't always load files automatically; you may need to refresh the page in your browser after you add the `script` element.

13.2.5 Running the program

Click Run. The Console panel should show a number between 3 and 7. Keep clicking Run to generate more random numbers.

Listings 13.1 and 13.2 repeat the HTML and JavaScript you've used. The JS Bin links for the two listings lead to the same bin. Running the program five times produces output something like this (it *is* random!):

```
> 5
> 7
> 7
> 3
> 4
```

> **Listing 13.1   Loading JavaScript with a script tag (HTML)**
> **(http://jsbin.com/lifugam/edit?html,js,console)**

```
<script src="http://output.jsbin.com/qezoce.js"></script>
```

Listing 13.2   Code in the JavaScript panel as well
(http://jsbin.com/lifugam/edit?html,js,console)

```
// requires the Number Generator module
var num = between(3, 7);
console.log(num);
```

When you run the program, JS Bin will first load and run the file specified in the script element's `src` attribute. Then it will run any code in the JavaScript panel. The loaded file and JavaScript panel code together form the following single program:

```
// From the loaded file
var between = function (lowest, highest) {

    var range = highest - lowest + 1;
    return lowest + Math.floor(Math.random() * range);

};

// From the JavaScript panel
var num = between(3, 7);
console.log(num);
```

When you click the Run button in the Console panel, it can take a moment for JS Bin to load the file specified in the `script` tag. Once the code runs, the random number is logged to the console.

13.3   *Importing the Number Generator—further examples*

You've seen how JS Bin assigns a code to each bin you create and how you can use that code to access individual files from your project. You created a random number generator function, `between`, and accessed the JavaScript file containing the code. One of the goals of splitting your work into modules is to use the same code in multiple projects by importing it rather than copying and pasting it; see figure 13.10.

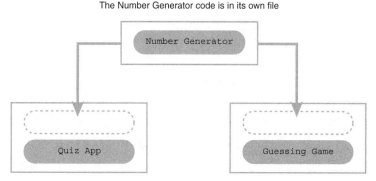

Figure 13.10   Importing the Number Generator function into two projects

Let's see that idea in action by importing the Number Generator into two other projects: the quiz app and the guessing game.

13.3.1 Picking random questions in the quiz app

It's time to randomize your quiz app. The new version of the app displays a random question from its question bank each time you call `quizMe` on the console:

```
> quiz.quizMe()
  5 x 6
> quiz.submit("30")
  Correct!
> quiz.quizMe()
  7 x 8
> quiz.submit("30")
  No, the answer is 56
```

Listing 13.4 shows the JavaScript for the main quiz app. You import the code for the between function by using a `script` element on the HTML panel (listing 13.3).

**Listing 13.3   Using the Number Generator with the quiz app (HTML)
(http://jsbin.com/ponogi/edit?html,js,console)**

```
<script src="http://output.jsbin.com/qezoce.js"></script>
```

**Listing 13.4   Using the Number Generator with the quiz app
(http://jsbin.com/ponogi/edit?html,js,console)**

```
var getQuiz = function () {          ◁─┐ Wrap the code in a function
    var qIndex = 0;                     │ to create a local scope

    var questions = [
        { question: "7 x 8", answer: "56" },
        { question: "12 x 12", answer: "144" },
        { question: "5 x 6", answer: "30" },
        { question: "9 x 3", answer: "27" }
    ];

    var getQuestion = function () {
        qIndex = between(0, questions.length - 1);    ◁─┐ Use the between function
        return questions[qIndex].question;              │ to pick a random question
    };

    var checkAnswer = function (userAnswer) {
        if (userAnswer === questions[qIndex].answer) {
            return "Correct!";
        } else {
            return "No, the answer is " + questions[qIndex].answer;
        }
    };
```

```
    return {
        quizMe: getQuestion,
        submit: checkAnswer
    };
};
```
Return an interface object from the getQuiz function

```
var quiz = getQuiz();
```
◁─┤ **Assign the interface returned from getQuiz to the quiz variable**

You use the between function to pick a random question from the question bank. The number of elements in the questions array is given by questions.length (every array has a length property) and the question indexes run from 0 to one less than the length. If there are four elements in the array, then the indexes run from 0 to 3. So, to pick a random index you use

```
qIndex = between(0, questions.length - 1);
```

You use the wrap-and-return module pattern from chapter 11, hiding your implementation (the code that makes everything work) inside the getQuiz function and returning the public interface as an object.

Follow the listing link to the game on JS Bin and test your knowledge of multiplication facts! The answers are stored as strings, so make sure you submit strings for the program to check: quiz.submit("30"), not quiz.submit(30).

13.3.2 *Using the between function in your guessing game*

Listing 13.6 shows the JavaScript code for your guessing game. At the console prompt, players have to guess a number between 5 and 10, inclusive:

```
> guess(7)
  Too high!
> guess(5)
  Too low!
> guess(6)
  Well done!
```

The app uses the between function, so you import it using a script element on the HTML panel (see the following listing).

Listing 13.5   Using the Number Generator in the guessing game (HTML)
(http://jsbin.com/tixina/edit?html,js,console)

```
<script src="http://output.jsbin.com/qezoce.js"></script>
```

Listing 13.6   Using the Number Generator in the guessing game
(http://jsbin.com/tixina/edit?html,js,console)

```
var getGuesser = function (lowest, highest) {          ⊲─┐  Wrap the code in a function
                                                           │  to create a local scope
    var secret = between(lowest, highest);      ⊲─────────┘

    return function (userNumber) {            ⊲─┐  Use the between function
        if (userNumber === secret) {            │  to pick a random number
            return "Well done!";
        } else if (userNumber > secret) {
            return "Too high!";               Return a function that players
        } else {                              use to make their guesses
            return "Too low!";
        }
    };
};
                                              ┐  Assign the returned function
var guess = getGuesser(5, 10);       ⊲────────┘  to the guess variable
```

Again, follow the listing link to JS Bin and get guessing!

Both the quiz app and the guessing game now import the same Number Generator file. The number generation code is in one place; there is *a single source of truth*. Any updates or fixes can be performed on that one file, and all the projects that use it will load the new version.

Importing one file is useful, but can you load more than one?

13.4 *Importing multiple files*

In chapters 7 and 11, you saw that an object can be used as a namespace, a way of organizing properties and methods so that only a single variable is required. As an example, you created spacer, a namespace of functions for formatting text on the console. The spacer namespace could be useful in a number of projects, whenever you want to format your text output with borders and boxes. Rather than copying and pasting the spacer code into every program where it's used, it seems like an obvious candidate to be saved to its own file and imported as needed. You can view the spacer code at http://jsbin.com/juneqo/edit?js.

Let's put spacer to work straight away. In listing 13.6 you updated your guessing game to import the between function and used it to generate the secret number to be guessed. Say you now want to format the feedback you give to players by wrapping the messages in boxes. That's what spacer is for! A game on the console will look something like this:

```
> guess(10)              > guess(5)              > guess(9)
  ++++++++++++             -----------             ==============
  + Too high! +           - Too low! -            = Well done! =
  ++++++++++++             -----------             ==============
```

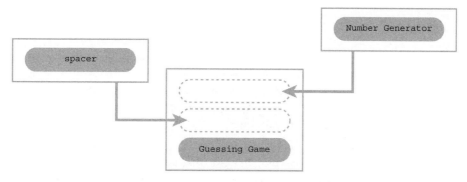

You can import as many modules as you need

Figure 13.11 Importing the `Number Generator` and `spacer` modules

Figure 13.11 shows the guessing game app importing the `Number Generator` and `spacer` modules.

The following listing shows the script elements added to the HTML panel to import the two modules you're using.

> **Listing 13.7 Using `spacer` and `between` in the guessing game (HTML) (http://jsbin.com/foqowa/edit?html,js,console)**

```html
<!-- Number Generator -->
<script src="http://output.jsbin.com/qezoce.js"></script>

<!-- spacer -->
<script src="http://output.jsbin.com/juneqo.js"></script>
```

Comments have been added to note which modules are being imported; JS Bin addresses aren't very user friendly, so it's helpful to make it clear what you're trying to load. The comments are HTML comments, so they look a little different from Java-Script comments.

The next listing shows the guessing game code using the two imported modules, between and spacer.

> **Listing 13.8 Using `spacer` and `between` in the guessing game (http://jsbin.com/foqowa/edit?html,js,console)**

```javascript
var getGuesser = function (lowest, highest) {
  var secret = between(lowest, highest);        // Use the imported between function

  return function (userNumber) {
    if (userNumber === secret) {
      return spacer.box("Well done!", 14, "=");   // ◁
    } else if (userNumber > secret) {
      return spacer.box("Too high!", 13, "+");    // ◁  Use the imported spacer namespace
    } else {
      return spacer.box("Too low!", 12, "-");     // ◁
```

```
    }
  };
};

var guess = getGuesser(5, 10);
```

Putting previously written and tested code into separate files like this also helps you focus on new code you're working on; listing 13.8 can be short and sweet because your trusted `spacer` code is packaged off in an external file.

When you import JavaScript, it's as if all of the imported code is joined to form a single file. If different imported files use the same variable names, it's possible for later code to inadvertently overwrite earlier code. Boom—you have variable collisions!

13.5 *Collisions—when imported code overwrites your variables*

You decide the boxed messages for your guessing game feedback are a bit too much. You'd like the feedback to look like this:

```
> guess(10)                      > guess(9)
  + T-o-o- -h-i-g-h-! +            = W-e-l-l- -d-o-n-e-! =
```

The messages take up less room but are nicely spaced out with dashes between characters. Fortunately, a friend of yours, Kallie, has been working on her own formatting functions and has kindly bundled them into a module you can import. The function you need is called `dasher` and is really easy to use:

```
dasher("message");     // m-e-s-s-a-g-e
dasher("Too low!");    // T-o-o- -l-o-w-!
```

You add a script element to the guessing game HTML panel to import Kallie's code, as shown next.

> **Listing 13.9   Importing Kallie's code (HTML)**
> **(http://jsbin.com/zusodu/edit?html,js,console)**

```
<!-- Number Generator -->
<script src="http://output.jsbin.com/qezoce.js"></script>

<!-- spacer -->
<script src="http://output.jsbin.com/juneqo.js"></script>

<!-- Kallie's code -->
<script src="http://output.jsbin.com/soxeke.js"></script>
```

No, I haven't shown you the JavaScript of Kallie's code. You know `dasher` is part of the interface, the variables and functions you're expected to use, and you know what `dasher` does; you shouldn't need to know *how* it does what it does, the implementation. Of course, you might (and probably should) be interested in the implementation, but you don't need to understand it in order to use the interface, the `dasher` function.

You update the guessing game to use the `dasher` function, as shown here.

Listing 13.10 Using Kallie's code
(http://jsbin.com/zusodu/edit?html,js,console)

```
var getGuesser = function (lowest, highest) {
  var secret = between(lowest, highest);

  return function (userNumber) {
    var msg;
    if (userNumber === secret) {
      msg = dasher("Well done!");
      return spacer.wrap(msg, msg.length + 4, "=");
    } else if (userNumber > secret) {
      msg = dasher("Too high!");
      return spacer.wrap(msg, msg.length + 4, "+");
    } else {
      msg = dasher("Too low!");
      return spacer.wrap(msg, msg.length + 4, "-");
    }
  };
};

var guess = getGuesser(5, 10);
```

Use dasher to space out your message

Use spacer.wrap to start and end the message with a character

Happy with your work, you run the program and make a guess. Error! What? Where has `spacer.wrap` gone? Figure 13.12 shows what happened in my browser.

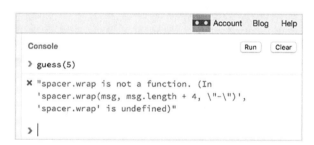

Figure 13.12 For some reason, the program can't find `spacer.wrap`.

There seems to be a problem with `spacer.wrap`, which has been a working part of your `spacer` namespace since chapter 7. Why has it chosen now to break? It's time to check inside Kallie's module. If you take a look at her code in the following listing, you might spot the problem.

Listing 13.11 Kallie's formatting code
(http://jsbin.com/soxeke/edit?js,console)

```
var spreader = function (text, character) {
  return text.split("").join(character);
};
```

Define a function to spread out text with a specified character

```
var spacer = function (text) {
    return spreader(text, " ");
};
```
Define a function to spread
out text with spaces

```
var dasher = function (text) {
    return spreader(text, "-");
};
```
Define a function to spread
out text with dashes

Kallie's code doesn't only include the dasher function; it also has a spacer function.
The three variables she has used, spreader, spacer, and dasher, are global variables.
Your spacer namespace also uses a global variable, spacer. Her spacer has overwrit-
ten your spacer, as shown in figure 13.13.

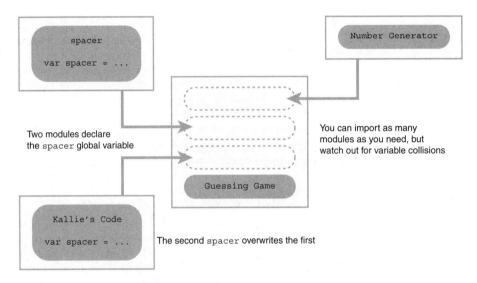

Figure 13.13   Two modules declare the same global variable, leading to a collision.

The problem isn't with the implementation of the functions—they work just fine—
it's with how the functions have been made available within the module. When variables are added to the global scope, possibly by different people in different modules, there's always the chance that the same name will be used in more than one
declaration.

13.5.1 *Variable collisions*

Your modules make their functionality available by using at least one global variable.
But what happens if the same variable is used by more than one module? Well, the last
module wins, assigning its own value to the variable. In the guessing game code, you
load two modules that use a global spacer variable and then you try to use that variable

later in the program. The following snippet shows how the second `spacer` overwrites the first, leading to an error when you try to use `spacer.wrap`.

```
// Code in first module
var spacer = {
    line : ...,
    wrap : ...,
    box : ...
};

// Code in second module
var spacer = function (text) { ... };

// Later in the code
spacer.wrap(msg, msg.length + 4, "=");   // ERROR! There is no spacer.wrap.
```

When one declaration supersedes another like this it's called a *variable collision*; the second variable declaration clobbers the first. You can appreciate why declaring lots of global variables is called *polluting the global namespace*—the more variables you declare, the greater the chance of collisions. Reduce the number of global variables by using namespaces, discussed next, and immediately invoked function expressions, discussed in section 13.6.

13.5.2 *Minimizing collisions by using namespaces*

Your `spacer` namespace module is well behaved because it uses only a single global variable. Rather than separate global variables for the `line`, `wrap`, and `box` functions, it uses an object as a namespace and assigns the functions to properties of the object. The object is then assigned to the single variable, `spacer`.

Kallie apologizes for the pollution her module caused—she's been busy—and updates the module to use a namespace, as shown in the next listing.

> **Listing 13.12   Kallie's formatting code in a namespace**
>   **(http://jsbin.com/moheka/edit?js,console)**

```
var kalliesCode = {
    spreader: function (text, character) {
        return text.split("").join(character);
    },

    spacer: function (text) {
        return kalliesCode.spreader(text, " ");
    },

    dasher: function (text) {
        return kalliesCode.spreader(text, "-");
    }
};
```

Wrap the functions in an object assigned to a single global variable

Add the spacer function as a property of the namespace object

Use dot notation when calling kalliesCode functions

You update your guessing game HTML to import the updated module (listing 13.13) and your JavaScript code to call the dasher function from within the kalliesCode namespace (listing 13.14).

> **Listing 13.13   Importing Kallie's namespace (HTML)**
> **(http://jsbin.com/seqahi/edit?html,js,console)**

```html
<!-- Number Generator -->
<script src="http://output.jsbin.com/qezoce.js"></script>

<!-- spacer -->
<script src="http://output.jsbin.com/juneqo.js"></script>

<!-- Kallie's code -->
<script src="http://output.jsbin.com/moheka.js"></script>
```

> **Listing 13.14   Using Kallie's code**
> **(http://jsbin.com/seqahi/edit?html,js,console)**

```javascript
var getGuesser = function (lowest, highest) {
  var secret = between(lowest, highest);

  return function (userNumber) {
    var msg;
    if (userNumber === secret) {
      msg = kalliesCode.dasher("Well done!");        // Call the dasher function
      return spacer.wrap(msg, msg.length + 4, "=");   //    from the kalliesCode
    } else if (userNumber > secret) {                //    namespace
      msg = kalliesCode.dasher("Too high!");
      return spacer.wrap(msg, msg.length + 4, "+");   // Happily use
    } else {                                          //    spacer.wrap
      msg = kalliesCode.dasher("Too low!");
      return spacer.wrap(msg, msg.length + 4, "-");
    }
  };
};

var guess = getGuesser(5, 10);
```

Follow the listing link to JS Bin, run the program, and play the game. Using a namespace has fixed the problem.

```
= W-e-l-l- -d-o-n-e-! =
```

Another important way of avoiding polluting the global namespace, this time by using functions, is covered next. It has a great name ... and here it is!

13.6   *Immediately invoked function expressions (IIFE)*

If the name of this section has immediately invoked a funky expression on your face, I hope it's one of curiosity, intrigue, and adventure rather than befuddlement, fear, or horror. *Immediately invoked function expressions* are just functions that you call straight away, without even bothering to use a variable. But why would you do that?

In section 13.5, you imported a module of code written by a friend, Kallie. (Honestly, you've known her for years.) Unfortunately, Kallie's global variables collided with yours (ouch!) and overwrote your beloved `spacer` namespace. You learned an important lesson about the dangers of global variables and vowed to do whatever you can to reduce pollution of the global namespace. You decide to review some of your code, on the lookout for global variables you can remove.

You start your review with the quiz app from earlier in the chapter. The following listing shows the structure of your code, with global variables, local variables, and the interface object.

> **Listing 13.15   Random quiz questions with two global variables**
> **(http://jsbin.com/ponogi/edit?html,js,console)**

```
var getQuiz = function () {            ◁─┤ Define a function to create
                                            local scope and assign it to
                                            a global variable, getQuiz

  var qIndex = 0;
  var questions = [ … ];                     Use var inside the
  var getQuestion = function () { … };       function to declare
  var checkAnswer = function (userAnswer) { … };   local variables

  return {
    quizMe: getQuestion,       Return an interface
    submit: checkAnswer        object to give users
  };                           access to some functions

};
                                    Call getQuiz and assign the
var quiz = getQuiz();       ◁─┤    interface returned to a
                                    global variable, quiz
```

The program declares two global variables: `getQuiz` and `quiz`. On the first line you define a function and assign it to `getQuiz`.

```
var getQuiz = function () { … };
```

Then, on the last line, you immediately call the function.

```
var quiz = getQuiz();
```

So, you declare `getQuiz` as a global variable—nasty pollution—and then use it only once before leaving it hanging around in the global scope like a bad smell. Shame on you! Remember, global variables run the risk of clobbering other global variables; they may seem fine in small pieces of code, but as projects grow and modules are created and imported, a faint whiff of unease soon builds to the furious stench of despair.

TIP   Avoid declaring *global* variables, polluting the global namespace. Reduce the number of global variables by using objects as namespaces. Declare *local* variables inside functions.

You can use an immediately invoked function expression to cut the number of global variables in half. To appreciate how to use an IIFE for the benefit of your programs, consider the following points:

- Recognizing function expressions
- Invoking functions
- Immediately invoking function expressions
- Returning information from an IIFE

13.6.1 *Recognizing function expressions*

You've been using function expressions since chapter 4. You've assigned them to variables and properties, passed them as arguments, and returned them from other functions.

```
var show = function (message) {      //
    console.log(message);            // Assign to a variable
};                                   //

var namespace = {
    show: function (message) {       //
        console.log(message);        // Assign to a property
    }                                //
};

tweets.forEach(function (message) {  //
    console.log(message);            // Pass as an argument to forEach
});                                  //

var getFunction = function () {
    var localMessage = "Hello Local!";

    return function () {             //
        console.log(localMessage);   // Return from a function
    };                               //
};
```

You've used functions to create blocks of code you can call on demand and to create local scopes, hiding variables you want to be private from the peeks and tweaks of users and programmers.

13.6.2 *Invoking functions*

To *invoke*, or *call*, a function, you use the *function invocation operator*, (), a pair of parentheses. Here's how to invoke the four example function expressions in the last section:

```
show("Hello World!");                // Call the show function

namespace.show("Hello World!");      // Call the show method

// Automatically called by forEach
```

```
var show = getFunction();          // getFunction returns a function
show();                            // Call the returned function
```

You pass arguments to the functions between the parentheses of the invocation operator. Any values that the functions return replace the function call.

13.6.3 *Immediately invoking function expressions*

You don't need to assign a function expression to a variable in order to invoke it. Just wrap the function expression in parentheses and append the function invocation operator:

```
(function () {
    console.log("Hello World!");
})();
```

Figure 13.14 shows an annotated version of the code pattern.

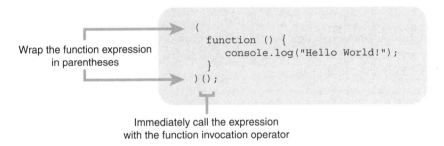

Wrap the function expression
in parentheses

```
(
    function () {
        console.log("Hello World!");
    }
)();
```

Immediately call the expression
with the function invocation operator

Figure 13.14   An immediately invoked function expression

The code in the function body runs immediately. But no global variable is used. The function expression has no impact on the global namespace. Breathe in the pollution-free, piquant freshness.

13.6.4 *Returning information from an IIFE*

So, immediately invoked functions reduce pollution and are great for hiding your privates. But there's more! Just like any other functions, immediately invoked functions can return values, such as objects acting as interfaces, giving you controlled access to the secret goodies inside the functions. (Note: please think carefully about just how much access to your privates is appropriate.)

Listing 13.16 demonstrates how an IIFE can return an interface object that you then assign to a variable. If you run the program, you can access the quiz interface at the console:

```
> quiz.quizMe()
  12 x 12
> quiz.submit("144")
  Correct!
```

```
var quiz = (function () {              Wrap the function
                                      in parentheses
    var qIndex = 0;
    var questions = [ ... ];                       Hide private
    var getQuestion = function () { ... };         variables within
    var checkAnswer = function (userAnswer) { ... };  the function

    return {
        quizMe: getQuestion,          Return the public
        submit: checkAnswer           interface as an object
    };

})();              Finish wrapping the function in
                   parentheses and invoke it with ()
```

You define a function, immediately invoke it, and assign the object returned to the quiz variable. Using an immediately invoked function expression just does away with the extra variable. Rather than

```
var getQuiz = function () {
    /* private */
    return interface;
};
var quiz = getQuiz();
```

you have

```
var quiz = (function () {
    /* private */
    return interface;
})();
```

You don't need to use the getQuiz variable.

The Crypt uses a number of constructors and functions and objects to build the game. You've seen the benefit of modules and immediately invoked function expressions; let's break the game code into modules.

13.7   *The Crypt—organizing code into modules*

Back at the start of this chapter, you saw how the growing amount of code in *The Crypt* is motivation for breaking the program into modules. Now that you've learned the hows and whys, it's time to do the deed.

The next listing shows the five HTML script elements you use to load the different modules that make up the game.

Listing 13.17 Importing modules for *The Crypt* (HTML)
(http://jsbin.com/zikuta/edit?html,js,console)

```
<!-- spacer -->
<script src="http://output.jsbin.com/juneqo.js"></script>
<!-- Player constructor -->
<script src="http://output.jsbin.com/nubijex.js"></script>
<!-- Place constructor -->
<script src="http://output.jsbin.com/dofuci.js"></script>
<!-- Map code -->
<script src="http://output.jsbin.com/dipaxo.js"></script>
<!-- Game initialization -->
<script src="http://output.jsbin.com/fisupe.js"></script>
```

Notice that the address for the `spacer` module is the same one you've been using throughout the chapter. That's the beauty of modules! You have a single file that's used in multiple projects. If you were to add a new formatting function to the `spacer` namespace, it would immediately be available to all of the projects that import the module.

The next listing shows the single line of JavaScript needed to get the game started.

Listing 13.18 Importing modules for *The Crypt*
(http://jsbin.com/zikuta/edit?html,js,console)

```
var game = theCrypt.getGame();
```

Run the game; it should work just the same in modular form. All of the functionality is defined in the modules; it requires minimal code to get the game started.

Apart from `spacer`, the modules for *The Crypt* all share the same namespace, `theCrypt` (figure 13.15). You start the game by calling the `getGame` method of the `theCrypt` namespace, `theCrypt.getGame()`;

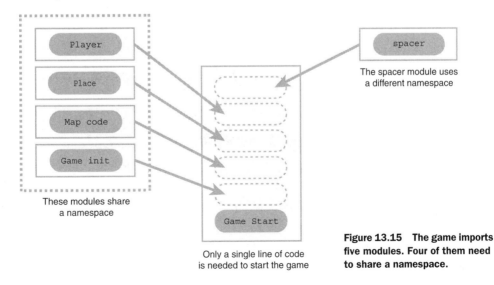

These modules share
a namespace

Only a single line of code
is needed to start the game

Figure 13.15 The game imports
five modules. Four of them need
to share a namespace.

The spacer module uses
a different namespace

You know that using a namespace is a good way to reduce the number of global variables and group related functions, but how can code in different module files share the same namespace?

13.7.1 *Sharing a namespace across modules*

Using what you've learned in this chapter, you want to do the following:

- Use a single global namespace, theCrypt, for all of the modules that form *The Crypt.*
- Assign to the namespace only those properties and functions that are needed by other modules.
- Hide everything else in the local scope of functions.

Modules add properties to the namespace theCrypt just as they would to any other object:

```
theCrypt.Player = Player;
```

But which module creates the namespace in the first place? Trying to access an undeclared variable will cause an error. But it would be inconvenient to have to load the modules in a certain order to ensure whichever one declares theCrypt is first. Fortunately, in browsers, global variables are automatically assigned to the special global object, window.

THE GLOBAL OBJECT, WINDOW

The window object is part of the way JavaScript works with global variables in browsers. You can test out global variable declarations and window at the console prompt:

```
> var test = "Hi"
  undefined
> test
  "Hi"
> window.test
  "Hi"
```

You declare a global variable, test, and it's automatically assigned as a property of window. Back at the prompt, try accessing a nonexistent global variable:

```
> theCrypt
  "Can't find variable: theCrypt"
```

An error is thrown (although your browser may display a slightly different error message). On the other hand, trying to access a nonexistent property of window doesn't throw an error; it returns undefined:

```
> window.theCrypt
  undefined
```

You can use the window object to check if theCrypt has been declared as a namespace without causing any errors.

USING WINDOW TO CHECK FOR GLOBAL VARIABLES

The next listing shows the `Player` module. Extra code has been wrapped around the constructor to modularize it.

Listing 13.19   The Player constructor as a module
(http://jsbin.com/nubijex/edit?js)

```
(function () {                          ←┤ Wrap the constructor in a
                                           function to create a local scope
    var Player = function (name, health) {
        /* unchanged implementation */      Don't touch the
    };                                      Player constructor

    if (window.theCrypt === undefined) {    Ensure there's a
        window.theCrypt = {};               global namespace
    }                                       called theCrypt

    theCrypt.Player = Player;           ←   Assign the Player
                                            constructor to the
}) ();              ←┤ Immediately invoke the    namespace
                      function expression
```

In listing 13.19 the `Player` module checks the `window` object to see if `theCrypt` has been declared as a global variable. If the module can't find `theCrypt`, then it declares it:

```
if (window.theCrypt === undefined) {
    window.theCrypt = {};
}
```

Once the module has ensured that the namespace is present, it adds the `Player` constructor as a property:

```
theCrypt.Player = Player;
```

The `Player` constructor is now available to other code that needs it, via the global variable `theCrypt`.

The next listing shows the `Place` module using the same global namespace.

Listing 13.20   The Place constructor as a module
(http://jsbin.com/dofuci/edit?js)

```
(function () {
    var Place = function (title, description) {
        /* unchanged implementation */
    };
    if (window.theCrypt === undefined) {
        window.theCrypt = {};               Assign the Place
    }                                       constructor to
    theCrypt.Place = Place;         ←──┘    the namespace
}) ();
```

Having each module check for theCrypt as a global variable on the window object means no one module is required to be loaded first because it's the one that creates the namespace. They all check for theCrypt. The first module to be loaded won't find it and will create it before using it. Modules loaded after the first will find theCrypt and assign to it the properties they want to be shared.

ASSIGNING NAMESPACE PROPERTIES TO LOCAL VARIABLES

You like the way a namespace cuts down on global variables, but you're not so keen on having to do more typing to use the shared properties. For example, the map code module needs to create places in *The Crypt* using the Place constructor:

```
var kitchen = new Place("The Kitchen", "You are in a kitchen…");
```

But you've moved the Place constructor into a namespace, theCrypt. You could change all of the references to Place in the map code:

```
var kitchen = new theCrypt.Place("The Kitchen", "You are in a kitchen…");
var library = new theCrypt.Place("The Old Library", "You are in a lib…");
```

But it can be easier to create a local Place variable and leave the original code alone:

```
var Place = theCrypt.Place;

var kitchen = new Place("The Kitchen", "You are in a kitchen…");
```

That's a handy way to reduce typing if you need to use a namespace property multiple times.

Having moved sections of code into their own modules, you can start to think carefully about what each module does. Could they be split into smaller modules that have more specific tasks? The next three chapters look at some common tasks and the code patterns that are often seen in programs that use and display data that changes: models, views, and controllers.

13.8 Summary

- Break up programs into modules, sections of code that can be loaded independently.
- Use the same module in multiple projects.
- Load modules in JS Bin by using an HTML script element:

  ```
  <script src="path/to/module.js"></script>
  ```

- Specify the location of the module file in the script element's src attribute.
- Minimize variable collisions, where one variable is overwritten by another, by using namespaces and immediately invoked function expressions.

- Create immediately invoked function expressions by wrapping a function definition in parentheses and appending the function invocation operator, ().

```
(function () {
    // Code to be executed immediately
}) ();
```

- Return an interface from the immediately invoked function expression. This is called the module pattern:

```
var game = (function () {
    // Local variables go here

    return {
        // Interface methods
    };
}) ();
```

- Make sure you load any modules that other modules depend on.

Models: working with data

In chapter 13, you saw how you can use modules to break a program into separate files. You can then work on the modules independently, easily switch between modules, and reuse them across multiple projects. You can even publish your modules and import published modules written by others.

This chapter maintains that spirit of modularization and reuse. You look at moving data out of constructors and functions. You represent the data simply so that multiple apps can use the data, even if the apps are written in different programming languages. You then consider how to feed that data into constructors and functions to build models that add extra functionality. Finally, you define map data for *The Crypt*, adding challenges to make the game more engaging.

14.1   *Building a fitness app—data and models*

Your development work has really gotten you noticed (*The Fruitinator!* was a global smash), and you're now part of a team developing a fitness application. Health-conscious users track their exercise, logging the date and duration of each session.

```
Mahesha
120 minutes on February 5th, 2017
35 minutes on February 6th, 2017

2 hours 35 minutes so far.
Great work!
```

The team is working on an Android version of the app using the Python programming language, an iOS version using Swift, and a web-based version using JavaScript. The same data will be used in all versions (figure 14.1).

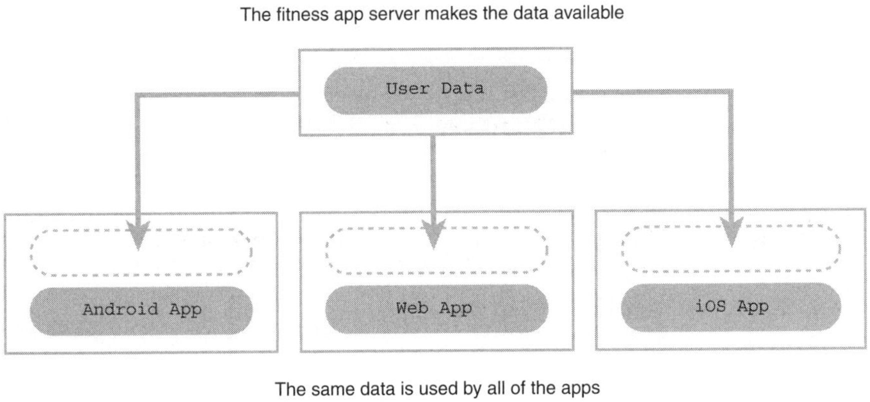

Figure 14.1   **The same data is used by the different versions of the app.**

Tasks involved in building the app include:

1 Retrieve user data as a string
2 Convert user data into user models
3 Display user data
4 Provide an interface for users to add sessions

The data is transferred across the internet as text. The format of the text is JSON, which you'll look at in chapter 20. As you'll see then, the text is easy to convert into a JavaScript object. The team has asked you to concentrate on the second task, building user models from user data.

14.1.1 Defining a User constructor

You've been asked to write JavaScript code to model a fitness app user. Your model needs to do the following:

1 Store the user's name.
2 Store a list of exercise sessions for the user, each with a date and duration.
3 Include a method for adding sessions to the list.
4 Include a method for retrieving data about the user.

Listing 14.1 shows your initial constructor function. You test it on the console:

```
> var user = new User("Mahesha")
  undefined
> user.addSession("2017-02-05", 120)
  120
> user.addSession("2017-02-06", 35)
  155
> user.getData().total
  155
```

Listing 14.1   The User constructor
          (http://jsbin.com/suzala/edit?js,console)

```
var User = function (name) {

    var sessions = [];                              Declare private
    var totalDuration = 0;                          variables

    this.addSession = function (sessionDate, duration) {

        sessions.push({                             Add a session
            "sessionDate" : sessionDate,            object to the
            "duration"    : duration                sessions array
        });

        totalDuration += duration;        ◁—┐  Add the current session's
                                               duration to the total
        return totalDuration;
    };

    this.getData = function () {          ◁—┐  Define a function to
        return {                               retrieve user data
            "name"     : name,
            "total"    : totalDuration,
            "sessions" : sessions.slice()   ◁—┐  Use slice to copy the
        };                                       sessions array
    };
};
```

The constructor includes a name parameter, some private variables declared using var, and two public methods assigned to the this object, addSession and getData. The getData method uses slice with no arguments to grab a copy of the sessions array.

(See chapter 8 for a reminder on array methods like `slice`.) Providing a copy of the session information prevents users from tweaking the `sessions` array outside the `add-Session` method. The object that `getData` returns also includes a `total` property, holding the total duration of the logged sessions.

When you create a JavaScript object using the `User` constructor, you create a user *model*. The model is more than just data; it includes private variables and public methods for managing the data, as shown in figure 14.2.

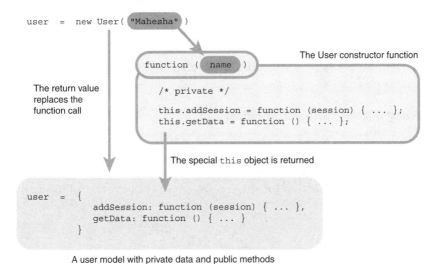

A user model with private data and public methods

Figure 14.2   A user model created by the `User` constructor function

If the model is more than the data, what does the data look like?

14.1.2 Getting a feel for the data as a JavaScript object

The data for a user is a simple JavaScript object:

```
var userData = {
    "name" : "Mahesha",
    "sessions" : [
        { "sessionDate" : "2017-02-05", "duration" : 120 },
        { "sessionDate" : "2017-02-06", "duration" : 35 },
        { "sessionDate" : "2017-02-06", "duration" : 45 }
    ]
};
```

You can access its properties, like `userData.name`. But it's still just data; it doesn't have the extra capabilities of a model built with the `User` constructer, like an `addSession` or `getData` method. The data object is shown again in figure 14.3 for comparison with figure 14.2.

```
user = {
        name: "Mahesha",
        sessions: [ ... ]
        }
```
User data as a simple JavaScript object

Figure 14.3   User data represented as a simple JavaScript object

Using simple JavaScript objects as the format for data is very common, even in other programming languages and especially on the web. Your team developing the fitness app is very happy that the user data is represented in such a well-supported form.

In order to make the most of the extra methods provided by a user model, addSession and getData, you need to define a function to build a model from the basic data object.

14.1.3 *Converting the data into a user model*

In listing 14.3, you define the buildUser function that takes data for a single user as a JavaScript object and creates a model by calling the User constructor. You test the buildUser function by creating a user model with it from a JavaScript object. Adding one extra exercise session for the created user produces the following output on the console:

```
> 240
```

You're using the User constructor from listing 14.1, so you import that by adding an HTML script element to the project (see chapter 13), as shown first in the next listing.

> **Listing 14.2   A function to build a user model from user data (HTML)**
> **(http://jsbin.com/zenire/edit?html,js,console)**

```
<!-- User constructor -->
<script src="http://output.jsbin.com/suzala.js"></script>
```

> **Listing 14.3   A function to build a user model from user data**
> **(http://jsbin.com/zenire/edit?html,js,console)**

```
var buildUser = function (userData) {

    var user = new User(userData.name);          ◁──┐ Create a new user object
                                                      with the User constructor
    userData.sessions.forEach(function (session) {
      user.addSession(                            ◁──┐ Add each
          session.sessionDate, session.duration);      session
    });

    return user;          ◁──┐ Return the newly
};                             created user model
```

```
var userData = {
  "name" : "Mahesha",
  "sessions" : [
    {"sessionDate": "2017-02-05", "duration": 120},
    {"sessionDate": "2017-02-06", "duration": 35},
    {"sessionDate": "2017-02-06", "duration": 45}
  ]
};
```
Create a JavaScript object to hold the user data

```
var user = buildUser(userData);
```
⟵ **Call buildUser to create a model from the data**

```
console.log(user.addSession("2017-02-15", 40));
```
⟵ **Add a session and log the total time returned**

With the `buildUser` function you can now upgrade plain user data, stored as a simple JavaScript object, to an enhanced user *model* that hides the data as private variables but adds methods to manage the state of the model and access a copy of the data.

14.1.4 What's next for the fitness app?

Your team is pleased with your work on the app; you've fulfilled the requirements for this chapter. The full set of requirements for the app is repeated here:

1 Retrieve user data as a string
2 Convert user data into user models
3 Display user data
4 Provide an interface for users to add sessions

You've completed the second requirement. You'll work on the others later in the book. For now, it's back to *The Crypt*. Can you separate the map data from the place models just as you separated user data from user models in the fitness app?

14.2 The Crypt—separating map data from the game

In this section you apply what you learned from working with the fitness app to *The Crypt*. In particular, you complete these tasks:

1 Use a basic JavaScript object to represent map data in the game
2 Add exit challenges to the map data
3 Update the `Place` constructor with methods to set and get challenges
4 Write a function to build place models from the map data

Currently, you build the map for *The Crypt* manually within the program by calling the `Place` constructor for each place you create and then by calling methods to add items and exits.

```
// Create two places
var kitchen = new Place(
    "The Kitchen",
    "You are in a kitchen. There is a disturbing smell."
);
```

```
var library = new Place(
    "The Old Library",
    "You are in a library. Dusty books line the walls."
);

kitchen.addItem("a piece of cheese");   // Add items separately
library.addItem("a rusty key");         //

kitchen.addExit("south", library);      // Add exits separately
library.addExit("north", kitchen);      //
```

The map data (the descriptions of places, exits, and items) are bound up with the
JavaScript that creates the objects used by the game; the only place in the code you
can find out about map locations is inside calls to the Place constructor.

```
var library = new Place(
    "The Old Library",                                   // Data inside
    "You are in a library. Dusty books line the walls."  // constructor
);
```

Details about exits and items for places are separated from the places themselves.

You saw in section 14.1 that data can be more easily shared when represented in a
common format; other programs and programming languages can read data formatted as simple JavaScript objects but don't know about your Place objects. If you separate the raw map data from the constructor function and methods like addItem and
addExit, it will be easier to define new maps, store them, switch them, and share them
(figure 14.4).

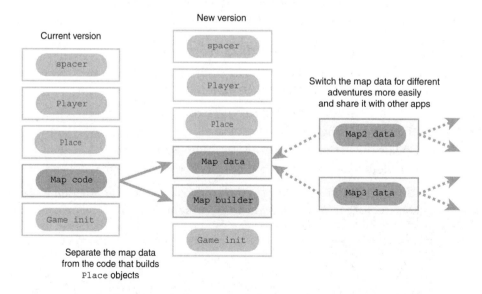

Figure 14.4   Splitting the map data from the map builder makes it easier to switch maps.

To achieve such a separation of data and game code, you have to decide what form the data will take and then write a function to convert the data into the `Place` models that the game uses.

14.2.1 Map data

A JavaScript object with a title, a list of places, and the name of the starting place will represent each map.

```
{
    "title": "The Dark House",
    "firstPlace" : "The Kitchen",
    "places" : [
        // Array of place objects
    ]
};
```

Each place within the `places` array will also be an object. The following snippet shows one such place:

```
{
    "title" : "The Kitchen",
    "description" : "You are in a kitchen. There is a disturbing smell.",
    "items" : [ "a piece of cheese" ],
    "exits" : [
        { "direction" : "south", "to" : "The Old Library" },
        { "direction" : "west",  "to" : "The Kitchen Garden" },
        { "direction" : "east",  "to" : "The Kitchen Cupboard" }
    ]
};
```

Each exit is an object with properties for its direction and the title of the place to which it leads. The data is compact and readable and keeps items and exits with the places to which they belong.

The following listing shows a section of map data. The four complete locations are on JS Bin.

> **Listing 14.4 Map data**
> **(http://jsbin.com/qonoje/edit?js,console)**

```
var mapData = {
  "title" : "The Dark House",
  "firstPlace" : "The Kitchen",

  "places" : [
    {
      "title" : "The Kitchen",
      "description" : "You are in a kitchen. There is a disturbing smell.",
      "items" : [ "a piece of cheese" ],
      "exits" : [
        { "direction": "south", "to": "The Old Library" },
        { "direction": "west",  "to": "The Kitchen Garden" },
```

Give each map a title ⟶ *(Include the title of the first location in the map)*

List all of the place objects in the places array

```
        { "direction": "east",  "to": "The Kitchen Cupboard" }
      ]
    },
    {
      "title" : "The Old Library",
      "description" : "You are in a library. Dusty books line the walls.",
      "items" : [ "a rusty key" ],
      "exits" : [
        { "direction" : "north", "to" : "The Kitchen" }
      ]
    },
    {
      "title" : "The Kitchen Garden", /* details on JS Bin */
    },
    {
      "title" : "The Kitchen Cupboard", /* details on JS Bin */
    }
  ]
};
```

The map data is only the description of each place; the constructed `Place` models will add the functionality your program expects.

14.2.2 Adding challenges to the map data

The Crypt, as it stands, lets you explore strange new worlds. You can find items in exotic locations. You can even pick up those items and add them to your hoard. But there's something missing. Your adventures are more like holidays (albeit with a bit of casual theft thrown in). You need to be challenged!

To make the game more fun, you add challenges to exits. When trying to go in a certain direction, you may be presented with a problem to solve. The game play will look something like this:

```
> game.go("south")
  *** A zombie sinks its teeth into your neck. ***

> game.use("a piece of cheese south")
  *** The zombie is strangely resilient. ***

> game.use("holy water south")
  *** The zombie disintegrates into a puddle of putrid goo. ***

> game.go("south")
  The Old Library
  You are in The Old Library…
```

The challenge prevented you from going south. To overcome the challenge, you had to use a particular item in the direction of the challenge.

```
game.use("holy water south")
```

If you don't have the required item, you have to go adventuring in a different direction, overcoming other challenges, until you find the item you need. So, how do you create challenges in the game?

All of the information about an adventure in *The Crypt* needs to be represented in its map data. At the moment, the exits from a place are simple:

```
{ "direction" : "south", "to" : "The Old Library" }
```

They have a direction and the title of the place to which they lead. To add a challenge to a particular exit, include a `challenge` property, like this:

```
{
    "direction" : "south",
    "to" : "The Old Library",
    "challenge" : {
        "message" : "A zombie sinks its teeth into your neck.",
        "success" : "The zombie disintegrates into a puddle of goo.",
        "failure" : "The zombie is strangely resilient.",
        "requires" : "holy water",
        "itemConsumed" : true,
        "damage" : 20
    }
}
```

Table 14.1 lists the properties of the challenge object along with their purpose and whether they're required.

Table 14.1 Challenge properties

Property	What is it for?	Required?
message	The message displayed to the player when they try to go in the direction of the exit and the challenge has not been overcome	Yes
success	The message displayed to the player when they use the item required to overcome the challenge	Yes
failure	The message displayed to the player when they try to use the wrong object to overcome the challenge	Yes
requires	The item required to overcome the challenge	Yes
itemConsumed	If the item is removed from the player's list of items once it is used	No
damage	The amount subtracted from the player's health when they try to go in the direction of the exit before they have overcome the challenge	No

To accommodate the challenges, you need to update the `Place` constructor.

14.2.3 Updating the Place constructor to include challenges

You have to update the `Place` model to allow for challenges. It needs an object in which to store the challenges, and methods, `addChallenge` and `getChallenge`, for adding and retrieving challenges for a specified direction. The next listing shows the changes to the `Place` constructor.

Listing 14.5   A Place constructor with challenges
             (http://jsbin.com/ruviso/edit?js,console)

```
var Place = function (title, description) {
  // other variables
  var challenges = {};                           Create an empty
                                                 object in which to
  // other methods                               store any challenges

  this.addChallenge = function (direction, challenge) {    The addChallenge method
    challenges[direction] = challenge;                     stores a challenge for a
  };                                                       specified direction.

  this.getChallenge = function (direction) {     The getChallenge method
    return challenges[direction];                returns the stored challenge
  };                                             for a specified direction.
};
```

You create a private `challenges` object to store any challenges. Just like for exits, you use directions as the keys for stored challenges. If a player must overcome a challenge before moving south, the details of the challenge will be stored in `challenges["south"]`.

To store a challenge use the `addChallenge` method, and to retrieve a challenge for a specified direction use the `getChallenge` method.

14.2.4 Using the map data to build a game map

Your implementation of *The Crypt* uses models created with the `Place` constructor linked with exits. Now that your map data is no longer tied up with the game logic, you need a way to convert the map into a set of place models.

You write a function called `buildMap` that takes a map data object as an argument and creates the place models, linked by their exits. It returns the model of the first place on the map, the starting point of the game.

```
var firstPlace = buildMap(mapData);
```

Figure 14.5 shows how the `buildMap` function uses `forEach` twice: first to create the place models and then to join the models by adding exits.

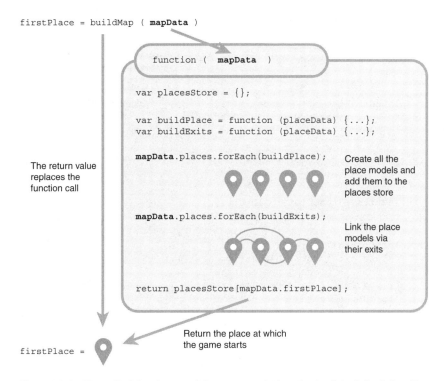

Figure 14.5   First, all of the place models are created; then they're linked via their exits.

The `buildMap` function is shown in listing 14.6 and follows these steps:

1   Create a model for each place (`buildPlace`)
  a   Call the `Place` constructor with the title and description
  b   Add any items to the newly created place model
  c   Put the place model in the places store
2   Add the exits and challenges for each place (`buildExits`)
  a   Retrieve the place model from the places store
  b   Add an exit to the model for each exit in the place's data
  c   Add a challenge for each exit in the place's data
3   Return the model for the first place in the game

**Listing 14.6   The map builder
(http://jsbin.com/paqihi/edit?js,console)**

```
var buildMap = function (mapData) {
  var placesStore = {};
```

```
var buildPlace = function (placeData) {
  var place = new theCrypt.Place(
      placeData.title,
      placeData.description
  );
```
Step 1a: Call the Place
constructor with the
title and description

```
  if (placeData.items !== undefined) {
    placeData.items.forEach(place.addItem);
  }
```
Step 1b: Add any items
to the newly created
place model

```
  placesStore[placeData.title] = place;
};
```
Step 1c: Put the place
model in the places store

```
var buildExits = function (placeData) {
  var here = placesStore[placeData.title];
```
Step 2a: Retrieve the place
model from the places store

```
  if (placeData.exits !== undefined) {
    placeData.exits.forEach(function (exit) {
      var there = placesStore[exit.to];
      here.addExit(exit.direction, there);
      here.addChallenge(
        exit.direction, exit.challenge);
    });
  }
};
```
Step 2b: Add an exit to the model
for each exit in the place's data

Step 2c: Add a challenge for
each exit in the place's data

```
mapData.places.forEach(buildPlace);
mapData.places.forEach(buildExits);
```
Start Step 1: Create a
model for each place

Start Step 2: Add the
exits for each place

```
  return placesStore[mapData.firstPlace];
};
```
Step 3: Return the model for
the first place in the game

The buildPlace function converts the data for a single place into a place model by using the Place constructor. Remember, the game modules use a global namespace, theCrypt (see chapter 13), so the constructor is accessed via theCrypt.Place. Before you can link the place models via their exits, all the place models need to exist. You call buildPlace for every place in the map data by iterating over the mapData.places array with forEach.

```
mapData.places.forEach(buildPlace);
```

Within buildPlace, you add each place you create to the placesStore object.

The buildExits function assigns the data for a place to a parameter, placeData, and grabs the matching place model from placesStore.

```
var here = placesStore[placeData.title];
```

It assigns the model to the here variable. Because place models have an addExit method, you can use here.addExit to add exits for the current model. The exits data looks like this:

```
"exits" : [
    { "direction": "south",
      "to": "The Old Library",
      "challenge" : {
        "message" : "A zombie sinks its teeth into your neck.",
        "success" : "The zombie disintegrates into a puddle of goo.",
        "failure" : "The zombie is strangely resilient.",
        "requires" : "holy water",
        "itemConsumed" : true,
        "damage" : 20
      }
    },
    { "direction": "west",  "to": "The Kitchen Garden" },
    { "direction": "east",  "to": "The Kitchen Cupboard" }
]
```

So, buildExits runs through the exit data, if it exists, and calls addExit and add-Challenge for each exit it finds.

```
placeData.exits.forEach(function (exit) {
    var there = placesStore[exit.to];
    here.addExit(exit.direction, there);
    here.addChallenge(exit.direction, exit.challenge);
});
```

The to property of each exit gives the title of the place to which the exit leads. The place model to which the exit leads can thus be found in placesStore by using exit.to as the key.

You add a challenge to every exit, whether or not a challenge is present in the map data.

```
here.addChallenge(exit.direction, exit.challenge);
```

If there's no challenge for the exit in the map data, then exit.challenge will be undefined. When you write code to work with challenges in chapter 16, you'll check if a challenge is undefined before trying to use it.

Et voila! By calling buildPlaces and buildExits for every place, you've created an interlinked map of place models for intrepid adventurers to explore. Will they find riches and glory? Will they discover enlightenment? Or will they meet their doom? Well, they'll need to start somewhere, and that's why the buildMap function returns the place model specified as the first model on the map.

```
return placesStore[mapData.firstPlace];
```

You've successfully separated the map data from the game implementation. The data is in a form that can be reused across projects and programming languages.

If you follow the JS Bin link for listing 14.6, you'll see that the full code wraps the buildMap function in an immediately invoked function expression and assigns build-Map to your global namespace, theCrypt. It's the same mechanism used for all of your modules, so it isn't shown in the printed listing.

14.2.5   *Bringing all the pieces together to run the game*

The game initialization module requires a tiny tweak. Here you update the call to buildMap, passing it the data from the new map data module.

Listing 14.7   Using the new map builder
(http://jsbin.com/mogano/edit?js,console)

```
var getGame = function () {

  var render = function () { … };

  var firstPlace = theCrypt.buildMap(theCrypt.mapData);    ◁─┐  Pass the map data
                                                             │  to the buildMap
  var player = new theCrypt.Player("Kandra", 50);           │  function
  player.addItem("The Sword of Doom");
  player.setPlace(firstPlace);

  render();

  // Return the public interface
  return {
    go: function (direction) { … },
    get: function () { … }
  };
};
```

The buildMap function returns the place where the adventure begins, and that is set as the player's location.

You also need to add an HTML script element to import the map data module in *The Crypt*. The next listing shows the HTML panel for the latest version of the game.

Listing 14.8   Using the map builder (HTML)
(http://jsbin.com/rulayu/edit?html,console)

```
<!-- spacer -->
<script src="http://output.jsbin.com/juneqo.js"></script>

<!-- Player constructor -->
<script src="http://output.jsbin.com/nubijex.js"></script>

<!-- Place constructor -->
<script src="http://output.jsbin.com/ruviso.js"></script>

<!-- map data (Kitchen example with challenge) -->
<script src="http://output.jsbin.com/jayici.js"></script>
```

```
<!-- map builder -->
<script src="http://output.jsbin.com/paqihi.js"></script>

<!-- Game initialization -->
<script src="http://output.jsbin.com/mogano.js"></script>
```

Have a play. It should work exactly as it did before, with the two commands `game.go` and `game.get` available. You won't spot the zombie (although it's there, lurking in the shadows of the map data)—you'll incorporate the challenges into the gameplay in chapter 16.

One of the aims of separating map data from the map building code was to more easily switch between maps. So because you've done so well, here's the exact same game code but with a different map file. (It's an old Jedi map trick!)

THE SPARROW
Map data: http://jsbin.com/woniqo/edit?js

Game: http://jsbin.com/dequzi/edit?console

You can take this whole modularization drive even further and separate the display of players and places from the models. Chapter 15 guides you on the next leg of your journey.

14.3 *Summary*

- Represent data in a form that's easy to reuse across projects, apps, and programming languages. Simple JavaScript objects are a common format for exchanging data on the web.
- Separate the data from the program logic to make it easier to switch between data sources.
- Define models that enhance the data, adding functionality and hiding private variables, ready to be used by other parts of your program.
- Define functions to create models from the data.

Views: displaying data

15

This chapter covers

- Presenting data with views
- Removing display code from constructors
- Passing the same model to multiple views

The console isn't the only place where you can display information for your users; I'm pretty sure you're keen to see how to output data on a web page! There are also desktop and phone applications, emails, and print documents to consider. Even on the console you may want the flexibility of a number of different formats for your output; maybe you want a simple text version and a fancy version with boxes and borders. You don't want to have to rewrite large portions of your programs to change the way they present information.

Views are focused modules of code that concentrate on displaying information. They take data and create visual output based on it. They may include controls like buttons and text boxes, but you'll leave that for part 3. Moving your display code into views lets you switch the type of output you want or display data in multiple ways without having to change other parts of your code, like the constructor functions for models.

In this chapter, you create views in the context of two examples, the fitness app and *The Crypt*. For the fitness app, you build a simple console view and then an enhanced version using the spacer namespace for formatting. For *The Crypt*, you separate out the display code that's currently in the `Player` and `Place` constructor functions, moving it into new player and place views.

All this modularization you've been pursuing throughout part 2 may seem like an uphill struggle, but the flexibility it gives you to update functionality by switching simple blocks of code in and out of a project is well worth the effort. And the views are magnificent!

15.1 Building a fitness app—displaying the latest user data

You and your team are hard at work writing a multiplatform fitness app that lets users log their exercise. The tasks involved in building the app include:

1 Retrieving user data as a string.
2 Converting user data into user models.
3 Displaying user data.
4 Providing an interface for users to add sessions.

You've already managed to convert a user's data from a simple JavaScript object into a user model with added functionality, including `addSession` and `getData` methods (see chapter 14). Now it's time to work on displaying the user data.

You're going to create two views, code that takes a user model and displays data from the model. Figure 15.1 shows how different views can work with the same single model to produce different output.

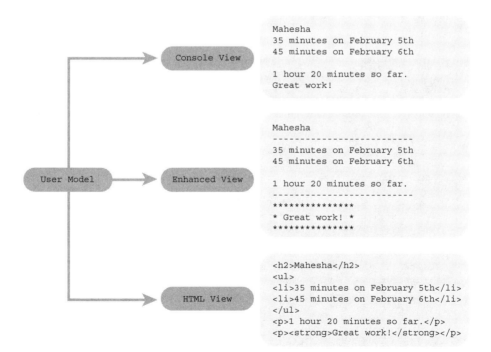

Figure 15.1   The same user model is used by different views to produce different output.

You're going to stick with console views for now, but in part 3 of *Get Programming with JavaScript,* you'll switch to views that generate HTML for output on a web page.

15.1.1   Creating your first fitness app view

Your first view for the fitness app is simple but effective, displaying user information on the console that looks like this:

```
Mahesha
35 minutes on 2017-02-05
45 minutes on 2017-02-06

80 minutes so far
Well done!
```

To produce the output you need a view and a user model:

```
var user = new User("Mahesha");      // Create a user model
user.addSession("2017-02-05", 35);
user.addSession("2017-02-06", 45);

userView.render(user);          // Pass the model to a view for display
```

In the listing 15.1 you define and immediately invoke a function that creates the user view, returning a simple interface object. You assign the interface to the userView variable. To test the view you call userView.render, which produces the display shown previously.

Listing 15.1   A simple user view
(http://jsbin.com/goqinep/edit?js,console)

```
var User = function (name) { /* unchanged from ch14 - on JS Bin */ };

var userView = (function () {                          Use a function
                                                      expression to create
  var getInfo = function (userData) {                 a local scope
    var infoString = "\n" + userData.name + "\n";

    userData.sessions.forEach(function (session) {    Define a function that
      infoString += session.duration + " minutes on ";  builds a string of info
      infoString += session.sessionDate + "\n";       from user data
    });

    infoString += "\n" + userData.total + " minutes so far";
    infoString += "\nWell done!\n";

    return infoString;                                Define the render function to
  };                                                  log the info for a user model

  var render = function (user) {                       Pass the data from the
    console.log(getInfo(user.getData()));             user model to getInfo
  };
```

```
    return {
      render: render
    };
```
Return a simple interface object that gives access to the render function

Immediately invoke the enclosing function expression

```
})();
```

```
var user = new User("Mahesha");
user.addSession("2017-02-05", 35);
user.addSession("2017-02-06", 45);
```
Create a user model and add two sessions

```
userView.render(user);
```
Display user info

You wrap the view code in an immediately invoked function expression to create a local scope, hiding implementation details, without the need for an extra global variable. (See chapter 13 for more on IIFEs and the perils of global pollution.)

The `User` constructor for user models from chapter 14 is included at the start of the listing. The user model provides a `getData` method that returns a simple JavaScript object:

```
{
    "name" : "Mahesha",
    "total" : 80,
    "sessions" : [
        { "sessionDate" : "2017-02-05", "duration" : 35 },
        { "sessionDate" : "2017-02-06", "duration" : 45 }
    ]
}
```

The view's `getInfo` function uses that data object to build the string of information shown before the listing.

But why stop at one view when you can have two?

15.1.2 *Using modules to switch fitness app views*

Ultimately, you'll present a number of views to your team from which they'll choose the best to go into production with the fitness app. The second view you add to your portfolio uses the formatting functions from the `spacer` namespace to add borders and boxes to the view's output. It's called `fitnessApp.userViewEnhanced`, and you can see the view's code as a module on JS Bin: http://jsbin.com/puculi/edit?js,console. It produces output like this:

```
Mahesha
---------------------------
35 minutes on 2017-02-05
45 minutes on 2017-02-06

80 minutes so far
---------------------------

**************
* Well done! *
**************
```

(The code for the second view is similar to the first. Here, I'm more interested in showing how multiple views can be used, so I've omitted the second view's code from the book.)

The next listing shows the HTML `script` elements used to import the `spacer` and `fitnessApp` modules. Notice, two view modules are imported.

> **Listing 15.2   Testing two user views (HTML)**
> **(http://jsbin.com/vamuzu/edit?html,js,console)**

```
<!-- spacer -->
<script src="http://output.jsbin.com/juneqo.js"></script>

<!-- fitnessApp.User -->
<script src="http://output.jsbin.com/fasebo.js"></script>

<!-- fitnessApp.userView -->
<script src="http://output.jsbin.com/yapahe.js"></script>

<!-- fitnessApp.userViewEnhanced -->
<script src="http://output.jsbin.com/puculi.js"></script>
```

The following listing shows the JavaScript used to test the two views you've created.

> **Listing 15.3   Testing two user views**
> **(http://jsbin.com/vamuzu/edit?html,js,console)**

```
var user = new fitnessApp.User("Mahesha");          Create a user model
user.addSession("2017-02-05", 35);                  and add two sessions
user.addSession("2017-02-06", 45);

fitnessApp.userView.render(user);              ⟵  Test the first user view

fitnessApp.userViewEnhanced.render(user);      ⟵  Test the enhanced user view
```

What lovely views! They both work well, displaying data from the same user model, so it will be easy to use whichever your team chooses. And it will be easy for you or others on the team to create more views if needed (that web view would be nice) without having to touch the user model code.

15.1.3 What's next for the fitness app?

You've created user models from data and displayed that data in a number of ways using views. Your next job is to give users a simple way to log their exercise sessions at the console, getting the views to re-render the display as the data changes. You'll do that by creating a fitness app *controller* in chapter 16.

15.2   *The Crypt—moving view code from Player and Place*

In the last section you saw how to create a *view* from scratch. You had a user *model* that provided data, and you wrote view code to display the data. In this section you work with existing models, `Player` and `Place`, from *The Crypt*. The code to display model

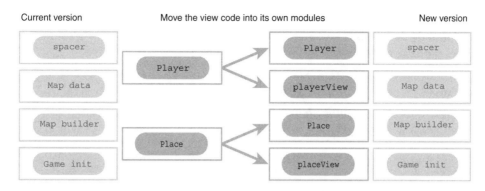

Figure 15.2 Move the view functions from the `Player` and `Place` models into their own modules

data is currently mixed in with the models themselves. Figure 15.2 shows all of the modules in the current and new versions of the game. To change to the new version, you'll separate the display code from the `Player` and `Place` models, creating two views, `playerView` and `placeView`.

You'll update players first and then places.

15.2.1 Creating a view for players

On the left of figure 15.3 are the functions currently defined in the `Player` model, before you make any changes. As it stands, the model includes six functions (on the top left) for the display of player information. You want the model to be concerned only with the management of player data, not with its display. The right of figure 15.3

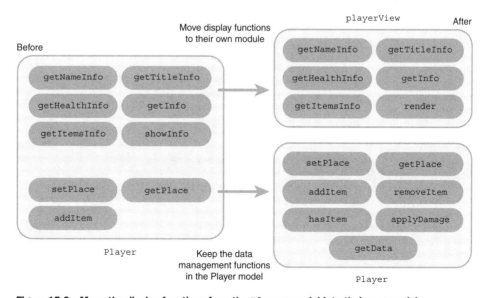

Figure 15.3 Move the display functions from the `Player` model into their own module.

shows an updated `Player` model with some extra methods to be added as well as a new module called `playerView`, concerned only with the display of player information. You create those two modules now.

THE MODEL

Models are more than just data. They provide methods for managing the data—adding, deleting, updating—and can prevent direct access to the data. To create a player model you call the `Player` constructor with the `new` keyword.

```
var player = new Player("Jahver", 80);
```

Listing 15.4 shows the new `Player` constructor. Although you don't want the `Player` model to bother with the display of its data, you do need to make that data available to any view that requires it. You still want to protect the private data from cheeky tweaks, so you create a method, `getData`, that returns a *copy* of the data. The data returned will look like this:

```
{
    "name" : "Jahver",
    "health" : 80,
    "items" : [ "a rusty key" ],
    "place" : "The Crypt"
}
```

In order to work with challenges in chapter 16, you add three more methods to the `Player` constructor: `hasItem`, `removeItem`, and `applyDamage`. If you head to JS Bin and run the code for the new constructor, you can perform the following actions at the console prompt (responses of `undefined` have been left out):

Create a player, add a couple of items, and get the player's data:

```
> var p = new theCrypt.Player("Dax", 10)
> p.addItem("a key")
> p.addItem("a lamp")
> p.getData()
  [object Object] {
    health: 10,
    items: ["a key", "a lamp"],
    name: "Dax"
  }
```

Use the new item methods to check if the player has an item and to remove an item:

```
> p.hasItem("a key")
  true
> p.hasItem("a sword")
  false
> p.removeItem("a key")
> p.getData().items
  ["a lamp"]
```

Apply damage to the player and check their health:

```
> p.applyDamage(2)
> p.getData().health
  8
> p.applyDamage(10)
> p.getData().health
  -2
```

> **Listing 15.4   The `Player` constructor**
> **(http://jsbin.com/yaneye/edit?js,console)**

```
(function () {

  var Player = function (name, health) {
    var items = [];
    var place = null;

    this.addItem = function (item) {
      items.push(item);
    };

    this.hasItem = function (item) {
      return items.indexOf(item) !== -1;
    };

    this.removeItem = function (item) {
      var itemIndex = items.indexOf(item);
      if (itemIndex !== -1) {
        items.splice(itemIndex, 1);
      }
    };

    this.setPlace = function (destination) {
      place = destination;
    };

    this.getPlace = function () {
      return place;
    };

    this.applyDamage = function (damage) {
      health = health - damage;
    };

    this.getData = function () {
      var data = {
        "name" : name,
        "health" : health,
        "items" : items.slice()
      };

      if (place !== null) {
        data.place = place.title;
      }
```

Return true if the specified item is in the items array

Remove the specified item from the items array

Subtract the specified damage from the player's health

Define a method to return a copy of the model's data

Use the slice method with no arguments to copy the items array

Include the title of the player's location if one has been assigned

```
      return data;                          Return the data object
  };
};

if (window.theCrypt === undefined) {
  window.theCrypt = {};
}
theCrypt.Player = Player;

})();
```

The `Player` constructor no longer assigns any display methods to the models it creates. The methods that are left from the previous version, `addItem`, `setPlace`, and `getPlace`, are purely for managing the player data the model holds. The display methods have been moved to the new view object.

Both `hasItem` and `removeItem` use the `indexOf` array method. If a specified item is in the `items` array, `indexOf` will return the index of that item. If the item is not in the array, `indexOf` will return -1.

```
["a key", "a lamp"].indexOf("a lamp");   // 1  -> second item in array
["a key", "a lamp"].indexOf("a sword");  // -1 -> not in array
```

The `removeItem` method also uses `splice` to remove an item from the `items` array.

```
items.splice(itemIndex, 1);
```

The first argument to `splice` is the index in the array at which to start removing items. The second argument is the number of items to remove. In `removeItem`, you want to remove a single specified item, so the second argument to `splice` is 1.

THE VIEW

Your player view will re-create the representation that used to be generated by the player objects themselves. To display a player, you call the view's `render` method, passing the player model as an argument:

```
theCrypt.playerView.render(kandra);
```

The `render` method calls `getInfo`, the function that builds up a string of player information, and displays the string returned on the console:

```
*****************************************
* Kandra (50)                          *
*****************************************
  Items:
   - a rusty key
   - a piece of cheese
*****************************************
```

The next listing shows the code for `playerView`. The interface assigned to `theCrypt.playerView` has the single method, `render`.

Listing 15.5   A player view
                      (http://jsbin.com/zucifu/edit?js,console)

```
(function () {

  var getNameInfo = function (playerData) {
    return playerData.name;
  };

  var getHealthInfo = function (playerData) {
    return "(" + playerData.health + ")";
  };

  var getItemsInfo = function (playerData) {
    var itemsString = "Items:" + spacer.newLine();

    playerData.items.forEach(function (item, i) {
      itemsString += "   - " + item + spacer.newLine();
    });

    return itemsString;
  };

  var getTitleInfo = function (playerData) {
    return getNameInfo(playerData) + " " + getHealthInfo(playerData);
  };

  var getInfo = function (playerData) {
    var info = spacer.box(
        getTitleInfo(playerData), 40, "*");
    info += "  " + getItemsInfo(playerData);       Use the player
    info += spacer.line(40, "*");                  data to build up
    info += spacer.newLine();                      a string of info

    return info;
  };

  var render = function (player) {
    console.log(getInfo(player.getData()));    ←⌐ Pass a copy of the
  };                                               player's data to getInfo

  if (window.theCrypt === undefined) {
    window.theCrypt = {};
  }

  theCrypt.playerView = {          Set the render
    render: render                 method as a property
  };                               of playerView

})();
```

render is the only function that produces any output that the user can see, logging the generated player information string to the console. In it, you pass the player's data to getInfo, and it passes the data on to the helper functions that each build a part of the overall information string.

You've split the player model from the player view. You'll see in chapter 17 how easy it is to change the view so it displays the player information on a web page rather than on the console. First, you follow the steps you used for players to create a model and a view for places in *The Crypt*.

15.2.2 Creating a view for places

Just as you did for players in the last section, you rewrite the constructor function for places so that it creates models that hold the data for each place and that provide some methods for manipulating that data. The models will also have a getData method so that views can get hold of a copy of each place's data for display. Then you create a view to log place data on the console. Figure 15.4 shows how the old model code will be split to form the new.

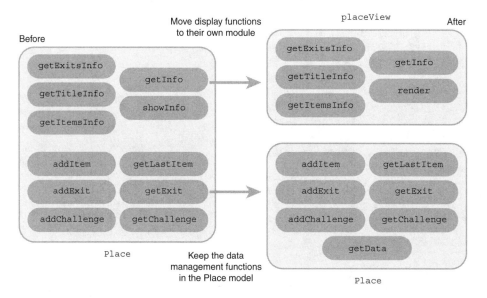

Figure 15.4   Move the display functions from the Place model into their own module

THE MODEL

Listing 15.6 shows a new version of the Place constructor, with its presentation code removed and a getData method added. The data returned by getData will have this form:

```
{
    "title" : "The Old Library",
    "description" : "You are in a dusty library. Books line the walls.",
    "items" : [ "a rusty key" ],
    "exits" : [ "west", "up" ]
}
```

The other methods are unchanged from previous incarnations of the constructor.

**Listing 15.6   A simplified `Place` constructor
                 (http://jsbin.com/vuwave/edit?js,console)**

```
(function () {

  var Place = function (title, description) {
    var exits = {};
    var items = [];
    var challenges = {};

    this.addItem = function (item) {
      items.push(item);
    };

    this.getLastItem = function () {
        return items.pop();
    };

    this.addExit = function (direction, exit) {
      exits[direction] = exit;
    };

    this.getExit = function (direction) {
      return exits[direction];
    };

    this.addChallenge = function (direction, challenge) {
      challenges[direction] = challenge;
    };

    this.getChallenge = function (direction) {
      return challenges[direction];
    };

    this.getData = function () {
      var data = {
        "title" : title,
        "description" : description,
        "items" : items.slice(),
        "exits" : Object.keys(exits)
      };

      return data;
    };
  };

  if (window.theCrypt === undefined) {
    window.theCrypt = {};
  }

  theCrypt.Place = Place;

})();
```

**Define a method to
return a copy of
the place's data**

**Use Object.keys to assign
an array of directions to
the exits property**

**Return the
data object**

Each place model links to destinations. The destinations are also place models. The destinations are stored in a place model's `exits` object. The keys of the `exits` object are the directions of the destinations. For example, `exits["south"]` might be the place model with a `title` property of `"The Old Library"`. The `Object.keys` method returns all of the keys of an object as an array. So, Object.keys(exits) returns all of the directions of exits from the current place, for example, ["south", "east", "west"].

The getData method in the Place constructor returns a copy of some of the data about a place, including an array of exit directions generated by using Object.keys(exits). The view will use that array to display the available exits from which players can choose to continue their adventures.

THE VIEW

Listing 15.7 shows the code for the place view module. How it works should be pretty familiar by now. It produces output on the console like this:

```
================
= The Kitchen =
================
You are in a kitchen. There is a disturbing smell.

Items:
   - a piece of cheese

Exits from The Kitchen:
   - east
   - south
========================================
```

Listing 15.7   A place view
(http://jsbin.com/royine/edit?js,console)

```
(function () {

  var getItemsInfo = function (placeData) {          ◁─┐ Pass the place's data
    var itemsString = "Items: " + spacer.newLine();     │ to the helper functions
    placeData.items.forEach(function (item) {
      itemsString += "   - " + item;
      itemsString += spacer.newLine();
    });
    return itemsString;
  };

  var getExitsInfo = function (placeData) {
    var exitsString = "Exits from " + placeData.title;
    exitsString += ":" + spacer.newLine();

    placeData.exits.forEach(function (direction) {
      exitsString += "   - " + direction;
      exitsString += spacer.newLine();
    });

    return exitsString;
  };

  var getTitleInfo = function (placeData) {
    return spacer.box(placeData.title, placeData.title.length + 4, "=");
  };
```

```
var getInfo = function (placeData) {                          Pass the place's
  var infoString = getTitleInfo(placeData);                   data to the main
  infoString += placeData.description;                        getInfo function
  infoString += spacer.newLine() + spacer.newLine();
  infoString += getItemsInfo(placeData) + spacer.newLine();
  infoString += getExitsInfo(placeData);
  infoString += spacer.line(40, "=") + spacer.newLine();
  return infoString;
};

var render = function (place) {
  console.log(getInfo(place.getData()));       Call getData to get
};                                             a copy of the place
                                               model's data
if (window.theCrypt === undefined) {
  window.theCrypt = {};
}

theCrypt.placeView = {
  render: render
};

})();
```

Just like the view module for players, the view for places calls some helper functions, in this case `getItemsInfo`, `getExitsInfo`, and `getTitleInfo`, from a main display function, `getInfo`, to build up a string of information about a model. The `render` function is the only one that produces output that the user can see, displaying the assembled place information on the console.

You now have model constructors and views for players and places. The data and the presentation of the data have been separated. The models are concerned only with the manipulation of the data and have nothing to do with its display. The views are concerned only with displaying the data and have nothing to do with changing it.

The views have been written to be used in the same way. They both have a `render` method that's passed the model to be displayed, as shown in the following snippet:

```
// Create some models
var kandra = new Player("Kandra", 50);
var library = new Place("The Library", "You are in a dusty library.");

// Use views to display the model info
playerView.render(kandra);
placeView.render(library);
```

As well as displaying information about players and places, you need to display messages to users as they play the game. They probably want to know if they've been bitten by a zombie or lacerated by a leopard!

15.3 *Talking to players—a message view*

As adventurers make their way around *The Crypt*, you need to let them know what's going on. You use the player view to give them updates on their health and the items they carry. You use the place view to display each place's title and description and to list its items and exits. You also need a way of displaying feedback when the players attempt an invalid action or succumb to their injuries.

```
> game.go("north")
  *** There is no exit in that direction ***
> game.get("a piece of cheese")
  *** That item is not here ***
> game.use("a lamp north")
  *** That doesn't help. The door is still locked. ***
```

To handle such messages, you create a message view. Like your other views, it has a single method in its public interface, render. You pass the text to be displayed to the render method:

```
theCrypt.messageView.render("That item is not here.");
```

The next listing shows the code for the view. The local getMessageInfo function returns a string for display, and the render function logs it to the console.

> **Listing 15.8   A message view**
> **(http://jsbin.com/jatofe/edit?js,console)**

```
(function () {

  var getMessageInfo = function (messageData) {
    return "*** " + messageData + " ***";     ⟵  Format the message to
  };                                              make it seem urgent

  var render = function (message) {
    console.error(getMessageInfo(message));   ⟵  Use console.error to log
  };                                              the message as an error

  if (window.theCrypt === undefined) {
    window.theCrypt = {};
  }

  theCrypt.messageView = {
    render: render
  };

})();
```

You use the console.error method in the render function. It's similar to console.log but developers use it to flag errors in programs. The console normally displays errors differently from standard logged messages. The errors are often shown in red. That suits your purposes for displaying messages to players on the console.

In chapter 14 you added challenges to the map data for *The Crypt*. You'll use the message view to display the various success and failure messages associated with each challenge. Knowing when to show those messages requires some code that checks user actions against challenges, updates player and place models as a result, and uses views to display the latest state of the game. You need *controllers*. Chapter 16 has you covered.

15.4 Summary

- Create views to display data from models.
- Maintain a separation of concerns where models manipulate data and views display data.
- Create multiple views to display the same model data in different ways.
- Keep the interface consistent for all views. For example, all of the views in this chapter have a render method as their interface. They can all be called the same way:

```
fitnessApp.userView.render(user);
fitnessApp.userViewEnhanced.render(user);
theCrypt.playerView.render(player);
theCrypt.placeView.render(place);
theCrypt.messageView.render(message);
```

Controllers:
linking models and views

16

This chapter covers

- Acting on user input
- Updating models in response to user actions
- Passing updated models to views for display
- Completing the console version of *The Crypt*

Part 2 of *Get Programming with JavaScript* has been about organizing your code. As your programs grow, that organization pays dividends, making it easier to focus on individual pieces, switch modules to alter functionality, and reuse code in multiple projects.

Breaking programs into modules encourages you to give each module a specific task. Chapters 14, 15, and 16 form a trilogy, with each chapter looking at a common task a module might perform. You met *models* in chapter 14 and *views* in chapter 15 and now you link them with *controllers*.

To see controllers in action and how they act on user input to manage models and update views, you continue your work on two projects: the fitness app and *The Crypt*. In the fitness app, users will log sessions of exercise, and in *The Crypt*, players will face puzzles to solve as they explore perilous places. But will they escape before their health reaches zero?

16.1   Building a fitness app—controllers

Your team members have been telling friends and family about the fitness app you're creating and they have a list of people lined up to test it out; they're a super-keen bunch and have been diligently logging their exercise on paper. Your work has gone well so far—what's left to do? Here are the requirements set out by the team:

1   Retrieve user data as a string.
2   Convert user data into user models.
3   Display user data.
4   Provide an interface for users to add sessions.

You've completed tasks 2 and 3, building models in chapter 14 and views in chapter 15. Task 1 involves retrieving data across the internet—you'll work on that in part 3. That leaves task 4—you need to provide a simple way for those eager fitness fanatics to log the sessions of exercise they complete.

You decide to provide a single command for users of the app to log their activity:

```
app.log("2017-02-07", 50)
```

The users call the `app.log` method, passing in the date of their session and the duration of their exercise in minutes. But how does that command reach the user model? And how does the view know to update the display? That's the job of the *controller.*

16.1.1   What does the controller do?

The controller orchestrates the other pieces of the program, reacting to user input and updating the models and views. Figure 16.1 shows the modules that your fitness app will load when opened in JS Bin. You already have data, the `User` constructor, and views from chapters 14 and 15. You need to create a controller to handle the interactions between the different parts.

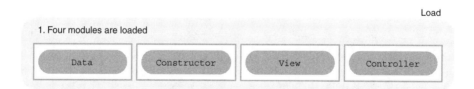

Figure 16.1   The four modules of the fitness app

Figure 16.2 shows how your controller is involved in initializing the app, using the `User` constructor to build a user model from the data. And when the app is running, the controller reacts to users calling `app.log` by adding the logged session to the user model and then passing the updated model to the view for display.

You know what the controller needs to do; how will you make it do it?

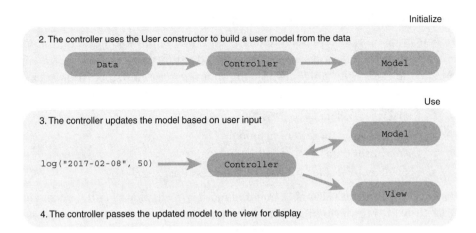

Figure 16.2   The tasks the controller performs in the fitness app

16.1.2 *Building the fitness app controller*

The snippets that follow show the kind of code you'd expect to see in the controller:

```
var user = buildUser(userData);      // Convert user data into a user model.

> app.log("2017-02-08", 50)          // When the user logs a session

user.addSession("2017-02-08", 50);   // the controller adds it to the model

fitnessApp.userView.render(user);    // and updates the view.
```

The first listing shows the full code for the controller.

Listing 16.1   The fitness app controller
(http://jsbin.com/goniro/edit?js,console)

```
(function () {
  var buildUser = function (userData) {          ◁— Define a function to
    var user = new fitnessApp.User(userData.name);    build a user model
                                                       from user data
    userData.sessions.forEach(function (session) {
      user.addSession(session.sessionDate, session.duration);
    });

    return user;                          Define an init function
  };                                      that initializes the app

  var init = function (userData) {    ◁—   Build a model from the
                                           user data and assign it
    var user = buildUser(userData);   ◁—   to the user variable

    fitnessApp.userView.render(user);      ◁— Pass the new user model
                                              to the view for display
```

```
      return {
        log: function (sessionDate, duration) {
          user.addSession(sessionDate, duration);
          fitnessApp.userView.render(user);
          return "Thanks for logging your session.";
        }
      };
    };

    if (window.fitnessApp === undefined) {
      window.fitnessApp = {};
    }

    fitnessApp.init = init;

})();
```

> **Return an interface with a single method, log**

> **Make the init method available by adding it to the fitnessApp namespace**

When the controller module is loaded, it adds its `init` function to the `fitnessApp` namespace. You'll be able to start the app by calling `init` and passing it the user data.

```
var app = fitnessApp.init(fitnessApp.userData);
```

The `init` function returns an interface with a single method, `log`. By assigning the returned interface to app, you let users record their sessions by calling `app.log`.

16.1.3 *Putting the pieces together for a working fitness app*

Listings 16.2 and 16.3 show the HTML and JavaScript for the fitness app on JS Bin. Running the program lets you log a session like this:

```
> app.log("2017-02-08", 55)
```

The controller adds your logged session to the user model and passes the updated model to the view, producing this output:

```
Mahesha
35 minutes on 2017-02-05
45 minutes on 2017-02-06
55 minutes on 2017-02-08

135 minutes so far
Well done!

Thanks for logging your session.
```

The following listing uses HTML `script` elements to load your four fitness app modules. The modules share properties, objects, and functions by assigning them to the `fitnessApp` namespace.

Listing 16.2   The fitness app (HTML)
(http://jsbin.com/huxuti/edit?html,js,console)

```
<!-- fitnessApp.userData -->
<script src="http://output.jsbin.com/tenuwis.js"></script>

<!-- fitnessApp.userView -->
<script src="http://output.jsbin.com/yapahe.js"></script>

<!-- fitnessApp.User -->
<script src="http://output.jsbin.com/fasebo.js"></script>

<!-- fitnessApp.controller -->
<script src="http://output.jsbin.com/goniro.js"></script>
```

The next listing shows the single line of JavaScript needed to initialize the program and make the `app.log` method available to users.

Listing 16.3   The fitness app
(http://jsbin.com/huxuti/edit?js,console)

```
var app = fitnessApp.init(fitnessApp.userData);
```

Run the program and have a go at logging some sessions.

16.1.4   What's next for the fitness app?

The last step for your app is to grab user data as text from across the internet and then convert that text into a JavaScript object ready to pass to `fitnessApp.init`. You'll return to your work on the app in chapter 20.

16.2   *The Crypt—adding a game controller*

Okay, this is it for *The Crypt* in part 2 of *Get Programming with JavaScript*. By the end of the chapter, you'll have a working console app with challenges for players to overcome and the danger of their health falling to zero, ending the game. There's one more piece of the puzzle needed to get the game fully working: a controller.

You have the data, the models, and the views for *The Crypt*. The *controller* is the module that ties everything together. It feeds the map data to the map builder and passes the model data to the views. It provides the interface that users will access to play the game and responds to player commands. That's quite a lot of jobs for one game module, so it's worth taking a minute to see how it fits in with the other modules that make up *The Crypt*.

Figure 16.3 shows all of the modules that make up *The Crypt*. The `Controller` module has replaced the module that used to be labelled "Game init." Now that you're working with models and views, it's more appropriate to call the module a controller. But why? What does the controller do?

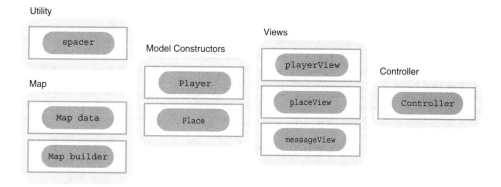

Figure 16.3   The modules that make up *The Crypt*

16.2.1 *What does the controller do?*

Your controller will initialize the game and act on user input while the game is running, updating models and views in response to the players' actions.

INITIALIZE THE GAME

When the game first loads, the controller will:

1 Use the Place constructor to build place models from the map data.
2 Use the Player constructor to build a player model.
3 Assign the place specified as first in the map data as the player's location.
4 Provide a UI.

Steps 1 and 2 are shown in figure 16.4.

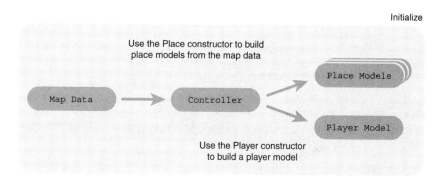

Figure 16.4   When the game loads, the controller builds the player and place models.

ACT ON USER INPUT

While the game is running, the controller will:

1   Check that player actions are valid.
2   Update player and place models.
3   Pass updated models to views for display.
4   Pass feedback messages to the message view.
5   Stop the game if the player's health reaches zero.

Steps 2, 3, and 4 are shown in figure 16.5.

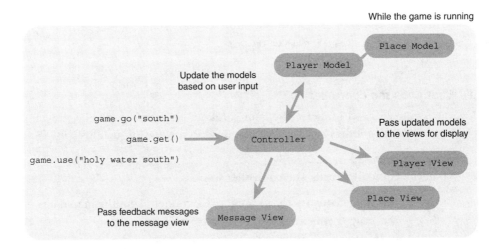

Figure 16.5   The controller responds to user actions and updates models and views.

The player model includes a getPlace method that the controller uses to access the player's current location (notice how the Place model is connected to the Player model in figure 16.5).

16.2.2   *Approaching the controller code*

You've seen what the controller does in *The Crypt* and are ready to explore the code that makes it work. Even though you've seen a lot of the code before, presenting it as one long listing can make it seem more daunting than it deserves, so your exploration is broken across sections.

- (16.3) The overall structure of the controller
- (16.4) Initializing the game, monitoring player health, updating the display, and ending the game
- (16.5) Handling player commands and challenges—get, go, and use
- (16.6) Running the game

Let the games begin!

16.3　The Crypt—the structure of the controller code

As you've seen, the controller has a number of tasks to perform to start, monitor, and end a game in *The Crypt*. To help you get a feel for how the parts make up the whole, listing 16.4 omits the function bodies and focuses on the variables in the code. You can see the full listing, function bodies and all, by following the link to JS Bin, and the code is also shown in the sections that follow in this chapter.

Listing 16.4　The game controller
(http://jsbin.com/yeqicu/edit?js)

```
(function () {

    var player;
    var inPlay = false;                          Use inPlay to flag when
                                                 the game is over

    var init = function (mapData, playerName) {
        /* Listing 16.5 */                       Build the map, create a
    };                                           player, and start the game

    var checkGameStatus = function () { /* 16.6 */ };

    var render = function () { /* 16.7 */ };        Call the views to
    var renderMessage = function (message) {/*16.7*/};  update the display

    var get = function () { /* 16.8 */ };
    var go = function (direction) { /* 16.9 */ };    Respond to user
    var use = function (item, direction) {/*16.10*/};  commands

    window.game = {
        get: get,              Assign the
        go: go,                interface to game,
        use: use,              a global variable
        init: init
    };

})();
```

Check if player health has dropped to zero

Listing 16.4 also includes comments pointing you to the listings in this chapter that investigate the missing function bodies.

It's time to start the game! And stop it! And monitor player health! And update the display! (Sorry for the excitement, but the full game is so close.)

16.4　The Crypt—starting and stopping the game

While the main game action takes place in the get, go, and use functions, you also need to easily start and stop the game and keep the display updated with the latest info. And now that players are facing cruel challenges, challenges that may drain their health, you need to check that they are still hale and hearty enough to carry on.

16.4.1 Initializing the game

To get the game started, it needs to be initialized by calling the init method.

```
game.init(map, playerName);
```

init builds the map, creates the player model, sets the player's location to the correct place, and then displays the player and place information, as shown in the following listing.

> **Listing 16.5   The init function**
> **(http://jsbin.com/yeqicu/edit?js)**

```
var player;                                          Declare a variable to record
var inPlay = false;                                  if the game is running

var init = function (mapData, playerName) {           Build the map, storing
    var firstPlace = theCrypt.buildMap(mapData);      the starting location

    player = new theCrypt.Player(playerName, 50);
    player.addItem("The Sword of Doom");          Set up the
    player.setPlace(firstPlace);                   player

    inPlay = true;                                   Update inPlay: the
                                                     game is now running
    render();          Display the place
};                     and player
```

You declare the player and inPlay variables outside the init function so other functions in the controller can access them. The buildMap function returns the starting place in the game, and then you set that place as the player's current location. The init function calls render to display the starting place and player information.

The render, get, go, and use functions use the inPlay variable. They perform their usual tasks only when inPlay is true. When a player's health drops to zero, the controller sets inPlay to false. For that to happen, you have to keep an eye on the player's health.

16.4.2 Monitoring player health

Whenever a player takes damage, you need to check if their health has reached zero, because that's "Game over, man. Game over!" The controller's checkGameStatus function does the checking, setting the isPlay variable to false if the player has succumbed to the litany of zombie bites, leopard lacerations, and nasty splinters they encounter, as shown in the next listing.

**Listing 16.6   Checking if health has dropped to zero
                 (http://jsbin.com/yeqicu/edit?js)**

```
var checkGameStatus = function () {
    if (player.getData().health <= 0) {
        inPlay = false;
        renderMessage("Overcome by your wounds...");
        renderMessage("...you fall to the ground.");
        renderMessage("- Your adventure is over -");
    }
};
```

Use getData to grab the player's data and check their health

Stop the game by setting inPlay to false

The condition uses the less than or equal to comparison operator, <=, to check if the health is less than or equal to zero.

```
player.getData().health <= 0
```

If the player has died, you stop the game and display a final message. If they're fit enough to carry on, checkGameStatus does nothing.

16.4.3 Updating the display—functions that use the view modules

Rather than calling the render methods of view modules directly, the controller uses its own functions. This makes it easier to switch to different view modules if required because the views are referenced in only one place, as shown in the following listing.

**Listing 16.7   Updating the display
                 (http://jsbin.com/yeqicu/edit?js)**

```
var render = function () {
    console.clear();
    if (inPlay) {
        theCrypt.placeView.render(player.getPlace());
        theCrypt.playerView.render(player);
    }
};

var renderMessage = function (message) {
    theCrypt.messageView.render(message);
};
```

Clear the display

Update the place and player display only if the game is in play

The init function gets things started, and then checkGameStatus, render, and render-Message are used throughout the game. The main action comes from the get, go, and use functions, with go and use making some tricky decisions based on items, exits, and challenges. It's time to investigate the player commands—make it so!

16.5   *The Crypt—giving commands and solving puzzles*

Users are permitted to take only a small set of actions when exploring *The Crypt*. The controller module assigns the following interface to the global `window` object:

```
window.game = {
    get: get,
    go: go,
    use: use,
    init: init
};
```

The user initiates actions in the game by calling the game controller interface methods at the console (`game.get()` or `game.go("south")`, for example). The game controller then creates, accesses, or updates models in response to the user's instructions and passes changed models to the views for display.

You've already looked at the `init` function; this section (16.5) steps through the `get`, `go`, and `use` functions. The `get` function hasn't evolved much, but the `go` function now checks for challenges. And `use` is a completely new function.

16.5.1   *Picking up items with game.get*

Players exploring *The Crypt* will find items as they travel from place to place. The items will help them to overcome challenges they may face. The `get` method gives them a way of picking up the items they find, as shown next.

Listing 16.8   The get function
                (http://jsbin.com/yeqicu/edit?js)

```
var get = function () {
    if (inPlay) {                                      ◁──┐ Get an item only if the
                                                            game is still active

        var place = player.getPlace();                 │ Retrieve the last item from
        var item = place.getLastItem();                │ the player's current location

        if (item !== undefined) {
                                                       ◁──┐ If an item was retrieved,
            player.addItem(item);                           add it to the player's list

            render();                                                      ◁──┐ Update the display to
                                                                                show the item has moved
        } else {
            renderMessage("There is no item to get");
        }

    } else {
        renderMessage("The game is over!");            ◁──┐ If inPlay is false, let
    }                                                        the player know
    return "";
};
```

An item is removed from the end of the place's list of items and added to the player's list of items. If the place has no items, `getLastItem` will return `undefined`.

Both the `go` and `use` functions involve checking challenges. A quick refresher is in order.

16.5.2 *Listing the properties of a challenge*

You're keen on the idea of challenges and want to add a splash of jeopardy. Players have had a health property right from the start of the book; you're ready to do dastardly damage to players as they meekly move around your maze.

You first saw challenges in *The Crypt* when developing map data in chapter 14, but you haven't put them to use until now. Two of the player commands, `go` and `use`, check for challenges in a specified direction, so it's worth reminding yourself of the properties that make up a challenge:

```
"challenge" : {
    "message" : "A zombie sinks its teeth into your neck.",
    "success" : "The zombie disintegrates into a puddle of goo.",
    "failure" : "The zombie is strangely resilient.",
    "requires" : "holy water",
    "itemConsumed" : true,
    "damage" : 20
}
```

Table 16.1 lists the properties of the challenge object along with their purpose and whether they are required.

Table 16.1   Properties of the challenge object

Property	What is it for?	Required?
message	The message displayed to the player when they try to go in the direction of the exit and the challenge has not been overcome.	Yes
success	The message displayed to the player when they use the item required to overcome the challenge.	Yes
failure	The message displayed to the player when they try to use the wrong object to overcome the challenge.	Yes
requires	The item required to overcome the challenge.	Yes
itemConsumed	If the item is removed from the player's list of items once it is used.	No
damage	The amount subtracted from the player's health when they try to go in the direction of the exit before they have overcome the challenge.	No
complete	Whether the challenge has been completed. Usually missing in the initial data, it's set to `true` during the game when a challenge is solved.	No

To retrieve a challenge from a place object, call `getChallenge`, specifying a direction:

```
place.getChallenge("south");
```

If there's no challenge in that direction, `getChallenge` returns `undefined`. The first command that uses challenges is `game.go`.

16.5.3   Moving with game.go

Players use the controller's go function to move from place to place. But if a lock or a leap or a leopard blocks their path, the controller needs to let them know. Players call go, specifying the direction in which they wish to travel:

```
> game.go("south")
```

The full go function is shown here. A walkthrough of the code follows the listing.

Listing 16.9   The go function (http://jsbin.com/yeqicu/edit?js)

```
var go = function (direction) {
  if (inPlay) {

    var place = player.getPlace();               Collect the
    var destination = place.getExit(direction);  info needed
    var challenge = place.getChallenge(direction);

    if (destination === undefined) {
      renderMessage("There is no exit in that direction");
    } else {

      if ((challenge === undefined) || challenge.complete) {

        player.setPlace(destination);       If there's no challenge or it's
        render();                           complete, move the player
                                            and update the display
      } else {

        if (challenge.damage) {             Apply any damage
          player.applyDamage(challenge.damage);   caused by the challenge
        }

        render();                           Update the display showing
                                            any changes to health
        renderMessage(challenge.message);

        checkGameStatus();                  Show the initial
      }                                     challenge message
    }
  } else {                                  Check if the player's health
    renderMessage("The game is over!");     has dropped to zero
  }
  return "";
};
```

The function starts by collecting the information it needs to act on the player's request:

```
var place = player.getPlace();
var destination = place.getExit(direction);
var challenge = place.getChallenge(direction);
```

It could be that there's no exit in the direction the player specified. You need to check for that:

```
if (destination === undefined) {
    renderMessage("There is no exit in that direction");
} else {
    // Check for challenges
}
```

Okay, say the player isn't walking into a wall and there's an exit in the direction specified. If there's no challenge, or if the player has completed the challenge, you can move them to the destination.

```
if ((challenge === undefined) || challenge.complete) {
    player.setPlace(destination);
    render();
} else {
    // Mention the leopard
    // and apply any damage.
}
```

The || symbol in the `if` condition is the logical OR operator. It lets you check a condition made up of two expressions at once. If either the first expression, `challenge === undefined`, or the second expression, `challenge.complete`, evaluates to `true`, then the whole condition is `true`. If both expressions evaluate to `false`, then the whole condition is `false`. (JavaScript also has a logical AND operator, `&&`, that evaluates to `true` if both expressions are `true`, and `false` otherwise.)

If the player hasn't completed a challenge, you need to apply any damage that the challenge causes (bumps, bruises, leopard bites, and so on).

```
if (challenge.damage) {
    player.applyDamage(challenge.damage);
}
```

Finally, update the display to show any changes to health, show the challenge's initial message, and check that the player's health is still above zero—the game remains in play.

```
render();
renderMessage(challenge.message);
checkGameStatus();
```

That takes care of player peregrinations. But what if there *is* a big, hungry cat blocking the path? How can players lick the leopard?

16.5.4 Licking the leopard with game.use

If a lock or a leap or a leopard blocks a player's path, the player can call the controller's use function to overcome the challenge. They specify the item to use and the direction in which to use it:

```
> game.use("a ball of wool", "south")
  *** The leopard chases the ball of wool, purring loudly. ***
```

The full use function is shown in listing 16.10. It has a number of nested if statements, but don't worry: the key decisions are shown in figure 16.6, and you venture down the rabbit hole to see how it works following the listing.

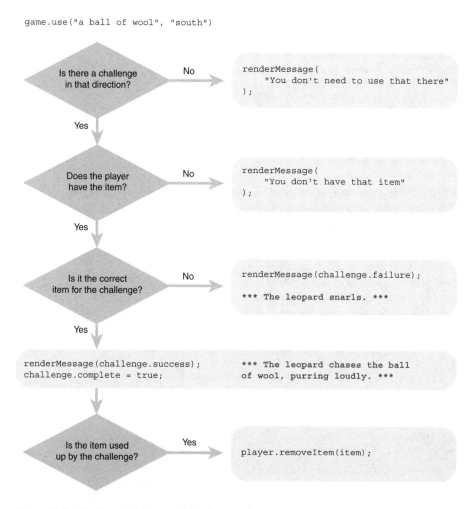

Figure 16.6   The key decisions made by the use function

Listing 16.10   **The use function**
                    (http://jsbin.com/yeqicu/edit?js)

```javascript
var use = function (item, direction) {
  if (inPlay) {

    var place = player.getPlace();                        // Get the challenge for
    var challenge = place.getChallenge(direction);        // the specified direction

    if ((challenge === undefined) || challenge.complete) {  // Check if the challenge
      renderMessage("You don't need to use that there");    // is complete or
    } else {                                                // doesn't exist

      if (player.hasItem(item)) {                         // Check if the player has
                                                          // the item specified
        if (item === challenge.requires) {                // Check if the item is the
                                                          // one required to overcome
                                                          // the challenge
          renderMessage(challenge.success);               // Display the success message and
          challenge.complete = true;                      // mark the challenge as complete

          if (challenge.itemConsumed) {                   // Remove the item from the
            player.removeItem(item);                      // player if it's consumed by
          }                                               // the challenge

        } else {
          renderMessage(challenge.failure);               // Display the failure
        }                                                 // message if the player
                                                          // has used the wrong item
      } else {
        renderMessage("You don't have that item");        // Let the player know they
      }                                                   // don't have the item
                                                          // they're trying to use
    }
  } else {
    renderMessage("The game is over!");
  }
  return "";
};
```

The function starts by collecting the information it needs to act on the player's request:

```javascript
var place = player.getPlace();
var challenge = place.getChallenge(direction);
```

It could be that there's no challenge in the direction the player specified. You need to check for that:

```javascript
if ((challenge === undefined) || challenge.complete) {
    renderMessage("You don't need to use that there");
} else {
    // There is a challenge to be overcome.
}
```

Some players are sneaky! You need to check that they have the item they're trying to use. If they don't, send them a polite message:

```
if (player.hasItem(item)) {
    // Check it's the right item
} else {
    renderMessage("You don't have that item");
}
```

Okay, so they're using an item they have against an actual challenge. Is it the right tool for the job? Let them know if it's not:

```
if (item === challenge.requires) {
    // Complete the challenge
} else {
    renderMessage(challenge.failure);
}
```

And finally, at the bottom of the rabbit hole, if they've passed all the checks, complete the challenge:

```
renderMessage(challenge.success);
challenge.complete = true;

if (challenge.itemConsumed) {
    player.removeItem(item);
}
```

Well done; you made it through the get, go, and use function wonderland. The pieces aren't too taxing, but when you have deeply nested ifs and buts, they can get quite hairy. Throw yourself a tea party! But don't be late for section 16.6—that's where your adventure really begins.

16.6 *The Crypt—running the game*

To get the game running, you need to include all of the modules you've created and then call the game.init method, passing it the map data and the player's name. Figure 16.7 shows all of the modules involved.

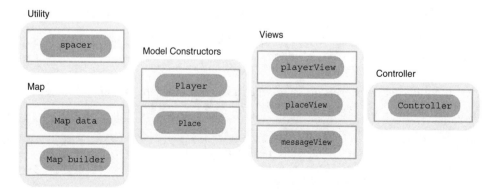

Figure 16.7 The many modules of *The Crypt*

The next listing shows the HTML `script` elements used to load the modules.

**Listing 16.11   Loading the game modules (HTML)
(http://jsbin.com/fociqo/edit?html,console)**

```
<script>
  console.log("Loading The Crypt ...");
</script>
```
⊲─┤ **Let players know the
modules are loading**

```
<!-- spacer -->
<script src="http://output.jsbin.com/juneqo.js"></script>

<!-- Place constructor -->
<script src="http://output.jsbin.com/vuwave.js"></script>

<!-- Player constructor -->
<script src="http://output.jsbin.com/nonari.js"></script>

<!-- player view -->
<script src="http://output.jsbin.com/zucifu.js"></script>

<!-- place view -->
<script src="http://output.jsbin.com/royine.js"></script>

<!-- message view -->
<script src="http://output.jsbin.com/jatofe.js"></script>

<!-- map data -->
<script src="http://output.jsbin.com/hozefe.js"></script>

<!-- map builder -->
<script src="http://output.jsbin.com/paqihi.js"></script>

<!-- game controller -->
<script src="http://output.jsbin.com/yeqicu.js"></script>
```

The HTML includes an initial `script` element that's different from the rest. It has no `src` attribute. Rather than linking to a file to load, it includes the JavaScript directly between the `script` tags. The module files can take a moment to load, so it's nice to give players feedback that something is happening. Putting the code in the HTML lets it run straight away; no need to wait for a file to load.

The following listing shows the code needed to get things up and running.

**Listing 16.12   Running the game
(http://jsbin.com/fociqo/edit?js,console)**

```
var playerName = "Jahver";
var map = theCrypt.mapData;

game.init(map, playerName);
```

Hide the JavaScript panel, run the game, and start exploring! Be careful though; challenges chip away at your health.

16.7 The Crypt—what's next for the app?

Congratulations! You've created a working console-based adventure game with swappable maps and a modular architecture (a fancy way of saying it's made up of lots of bits).

Part 2 of *Get Programming with JavaScript* was all about organizing your code to better cope with larger programs. Your knowledge of private variables, modules, models, views, and controllers equips you to cope with more ambitious projects. By sticking to the console, you were able to focus on the key JavaScript language concepts; now it's time to make the jump to HTML and web interfaces. As you'll see, the work you've done building a well-organized program will make your first steps as a web developer much easier.

16.8 Summary

- Use a *controller* to manage the models and the views. The controller updates the models in response to user input and passes data from the models to the views for display.

JavaScript in the browser

U p to this point in *Get Programming with JavaScript*, you've been using the console as the way of interacting with your programs. You've been able to focus on the JavaScript code. Now it's time to start using a web page as the user interface, using HyperText Markup Language (HTML) to specify headings, paragraphs, and list items for presentation; and buttons, drop-down lists, and text boxes for user input. You use templates as an efficient way to generate HTML from your data and XMLHttpRequest objects to load extra data for your web pages.

Part 3 shows you how to organize files on your own computer rather than on JS Bin and suggests some next steps as you continue your JavaScript adventure. *The Crypt* gets an HTML makeover and the ability to load locations one at a time as players explore the worlds you create for them.

17

HTML:
building web pages

This chapter covers

- Using HTML to display static content
- Tags, elements, and attributes
- Common HTML elements
- Manipulating web page content with JavaScript
- Switching to HTML-based views in *The Crypt*

JavaScript is associated with adding interactivity to web pages: reacting to users clicking buttons and selecting from drop-down menus, for example, and updating parts of a page with new content. Having learned the fundamentals of the language, you're almost ready to take that step to interactivity and dynamic content. Your focus is still on JavaScript, but you need to learn enough HTML to see how JavaScript can be used to create and manipulate the content of a web page. JS Bin still has you covered while you learn; you can add HTML and view the resulting web page in the Output panel. In chapter 21 you'll see how to move on from the JS Bin sandbox and organize your own HTML, CSS, and JavaScript files.

You've spent a lot of time building *The Crypt* in a modular fashion. That work pays off in this chapter when you see how easy it is to switch from displaying output on the console to displaying it on a web page. It will just take a few lines of code—it's almost magical.

17.1   HTML, CSS, JavaScript—building a web page

You want to build a movie reviews web page, My Movie Ratings, that displays information about your favorite movies and lets you rate them (figure 17.1). To build the page you use three languages:

- *HTML*—You use HTML to annotate the text of the page and specify media to be loaded; headers, paragraphs, lists, images, and buttons are all specified with HTML. This is your base layer, the essential content, the information you want visitors to find and read.
- *CSS*—You use the Cascading Style Sheets language to specify the look of the page, its colors, fonts, margins, borders, and so on. This is your presentation layer, a visual treat that enhances the content.
- *JavaScript*—You use the JavaScript language to add interactivity to the page; you respond to button clicks, filter content, load extra data, and pop-up messages with JavaScript. This is your behavior layer, a subtle dash of user interface magic that smooths the way and can improve the user's experience and efficiency.

Figure 17.1 includes three screenshots of the My Movie Ratings page and shows how the CSS and JavaScript layers build on the HTML foundation.

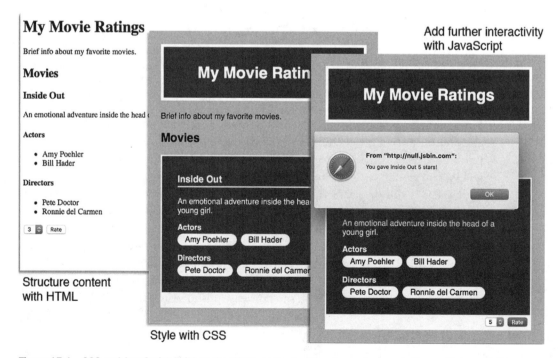

Figure 17.1   CSS and JavaScript build on the HTML content with enhanced presentation and interactivity.

Even without CSS and JavaScript, on the left of figure 17.1, the key information about the movie is accessible. The CSS adds visual styles, a sense of identity, and (hopefully) design that guides and delights the visitor. Finally, on the right, the figure shows a message that has been popped up using JavaScript after a user clicked the Rate button.

Take a look at your My Movie Ratings pages on JS Bin. There's the base HTML version at http://jsbin.com/sayayim/edit?output and the version with CSS and JavaScript at http://jsbin.com/hikuzi/edit?output. (You may have to run the JavaScript to make the Rate button work.)

17.1.1 *Loading the layers*

If you had your own website, jahvers.crypt, you'd load the My Movie Ratings web page by pointing your browser at the page's URL, jahvers.crypt/movies.html, say. The browser loads the HTML document, movies.html, sent by the server at that address. The movies.html document may contain CSS and JavaScript code within it, between `style` and `script` tags, respectively:

```
<head>
    <title>My Movie Ratings</title>

    <style>
        /* CSS goes here */
    </style>

    <script>
        /* JavaScript goes here */
    </script>
</head>

<body>
    <!-- Page content for display goes here -->
</body>
```

Don't worry about all the HTML tags for now; we cover them in section 17.2. You're well aware of the benefits of modularization (that's what part 2 was all about!), so you'll be pleased to know that HTML documents can load CSS files as well as JavaScript files:

```
<head>
    <title>My Movie Ratings</title>

    <link rel="stylesheet" href="movies.css" />
    <script src="movies.js"></script>
</head>

<body>
    <!-- Page content for display goes here -->
</body>
```

You've seen the `script` tags for loading JavaScript modules before; the `link` tag does a similar job for loading CSS. When your browser is reading through your HTML document, ready to display it, it will load the CSS and JavaScript files it finds specified by the link and script elements. You'll take a proper look at organizing your own HTML, CSS, and JavaScript files in chapter 21. For now, JS Bin does the work for you.

17.1.2 Loading the layers in JS Bin

When working on your projects, or bins, on JS Bin, you can add code to three panels: HTML, CSS, and JavaScript. JS Bin automatically merges the code from the three panels, embedding the CSS and JavaScript into the HTML and showing the resulting web page on its Output panel.

You won't spend much time working on CSS in *Get Programming with JavaScript*, but where it's used in examples, you can always take a look at the CSS panel yourself; the code used is mostly straightforward. You return to JavaScript in section 17.3, after saying a brief hello to HTML.

17.2   *HTML—a very short introduction*

For My Movie Ratings, your movie reviews website, you want headings, lists of actors and directors, a choice of possible ratings, and a button to submit your verdict. You need a way of specifying that this text is a heading but that text is a list item; here's a drop-down list and there's a button. You're not on the console anymore, Dorothy—you've left the monochrome world of spaces and new-line characters and entered the wonderful, colorful land of HTML. (Rest assured. There are no flying monkeys in this chapter.)

You use HTML to annotate text and to identify media that you want to embed in a document. The annotations specify the role that each section of text plays within the structure of the document. The media can be images, video, audio, or some other format.

The markup itself takes the form of *tags*. In a document, a section of text might be a heading, a paragraph, a list item, or a quotation, for example, and there are tags to mark up those sections of text. Here's a heading and a paragraph, each marked up with an opening and closing tag:

```
<h1>My Movie Ratings</h1>

<p>Brief info about my favorite movies.</p>
```

You wrap each section of text with an opening and closing tag. The heading has <h1> and </h1>, the paragraph <p> and </p>. Together, each opening and closing tag pair specifies an *element*. The h1 tags specify a heading element; the p tags specify a paragraph element.

When a web browser loads an HTML document, it sees the tags and creates the corresponding element in its model of the page in memory. The tags specify what type of element to create and the text between the tags forms the content of the element.

17.2.1 Starting with an empty page

Before you start adding content to pages, take a look at the HTML that constitutes a bare-bones web page. If you create a new bin on JS Bin and view the HTML panel, you'll see the following markup. (I've reformatted it slightly.)

```
<!DOCTYPE html>

<html>
    <head>
        <meta charset="utf-8">
        <title>JS Bin</title>
    </head>

    <body>

    </body>
</html>
```

The DOCTYPE in the first line gives the browser information about the version of HTML you're using and helps it decide how to process and display the page. HTML has evolved over the years, and a number of versions and variations are specified by complicated-looking document type declarations. Fortunately, <!DOCTYPE html> is a neat shorthand for the latest version (currently HTML5).

You wrap the whole document, after the document type, in html tags. Within the document, there are two sections, head and body. The head section contains information about the document: its title and character encoding. The body section is where the main content of the page goes—the content that will be displayed to the user when they visit the web page. All of your pages will use the same basic structure shown here.

17.2.2 Adding some content

Figure 17.2 shows some text for My Movie Ratings added between the body tags of a new JS Bin document. The text has been marked up with appropriate HTML tags to denote headings, subheadings, and paragraphs.

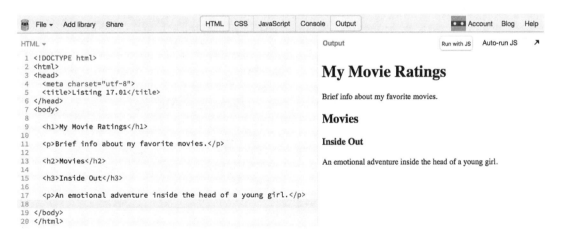

Figure 17.2 The hierarchy of headings and the paragraphs

The browser represents the hierarchy of headings, h1, h2, h3, by using different font sizes. The following listing shows the HTML used between the body tags for the web page.

Listing 17.1   My Movie Ratings—headings and paragraphs (HTML)
(http://jsbin.com/nosiwi/edit?html,output)

```
<body>                                              ⟵  Put the content to be displayed on
                                                       the web page between the body tags
    <h1>My Movie Ratings</h1>                   ⟵   Use an h1 tag for the
                                                    main heading on a page
    <p>Brief info about my favorite movies.</p>

    <h2>Movies</h2>                             ⟵   Use heading tags h2, h3, and so on for
                                                    headings of decreasing importance
    <h3>Inside Out</h3>

    <p>An emotional adventure inside the head of a young girl.</p>   ⟵

</body>                                             Wrap paragraphs in p tags
```

17.2.3 *Marking up a list*

Each movie includes a list of actors and a list of directors. Use the li tag to mark up list item elements. A single list item for an actor looks like this:

```
<li>Amy Poehler</li>
```

The list items need to be part of a list. You can have an ordered list, if the order of the items matters, or an unordered list, if it doesn't. Use ol tags for an ordered list and ul tags for an unordered list. Figure 17.3 shows the output for lists of actors and directors. Listing 17.2 shows the new code.

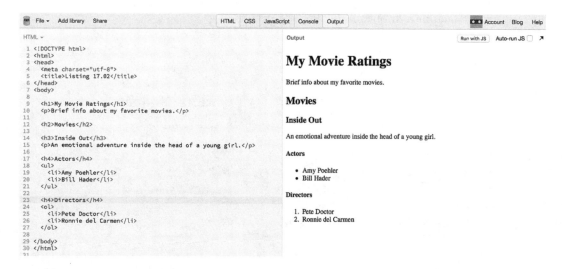

Figure 17.3   The browser renders the ordered list with numbers and the unordered list with bullets.

Listing 17.2   Ordered and unordered lists (HTML)
(http://jsbin.com/vegahe/edit?html,output)

```
<body>

  <h1>My Movie Ratings</h1>
  <p>Brief info about my favorite movies.</p>

  <h2>Movies</h2>

  <h3>Inside Out</h3>
  <p>An emotional adventure inside the head of a young girl.</p>

  <h4>Actors</h4>
  <ul>
    <li>Amy Poehler</li>
    <li>Bill Hader</li>
  </ul>

  <h4>Directors</h4>
  <ol>
    <li>Pete Doctor</li>
    <li>Ronnie del Carmen</li>
  </ol>

</body>
```

Use ul tags to create an unordered list

Put each of the list items between opening and closing li tags

Use ol tags to create an ordered list

As you can see in figure 17.3, the browser automatically adds numbers for an ordered list and bullets for an unordered list.

17.2.4 *Some common HTML elements*

Figure 17.4 is a screenshot of a web page made up of some common HTML elements. The content of each element describes the element. You can visit the page on JS Bin: http://jsbin.com/nuriho/edit?html,css,output.

The tags used to create the page in figure 17.4 are shown in table 17.1. There are plenty more HTML tags, but these are enough for you to work with for now.

Table 17.1   Some common HTML elements for wrapping content

Tag	Element	What is it for?
`<h1>`	Heading	Main heading for a document or part of a document
`<h2>`...`<h6>`	Subheading	Subheadings in decreasing order of importance
`<p>`	Paragraph	Paragraphs
`<div>`	Division	Wraps a set of elements that belong together as a section of a document

Table 17.1   Some common HTML elements for wrapping content *(continued)*

Tag	Element	What is it for?
`<ol>`	Ordered list	Wraps a set of list items where the order of the items is important (e.g., a numbered list)
`<ul>`	Unordered list	Wraps a set of list items where the order of the items is not important (e.g., a bulleted list)
`<li>`	List item	Wraps a single item in an ordered or unordered list
`<head>`	Head	Wraps elements that provide meta-information about a document and load extra code needed by the document
`<body>`	Body	Wraps the main content of the page, the content that is displayed directly on the web page

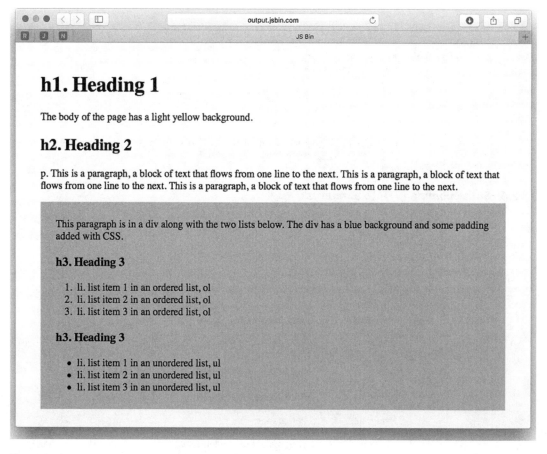

Figure 17.4   A web page with self-describing HTML elements

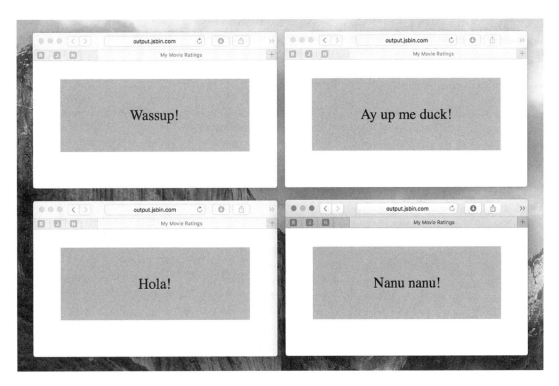

Figure 17.5   Random greetings from a web page

17.3   *Adding content to a web page with JavaScript*

Looking for ways to add interest to the site, you decide to welcome visitors to your My Movie Ratings web page with a random greeting. To test out the idea, you create a minimal page. Figure 17.5 shows what you're aiming for, with four visits to the page producing four different greetings.

Refreshing the page generates a new random greeting. Try it out on JS Bin at http://output.jsbin.com/mikura.html. The next two listings show how to create the page. Run the JavaScript to make the message appear.

> **Listing 17.3   Adding content to a paragraph with JavaScript (HTML)**
> **(http://jsbin.com/mikura/edit?html,js,output)**

```
<p id="greeting">Welcome!</p>
```

> **Listing 17.4   Adding content to a paragraph with JavaScript**
> **(http://jsbin.com/mikura/edit?html,js,output)**

```
function getGreeting () {
  var hellos = [            ⟵—| Create an array
    "Nanu nanu!",                of greetings
```

```
        "Wassup!",
        "Yo!",
        "Hello movie lover!",
        "Ay up me duck!",                              Generate a
        "Hola!"                                        random index
    ];                                                 from zero to one
                                                       less than the
    var index = Math.floor(Math.random() * hellos.length);  ◁──┘  length of the array

    return hellos[index];
    }

    function updateGreeting () {
      para.innerHTML = getGreeting();
    }
                                                      Get a reference to
 var para = document.getElementById("greeting");   ◁──┘  the paragraph

    updateGreeting();                ◁──┤  Set the content of the paragraph
                                         to a random greeting
```

To generate the effect, you follow these steps:

1 Assign an id to an element in the HTML
2 Use the id to get a reference to the element in JavaScript
3 Use the reference to update the element's contents

17.3.1 *Getting an element by its id*

You display the greeting in a paragraph element. To set the greeting, you need to get hold of a reference to that paragraph in JavaScript. You give the HTML element a unique id attribute:

```
<p id="greeting">Welcome!</p>
```

To get a reference to the element in a JavaScript program, you use the document.get-ElementById method, passing the id of the element as an argument:

```
var para = document.getElementById("greeting");
```

The web browser makes the document object available to your JavaScript code. The document object has properties and methods that allow you to interact with the hierarchy of elements on a page.

   You obtained a reference to the paragraph element by using document.get-ElementById. Having assigned the reference to the para variable, you can now use para to manipulate the element. You update the content of the paragraph by setting the element's innerHTML property.

```
para.innerHTML = "Ay up me duck!";
```

The original content of the paragraph is replaced and becomes

```
<p id="greeting">Ay up me duck!</p>
```

17.3.2 Function declarations

You're now using function declarations rather than function expressions when defining named functions for later use.

```
var sayHello = function () {   //
    console.log("Hello");      // function expression assigned to variable
};                             //

function sayHello () {         //
    console.log("Hello");      // function declaration
}                              //
```

Function declarations were mentioned in chapter 4 as an alternate syntax for defining functions. You've been using expressions up until now to be consistent with the assignment of values, objects, arrays, and functions to variables.

```
var num = 4;
var movie = {};
var actors = [];
var getRating = function () {};
```

It's more common to see function declarations for named functions, so you've switched to declarations for part 3 of *Get Programming with JavaScript.*

17.3.3 What, no JavaScript?

Occasionally, visitors will arrive at your site on devices that either don't have JavaScript or have it disabled. Or they'll be on a slow network, maybe at a hotel or on a train, where it takes longer (much longer!) to load any JavaScript modules for the page. If your page relies on JavaScript to display its content, visitors may be presented with an empty space. Whenever possible, consider including initial content in the page so that visiting is not a useless waste of time. Content should be available to everyone, with the extra flexibility, fluidity, and flashiness that JavaScript brings layered on top for those whose devices can handle it.

For your random greeting test, you included a greeting, "Welcome!", in the initial HTML (listing 17.3). A random greeting is a nice bit of fun but isn't essential.

Having seen how to add some text to a paragraph, you now step things up and add a whole series of elements at once.

17.4 Displaying data from an array

Each movie on My Movie Ratings has a title and a one-line summary. Figure 17.6 shows a list of three movies on the site.

My Movie Ratings

- **Inside Out**

  An emotional adventure inside the head of a young girl.

- **Tomorrowland**

  Recreating the hope and wonder of previous generations.

- **The Wizard of Oz**

  Strangers find friendship and strength on a long walk.

Figure 17.6   A list of movies

Given some movie data, you can loop through the movies and insert them into an existing element on the page. The movie data looks like this:

```
var moviesData = [
    {
        "title" : "Inside Out",
        "summary" : "An emotional adventure inside the head of a young girl."
    },
    {
        "title" : "Tomorrowland",
        "summary" : "Recreating the hope and wonder of previous generations."
    },
    {
        "title" : "The Wizard of Oz",
        "summary" : "Strangers find friendship and strength on a long walk."
    }
];
```

You place a div element with an id of movies on the page, as shown in the following listing. Use div elements as containers to collect groups of related elements together.

Listing 17.5   **Building HTML with JavaScript (HTML)**
              (http://jsbin.com/jakowat/edit?html,js,output)

```
<body>
    <h1>My Movie Ratings</h1>

    <div id="movies"></div>
</body>
```

Each movie will be a list item in an unordered list. The browser automatically adds the bullets for list items in an unordered list. The next listing shows the JavaScript used to display the movies.

```
var moviesData = [ /* As above */ ];

function getMovieHTML (movie) {                         Use the getMovieHTML
  var html = "<h3>" + movie.title + "</h3>";            function to generate a string
  html += "<p>" + movie.summary + "</p>";               of HTML for a single movie
  return html;
}                                                       Use the getMoviesHTML
                                                        function to generate a string
function getMoviesHTML (movies) {                       of HTML for an array of movies
  var html = "";

  movies.forEach(function (movie) {                     Wrap the response from
    html += "<li>" + getMovieHTML(movie) + "</li>";     getMovieHTML in li tags
  });                                                    to create a list item

  return "<ul>" + html + "</ul>";                        Wrap all list items in an
}                                                        unordered list with ul tags

function render (movies) {
  var moviesDiv = document.getElementById("movies");     Update the innerHTML of the
  moviesDiv.innerHTML = getMoviesHTML(movies);           element with an id of movies
}

render(moviesData);                                      Call the render method,
                                                         passing it the data it needs
```

The `getMovieHTML` method builds up the HTML for a single movie by sandwiching the properties of the `movie` object between appropriate opening and closing tags.

```
var html = "<h3>" + movie.title + "</h3>";
html += "<p>" + movie.summary + "</p>";
```

The `getMoviesHTML` method iterates over the array of movies, building up the HTML for all of the movies as it goes. It uses `getMovieHTML` to get the HTML for each movie, wrapping the returned strings in `li` tags to create list item elements.

```
movies.forEach(function (movie) {
    html += "<li>" + getMovieHTML(movie) + "</li>";
});
```

It then wraps the HTML for the list of items in opening and closing `ul` tags for an unordered list and returns the complete HTML string.

```
return "<ul>" + html + "</ul>";
```

The `getMoviesHTML` function returns HTML that looks like the following (but without the line breaks and extra spaces):

```
<ul>
    <li>
        <h3>Inside Out</h3>
```

```
            <p>An emotional adventure inside the head of a young girl.</p>
        </li>
        <li>
            <h3>Tomorrowland</h3>
            <p>Recreating the hope and wonder of previous generations.</p>
        </li>
        <li>
            <h3>The Wizard of Oz</h3>
            <p>Strangers find friendship and strength on a long walk.</p>
        </li>
    </ul>
```

The render method is the one that changes the page. It gets a reference to the target div on the page and sets its innerHTML property with the HTML string returned by getMoviesHTML.

```
var moviesDiv = document.getElementById("movies");
moviesDiv.innerHTML = getMoviesHTML(movies);
```

To reduce the number of global variables, you could wrap the getMovieHTML, get-MoviesHTML, and render functions in an immediately invoked function expression (IIFE—see chapter 13) that returns just render in its interface. The listing has been kept simple to help focus on the generation of HTML and how to update an element on a web page.

17.5   *The Crypt—displaying players and places with web views*

You've split the program for *The Crypt* across multiple modules, sections of code that can be loaded independently. The modules perform different tasks: you have data, models, views, and a controller (figure 17.7).

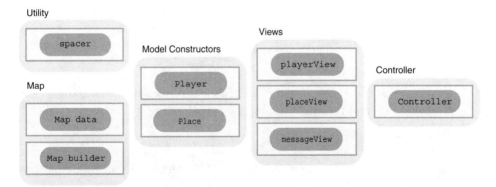

Figure 17.7   The modules that make up *The Crypt*

The promise of modules is that you can switch them easily to change the behavior of the program. It's time to make good on that promise. To build your first HTML version of *The Crypt*, follow these steps:

1 Update the player view (two lines of code)
2 Update the place view (two lines of code)
3 Create an HTML page that has `script` elements to load all of the game modules and that has placeholders for the player and place views to fill

You won't see the output until all of the pieces are in place. But to get a sense of what you're building, figure 17.8 shows your first HTML game in action. The web page output shows the current states of the player and place. You enter commands at the console.

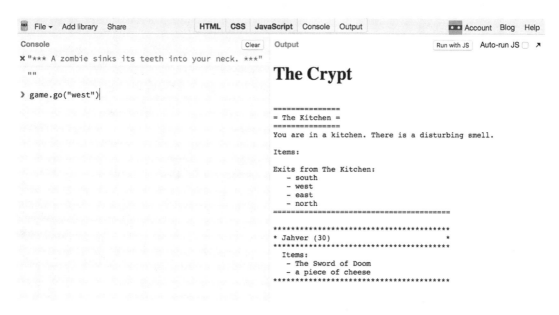

Figure 17.8 *The Crypt* with commands and messages on the Console panel and updates on the Output panel

Before looking at the updated versions of the player and place views, take time to consider the awesome power of your modular approach. The single method that displays information for each view is the `render` method. To reflect its beauty and simplicity, it gets the following section all to itself.

17.5.1 *Updating the player and place view modules—the render method*

In moving from a console application to a web application, you update the player and place views. The new versions display information by inserting text into an element on a web page rather than logging the information to the console. Those are the only changes you make (figure 17.9), and the changes themselves are small.

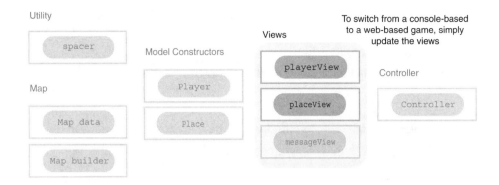

Figure 17.9   You only need to change the views to switch to a web-based version of *The Crypt*.

The views in chapter 15 use `console.log` in a single method, the `render` method. That was by design; you have a single place where changes need to be made.

The `render` method for the console-based player view looks like this:

```
function render (player) {
    console.log(getInfo(player.getData()));
};
```

The `render` method for the console-based place view looks like this:

```
function render (place) {
    console.log(getInfo(place.getData()));
};
```

Using what you've learned in this chapter about updating web page elements, the new place view's `render` method looks like this:

```
function render (place) {
    var placeDiv = document.getElementById("place");
    placeDiv.innerHTML = getInfo(place.getData());
};
```

The new player view's `render` method looks almost identical:

```
function render (place) {
    var playerDiv = document.getElementById("player");
    playerDiv.innerHTML = getInfo(player.getData());
};
```

Those really are the only changes to the JavaScript that you need. The new methods use `document.getElementById` to get references to elements on the web page. Until you create the web page in listing 17.9, those elements won't exist, so you can't test your new views. Be patient; their time will come.

17.5.2 Updating the player and place view modules—the listings

Listing 17.7 shows the new player view with its updated render method. Everything else is the same as it's been since chapter 15, so function bodies have been omitted in print. The JS Bin link is there so you can check the full listing if you want. The meaning of "use strict" is discussed after the listings for both views.

Listing 17.7 A web-based player view
(http://jsbin.com/cehexi/edit?js,console)

```
(function () {
    "use strict";

    function getNameInfo (playerData) { … }
    function getHealthInfo (playerData) { … }
    function getItemsInfo (playerData) { … }
    function getTitleInfo (playerData) { … }
    function getInfo (playerData) { … }

    function render (player) {

        var playerDiv = document.getElementById("player");

        playerDiv.innerHTML = getInfo(player.getData());

    }

    if (window.theCrypt === undefined) { window.theCrypt = {}; }
    theCrypt.playerView = { render: render };
})();
```

Update the render method to work with web page elements

Get a reference to the div element with an id of "player"

Set the content of the div to the string produced by the getInfo method

The next listing shows the new place view with its updated render method.

Listing 17.8 A web-based place view
(http://jsbin.com/cakine/edit?js,console)

```
(function () {
    "use strict";

    function getItemsInfo (placeData) { … }
    function getExitsInfo (placeData) { … }
    function getTitleInfo (placeData) { … }
    function getInfo (placeData) { … }

    function render (place) {

        var placeDiv = document.getElementById("place");

        placeDiv.innerHTML = getInfo(place.getData());

    }

    if (window.theCrypt === undefined) { window.theCrypt = {}; }
    theCrypt.placeView = { render: render };
})();
```

Update the render method to work with web page elements

Get a reference to the div element with an id of "place"

Set the content of the div to the string produced by the getInfo method

Those changes to the render methods are all you need to move the display of player and place information to the web page from the console. For now, the user continues to give commands via the console.

17.5.3 Using JavaScript's strict mode

JavaScript is in use on millions of web pages. Those pages need to continue working even as JavaScript evolves and matures. To opt into more recent ways of using the language that alert you to more errors you might have made, optimize how the language works, and prepare the way for further developments, you can run your code in *strict mode*. To enable strict mode for a function, add `"use strict"` at the top of the function.

All of your code throughout the book could have been run in strict mode, but I felt it might be distracting while learning the basics. Modules in part 3 will all be in strict mode; listing 17.8 is the first module in part 3, which is why it's being introduced at this point. Find out more at www.room51.co.uk/js/strict-mode.html.

17.5.4 Loading modules and adding placeholders in the HTML

The next listing shows the complete HTML for your first web-based version of *The Crypt*. It includes `script` tags to load all of the modules you need.

**Listing 17.9   A web-based The Crypt game (HTML)
(http://jsbin.com/zaxaje/edit?html,console,output)**

```
<!DOCTYPE html>
<html>
<head>
  <meta charset="utf-8">
  <title>The Crypt</title>          ◁─┐  Update the
</head>                                  │  title element

<body>                                      Include a div with an id of
  <h1>The Crypt</h1>                        "place" for place information

  <div id="place"></div>           ◁─┐   Include a div with an id of
                                      │   "player" for player information
  <div id="player"></div>          ◁─┘

  <!-- Modules -->                 ◁─┐  Load all of the modules
                                      │  needed to run the game
  <!-- spacer -->
  <script src="http://output.jsbin.com/juneqo.js"></script>

  <!-- Place constructor -->
  <script src="http://output.jsbin.com/vuwave.js"></script>
  <!-- Player constructor -->
  <script src="http://output.jsbin.com/nonari.js"></script>

  <!-- player view -->
  <script src="http://output.jsbin.com/cehexi.js"></script>
  <!-- place view -->
  <script src="http://output.jsbin.com/cakine.js"></script>
  <!-- message view -->
  <script src="http://output.jsbin.com/jatofe.js"></script>
```

```
<!-- map data -->
<script src="http://output.jsbin.com/hozefe.js"></script>
<!-- map builder -->
<script src="http://output.jsbin.com/paqihi.js"></script>

<!-- game controller -->
<script src="http://output.jsbin.com/yeqicu.js"></script> </body>
</html>
```

You set the title of the page using a `title` element in the `head` section. The page title isn't always visible when working in the JS Bin editing environment but is normally used by browsers to label tabs and windows showing the page and when saving the page as a bookmark or favorite. The `script` tags for loading modules are added just before the closing `body` tag. This ensures that the two `div` elements used by the program are on the page before any code tries to update them with player and place information.

Unfortunately, because your views use the `spacer` namespace to format the generated text with line breaks and spaces for the console, and web pages don't honor those line breaks and spaces, all of the player and place information runs together. Although the output isn't quite what you wanted, you can still play the game, as shown in figure 17.10.

Figure 17.10   The text output runs together but the game is playable.

17.5.5 *Adding a touch of CSS*

You have one more panel up your sleeve on JS Bin! The CSS panel is used for specifying how you want elements to look on a page: their size, color, margins, borders, and so on. With a couple of lines of CSS, you can tell the browser to honor the line breaks generated by your view modules and use a font that gives the same amount of space to each character, just like the font on the console.

The next listing shows the code to add to the CSS panel.

**Listing 17.10   A web-based The Crypt game (CSS)
(http://jsbin.com/toyahi/edit?css)**

```
div {
  white-space: pre;
  font-family: monospace;
}
```

The first rule tells the browser to preserve the white space (that is, spaces and line breaks) of text content in `div` elements. The second specifies that the browser should use a monospace font for text in `div` elements. Your page uses `div` elements for the player information and for the place information. The output on the web page is now formatted as it was on the console. Refer to figure 17.8 to see the nicely formatted output.

17.5.6 *Playing the game*

You still issue game instructions via the console as methods of `game`. The methods available are `get`, `go`, and `use`. Run the program at http://jsbin.com/toyahi/edit?console,output and have a go at playing the game, issuing commands on the console like this:

```
> game.get()
> game.go("south")
> game.use("a rusty key", "north")
```

Using line breaks and spaces to format the output isn't the best approach. It would be better to use appropriate HTML tags (for headings, paragraphs, and lists) to convey the structure of the different pieces of information in the output. You'll look at better ways of formatting the player and place information using HTML in chapter 19 when you investigate templates.

The current version of *The Crypt* is a bit of a hybrid. Although you make use of HTML to display some information, you still force players to enter commands on the console. In chapter 18 you'll discover how to use simple form elements like buttons, drop-down lists, and text boxes to let players interact with the game directly on the web page. To prepare the way for that fully HTML-based version, you finish this chapter by repeating the changes you made to the place and player views but this time for the message view.

17.5.7 *Preparing the message view*

In order to make the UI 100% web page based, you need to update the message view so that it displays messages on the web page rather than on the console. The following listing shows the new module code.

**Listing 17.11   A web-based message view
(http://jsbin.com/nocosej/edit?js,console)**

```
(function () {
    "use strict";
```

```
    function getMessageInfo (message) {
        return "*** " + message + " ***";
    }

    function render (message) {
        var messageDiv = document.getElementById("messages");     Display the message
        messageDiv.innerHTML = getMessageInfo(message);           on the page
    }

    function clear () {                                            Define a method to
        var messageDiv = document.getElementById("messages");     clear any displayed
        messageDiv.innerHTML = "";                                messages
    }

    if (window.theCrypt === undefined) {
        window.theCrypt = {};
    }

    theCrypt.messageView = {
        render: render,              Include the clear
        clear: clear          ◁───┤  method in the
    };                               interface
})();
```

The view will need an element with an id of messages. It also adds a clear method for removing messages from the page.

17.6 Summary

- Annotate text with HTML to specify the role the text plays in the structure of a document. For example, the text is a heading, a list item, or a paragraph.

- Precede an HTML document with its document type:

  ```
  <!DOCTYPE html>
  ```

- Use html tags to wrap the entire document:

  ```
  <html> … </html>
  ```

- The head element of a document contains information about the document, for example, its title and character encoding:

  ```
  <head>
      <meta charset="utf-8">
      <title>My Web Page</title>
  </head>
  ```

- The body element of a document contains the content to be displayed on the web page:

  ```
  <body> … </body>
  ```

- Use tags appropriate to the content. Among many more tags, there are headings `<h1>`, `<h2>`, … , `<h6>`; paragraphs `<p>`; list items `<li>`; and lists `<ol>` and `<ul>`.

- Add `id` attributes to opening tags to uniquely identify elements on the page.

```
<p id="message"></p>
```

- From JavaScript, get a reference to an HTML element by using the `document.getElementById` method:

```
var para = document.getElementById("message");
```

- Change the content of an element by setting its `innerHTML` property:

```
para.innerHTML = "New text for the paragraph.";
```

Controls: getting user input

We love buttons! Whether we're buying books on Amazon, liking a tweet, or sending that late-night drunken email, we find it hard to resist clicking those alluring, colorful buttons. Well, it's time for you to issue your own calls to action and start adding buttons to your pages. And while you're at it, you need to make space for text boxes and drop-down lists too.

In chapter 17 you made the jump to HTML and used JavaScript to add content to a web page. To get user input, however, you stuck with the console. In these days of flashy web apps you want the users to interact solely via the web page; they shouldn't have to know JavaScript and go searching for the console to use the programs you write for them.

This chapter introduces the HTML input, select, and button elements, letting users type information and commands into a text box, choose from a drop-down list, and initiate actions by clicking buttons. You see how to set up functions that are automatically called when a button is clicked.

It's fun to click buttons, so let's start with those. *Click!*

18.1 Working with buttons

You're building a My Movie Ratings website (see chapter 17) and have been testing random greetings when visitors arrive at the site. You want to give visitors the ability to check out more greetings without reloading the whole page. You decide to add a button to your test page that updates the display with a random greeting (figure 18.1).

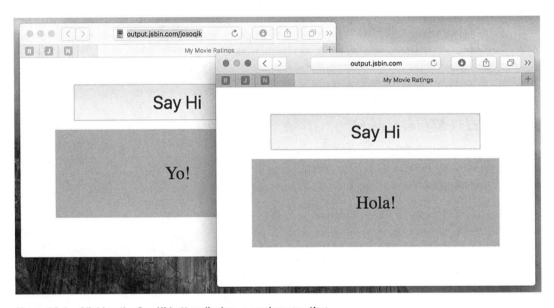

Figure 18.1 Clicking the Say Hi button displays a random greeting.

Clicking the Say Hi button displays the greeting. But how? How can you make your JavaScript program respond to a user clicking the button? You need to do three things:

1 Add a `button` HTML element to the page
2 Write a function to update the greeting
3 Get the button to call the function when it's clicked

18.1.1 Adding a button to a page

Well, for starters, you need a button on the page. HTML includes a `button` element. Put the button text between the tags (figure 18.2):

```
<button>Button 1</button>
```

```
HTML ▾
1 <button>Button 1</button>
2 <button>Button 2</button>
3 <button>Button 3</button>|
```

Output

| Button 1 | Button 2 | Button 3 |

Figure 18.2   The HTML for three buttons and the output generated

To work with the button in JavaScript, you give it a unique `id` attribute in HTML.

```
<button id="btnGreeting">Say Hi</button>
```

The following listing shows the key HTML for the My Movie Ratings test page. The paragraph with `id` of `"greeting"` is where you'll insert the random greeting later.

> **Listing 18.1   My Movie Ratings greetings with button (HTML)**
> **(http://jsbin.com/josoqik/edit?html,output)**

```
<button id="btnGreeting">Say Hi</button>

<p id="greeting">Welcome!</p>
```

The output was shown in figure 18.1. Feel free to take a peek at the CSS panel on JS Bin if you're interested in how the styling is applied.

18.1.2   Writing functions to update the greeting

In chapter 17 you wrote two functions, `getGreeting` and `updateGreeting`, that chose a random welcome message and updated the display.

```
function getGreeting () {
    // Return random greeting
};
function updateGreeting () {
    para.innerHTML = getGreeting();
};
var para = document.getElementById("greeting");
updateGreeting();
```

The `updateGreeting` function updates the display by setting the `innerHTML` property of the paragraph element, `para`.

So you have your button and paragraph in place in the HTML and you have a function to update the paragraph. Now you want the button to call the `updateGreeting` function when a user clicks it.

18.1.3   Listening for clicks

Click—"Wassup!" … *Click*—"Hola!" … *Click*—"Ay up me duck!"

"Dear button, please call my `updateGreeting` function whenever someone clicks you," is the instruction you want to send. To give the button an instruction like that, you need a reference to the button in JavaScript.

```
var btn = document.getElementById("btnGreeting");
```

Once you have a reference to the button, `btn`, you can tell the button to call a function whenever the button is clicked:

```
btn.addEventListener("click", updateGreeting);
```

The `addEventListener` method tells the button (or whichever element it's called from) to call a specified function whenever a specified *event* occurs—in this case whenever the button is clicked. It's like the `updateGreeting` function is waiting, or *listening*, for the button to be clicked.

Listing 18.2 shows the final listing for your random greetings test page. It's the same as the listing from chapter 17 but with the two lines of button code added. The code is wrapped in an immediately invoked function expression to avoid polluting the global namespace. It also includes a `use strict` statement to instruct the browser to use strict mode (see section 17.5.3).

**Listing 18.2   My Movie Ratings greetings with button
(http://jsbin.com/josoqik/edit?js,output)**

```
(function () {
  "use strict";

  function getGreeting () {
    var hellos = [ "Nanu nanu!", "Wassup!", "Yo!", "Hello movie lover!",
      "Ay up me duck!", "Hola!" ];

    var index = Math.floor(Math.random() * hellos.length);

    return hellos[index];
  };

  function updateGreeting () {
    para.innerHTML = getGreeting();
  };

  var btn = document.getElementById("btnGreeting");      ⟵┘ Get a reference
  var para = document.getElementById("greeting");            to the button

  btn.addEventListener("click", updateGreeting);      ⟵┐ Tell the button to call
                                                         the updateGreeting
  updateGreeting();                                       function whenever
                                                           it's clicked
})();
```

Take a look back at chapter 12 for a reminder of how to use `Math.floor` and `Math.random` to generate a random index for an array.

A marvelous menagerie of events

Clicks aren't the only events that functions can listen out for; mouse moves, page scrolling, keys on the keyboard being pressed, and images loading are some others, and taps, flicks, force presses, and shakes are some new events appearing for touch-enabled and mobile devices.

You'll keep it simple and stick with button clicks for now, but if you're interested in the marvelous menagerie of possible events, check out the event reference on the Mozilla Developer Network at https://developer.mozilla.org/en-US/docs/Web/Events.

18.2 Using a select element to choose an option

The My Movie Ratings website lets users rate movies. They choose a rating from a drop-down menu and click the Rate button. The page then shows a message with their rating (figure 18.3).

Figure 18.3 Clicking the Rate button pops up a message with your rating.

To implement the rating system, you need to do four things:

1 Add a `select` HTML element to the page with `option` elements for each rating
2 Add a `button` HTML element to the page with "Rate" as its text
3 Write a function to pop up the message with the rating
4 Tell the button to call the function when clicked

18.2.1 *Adding a select element to the page*

Web browsers render the select element as a drop-down list. You use option elements to specify the choices in the list (figure 18.4).

```
<select id="movies">
    <option>Inside Out</option>
    <option>Tomorrowland</option>
    <option>The Wizard of Oz</option>
</select>
```

Test it out on JS Bin. Create a new bin with the HTML, Console, and Output panels open. Replace the contents of the HTML panel with the select code in the previous snippet. You should see the drop-down list appear on the Output panel. At the console prompt, enter these commands:

```
> var dd = document.getElementById("movies")
  undefined
> dd.value
  Inside Out
```

Choose a different film from the drop-down list on the Output panel. Then use Java-Script to check its new value:

```
> dd.value
  The Wizard of Oz
```

You can update the drop-down's selected value from JavaScript too:

```
> dd.value = "Tomorrowland"
  Tomorrowland
```

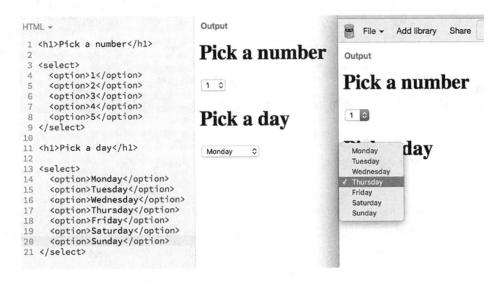

Figure 18.4   Two select elements in HTML, displayed on a web page and with a selection in progress

The value set in JavaScript is selected on the Output panel.

Figure 18.4 shows the HTML for two `select` elements and how they're rendered on a web page.

The next listing shows the HTML for the body of the My Movie Ratings main page, with a `select` element and a `button` to rate the film shown.

Listing 18.3 My Movie Ratings with a drop-down list (HTML)
(http://jsbin.com/hikuzi/edit?html,output)

```html
<h1>My Movie Ratings</h1>
<p>Brief info about my favorite movies.</p>

<h2>Movies</h2>

<div id="movieBox">

  <h3 id="movie">Inside Out</h3>
  <p>An emotional adventure inside the head of a young girl.</p>

  <h4>Actors</h4>
  <ul>
    <li>Amy Poehler</li>
    <li>Bill Hader</li>
  </ul>

  <h4>Directors</h4>
  <ul>
    <li>Pete Doctor</li>
    <li>Ronnie del Carmen</li>
  </ul>

  <div class="controls">

    <select id="rating">
      <option>1</option>
      <option>2</option>
      <option selected>3</option>
      <option>4</option>
      <option>5</option>
    </select>

    <button id="rate">Rate</button>

  </div>
</div>
```

Add a drop-down list by using a select element

Add choices to the list with option elements

Specify which choice is initially selected

Add a button element

Notice that you can add an attribute of `selected` to have that option selected when the drop-down list is shown on the web page.

18.2.2 *A function to rate movies and a button to call it*

To rate a movie, you need a function that gets the user's choice from the drop-down list, gets the value of the selected option in the `select` element, and pops up a message that includes that value, shown in listing 18.4.

Listing 18.4   My Movie Ratings with a drop-down list
(http://jsbin.com/hikuzi/edit?js,output)

```
(function () {
  "use strict";

  var rateButton = document.getElementById("rate");          Collect references
  var ratingList = document.getElementById("rating");         to the elements
  var movie = document.getElementById("movie");               you're using

  function rateMovie () {
                                                             Get the selected option
    var rating = ratingList.value;                ⊲⎤        from the drop-down

    var movieTitle = movie.innerHTML;              ⊲—  Get the title of the movie

    alert("You gave " +                                      Use the alert function to
      movieTitle + " " + rating + " stars!");                pop up a message

    // Save the rating to the database
  }

  rateButton.addEventListener("click", rateMovie);   ⊲⎤    Tell the button to call
                                                             the rateMovie function
})();                                                        when clicked
```

The `value` property of the drop-down list gives you the user's rating. You call the
`alert` function, provided by the browser, to display the rating in a pop-up dialog box.
Having wrapped the code in a function, `rateMovie`, you use `addEventListener` to tell
the Rate button to call `rateMovie` whenever it's clicked.

Your users can choose a rating from a list. But what if you want to give them more
freedom to express themselves?

18.3   Reading user input with text boxes

Congratulations, the My Movie Ratings site now lets users rate movies! Your success
gets you thinking—what about comments? Why not get users to add a brief comment
with their ratings? Figure 18.5 shows the site with two comments added and a third
in progress.

Users type their comment into the text box, pick a rating from the drop-down list,
and click the Rate button. Rather than popping up a message, you now add their comment and rating to the comments section for the movie. To add comments to the site,
you need to do five things:

1 Add a text box to the page
2 Add an unordered list to the HTML as a place for comments to go
3 Get a reference to the text box in JavaScript and access its value
4 Get a reference to the comments list in JavaScript
5 Update the `rateMovie` function to append a comment to the comments list

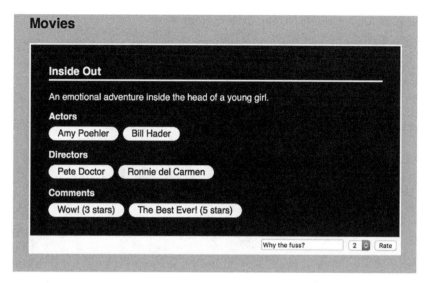

Figure 18.5　The movie has a text box to add comments and a section to display them.

18.3.1　*Adding a text box to the page*

To add a text box to the page, you use an `input` HTML element with its `type` attribute set to `"text"`. Include an `id` attribute to reference the element from JavaScript.

```
<input type="text" id="txtComment" />
```

The `input` element displays form controls on a web page. It doesn't wrap any other content so is written as a *self-closing* tag. There's no opening and closing tag pair. Notice the forward slash at the end of the tag; it shows you that this tag doesn't need a closing tag. The text box goes in the `"controls"` div along with the ratings drop-down list and the Rate button.

```
<div class="controls">

    <input type="text" id="txtComment" />

    <select id="rating"> <!-- options for ratings --> </select>
    <button id="rate">Rate</button>

</div>
```

The `input` element with a `type` attribute set to `"text"` is displayed as a text box on the page. Other common `type` attributes for input elements include `password`, `submit`, `checkbox`, and `radio`. Browser makers such as Microsoft, Apple, Google, Mozilla, and Opera are working to improve support for new types like color pickers, date pickers, and sliders. To find out more about types of input elements, you can visit the Mozilla Developer Network at https://developer.mozilla.org/en/docs/Web/HTML/Element/Input.

18.3.2   Adding an unordered list to display the comments

You use a `ul` element for the list of comments, preceding it by a heading. You give the list an `id` attribute so you can add list items using JavaScript.

```
<h4>Comments</h4>
<ul id="comments"></ul>
```

You add the comments list after the Actors and Directors lists.

18.3.3   Getting references to the new elements

In order to read comments typed into the text box and to add list items to the list of comments, you need to get a reference to the two elements in your JavaScript code.

```
var commentsList = document.getElementById("comments");  // The list
var commentBox = document.getElementById("txtComment");  // The text box
```

The text entered by the user in the text box is accessed via its `value` property. To see the `value` property in action, you can access and update it at the console. Visit the My Movie Ratings page at http://jsbin.com/nevaxit/edit?console,output, type "Great Movie!" into the text box, and then type these commands at the console prompt:

```
> var txt = document.getElementById("txtComment")
  undefined
> txt.value
  Great Movie!
> txt.value = "Rubbish!"
  Rubbish!
```

The last command will update the contents of the text box on the web page.

18.3.4   Updating the rateMovie function

The next listing shows all of the assembled pieces. The comment from the text box and the rating from the drop-down list are appended as a list item to the existing list of comments.

> ### Listing 18.5   Movies, comments, and a random greeting
> (http://jsbin.com/nevaxit/edit?js,output)

```
(function () {
  "use strict";

  function getById (id) {                          Define a function with
      return document.getElementById(id);          a shorter name to get
  }                                                 elements by id

  var rateButton = getById("rate");
  var ratingList = getById("rating");
  var movie = getById("movie");

  var commentsList = getById("comments");          Get references to the
  var commentBox = getById("txtComment");          elements used for comments
```

```
function rateMovie () {
    var rating = ratingList.value;
    var movieTitle = movie.innerHTML;

    var comments = commentsList.innerHTML;

    var comment = commentBox.value;

    comments += "<li>" + comment + " (" + rating +
        " stars)</li>";

    commentsList.innerHTML = comments;

    commentBox.value = "";
}

rateButton.addEventListener("click", rateMovie);

/* Random greeting code - see listing 18.2 */

})();
```

Get the current list items in the comments list

Read the text in the text box

Append a new comment and rating using the += operator

Update the comments list

Remove the comment from the text box

Tell the button to call rateMovie when it's clicked

In the listing, you need to get references to five HTML elements. Rather than typing out document.getElementById(id) each time, you create a function that does the same job but with a shorter name, getById.

Listing 18.6 shows the updated HTML including the text box, comments list, and a span element for your random greetings. A span wraps text *inline*, within a paragraph, for example, and lets you describe the purpose of the text it wraps, in this case with an id of "greeting", style it differently (change the color, make it bold, change its size), and access it via JavaScript (to add a random greeting, for example).

The contents of the body element are shown here, and some items have been omitted or compressed because they're unchanged from listing 18.3. Everything is on JS Bin.

Listing 18.6 Movies, comments, and a random greeting (HTML) (http://jsbin.com/nevaxit/edit?html,output)

```
<h1>My Movie Ratings</h1>

<p>Brief info about my favorite movies.
  <span id="greeting">Welcome!</span></p>

<h2>Movies</h2>

<div id="movieBox">
  <h3 id="movie">Inside Out</h3>
  <p>An emotional adventure inside the head of a young girl.</p>

  <h4>Actors</h4><ul> <!-- actors --> </ul>
  <h4>Directors</h4><ul> <!-- directors --> </ul>

  <h4>Comments</h4>
  <ul id="comments"></ul>
```

Include a span for random greetings

Add an unordered list to display comments and ratings

```
<div class="controls">
  <input type="text" id="txtComment" />        ◁─┐   Add a text box for users
                                                  │   to enter comments
  <select id="rating">
    <!-- options for ratings -->
  </select>
  <button id="rate">Rate</button>
</div>
</div>
```

Try out the web page at http://output.jsbin.com/nevaxit. Add some comments and ratings and add them to the list. And check out the random greetings.

18.3.5　*Styling the examples with CSS*

Many of the examples in part 3 of *Get Programming with JavaScript* have had colors, fonts, margins, borders, and so on set with CSS rules on the CSS panel. Although the book doesn't teach CSS directly, please have a look at the CSS rules. Taken one at a time, most of them are easy to follow. Try changing some values or deleting some or all of the rules. Although they may make the page look nicer, all examples should work just fine without them.

18.4　*The Crypt—player commands via a text box*

Players exploring *The Crypt* have been entering their get, go, and use commands at the console prompt. You can now move user input to the game's web page with commands entered via a text box, as shown in figure 18.6.

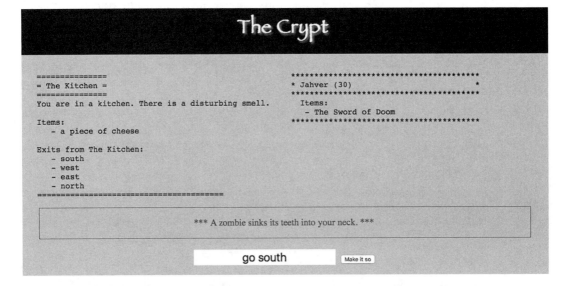

Figure 18.6　Commands are now entered into a text box at the bottom of the page.

In order to create a web-based set of user controls, you need to do three things:

1   Add a text box and button to the page.
2   Write a function to convert the text in the text box into game commands.
3   Write a function to be called when the button is clicked.

You could update the code in the controller module to include the two new functions. But the controller module works nicely already, setting up the game and working with the models and views for players, places, and messages (see chapter 16). A better plan is to add a separate module that deals with the commands entered into the text box, calling on the existing controller to execute the get, go, and use methods as necessary. Figure 18.7 shows the modules used by *The Crypt*, including the new *Commands* module.

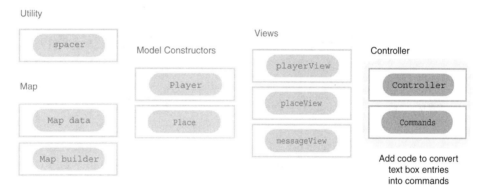

Figure 18.7   Modules for *The Crypt*, including a Commands module to execute commands via a text box

Get started by adding a text box and button to the HTML for the page.

18.4.1 *Adding controls to the page*

You need a way for users to enter the command string and submit it. The following listing shows the HTML added to your *The Crypt* web page for the text box and button. The player, place, and messages div elements are initially empty, which is why they can't be seen on the Output panel.

**Listing 18.7   Adding controls to *The Crypt* (HTML)
(http://jsbin.com/rijage/edit?html,output)**

```
<h1>The Crypt</h1>

<div id="place"></div>
<div id="player"></div>
<div id="messages"></div>
```

```
<div id="controls">
  <input type="text" id="txtCommand">          Add a text box with an
  <button id="btnCommand">Make it so</button>   id of txtCommand
</div>

<!-- Include all of the modules -->                Add a button with an
                                                    id of btnCommand
```

Your controls, the text box and button, are now on the page and they have id attributes set so they can be accessed using JavaScript.

18.4.2 Mapping text box entries to game commands

Table 18.1 shows how the commands entered into the text box will match up with the methods from the controller module created in chapter 16.

Table 18.1 Comparing text box commands with methods from the controller module

Text box command	Controller method
get	game.get()
go north	game.go("north")
use a rusty key north	game.use("a rusty key", "north")

As you can see, the text box commands should make it easier for users to play the game. So how do you translate the text box input into commands that the controller understands?

18.4.3 Issuing orders with split, join, pop, and shift

The user will type a command into a text box. You need to convert that command into an action that the program will take, as shown in table 18.1. To call the correct controller method (get, go, or use) based on the command entered in the text box, you first represent the command by a JavaScript object. The object will have a type property that matches the controller method that you need to call. Table 18.2 shows the commands and the command objects that they should generate.

Table 18.2 Command objects

Text box command	Command object

get	{
	    type: "get"
	}

go north	{
	    type: "go",
	    direction: "north"
	}

Table 18.2   Command objects

Text box command	Command object
`use a rusty key north`	```{ type: "use", item: "a rusty key", direction: "north" }```

The first word of each text box command gives you the `type` of the command object. To get at the separate words of the command, you convert the string into an array of words using `split`.

```
var commandWords = commandString.split(" ");
```

For example, `"get a rusty key"` becomes `["get", "a", "rusty", "key"]`. The `shift` array method removes and returns the first element in an array. That's perfect for grabbing the command `type` for your command object.

```
var commandWords = commandString.split(" ");
var command = {
    type: commandWords.shift();
};
```

The command word is no longer in the array. `["get", "a", "rusty", "key"]` becomes `["a", "rusty", "key"]`.

For `go` and `use`, you grab the `direction`, the last element in the `commandWords` array, by using the `pop` array method.

```
command.direction = commandString.pop();
```

If there are any elements left in the `commandWords` array, you join them back together to form the name of an item.

```
command.item = commandWords.join(" ");
```

For example, `["a", "rusty", "key"]` is joined to become `"a rusty key"`.

The next listing shows a function that converts a command string into a command object using the ideas just discussed.

Listing 18.8   Converting a command string into a command object
(http://jsbin.com/repebe/edit?js,console)

```
function parseCommand (commandString) {

    var commandWords = commandString.split(" ");
```
Split the command string into
an array of separate words

```
var command = {
  type: commandWords.shift();
};

if (command.type === "go" || command.type === "use") {
  command.direction = commandWords.pop();
}

command.item = commandWords.join(" ");

return command;
};
```

Create an object and assign it to the command variable

Check if the type is go OR use

Remove the first word in the array and assign it to the type property

Remove the last word in the array and assign it to the direction property

Join any remaining words to form the name of an item

With the command object in hand you can now call the matching method of the game controller. To organize the different possible command types, use a control structure tailor made for deciding between many options: the `switch` block.

18.4.4 Deciding between options with switch

You want to take different actions depending on which command was issued. You could use a series of if-else blocks. But a `switch` block is an alternative that some programmers feel is neater. `switch` lets you define a series of code blocks and execute certain blocks depending on the value of a variable or property. Here's an example comparing the two approaches, using `command.type` as the `switch` variable:

```
switch (command.type) {

  case "get":                      if (command.type === "get") {
    game.get();                        game.get();
    break;                         }

  case "go":                       else if (command.type === "go") {
    game.go(command.direction);        game.go(command.direction);
    break;                         }

  case "use":                      else if (command.type === "use") {
    game.use(command.item,             game.use(command.item,
      command.direction);                command.direction);
    break;                         }

  default:                         else {
    game.renderMessage(                game.renderMessage(
      "I can't do that");              "I can't do that");
}                                  }
```

If the value of `command.type` is "get", then the code in the first `case` block is executed. If the value of `command.type` is "go", then the code in the second `case` is executed. Without the `break` statement, the `switch` block would continue to execute all of the `case` blocks after the first one matched. You can include a `default` case with code to be executed if no other conditions are matched.

There's not much difference between the two approaches; it's a bit easier to read the condition in the `switch` block, but you have the extra `break` statements. Once again, it comes down to personal preference: if you think the `switch` block is neater, use it; just don't forget the `break` statements.

Listing 18.9 shows the `switch` block for *The Crypt* in context, as part of a `doAction` function.

18.4.5 Making it so—listening for button clicks

The final piece of the UI puzzle is to link the JavaScript to the HTML. You need the button to call the `doAction` function from listing 18.9 whenever it's clicked:

```
var commandButton = document.getElementById("btnCommand");

commandButton.addEventListener("click", doAction);
```

The `doAction` function retrieves the text from the text box:

```
var txtCommand = document.getElementById("txtCommand");
var commandString = txtCommand.value;
```

The `doAction` function then parses the command string to create a command object. It uses a `switch` block to call the matching controller method. Listing 18.9 shows how the pieces fit together for the command module. It uses the `parseCommand` function from listing 18.8, which can be seen on JS Bin. Note that the JS Bin listing is for reference; the module won't run in isolation on JS Bin but will throw an error.

Listing 18.9   The command module
(http://jsbin.com/qedubi/edit?js,console)

```
(function () {
  "use strict";

  function parseCommand (commandString) { /* listing 18.8 */ }

  function doAction = () {

    var txtCommand = document.getElementById("txtCommand");      Assign the text from
    var commandString = txtCommand.value;                        the text box to the
                                                                 commandString
                                                                 variable

    var command = parseCommand(commandString);          Parse the text and assign the
                                                         command object created to
                                                         the command variable

    theCrypt.messageView.clear();                    Clear old messages
                                                     from the message view
    switch (command.type) {
      case "get":
        game.get();
        break;

      case "go":
        game.go(command.direction);
        break;
```

```
      case "use":
        game.use(command.item, command.direction);
        break;

      default:
        theCrypt.messageView.render("I don't know how to do that");
    }

    txtCommand.value = "";                    Clear the text box and give it the
    txtCommand.focus();                       focus, ready for the next command
  }

  var commandButton =                         Get a reference to the
    document.getElementById("btnCommand");    button on the page

  commandButton.addEventListener("click", doAction);     Tell the button to call
})();                                                     the doAction function
                                                         whenever it's clicked
```

You like to smooth the path for the players, so, after the `switch` block, you clear the user's command from the text box by setting its `value` property to an empty string. And because you *really* care, you put the cursor in the text box, ready for their next command, by calling the text box's `focus` method. Just before the `switch` block, you also use the message view's `clear` method, added at the end of chapter 17, to clean up any old messages.

The code for the command module is wrapped inside an immediately invoked function expression. As soon as the script is loaded by the web page, it will be executed and the event listener will be added to the button element.

18.4.6 *Enter The Crypt*

Rather than changing the existing, working code of the Controller module, you created a new module, the Commands module, that parses a player's commands and calls the controller's public methods, `get`, `go`, and `use`. That's neat! The controller is independent of the player interface; it's the same one that worked in the console-based game and it will work with new interfaces—could you add a button to get items in a room?

Figure 18.8 shows a game of *The Crypt* in progress with a message being displayed to a player via the message view.

Listing 18.7 included the HTML for the latest version of the game but you need to change the message view `script` element and add one for the new Commands module:

```
<!-- message view -->
<script src="http://output.jsbin.com/nocosej.js"></script>

<!-- Web Page Controls -->
<script src="http://output.jsbin.com/qedubi.js"></script>
```

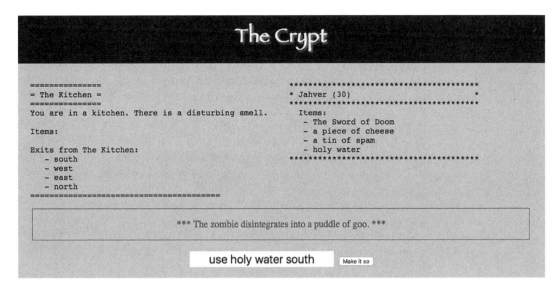

Figure 18.8 *The Crypt* in progress showing a message to the player

Play the game at http://output.jsbin.com/depijo, and see the HTML and JavaScript at http://jsbin.com/depijo/edit?html,javascript. Be careful not to step in the zombie!

18.5 Summary

- To use controls like buttons, drop-down lists, and text boxes, you need an HTML element for the control, an id attribute on the element, and a reference to the element in JavaScript. You can then access the value properties of text boxes or drop-down lists and specify a function to call when a button is clicked.

- Use a button element to display a button on the page. Include the text to be shown on the button between the opening and closing tags:

```
<button>Click Me!</button>
```

- Include an id attribute in the opening tag so that the button can be accessed from JavaScript code:

```
<button id="messageButton">Click Me!</button>
```

- Use the button's id to get a reference to the button in JavaScript:

```
var btn = document.getElementById("messageButton");
```

- Define a function that can be called when the button is clicked:

```
var showMessage = function () {
    var messageDiv = document.getElementById("message");
    messageDiv.innerHTML = "You clicked the button!";
};
```

- Add an event listener to the button to call a function when the button is clicked:

```
btn.addEventListener("click", showMessage);
```

- Use an input element with its type attribute set to text to display a text box on the page. input elements don't have closing tags:

```
<input type="text" id="userMessage" />
```

- Get or set the text in a text box by using its value property:

```
var txtBox = document.getElementById("userMessage");
var message = txtBox.value;
```

- Use a select element with option elements to display a drop-down list:

```
<select>
    <option>Choice 1</option>
    <option>Choice 2</option>
    <option>Choice 3</option>
</select>
```

- Execute code depending on the value of a variable or property by using a switch block:

```
switch (command.type) {
    case "go":
        // Execute code when command.type === "go"
        break;

    case "get":
        // Execute code when command.type === "get"
        break;

    default:
        // Execute code if no other cases match
}
```

Templates: filling placeholders with data

You want your websites to be easy to navigate and a pleasure to use. Their designs should consider what content to include on each page, its accessibility and usability, the look and feel, and the overall user experience. Members of your team, building and maintaining a site, will have different strengths; even as a team of one, it makes sense to focus on different aspects of a site at different times.

Get Programming with JavaScript has favored a modular approach to developing applications, and you've seen that although there may be more pieces to manage, the management of each piece is simpler, more flexible, and more focused. But in moving from pure JavaScript in part 2 to JavaScript and HTML in part 3, there has been an unwelcome crossing of the streams. You now have views that mix data and JavaScript with HTML to produce their output (see chapter 17—or better yet, read on):

```
var html = "<h3>" + movie.title + "</h3>";
html += "<p>" + movie.summary + "</p>";
```

This chapter shows you how to untangle the HTML from the data and the JavaScript by using templates. The designers on your team can focus on their HTML and avoid the tricky JavaScript syntax. And, as ever with a modular approach, isolating the pieces improves flexibility, swapability, and maintainability. Don't cross the streams!

19.1   Building a news page—breaking news

In chapters 14, 15, and 16 you worked on a fitness app that let users log their sessions of exercise; you're part of a team of developers working on the app for different devices and platforms. Well, the fitness app is gaining a lot of attention; early reports from testers are positive and there's quite a buzz on social media. You decide to create a news page for the team, to keep developers, testers, and other interested parties up to date with the work you're doing.

Figure 19.1 shows the news page with two news items. All team members contribute to the news page, adding their items to a central content management system (CMS). Someone else manages the CMS and provides you with the news items as JavaScript data. Your job is to turn the data into HTML for the news page.

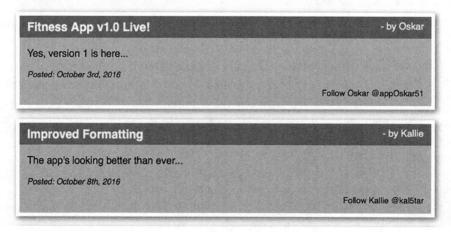

Figure 19.1   Fitness App News with two news items

19.1.1 *Comparing the news item data and HTML*

The team members are keen and update the news on the content management system regularly. The CMS provides you with data in this form:

```
var posts = [
    {
      title: "Fitness App v1.0 Live!",
      body: "Yes, version 1 is here...",
      posted: "October 3rd, 2016",
      author: "Oskar",
      social: "@appOskar51"
    },
    {
      title: "Improved Formatting",
      body: "The app's looking better than ever...",
      posted: "October 8th, 2016",
      author: "Kallie",
      social: "@kal5tar"
    }
];
```

A designer on the team writes the HTML for a single news item:

```
<div class="newsItem">
    <h3>Fitness App v1.0 Live!<span> - by Oskar</span></h3>
    <p>Yes, version 1 is here...</p>
    <p class="posted"><em>Posted: October 3rd, 2016</em></p>
    <p class="follow">Follow Oskar @appOskar51</p>
</div>
```

Each item is wrapped in a `div` element and is made up of a heading and three paragraphs. The heading includes a `span` element for the author of the post. (You use the span to style the author differently from the rest of the heading with CSS.) How do you construct the finished HTML news item from the data?

19.1.2 *Constructing the HTML by string concatenation*

Up to this point, you've been constructing strings for display piece by piece by using string concatenation. For a news item you do something like this:

```
var item = '<div class="newsItem"><h3>' + post.title;
item += '<span> - ' + post.author + '</span></h3>';
item += '<p>' + post.body + '</p>';
item += '<p class="posted"><em>Posted: ' + post.posted + '</em></p>';
item += '<p class="follow">Follow ' + post.author + ' ';
item += post.social + '</p></div>';
```

A big drawback to this approach is the way it mixes up JavaScript and data with HTML. There are some fantastic designers on your team who know HTML inside out but who are not so confident with JavaScript. They'll happily piece together the structure of a news item with HTML, but all the `var` and `+=` and dot notation are a mystery.

And even if they were okay with JavaScript, updating the code isn't exactly a walk in the park; I'm looking at you, quotation marks! There is a better way: let the HTML experts stick to what they know best.

19.1.3 Designing with HTML templates

You want the designers to come up with some elegant, well-structured HTML for a generic news item, and you'll then fill it with the latest data. You want them to provide you with a *template* for a news item.

```html
<div class="newsItem">
    <h3>{{title}}<span> - {{author}}</span></h3>
    <p>{{body}}</p>
    <p class="posted"><em>Posted: {{posted}}</em></p>
    <p class="follow">Follow {{author}} {{social}}</p>
</div>
```

That's much neater than all that string concatenation, right? There's no potential confusion with single and double quotation marks, and the different *fields* of the data (title, body, author, posted, social) are clearly identified as *placeholders* with double curly braces.

But if the template is included with the HTML, won't it appear on the web page? Not if you wrap it in `script` tags.

19.1.4 Using script tags for templates

The HTML templates are kept with the rest of the HTML for a web page, placed within `script` tags. Use a nonstandard `type` attribute for the `script` element, and then when the browser is loading the page it won't recognize the `type` and will ignore the template. The content of the `script` element won't appear as part of the output—the visible web page—and won't be run as JavaScript either.

```html
<script type="text/template" id="newsItemTemplate">
    <div class="newsItem">
        <h3>{{title}}<span> - {{author}}</span></h3>
        <p>{{body}}</p>
        <p class="posted"><em>Posted: {{posted}}</em></p>
        <p class="follow">Follow {{author}} {{social}}</p>
    </div>
</script>
```

If the `script` element has a `type` of `"text/javascript"` or if the `type` is missing, the browser will try to execute its contents as JavaScript code. But with a `type` of `"text/template"`, the browser simply passes over the contents.

Although the browser will ignore the template when rendering the page, you can still access it from JavaScript via its `id` attribute.

```js
var templateScript = document.getElementById("newsItemTemplate");
var templateString = templateScript.innerHTML;
```

The first listing shows the contents of the body element for your news page. There's a heading, a div for the news items, and your template wrapped in a script tag.

Listing 19.1   Fitness App News (HTML)
(http://jsbin.com/viyuyo/edit?html,output)

```
<h1>Fitness App News</h1>

<div id="news"></news>                                    Include a div in which to
                                                           place the news items

<script type="text/template" id="newsItemTemplate">
  <div class="newsItem">
    <h3>{{title}}<span> - by {{author}}</span></h3>      Use a script
    <p>{{body}}</p>                                       element to wrap
    <p class="posted"><em>Posted: {{posted}}</em></p>     the news item
    <p class="follow">Follow {{author}} {{social}}</p>    template
  </div>
</script>
```

You only need to find a way to replace the placeholders with the actual data, and you'll have news items ready for publication. You need to learn how to replace one string, a placeholder, with another, some data.

19.2   Replacing one string with another

To switch one string for another, you use the replace string method, passing the string to find as the first argument and the string with which to replace it as the second. The method returns a new string. The following listing shows how to replace the string "{{title}}" with the string "Fitness App v1.0 Live!". It produces the following output on the console:

```
> <h3>{{title}}</h3>
> <h3>Fitness App v1.0 Live!</h3>
```

Listing 19.2   Replacing one string with another
(http://jsbin.com/jeyohu/edit?js,console)

```
var before = "<h3>{{title}}</h3>";
                                                           Look for the first
var after = before.replace(                                string and replace
            "{{title}}", "Fitness App v1.0 Live!");        it with the second

console.log(before);            The original string
console.log(after);             is not changed
```

The replace method searches the string to which it is attached, returning a new string.

```
before.replace(string1, string2);
```

This snippet searches the string stored in the variable before.

19.2.1 *Chaining calls to replace*

The replace method acts on strings. It also returns a string. This means replace can be called on its own return value, allowing you to chain calls like this:

```
template
    .replace("{{title}}", "Fitness App v1.0 Live!")
    .replace("{{author}}", "Oskar");
```

If template is the string "<h3>{{title}}<span> - by {{author}}</span></h3>", then the previous snippet works through the following steps. First, the {{title}} placeholder is replaced:

```
"<h3>{{title}}<span> - by {{author}}</span></h3>"
    .replace("{{title}}", "Fitness App v1.0 Live!")
    .replace("{{author}}", "Oskar");
```

Then the {{author}} placeholder is replaced:

```
"<h3>Fitness App v1.0 Live!<span> - by {{author}}</span></h3>"
    .replace("{{author}}", "Oskar");
```

The final result is

```
"<h3>Fitness App v1.0 Live!<span> - by Oskar</span></h3>";
```

Listing 19.3 shows an example of chaining two calls to replace. It produces the following output on the console:

```
> Follow {{author}} {{social}}
> Follow Oskar @appOskar51
```

> **Listing 19.3   Chaining calls to replace**
> **(http://jsbin.com/rebugu/edit?js,console)**

```
var data = { author : "Oskar", social : "@appOskar51" };
var before = "Follow {{author}} {{social}}";

var after = before                                        Call replace on the
        .replace("{{author}}", data.author)  ◁─────      original string
        .replace("{{social}}", data.social);  ◁──┐
                                                 │       Call replace on the
console.log(before);                             │       value returned by
console.log(after);                              └───    the first call
```

The calls to replace were written across multiple lines in listing 19.3. This has no impact on the program but makes it easier for someone reading the code to pick out the separate calls. When methods can be chained with dot notation, like replace, they are said to have a *fluent interface.* Programmers often design whole suites of objects and methods to use fluent interfaces so they become easier to use, read, and understand.

19.3   *While loops—replacing a string multiple times*

Knowing how to use `replace` to swap one string for another, you write code to test it out for the news page. Figure 19.2 shows what a news item template looks like before you replace its placeholders.

Figure 19.2   A news item with all of its placeholders showing

The data for a news item is a JavaScript object with five properties: `title`, `body`, `author`, `posted`, and `social`:

```
var data = {
    title: "Fitness App v1.0 Live!",
    body: "Yes, version 1 is here...",
    posted: "October 3rd, 2016",
    author: "Oskar",
    social: "@appOskar51"
};
```

You call `replace` for each of the properties and, at first, you think things have gone well. Figure 19.3 shows the rendered news item.

Figure 19.3   A news item—one of the `{{author}}` placeholders has not been replaced (bottom right).

Close, but no Pulitzer! One of the placeholders hasn't been replaced. There's still a stubborn {{author}} in the bottom right of the news item. The following listing shows the code you used. What went wrong?

> **Listing 19.4   Calling replace once for each property**
> **(http://jsbin.com/quroha/edit?js,html,output)**

```
var data = {
    title: "Fitness App v1.0 Live!",
    body: "Yes, version 1 is here...",
    posted: "October 3rd, 2016",
    author: "Oskar",
    social: "@appOskar51"
};

var templateScript =                                       Get a reference to the script
    document.getElementById("newsItemTemplate");           element that holds the template
```

Extract
the HTML
for the
template
```
var templateString = templateScript.innerHTML;

var newsItemHTML = templateString
    .replace("{{title}}", data.title)
    .replace("{{author}}", data.author)               Replace each
    .replace("{{posted}}", data.posted)               placeholder with
    .replace("{{body}}", data.body)                   its property value
    .replace("{{social}}", data.social);
```
```
                                                          Get a reference to
var newsContainer = document.getElementById("news");  ◁── the div that will hold
                                                          the news item
```
```
newsContainer.innerHTML = newsItemHTML;   ◁──
                                             Inject the news item
                                             HTML into the div
```

The problem is, the replace method replaces only the first occurrence of the string it's trying to match. The news item template has two {{author}} placeholders and you replace only one of them. Have a go at fixing the problem yourself, by calling replace twice for the same placeholder.

The template and replace code are all a bit too *tightly coupled*. If the designer changes the template to include the {{author}} placeholder a third time (maybe for an email link or a short bio), you'll have to dig back into the JavaScript and update the code to add another call to replace.

You want code that automatically keeps calling replace while there are placeholders to fill. How can you call replace the correct number of times?

19.3.1 *Repeating code while a condition is met*

All of the placeholders in your news item template need to be replaced with the corresponding data. For example, both instances of {{author}} should be filled with Oskar, as shown in the top right and bottom right of figure 19.4.

Figure 19.4   Both author placeholders have been replaced with Oskar (top right and bottom right).

Your code should keep calling `replace` while it finds a placeholder for each property. In pseudocode (pretend code) it should look something like this:

```
while there is a placeholder {
    replace the placeholder with data
}
```

The code block between the curly braces should keep being repeated while there's a placeholder. Once no placeholder is found, the code block can be skipped. Here's how to accomplish that goal in JavaScript:

```
while (filled.indexOf(placeholder) !== -1) {
    filled = filled.replace(placeholder, data.property);
}
```

You'll dig into the details shortly, so don't worry too much if you don't follow everything yet. But you should be able to appreciate the gist of what the code is doing. Let's look at how the `while` loop works in general.

19.3.2   *The while loop*

The `while` loop keeps calling `replace` while a placeholder is found in the `filled` string. When no placeholder is found, execution continues after the code block. In general, the `while` loop lets you repeatedly execute a block of code while a condition is `true`. The structure of a `while` loop looks like this:

```
while (condition) {
    // Code to execute if condition is true.
}
```

The loop first evaluates the condition. If it evaluates to `true`, then the code block is executed, just like an `if` statement. Unlike an `if` statement, once the code block has been executed, the `while` loop evaluates the condition again. If the condition still evaluates to `true`, then the block is executed again. The loop keeps executing the code block while the condition is `true`. If the condition is `false`, then the code block is skipped and the program continues with the statements after the block.

The next listing shows a while loop being used to display whole numbers from 1 to 10.

```
var count = 1;

while (count < 11) {                  Use the increment
    console.log(count);               operator, ++, to add 1
    count++;                          to the value of count
}
```

Once the count variable reaches 11, the condition will evaluate to `false` and the value of count won't be logged to the console. The code block should always change the value of a variable used in the condition. Otherwise, if the condition's value starts as true, it will never become `false` and the loop will become an *infinite loop*. In listing 19.5, you use the increment operator, ++, to add 1 to the value of count. Three different ways of adding 1 to the value of a count variable are shown here:

```
count = count + 1;
count += 1;
count++;
```

19.3.3   *Replacing a string while it can be found*

You can use a while loop to replace multiple occurrences of a placeholder. First, check if the placeholder you want to replace is present with the indexOf method. indexOf returns -1 if a string can't be found. If the placeholder is found, then indexOf won't return -1. Use that fact in the condition of a while loop:

```
while (filled.indexOf(placeholder) !== -1) {
    // Make changes to filled
}
```

Listing 19.6 uses a while loop to keep replacing a string until it's no longer found. It produces the following output on the console:

```
> Starting replacement...
> {{title}} by Oskar. Follow {{author}} {{social}}
> {{title}} by Oskar. Follow Oskar {{social}}
> ...replacement finished.
```

```
var template = "{{title}} by {{author}}. Follow {{author}} {{social}}";

var filled = template;                           Use a second variable so
                                                 that the initial template
console.log("Starting replacement...");          is unchanged
```

```
while (filled.indexOf("{{author}}") !== -1) {
    filled = filled.replace("{{author}}", "Oskar");
    console.log(filled);
}
console.log("...replacement finished.");
```

Check if the placeholder can be found

Replace the placeholder with a value

The code first logs that it's starting the replacement process. The `while` loop then executes its code block twice, replacing one instance of {{author}} and then the other. With no more instances of {{author}} to find, `filled.indexOf("{{author}}")` returns `-1` and the `while` loop ends. Execution continues after the loop, and the code concludes by logging that the replacement process has finished.

19.3.4 *Replacing strings with regular expressions*

There's an alternative way of replacing strings. It uses *regular expressions*, a powerful but often complicated way of specifying patterns of characters you want to match and replace. Regular expressions are a little beyond the scope of the book, but you can investigate a number of examples on the *Get Programming with JavaScript* website at www.room51.co.uk/js/regexp.html.

19.4 *Automating placeholder replacement for templates*

The fitness app uses data for user exercise sessions, and its news page uses data for news items. The quiz app uses data for sets of questions and answers, and *The Crypt* uses data for its maps. It would be great to use HTML templates to display all kinds of data you might find in your projects. But you don't want to have to reinvent the `while` every time you need to fill placeholders with data. So, what's the key to automating template use?

19.4.1 *Matching template placeholders with object properties*

Figure 19.5 shows a news item from the fitness app news page again. The placeholders have yet to be filled with data.

Figure 19.5   A news item with placeholders unfilled

The data that will fill the placeholders looks like this:

```
var data = {
    title: "Fitness App v1.0 Live!",
    body: "Yes, version 1 is here...",
    posted: "October 3rd, 2016",
    author: "Oskar",
    social: "@appOskar51"
};
```

The property names of the news item data object, its *keys*, match the names of the placeholders in the template. For each key, you want to keep replacing its matching placeholders while they can be found.

1 Start with title and keep replacing {{title}} with Fitness App v1.0 Live! until there are no more {{title}} placeholders to replace.
2 Move on to body and keep replacing {{body}} with Yes, version 1 is here... until there are no more {{body}} placeholders to replace.
3 Repeat the process for each key until all of the keys have had all of their placeholders replaced.

You can get an array of all of the news item's property names by using the Object .keys method.

```
var keys = Object.keys(data);
```

For the news item, keys = ["title", "body", "posted", "author", "social"].

Armed with the keys, you can easily create the placeholders and replace them with values in the template. Remember, you can use square bracket notation to retrieve the value for a key:

```
data["title"];    // "Fitness App v1.0 Live!"
data["author"];   // "Oskar"
```

And if you have a property's key, you can also build the placeholder you need to match in the template:

```
var placeholder = "{{" + key + "}}";
```

The *key* for a property is well named; you use it to unlock the value of the property and its placeholder (table 19.1).

Table 19.1 A property's keys are used to access its value and build its placeholder

Key	Value	Placeholder
title	data["**title**"]	{{**title**}}
body	data["**body**"]	{{**body**}}
posted	data["**posted**"]	{{**posted**}}

19.4.2 Filling all of the placeholders for each key

It's time to bring all of the parts together and write some code that will not only fill templates with data for the fitness app news page but will also work with any data and matching templates. Listing 19.7 shows a `fill` function that uses the ideas from the previous section, iterating over the keys of a data object and replacing the placeholders with values.

Listing 19.7 A function to fill templates with data
(http://jsbin.com/bazika/edit?js,output)

```
function fill (template, data) {

    Object.keys(data).forEach(function (key) {          ⟵  Iterate over each
                                                              key in the data
        var placeholder = "{{" + key + "}}";       Use the key to build a placeholder
        var value = data[key];                     and retrieve the data value

        while (template.indexOf(placeholder) !== -1) {      Keep replacing the
            template = template.replace(placeholder, value);  placeholder with
        }                                                     the value until the
                                                              placeholder can't
    });                                                       be found

    return template;          ⟵  Return the filled
}                                 template
// Test the fill function

var data = {
    title: "Fitness App v1.0 Live!",
    body: "Yes, version 1 is here...",
    posted: "October 3rd, 2016",
    author: "Oskar",
    social: "@appOskar51"
};

var templateScript =                                       Collect the template
        document.getElementById("newsItemTemplate");       and news container
var templateString = templateScript.innerHTML;             reference from the
var newsContainer = document.getElementById("news");       web page

newsContainer.innerHTML = fill(templateString, data);      ⟵

                                 Fill the template with the data
                                 and update the news display
```

Listing 19.7 also includes code to test the `fill` function. On the last line, it sets the contents of a `div` element with the HTML returned by the function.

19.4.3 Building a list of items using a template

You're already smiling. Yes, the fitness app news page features a list of news items. And yes, your template `fill` function works with only a single news item. But you know the power of `forEach` for working with lists. Writing a `fillList` function is a snap, as shown here.

> **Listing 19.8   Building a list using a template**
> **(http://jsbin.com/hilecu/edit?js,output)**

```
function fill (template, data) { /* Listing 19.7 */ }

function fillList (template, dataArray) {
    var listString = "";

    dataArray.forEach(function (data) {          Call the fill function for
      listString += fill(template, data);        every item, building up
    });                                          the list string

    return listString;
}

// Test the function
var posts = [
    {
      title: "Fitness App v1.0 Live!",
      body: "Yes, version 1 is here...",
      posted: "October 3rd, 2016",
      author: "Oskar",
      social: "@appOskar51"
    },
    {
      title: "Improved Formatting",
      body: "The app's looking better than ever...",
      posted: "October 8th, 2016",
      author: "Kallie",
      social: "@kal5tar"
    }
    /* Two more items on JS Bin */
];

var templateScript = document.getElementById("newsItemTemplate");
var templateString = templateScript.innerHTML;
var newsContainer = document.getElementById("news");

newsContainer.innerHTML =                         Fill the template for every news
        fillList(templateString, posts);          item and update the display with
                                                  the completed HTML string
```

In the `fillList` function in listing 19.8, you use the `forEach` method to iterate over the array of data objects, `dataArray`, passing each one to the `fill` function and appending the filled templates it returns to `listString`.

Now that you have the two template functions you need, you're keen to get the scoop on the finished fitness app news page.

19.5   Building a news page—news just in

It's time to get modular. You know how the fitness app team rolls; they love to share code but they hate pollution. They want to see a finished news page with separate data and template modules. Figure 19.6 shows the setup.

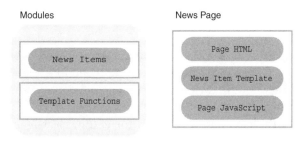

Figure 19.6   The page includes the news item template and JavaScript code and imports two modules.

The news page on JS Bin includes the news item template inside a `script` element and code in the JavaScript panel that uses the modules and template to display the news items. The finished web page with two news items displayed was shown in figure 19.1.

To finish your work on the news page, first create the modules and then import them into the web page. Read all about it in the next two sections.

19.5.1   Creating the templates and data modules

Put the template functions into one module and the news data into another. Use namespaces to avoid creating too many local variables.

TEMPLATING FUNCTIONS

The next listing shows how the two templating functions from listings 19.7 and 19.8 are packaged into a templates module.

Listing 19.9   The templates module
              (http://jsbin.com/pugase/edit?js,console)

```
(function () {
    "use strict";

    function fill (template, data) { /* see listing 19.7 */ }

    function fillList (template, dataArray) { /* see Listing 19.8 */ }

    if (window.gpwj === undefined) {         Ensure gpwj exists in
        window.gpwj = {};                    the global namespace
    }

    gpwj.templates = {          Add the two
        fill: fill,             template functions
        fillList: fillList      to gpwj.templates
    };

})();
```

You use a new namespace, `gpwj` (from *Get Programming with JavaScript*); the templates module will be useful in so many projects that it's worth having it as part of a general utilities namespace rather than in with the fitness app or *The Crypt* or wherever else it will be used. To call the functions, include the namespace:

```
var newsItemHTML = gpwj.templates.fill(newsItemTemplate, data);
```

NEWS DATA

For the real-world news page, the data will come from a central content management system. You mimic the CMS news feed by creating a module that supplies dummy data. You can swap the module for one with a live CMS connection further down the line.

The next listing includes the data and a function for getting it assigned to the `fitnessApp.news` namespace.

Listing 19.10   A news page data module
(http://jsbin.com/fupiki/edit?js,console)

```
(function () {
  "use strict";                    Include an array of news
                                   items rather than getting
  var posts = [                    data from the CMS
    {
      title: "Fitness App v1.0 Live!",
      body: "Yes, version 1 is here...",
      posted: "October 3rd, 2016",
      author: "Oskar",
      social: "@appOskar51"
    }
    /* more data on JS Bin */
  ];

  function getNews (numItems) {          Return the specified
    return posts.slice(0, numItems);     number of news items
  }

  if (window.fitnessApp === undefined) {    Ensure the fitnessApp
    window.fitnessApp = {};                 global namespace exists
  }

  fitnessApp.news = {          Add a news namespace
    getItems: getNews          to the fitnessApp
  };                           namespace

})();
```

To get news items, call `getItems`, specifying the number of items you want. For example, to get three news items you'd use the following code:

```
var itemsData = fitnessApp.news.getItems(3);
```

The real news data module that retrieves items from the CMS will use the same interface as listing 19.10. In other words, its news will also be accessed by calling its get-Items method. By using the same interface, you can easily swap modules from your static version to the dynamic CMS version.

19.5.2 Importing the modules

To provide your readers with the latest headlines on developments from the fitness app team, you create the simple news page HTML shown here.

Listing 19.11   A modular news page (HTML)
(http://jsbin.com/vemufa/edit?html,output)

```
<h1>Fitness App News</h1>

<div id="news"></news>
```
Include a div for the news items

```
<script type="text/template" id="newsItemTemplate">
  <div class="newsItem">
    <h3>{{title}}<span> - by {{author}}</span></h3>
    <p>{{body}}</p>
    <p class="posted"><em>Posted: {{posted}}</em></p>
    <p class="follow">Follow {{author}} {{social}}</p>
  </div>
</script>
```
Put HTML templates in the page inside script tags

```
<!-- templates module -->
<script src="http://output.jsbin.com/pugase.js"></script>

<!-- news items data -->
<script src="http://output.jsbin.com/fupiki.js"></script>
```
Import the templating and data modules

To bring all of the pieces together, you add JavaScript that retrieves the template from the page, fills it with the news item data, and updates the news div with the generated HTML, as in the next listing.

Listing 19.12   A modular news page
(http://jsbin.com/vemufa/edit?js,output)

```
var templateScript =
    document.getElementById("newsItemTemplate");
var templateString = templateScript.innerHTML;
var newsContainer = document.getElementById("news");
```
Grab the pieces you need from the page

```
var newsData = fitnessApp.news.getItems(3);
```
Use the news data module to retrieve three news items

```
newsContainer.innerHTML =
    gpwj.templates.fillList(templateString, newsData);
```
Use the template module to generate the news items HTML and update the page

Using templates is a common way to generate HTML from an application's data. There are many JavaScript templating libraries freely available for general use; Handlebars, Moustache, and Pug are three popular examples.

Stop the press! Your team members love the neat, modular, reusable approach you've taken and vow to add new news items every day. Some of them have already started incorporating the gpwj.templates functions into their own applications. You decide to do the same, as you return to *The Crypt*.

19.6   *The Crypt—improving the views*

In chapter 17 you created some web-based views for players and places. The information they displayed, originally intended for the console, was formatted with spaces, line breaks, and boxes and borders from the spacer namespace, rather than HTML. Now that you've seen how templates can be used to separate markup and JavaScript, it's time to improve the views so that appropriate HTML tags are used to wrap data in *The Crypt*.

Figure 19.7 shows what *The Crypt* will look like after the changes. Switching to HTML from plain text makes it possible to style the output with CSS, leading to much greater potential for visually interesting designs. Figure 19.8 shows the modules for the project with new and updated modules highlighted.

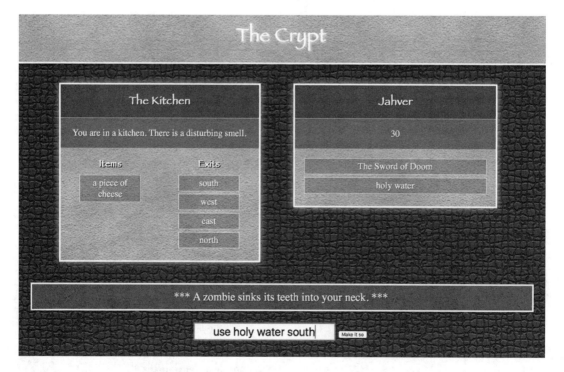

Figure 19.7   The latest version of *The Crypt* uses HTML templates to build page elements.

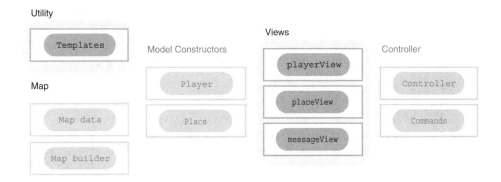

Figure 19.8 Modules in *The Crypt* with new or updated modules highlighted

You created the Templates module earlier in the chapter. Now you create templates and update the views to use them.

19.6.1 *Creating HTML templates for all of the views*

The following listing shows all of the templates for *The Crypt* embedded within HTML `script` tags. They're part of a full web page on JS Bin.

Listing 19.13   The Crypt with Templates (HTML)
(http://jsbin.com/yapiyic/edit?html,output)

```
<script type="text/template" id="itemTemplate">
    <li>{{item}}</li>
</script>
```
> Use script tags to include HTML templates in the page

```
<script type="text/template" id="playerTemplate">
    <h3>{{name}}</h3>
    <p>{{health}}</p>

    <ol id="playerItems"></ol>
</script>
```
> Give the script tags a nonstandard type attribute so they're not executed

```
<script type="text/template" id="placeTemplate">
    <h3>{{title}}</h3>
    <p>{{description}}</p>

    <div class="placePanel">
        <h4>Items:</h4>
        <ol id="placeItems"></ol>
    </div>

    <div class="placePanel">
        <h4>Exits:</h4>
        <ol id="placeExits"></ol>
    </div>
</script>
```
> Include an id attribute so the script elements can be accessed from JavaScript

> Include an ordered list element in the template as a container for list items

> Give the list containers ids so the items can be added from JavaScript

```
<script type="text/template" id="messageTemplate">
    <p>*** {{message}} ***</p>
</script>
```

There's no JavaScript mixed with the templates. A web designer used to working in HTML could use their knowledge to update the templates without having to unpick the HTML from any other code. Clearly, this separation of concerns makes the templates neater, easier to read, and easier to use for anyone involved in building the application.

19.6.2   *Updating the views to use the new templates*

With the template strings for *The Crypt* now embedded as HTML on the page, you need to update the view modules to grab the template strings and fill them with a message or with data from the player and place models. Listings 19.14, 19.15, and 19.16 show the new view code. *Note: The views are designed to be used by the controller and won't work in isolation.* The links to JS Bin are included so you can copy, clone, or change the code if you choose.

MESSAGES

The simplest view is the message view. Here's the updated code.

> **Listing 19.14   A message view using templates**
> **(http://jsbin.com/jojeyo/edit?js,console)**

```
(function () {
  "use strict";

  var messageDiv = document.getElementById("messages");        Collect references
  var templateScript =                                         to elements on the
    document.getElementById("messageTemplate");                web page
  var template = templateScript.innerHTML;

  function render (message) {
    var data = { message: message };          Define a function to fill
    messageDiv.innerHTML =                     the message template
      gpwj.templates.fill(template, data);     and update the display
  }

  function clear () {                    Define a function to
    messageDiv.innerHTML = "";           empty the message div,
  }                                      clearing the display

  if (window.theCrypt === undefined) {
    window.theCrypt = {};
  }

  theCrypt.messageView = {          Add both functions
    render: render,                 to the messageView
    clear: clear                    namespace
  };

})();
```

The messages passed to the `render` method for the message view are just strings. The `template.fill` method expects objects (it uses object keys to create placeholders and find values), so `render` creates an object, `data`, from the message to use as the argument.

A message of "hello" becomes { message : "hello" }. The fill method will then replace the {{message}} placeholder with the value "hello".

PLAYERS

The player view is slightly more complicated than the message view because players have items. As well as having a template string to display the player's name and health, the player view needs another for the items.

The next listing shows the new player view. The code relating to items is shown in bold.

> ### Listing 19.15 A player view using templates
> (http://jsbin.com/suyona/edit?js,console)

```
(function () {
  "use strict";

  var playerDiv = document.getElementById("player");
  var playerScript = document.getElementById("playerTemplate");
  var itemScript = document.getElementById("itemTemplate");

  var playerTemplate = playerScript.innerHTML;
  var itemTemplate = itemScript.innerHTML;

  function render (player) {
    var data = player.getData();
    var itemsDiv;

    var items = data.items.map(function (itemName) {      Use map to create an array
      return { item : itemName };                          of item objects from the
    });                                                    array of item name strings

    playerDiv.innerHTML =                                  Add the HTML generated
      gpwj.templates.fill(playerTemplate, data);          from the player template
                                                          to the page
    itemsDiv = document.getElementById("playerItems");

    itemsDiv.innerHTML =                                   Add the items HTML to
      gpwj.templates.fillList(itemTemplate, items);        the playerItems div
  }

  if (window.theCrypt === undefined) {
    window.theCrypt = {};
  }

  theCrypt.playerView =  {
    render: render
  };

})();
```

Get a reference to the playerItems div that has just been added to the page

The player's items data is an array of strings. Because fillList expects an array of objects, you use map to transform the array from strings to objects. You pass a function to the map method and map builds a new array, with each new element created by the function. The array ["a lamp", "a key"] becomes [{ item : "a lamp" }, { item : "a key" }].

The items HTML generated by `fillList` can't be added to the page until the player HTML has been added because the player HTML includes the `ol` element that will contain the items.

```
//Add the filled player template to the page.
playerDiv.innerHTML = gpwj.templates.fill(playerTemplate, data);

// Get a reference to the playerItems ol that's just been added to the page
itemsDiv = document.getElementById("playerItems");

// Add the HTML for the list of items to the playerItems ol element
itemsDiv.innerHTML = gpwj.templates.fillList(itemTemplate, items);
```

PLACES

The places view is the most complicated because places have items *and* exits. But the method for displaying exits is the same as that for items, so the extra complication is just a touch of repetition. The exits data is an array of strings, just like the items data. The same template can be used for both.

The following listing shows the updated place view. The code for exits is in bold.

Listing 19.16   A place view using templates
(http://jsbin.com/yoquna/edit?js,console)

```
(function () {
  "use strict";

  var placeDiv = document.getElementById("place");
  var placeScript = document.getElementById("placeTemplate");
  var itemScript = document.getElementById("itemTemplate");

  var placeTemplate = placeScript.innerHTML;
  var itemTemplate = itemScript.innerHTML;

  function render (place) {
    var data = place.getData();
    var itemsDiv;
    var exitsDiv;

    var items = data.items.map(function (itemName) {
      return { item : itemName };
    });

    var exits = data.exits.map(function (exitName) {      Use map to get an
      return { item : exitName };                         array of objects from
    });                                                   an array of strings

    placeDiv.innerHTML =
      gpwj.templates.fill(placeTemplate, data);

    itemsDiv = document.getElementById("placeItems");
    itemsDiv.innerHTML =
      gpwj.templates.fillList(itemTemplate, items);
```

```
      exitsDiv = document.getElementById("placeExits");
      exitsDiv.innerHTML =
        gpwj.templates.fillList(itemTemplate, exits);
    }

    if (window.theCrypt === undefined) {
      window.theCrypt = {};
    }

    theCrypt.placeView = {
      render: render
    };

})();
```

> Once it's been added,
> get a reference to the
> placeExits ol and fill it
> with the exits HTML

Once again, map is used to convert an array of strings into an array of objects, this time for both items and exits.

19.6.3 *Enter The Crypt*

Listing 19.13 on JS Bin is a working example of *The Crypt* using templates and the three new views. The scripts to import the new modules are shown here:

```
<!-- gpwj.templates -->
<script src="http://output.jsbin.com/pugase.js"></script>

<!-- player view -->
<script src="http://output.jsbin.com/suyona.js"></script>
<!-- place view -->
<script src="http://output.jsbin.com/yoquna.js"></script>
<!-- message view -->
<script src="http://output.jsbin.com/jojeyo.js"></script>
```

Make your way to http://output.jsbin.com/yapiyic and have a play.

19.7 *Summary*

- Use the replace string method to replace one string with another:

  ```
  "One too three".replace("too", "two");      // Returns "One two three"
  ```

- Chain calls to replace to swap multiple strings:

  ```
  "One too three".replace("One", "Far").replace("three", "long");
  // Returns "Far too long"
  ```

- Use a while loop to execute a block of code while a condition remains true.

  ```
  var count = 10;

  while (count > 5) {          // Displays 10 9 8 7 6 on separate lines
      console.log(count);
      count = count - 1;
  }
  ```

- Use the map array method to create a new array based on the elements of an existing array. The function passed to map as an argument returns a new value based on an old value:

```
var planets = ["Mercury", "Venus"];

var bigPlanets = planets.map(function (oldValue) {
    return oldValue + " becomes " + oldValue.toUpperCase();
});

// bigPlanets === ["Mercury becomes MERCURY", "Venus becomes VENUS"]
```

- Use template strings with placeholders to avoid mixing JavaScript with display strings:

```
var templateString = "<h3>{{title}}</h3><p>{{body}}</p>";
```

- Embed template strings in HTML by using script tags with nonstandard type attributes.

```
<script type="text/template" id="postTemplate">
    <h3>{{title}}</h3><p>{{body}}</p>
</script>
```

- Access the template from JavaScript via the script tag's id attribute and the element's innerHTML property:

```
var templateString = document.getElementById("postTemplate").innerHTML;
```

- Fill a template with data from an object. It returns a string with the placeholders replaced by the properties of the object:

```
var data = {title: "Out of Office", body: "I'm going on an adventure!"};
var template = "<h3>{{title}}</h3><p>{{body}}</p>";
gpwj.templates.fill(template, data);
// Returns "<h3>Out of Office</h3><p>I'm going on an adventure!</p>"
```

XHR: loading data

This chapter covers

- Loading data with the `XMLHttpRequest` object
- Calling functions once the data loads
- Updating views with loaded data
- JavaScript Object Notation (JSON)
- Converting JSON text into JavaScript objects

A calendar or movies database or adventure game can use a lot of data. A news site may have up-to-the-minute updates with breaking news and sports scores. It's not always desirable to load all of the data at once or for a visitor to have to keep refreshing a web page to get the latest information. It would be great if a page could access just the pieces of new data it needs to stay fresh, even after it has loaded. Stock prices, tweets, comments, scores, and, yes, the current health of zombies can all be updated independently without a full page reload.

This chapter shows you how to reach out across the internet and grab data for your apps while they're running. In particular, you load exercise data as you switch between users in the fitness app, and you load location data, tomb by tomb, as players solve the riddles of *The Crypt*.

20.1   *Building a fitness app—retrieving user data*

You and your team have been building a fitness app that lets users track their exercise (see chapters 14 to 16). The app can convert JavaScript data into user models, use a choice of views to display user info on the console, and accept user input at the console prompt. The tasks you were given for the project are these:

1 Retrieve user data as a string.

2 Convert user data into user models.

3 Display user data.

4 Provide an interface for users to add sessions.

You've completed tasks 2, 3, and 4, and now it's time to retrieve user data over the internet. You want to be able to switch between users while using the app, as shown in figure 20.1.

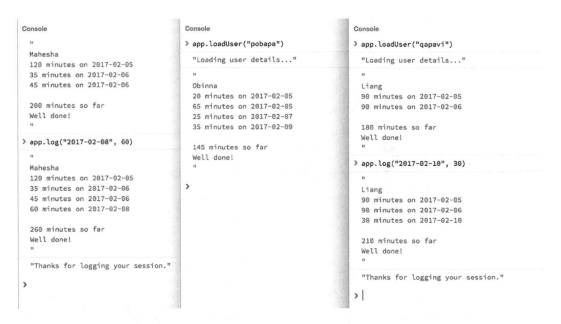

Figure 20.1   Switching between users while using the fitness app

Figure 20.1 shows an `app.loadUser` method being called to load data for second and third users. Before you can get your hands on the data, you need some way of specifying the location of the data for each user.

20.1.1   *Locating the user data*

Different team members are working on versions of the fitness app for different platforms and devices. But all of the versions will use the same data, provided by the central fitness app server, as shown in figure 20.2.

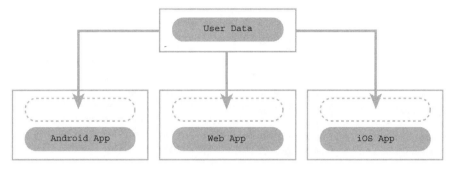

The same data is used by all of the apps

Figure 20.2   The same data is used by all of the apps.

Up until now, while developing the app, you've been using a static data file for a single user. You want to be able to swap between users without reloading the whole app and without loading the data for all of the users at once (you're hoping for *lots* of users!). You decide to define a `loadUser` method that will load user data for a given user ID and display it on the console:

```
> app.loadUser("qiwizo")
  Loading user details...

  Mahesha
  120 minutes on 2017-02-05
  35 minutes on 2017-02-06
  45 minutes on 2017-02-06

  200 minutes so far
  Well done!
```

Your IDs for the fitness app correspond to files on JS Bin; in a real application they may be IDs from a database or maybe unique usernames. Each file contains the data for just one user. For example, here's Mahesha's data at http://output.jsbin.com/qiwizo.json:

```
{
  "name" : "Mahesha",
  "sessions" : [
    {"sessionDate": "2017-02-05", "duration": 120},
    {"sessionDate": "2017-02-06", "duration": 35},
    {"sessionDate": "2017-02-06", "duration": 45}
  ]
}
```

So, how do you load data for a player while your program is running? The secret lies with the strangely named `XMLHttpRequest` object. But before you load up its secrets, it'll be worth getting a better sense of the steps involved in working with the remote data.

20.1.2 *Loading the user data—an outline*

You need to load user data for the fitness app. Whenever a user calls the `loadUser` method, your app needs to reach out across the internet, find the data, retrieve it, and then use it. To do all that, the app will need the following:

- A user ID
- A URL at which to find the data
- A function to call once the data is retrieved

The third requirement is worth considering further. The data is across the internet, possibly across the world, on another machine. It will take time for the data to be found and retrieved (hopefully milliseconds, but maybe seconds). Your program needs the data before it can use it to create a new `User` and update the display. You define a function, called a *callback function*, that will be called when the data is loaded. You've come across callback functions before: when working with buttons in chapter 18, you asked for a function to be called when a button was clicked. It was as if the function were listening for the click event to happen. For loading user data, your callback function is listening for a load event to happen. Your code for loading user data and using it to update the app will be something like this:

```
function updateUser (userData) {
    // Create a new User from the data
    // Use a view to update the display
}

function loadData (id, callback) {
    // Build a URL using the id

    // Let the app know to run the callback function when the data loads

    // Tell the app to go and get the data from the URL
}

loadData("qiwizo", updateUser);
```

You pass the `loadData` function the `id` of the user, `qiwizo`, and a function to call when the data has loaded, `updateUser`.

You have a sense of the steps involved in retrieving the data you need. It's time to study the specifics.

20.1.3 *Loading the user data—the XMLHttpRequest constructor*

Yes, the `XMLHttpRequest` constructor has a funny name, although the request bit's okay. You want to *request* information from a computer, a *server,* somewhere in the world. You can research XML and HTTP as homework. From now on, apart from in code, I'll call it the XHR constructor. Short. Snappy. Cuddly?

The XHR constructor is provided by the browser. You use it to create XHR objects that include methods for requesting resources from across the internet. You pass an XHR object a URL and a function to call, and when it loads the data it will call your function. Figure 20.3 shows the data retrieved when an XHR object is used to load the data for a user in the fitness app.

```
Console
"{
  \"name\" : \"Mahesha\",
  \"sessions\" : [
    {\"sessionDate\": \"2017-02-05\", \"duration\": 120},
    {\"sessionDate\": \"2017-02-06\", \"duration\": 35},
    {\"sessionDate\": \"2017-02-06\", \"duration\": 45}
  ]
}"
```

Figure 20.3 The string of data returned by an XHR object

Listing 20.1 has the code, which includes these five steps, required to make the request for the data.

1 Use the XHR constructor to create an XHR object
2 State or build the URL
3 Give the XHR object a function to call when the data has loaded
4 Call the open method, passing it the URL
5 Call the send method to start the request

Listing 20.1 Using an XHR object to load user data
(http://jsbin.com/qakofo/edit?js,console)

```
var xhr = new XMLHttpRequest();
```
Step 1: Use the XHR constructor to create a new XHR object

```
var url = "http://output.jsbin.com/qiwizo.json";
```
Step 2: Store a URL at which to find the data

```
xhr.addEventListener("load", function () {
  console.log(xhr.responseText);
});
```
Step 3: Tell the XHR object to call a function when the data has loaded

```
xhr.open("GET", url);
```
Step 4: Call open, specifying the URL

```
xhr.send();
```
Step 5: Call send to start the request

You call the XHR constructor with the new keyword and it creates and returns an XHR object. You call the object's methods to set up and start the request. You provide a function to call once the data is loaded; in listing 20.1 you use a function expression as the second argument to addEventListener, but you could also use the name of a previously defined function. Once loaded, the data is automatically assigned to the responseText property of the XHR object and your callback function can access the data via that property. The first argument to the open function, GET, is the *HTTP method* or *verb* for the request. You stick with GET for this chapter because you're getting data, but there are other verbs, like POST, PUT, and DELETE.

You can see in figure 20.3 that the data is returned as text. The text is shown between double quotation marks (the very first character and the very last). The data is in a format called JavaScript Object Notation (JSON), which is discussed in more detail in section 20.2. Because it's text, a string, you can't access the data as you would a JavaScript object, with expressions such as data.name or data["sessions"].

Happily, there's a simple way to convert the JSON text into a JavaScript object.

20.1.4 *Loading the user data—parsing the XHR response with JSON.parse*

The XHR request runs your callback function once it has loaded the data for a fitness app user. The data, as a string, is automatically assigned to the responseText property of the XHR object. In order to translate the string into a JavaScript object with properties you can access, like name and sessions, you use the JSON.parse JavaScript method.

```
var dataAsObject = JSON.parse(dataAsString);
```

Figure 20.4 shows what the user data looks like once you parse it and log it to the console. Rather than just a string, it's now an *object* with properties (compare figures 20.3 and 20.4).

```
Console
[object Object] {
  name: "Mahesha",
  sessions: [[object Object] {
  duration: 120,
  sessionDate: "2017-02-05"
}, [object Object] {
  duration: 35,
  sessionDate: "2017-02-06"
}, [object Object] {
  duration: 45,
  sessionDate: "2017-02-06"
}]
}
```

Figure 20.4   Once the JSON text has been parsed, you have a standard JavaScript object.

The following listing updates listing 20.1, parsing the loaded text to obtain a JavaScript object, before logging the data to the console.

```
var xhr = new XMLHttpRequest();
var url = "http://output.jsbin.com/qiwizo.json";

xhr.addEventListener("load", function () {                    Parse the JSON
  var data = JSON.parse(xhr.responseText);              ◁──  text to obtain a
  console.log(data);                                         JavaScript object
});

xhr.open("GET", url);
xhr.send();
```

You should have a big smile on your face. With just a few lines of code, you can access data from anywhere in the world. (Well, from the server hosting your web page. But that could be anywhere.) Big hugs.

All of the apps developed in *Get Programming with JavaScript* could benefit from an easy way to access data on JS Bin; the bin codes it generates, like `qiwizo`, are a bit fiddly. In the next section, you package the XHR code into a `load` function that makes retrieving data even easier.

20.1.5   *Loading JS Bin data—a handy function*

The quiz app, the My Movie Ratings page, the fitness app news page, and *The Crypt* could all use the ability to load data while running, just like the fitness app itself. To streamline the process of loading data from JS Bin, you create a module, *Bin Data*.

As a general utility function, you add the `load` function to the `gpwj` namespace, already home to templating functions (see chapter 19). To load the data in a JS Bin file, you use code of the following form:

```
function doSomethingWithData (data) {
    // Do something amazing with the data
}

gpwj.data.load("qiwizo", doSomethingWithData);
```

The next listing shows the function in action. It produces the output in figure 20.4.

```
(function () {
  "use strict";

  function loadData (bin, callback) {                        Use the bin code
    var xhr = new XMLHttpRequest();                          to construct
    var url = "http://output.jsbin.com/" + bin + ".json";  ◁──  the URL

    xhr.addEventListener("load", function () {              Pass the loaded
      var data = JSON.parse(xhr.responseText);              data to the
      callback(data);                                   ◁── callback function
    });
```

```
    xhr.open("GET", url);
    xhr.send();
  }

  if (window.gpwj === undefined) {
    window.gpwj = {};
  }

  gpwj.data = {
    load: loadData
  };
}) ();

gpwj.data.load("qiwizo", console.log);
```

Test the function, telling
it to call console.log
with the loaded data

You use the load function to grab location data in *The Crypt* in section 20.3. Data-loading versions of the other projects in the book are available on the *Get Programming with JavaScript* website at www.room51.co.uk/books/getprogramming/projects/. The fitness app gets the upgrade right now.

20.1.6 Building the fitness app

The fitness app team is excited to see the working prototype of the console-based program. There are three tasks remaining:

1 Update the controller module to use the new load function for user data
2 Use script elements to load the modules the app uses
3 Add a line of JavaScript to initialize the app

The new controller is shown here. It has a loadUser function that calls the gpwj.data .load method. Both loadUser and log are returned from the init method as an interface.

**Listing 20.4   The fitness app controller
            (http://jsbin.com/nudezo/edit?js,console)**

```
(function () {
  "use strict";

  var user = null;

  function buildUser (userData) { /* Listing 14.3 */ }

  function updateUserFromData (userData) {
      user = buildUser(userData);
      fitnessApp.userView.render(user);
  }

  function loadUser (id) {
    gpwj.data.load(id, updateUserFromData);
    return "Loading user details...";
  }
```

Create a user from
the loaded data and
update the display

Load user data and
invoke the callback
function

```
function log (sessionDate, duration) {
  if (user !== null) {
      user.addSession(sessionDate, duration);
      fitnessApp.userView.render(user);
      return "Thanks for logging your session.";
  } else {
      return "Please wait for user details to load.";
  }
}
```

Define a function to let users log their sessions

```
function init (id) {
  loadUser(id);

  return {
    log: log,
    loadUser: loadUser
  };
}
```

Load the data for an initial user

Return an interface object

```
if (window.fitnessApp === undefined) {
  window.fitnessApp = {};
}

fitnessApp.init = init;
})();
```

Because the app loads user data while running, there's a chance a user may try to log an exercise session before the data has loaded (the fitness app users are *super*-keen). The log method makes sure the user has been set, user !== null, before allowing logging to take place. Remember, null is a special JavaScript value often used to signify that an object is expected but is missing or not yet assigned.

With all the pieces in place, it's simply a matter of gathering them together and firing the starting pistol. The four fitness app modules are shown in figure 20.5, with the Bin Data module replacing the module that provided static data.

Figure 20.5   The modules that make up the fitness app

You haven't had to alter the User constructor or view. The next listing shows the script elements used to load the four modules.

**Listing 20.5   The fitness app (HTML)
(http://jsbin.com/mikigo/edit?html,console)**

```
<!-- fitnessApp.User -->
<script src="http://output.jsbin.com/fasebo.js"></script>

<!-- fitnessApp.userView -->
<script src="http://output.jsbin.com/yapahe.js"></script>
```

```
<!-- fitnessApp.controller -->
<script src="http://output.jsbin.com/nudezo.js"></script>

<!-- gpwj.data -->
<script src="http://output.jsbin.com/guzula.json"></script>
```

The following listing shows the JavaScript that fires the starting pistol, calling fitnessApp.init with the JS Bin code for an initial user.

> **Listing 20.6   The fitness app**
> **(http://jsbin.com/mikigo/edit?js,console)**

```
var app = fitnessApp.init("qiwizo");
```

The best place to see the app in action is on JS Bin, but figure 20.1 at the start of the chapter shows a user loading and logging sessions.

You're thrilled with the working app and so is the development team. But there's something missing (apart from actually being able to save data somewhere). Isn't part 3 of *Get Programming with JavaScript* all about HTML-based apps? Why are you back at the console?

20.1.7   *The fitness app—what's next?*

Figure 20.6 shows what you're really after—an HTML-based fitness app with dropdown lists, text boxes, and buttons. You can choose users from a list, load their details, and log new sessions. With all you've learned in the book, could you build the app? There's nothing like jumping in and trying to build something yourself for helping

Fitness App

Mahesha ⬍   Load Sessions

Mahesha

120 minutes on 2017-02-05
35 minutes on 2017-02-06
45 minutes on 2017-02-06

200 minutes so far

Well done!

Log a session...

Date

Duration
     (minutes)

Add Session

Fitness App

Obinna ⬍   Load Sessions

Obinna

20 minutes on 2017-02-05
65 minutes on 2017-02-05
25 minutes on 2017-02-07
35 minutes on 2017-02-09

145 minutes so far

Well done!

Log a session...

Date

Duration
     (minutes)

Add Session

Fitness App

Liang ⬍   Load Sessions

Liang

90 minutes on 2017-02-05
90 minutes on 2017-02-06

180 minutes so far

Well done!

Log a session...

Date

Duration
     (minutes)

Add Session

Figure 20.6   The fitness app using web-based views

you learn. There's no pressure, no race, and no failure; be brave and curious, make mistakes, and ask for help. Even if you don't make it to the finish line, you're sure to learn lots along the way, get a great JavaScript workout, and build your coding muscles. And once you've tried it for yourself, you can sneak a peek at http://jsbin.com/vayogu/ edit?output to see one way of piecing it together. (Don't forget to run the program.)

And if it's an HTML-based data-driven app that you're after, there's no better place to see it in action than in *The Crypt*.

But first, as promised, here's a very brief introduction to the JSON data format.

20.2   JSON—a simple data format

JSON is a data format that's easy for humans to read and write and easy for computers to parse and generate. It has become very popular as a format for exchanging data on the web. Here's a calendar event written in JSON:

```
{
    "title" : "Cooking with Cheese",
    "date" : "Wed 20 June",
    "location" : "The Kitchen"
}
```

The format should be very familiar; it's based on a subset of JavaScript. Property names and strings must be enclosed in double quotation marks. Property values can be arrays or nested objects. Here is some calendar data for June:

```
{
  "calEvents" : [
    {
      "title" : "Sword Sharpening",
      "date" : "Mon 3 June",
      "location" : "The Crypt"
    },
    {
      "title" : "Team Work Session",
      "date" : "Mon 17 June",
      "location" : "The Crypt"
    },
    {
      "title" : "Cooking with Cheese",
      "date" : "Wed 20 June",
      "location" : "The Kitchen"
    }
  ]
}
```

Values can also be numbers, booleans, `null`, and `undefined`. That's as much as you need. (There's not much more to JSON, to be honest. The full specification is at http://json.org. You may be surprised at how brief it is—you have to love those train track diagrams for efficiency!)

JSON data is transferred as text. So, how do you convert it into objects and arrays that can be used in a JavaScript program?

20.2.1 *Converting JSON into objects and arrays with JSON.parse*

You turn JSON as text into JavaScript objects by passing it to the `JSON.parse` method. You can then access the properties or elements in the data using dot or bracket notations. If you've used an XHR object to send a request for a single calendar event as JSON, you can convert the response to a JavaScript object like this:

```
var calEvent = JSON.parse(xhr.responseText);

calEvent.title;    // Cooking with Cheese
calEvent.date;     // Wed 20 June
calEvent.location; // The Kitchen
```

That's quite a brief introduction to JSON, but seeing as the whole book is about JavaScript, it should be enough.

It's time to load map data, mysterious room by mysterious room, as you return to *The Crypt*.

20.3   *The Crypt—loading a map on demand*

Adventures in *The Crypt* involve exploring ancient tombs, sprawling spaceships, and mysterious forests. Each adventure may cover dozens of locations with little chance of completion in a single sitting. Rather than loading the whole map at the start of a game, it might make more sense to load places only when a player visits them. The game can store the JSON data for each place in a separate file on JS Bin and use `XMLHttpRequest` to load the files when needed.

Figure 20.7 shows only the first location, loaded at the start of a game. The loaded data includes the JS Bin file codes for the exits from the location. The data file for the location south of the The Kitchen has the code `kacaluy`, for example.

The data for each place on the map is loaded only when a player moves to that place. Figure 20.8 shows the same map once a player has moved south from The Kitchen. The data for The Old Library has now been loaded.

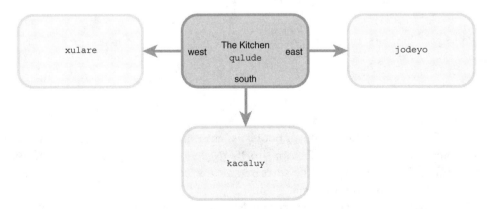

Figure 20.7   At the start of the game, only the initial place data is loaded.

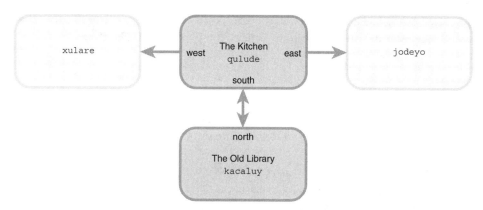

Figure 20.8 The data for The Old Library has been loaded because the player moved there.

To allow step-by-step loading like this, you have to include the JS Bin file codes for each place's exits in its map data.

20.3.1 Specifying exits with JS Bin file codes

Say a game in *The Crypt* starts in The Kitchen. At first, the game will load only the data for The Kitchen, not for any other places on the map. That's a lot less data loaded at the start of the game. The next listing shows the data for that single location. (The challenges have been left out so you can focus on the ids.)

Listing 20.7   The JSON data for The Kitchen
                    (http://output.jsbin.com/qulude.json)

```
{
  "title" : "The Kitchen",
  "id" : "qulude",
  "description" : "You are in a kitchen. There is a disturbing smell.",
  "items" : [ "a piece of cheese" ],
  "exits" : [
    {
      "direction" : "south",
      "to" : "The Old Library",
      "id" : "kacaluy"                  ◁
    },
    {
      "direction" : "west",
      "to" : "The Kitchen Garden",       Include the code for the
      "id" : "xulare"            ◁       destination of each exit
    },                                   so its data can be loaded
    {                                    if it is visited
      "direction" : "east",
      "to" : "The Kitchen Cupboard",
      "id" : "jodeyo"                   ◁
    }
  ]
}
```

Each place has a unique id that corresponds to the JS Bin code of the file where its data is stored. You use the id to construct a place's URL like this:

```
var url = "http://output.jsbin.com/" + id + ".json";
```

Players will move back and forth around the map, solving puzzles, collecting treasure, dissolving zombies, and licking leopards. They're likely to visit some locations several times, and you'd like to avoid loading the same data again and again.

20.3.2 *Using a cache—load each place only once*

Whenever you create a new place from loaded data, you store it in a cache, using the place's id as the key. Further requests for a place can be given the stored place from the cache, avoiding repeatedly loading the same data from JS Bin.

```
var placeStore = {};      // Set up an object to store the loaded places

placesStore[placeData.id] = place;    // Use the place's id as the key
```

20.3.3 *Replacing the Map Data and Map Builder modules with Map Manager*

The map builder for *The Crypt* used to take data for the whole map, create all of the place models, and then add the items, exits, and challenges to the places. Once it had done that for the whole map, it would return the first place and the game was ready to play. You now load one place at a time; you need a function to load the individual place data and a function to build a single place model from the loaded data.

Listing 20.8 shows the code for a new Map Manager module that will replace the map-building code you were using in previous versions of *The Crypt* (figure 20.9). The

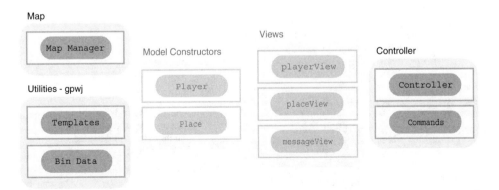

Figure 20.9   The modules for *The Crypt* with new or updated modules highlighted

Map Manager module makes a single method available in its interface, `loadPlace`. Use it with a previously defined callback function or a function expression:

```
// Use a previously defined function as the callback
theCrypt.map.loadPlace("qiwizo", doSomethingWithPlace);

// Use a function expression as the callback
theCrypt.map.loadPlace("qiwizo", function (place) {
    // Use the place model
});
```

Listing 20.8   Map Manager
(http://jsbin.com/xesoxu/edit?js)

```
(function () {
  "use strict";
  var placesStore = {};                              ⟵⎦ Use an object to act as a
                                                         cache for loaded places
  function addPlace (placeData) {
      var place = new theCrypt.Place(                    Create a Place object
          placeData.title, placeData.description);       from the place data

      placesStore[placeData.id] = place;          ⟵⎤
                                                      Cache the newly created
      if (placeData.items !== undefined) {            place in placesStore,
          placeData.items.forEach(place.addItem);     using its id as a key
      }

      if (placeData.exits !== undefined) {
          placeData.exits.forEach(function (exit) {
              place.addExit(exit.direction, exit.id);   ⟵   Add the place id as an
              place.addChallenge(                            exit for the specified
                  exit.direction, exit.challenge);           direction
          });
      }
      return place;                          ⎤ Include a callback parameter
  }                                            for a function to be called
                                            ⎦ with the loaded place
  function loadPlace (id, callback) {    ⟵
      var place = placesStore[id];

      if (place === undefined) {                    ⟵⎤ Only load the place data
          gpwj.data.load(id, function (placeData) {   ⎦ if it is not in the cache

              var place = addPlace(placeData);
              callback(place);                         ⎤ Call the callback with a
                                                         place newly constructed
          });                                         ⎦ from the data
      } else {
          callback(place);           ⟵⎤ If the place has already been
      }                                ⎦ loaded, call the callback with
  }                                       the cached place

  if (window.theCrypt === undefined) {
      window.theCrypt = {};
  }
```

Check the cache for the requested place ⟶

Use the Bin Data module to load the data ⟶

```
    theCrypt.map = {
        loadPlace: loadPlace
    };

}) ();
```

The Map Manager is made up of two functions. Let's explore them in turn.

ADDING A PLACE TO THE STORE
The addPlace function uses the Place constructor to create a model from the data; adds items, exits, and challenges; stores the place in the cache; and returns it.

```
function addPlace (placeData) {
    // Create a place model

    // Store place in cache

    // Add items
    // Add exits and challenges

    // Return the new place model
}
```

There's nothing more to say for the function; apart from the cache, you've seen it all before.

LOADING THE DATA FOR A SINGLE PLACE
When you call the loadPlace function, you give it the id of the place you want and a callback function. Your callback will be called with the place model for the id as an argument.

```
callback(place);
```

But where does the loadPlace function get the place model from? First, it tries the cache. If the place isn't there, it loads the place data from JS Bin.

```
var place = placesStore[id];    // Try to get the place from the cache

if (place === undefined) {
    // The place is not in the cache, so
    // load the place data from JS Bin and
    // pass the place to the callback
    callback(place);
} else {
    // The place was in the cache, so
    // pass it to the callback
    callback(place);
}
```

If the loadPlace function has to load the data, it uses the Bin Data module's load function to get it from JS Bin. The place wasn't in the cache, so the code passes the place data to addPlace, to create and store the model, before passing the new place model to the callback.

```
gpwj.data.load(id, function (placeData) {
    var place = addPlace(placeData);    // Create and store a place model
    callback(place);       // Pass the new place model to the callback
});
```

Now you know how the data loading works, you put it to use in the game controller, for loading an initial location and for moving a player to a new location.

20.3.4 *Updating the game controller to use the Map Manager*

You'll need to update two controller methods to make use of the new Map Manager. The init method used to call buildMap to build the whole map for an adventure. Now it will call loadPlace to load only the first place in the game. And because places are no longer preloaded, the go method will need to call loadPlace to retrieve a place from the cache or load it from JS Bin.

The next listing shows the two updated methods in the context of the controller.

Listing 20.9   The game controller using the Map Manager
(http://jsbin.com/vezaza/edit?js)

```
(function () {
  "use strict";

  var player;
  var inPlay = false;

  function init (firstPlaceId, playerName) {                    Use loadPlace to load the
    theCrypt.map.loadPlace(                                     first place in the game
      firstPlaceId, function (firstPlace) {                     and run the init code

        player = new theCrypt.Player(playerName, 50);
        player.addItem("The Sword of Doom");
        player.setPlace(firstPlace);

        inPlay = true;
        render();

    });
  }

  function go (direction) {
    if (inPlay) {
      /* Declare variables */

      if (destination === undefined) {
        renderMessage("There is no exit in that direction");
      } else {
        if ((challenge === undefined) || challenge.complete) {      Load the place to
          theCrypt.map.loadPlace(                                   which the player
            destination, function (place) {                         is moving
              player.setPlace(place);
              render();                                    Once loaded, set the place
          });                                              as the player's location
        } else {                                           and update the display
          // Apply challenge
```

```
        }
      }
    } else {
      renderMessage("The game is over!");
    }
  }

  /* Other functions */                    Assign the public
                                        ◄─┘ interface
  window.game = { ... };

})();
```

The `init` method can't do the bulk of its work until the starting place has been loaded. Most of its code, therefore, is inside the callback function passed to `load-Place`. Similarly, the `go` method gets the place with `loadPlace` before setting it as the player's new location.

20.3.5 Building the game page

All that's left is to import the modules and add a few lines of JavaScript to initialize the game.

The following listing shows the full HTML for the game. The messages `div` and the text box for commands have been moved above the place and player sections.

> **Listing 20.10   The Crypt (HTML)**
>   **(http://jsbin.com/cujibok/edit?html,output)**

```html
<!DOCTYPE html>
<html>
<head>
  <meta charset="utf-8">
  <title>The Crypt</title>
</head>
<body>

  <h1>The Crypt</h1>

  <div id="messages" class="hidden"></div>

  <div id="controls">
    <input type="text" id="txtCommand" />
    <input type="button" id="btnCommand" value="Make it so" />
  </div>

  <div id="views">
    <div id="place"></div>
    <div id="player"></div>
  </div>

  <!-- Templates -->

  <script type="text/x-template" id="itemTemplate">
      <li>{{item}}</li>
  </script>
```

```
<script type="text/x-template" id="playerTemplate">
    <h3>{{name}}</h3>
    <p>{{health}}</p>
    <ol id="playerItems"></ol>
</script>

<script type="text/x-template" id="placeTemplate">
    <h3>{{title}}</h3>
    <p>{{description}}</p>

    <div class="placePanel">
      <h4>Items</h4>
      <ol id="placeItems"></ol>
    </div>

    <div class="placePanel">
      <h4>Exits</h4>
      <ol id="placeExits"></ol>
    </div>
</script>

<script type="text/x-template" id="messageTemplate">
    <p>*** {{message}} ***</p>
</script>

<!-- Modules -->

<!-- gpwj.templates -->
<script src="http://output.jsbin.com/pugase.js"></script>
<!-- gpwj.data -->
<script src="http://output.jsbin.com/guzula.js"></script>

<!-- Place constructor -->
<script src="http://output.jsbin.com/vuwave.js"></script>
<!-- Player constructor -->
<script src="http://output.jsbin.com/nonari.js"></script>

<!-- player view -->
<script src="http://output.jsbin.com/suyona.js"></script>
<!-- place view -->
<script src="http://output.jsbin.com/yoquna.js"></script>
<!-- message view -->
<script src="http://output.jsbin.com/jojeyo.js"></script>

<!-- map manager -->
<script src="http://output.jsbin.com/xesoxu.js"></script>

<!-- game controller -->
<script src="http://output.jsbin.com/vezaza.js"></script>
<!-- Web Page Controls -->
<script src="http://output.jsbin.com/xoyasi.js"></script>
</body>
</html>
```

The next listing shows the JavaScript initialization code. It now specifies the JS Bin code for the data file of the first place in the game.

Listing 20.11   The Crypt
                (http://jsbin.com/cujibok/edit?js,output)

```
var playerName = "Kandra";
var firstPlaceId = "vitewib";

game.init(firstPlaceId, playerName);
```

**Specify the id of the JS
Bin file for the first
place on the map**

20.3.6 *Enter The Crypt*

Fantastic! The templates for the game are organized with the rest of the HTML; if the design needs changing, the templates are easy to find and there's no intertwining of JavaScript, data, and HTML to wrangle. Simpler maintenance, fewer mistakes, and happier designers. Win, win, win!

Now, you just need to survive *The Crypt*. Test your strength, skill, and stamina and play the game on JS Bin at http://output.jsbin.com/cujibok. Good luck!

20.4   *Summary*

- Use XMLHttpRequest objects to load resources for a web page without reloading the whole page.

- Transfer data for your applications using JSON, a lightweight, readable, JavaScript-based data exchange format.

- To load data, create an XMLHttpRequest object, set an event listener for the load event, call the open method with the URL of the resource, and finally call the send method:

```
var xhr = new XMLHttpRequest();
xhr.addEventListener("load", function () {
    // Use xhr.responseText
});
xhr.open("GET", url);
xhr.send();
```

- Access JSON data when the load event has fired via the responseText property of the XHR object.

- Convert the JSON data string into a JavaScript object by passing it to the JSON.parse method:

```
var data = JSON.parse(xhr.responseText);
```

- Use a JavaScript object as a cache. Place loaded data or models into the cache and check the cache before using XHR.

21

Conclusion:
get programming
with JavaScript

This chapter covers

- Carrying on your good work
- Working locally with files
- Books and resources

So, how do you get programming with JavaScript?

Well, you just get programming with JavaScript.

If you really want to understand programming, you have to jump in and write programs. Reading books and pondering code can be fun and informative, but it's trying to solve problems and create code yourself that really builds up your skills, experience, and resilience. But you're not alone. In this chapter you look at ways you can get help if you get stuck on a project or are just curious about how things work. First, you investigate using JavaScript in web pages saved on your own computer, rather than on JS Bin.

21.1 *Working locally with files*

JS Bin and other online coding sites are great for trying out your ideas and checking that your code works. But you want to break out from the sandbox and create your own sites. This section looks at writing and saving your files locally (on your own computer) and opening them in your browser.

21.1.1 *Writing code*

JavaScript and HTML files are just text files. You can write them in any text editor. Notepad for Windows and TextEdit on OS X would both do the job, although they're very basic. More advanced text editors perform syntax highlighting, using colors to differentiate keywords from variables, arguments, strings, and so on, and they perform code completion, suggesting what you might be trying to type and letting you insert the suggestions quickly. Some popular editors are Sublime Text, BBEdit, Notepad++, Atom, and Emacs.

There are also integrated development environments (IDEs) that provide extra tools that let you manage projects, collaborate, track versions, merge files, minify and compress files, and lots more. Examples are Visual Studio, Dreamweaver, Eclipse, and WebStorm. Figure 21.1 shows three editors with increasing levels of project support.

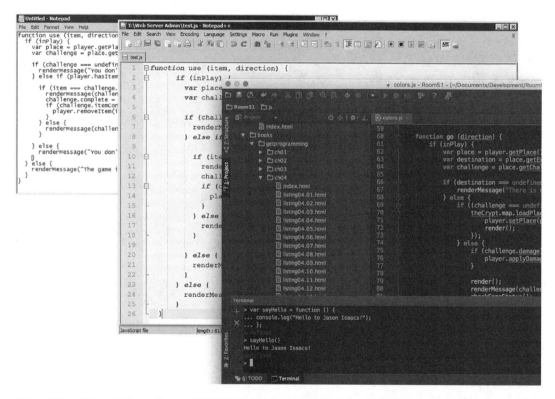

Figure 21.1   Notepad, Notepad++, and WebStorm provide increasing levels of project support.

21.1.2 *Saving files*

Save your files in an organized way, with sensible folders splitting them into types or subprojects. Figure 21.2 shows a possible structure of files for *The Crypt*. There are separate folders for style sheets, JavaScript files, and game maps. The main HTML file is

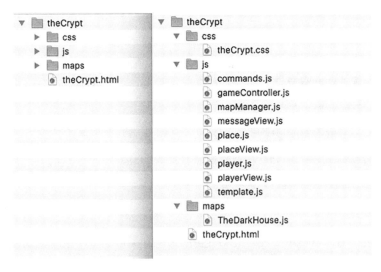

Figure 21.2 A possible structure of folders and files for *The Crypt*

in the root of the project. Various project folders from *Get Programming with JavaScript* are available in its GitHub repository: https://github.com/jrlarsen/GetProgramming.

The files have names that represent their purpose. Just because JS Bin assigns random names to files, that doesn't mean you should. The following listing shows the HTML file for the game with the `script` elements used to load the JavaScript. There's also a `link` element in the `head` section that loads the CSS file that styles the page. The templates have been omitted because they haven't changed.

Listing 21.1 script elements in theCrypt.html

```
<!DOCTYPE html>
<html lang="en">
<head>
    <meta charset="UTF-8">
    <link rel="stylesheet" href="css/theCrypt.css" />        Load the CSS file to set
    <title>The Crypt</title>                                 the styles for the page
</head>
<body>

<h1>The Crypt</h1>

<div id="player"></div>
<div id="place"></div>
<div id="messages"></div>

<p id="controls">
    <input type="text" id="txtCommand">
    <button id="btnCommand">Make it so</button>
</p>
```

```
<!-- Templates -->
    <!-- unchanged - see previous chapters -->
<!-- Modules -->
<script src="maps/TheDarkHouse.js"></script>
<script src="js/mapManager.js"></script>
<script src="js/template.js"></script>
<script src="js/player.js"></script>
<script src="js/place.js"></script>
<script src="js/playerView.js"></script>
<script src="js/placeView.js"></script>
<script src="js/messageView.js"></script>
<script src="js/gameController.js"></script>
<script src="js/commands.js"></script>
</body>
</html>
```

You can use relative paths to load the script files.

The paths used in the `src` attributes to tell the browser where to find the files to load are relative to theCrypt.html. For example, maps/TheDarkHouse.js means "starting from the same folder as theCrypt.html, find the maps folder, and in that folder find the file called TheDarkHouse.js."

21.1.3 *Opening your pages in a browser*

In your browser menu, choose File > Open and browse your filesystem for theCrypt.html. The page should open in the browser.

21.1.4 *Concatenating and minifying files*

If you were hosting your project on a web server for users to access over the internet, it would be better to place all of your JavaScript modules into a single file. For each `script` element, the browser will make a request to the server for the file specified by the `src` attribute. If all of the files are needed to make the application work, then it will be quicker to load one large file rather than many small files.

You can see a version of *The Crypt* on JS Bin with all of the JavaScript in the one bin: http://jsbin.com/xewozi/edit?js,output.

While developing the application, using separate files helps with focus, reuse, and flexibility. But when the time comes to publish the app, merging the files will help the code load more quickly. You can copy the code by hand into a single file, but there are tools to help. They may be a bit advanced for beginners, but if you're interested, look out for Grunt, Gulp, Browserify, and CodeKit.

The tools will also *minify* your code, squashing it down into a smaller file. When the browser runs your JavaScript, it doesn't need the spaces and line breaks that help *you* read the code. It doesn't need well-named variables either; a, b, and c will do the job just as well as `loadData`, `checkGameStatus`, and `renderMessage`. The tools will strip the spaces and rename the variables to create a smaller file that does exactly the same job. The next two listings show the same code, the use function from *The Crypt* controller module.

Listing 21.2 The use function (minified)

```
function r(e,a){if(s){var o=l.getPlace(),i=o.getChallenge(a);void
0===i||i.complete===!0?t("You don't need to use that
there"):l.hasItem(e)?e===i.requires?(t(i.success),i.complete=!0,i.itemConsume
d&&l.removeItem(e)):t(i.failure):t("You don't have that item")}else t("The
game is over!")}
```

Listing 21.3 The use function

```
function use (item, direction) {
    if (inPlay) {
        var place = player.getPlace();
        var challenge = place.getChallenge(direction);

        if (challenge === undefined || challenge.complete === true) {
            renderMessage("You don't need to use that there");
        } else if (player.hasItem(item)) {

            if (item === challenge.requires) {
                renderMessage(challenge.success);
                challenge.complete = true;
                if (challenge.itemConsumed) {
                    player.removeItem(item);
                }
            } else {
                renderMessage(challenge.failure);
            }

        } else {
            renderMessage("You don't have that item");
        }
    } else {
        renderMessage("The game is over!");
    }
}
```

You can probably appreciate that file-size savings can be significant.

21.2 *Getting help*

The fact that you've read this book shows you appreciate guided, organized instruction. Once you're up and running, though, it's great to be able to dip in and out of resources, look things up, and ask for help with specific problems. For reference, a great site is the Mozilla Developer Network (https://developer.mozilla.org) which has documentation and examples for HTML, CSS, JavaScript, and more. For answers to specific questions, join the forums at stackoverflow (http://stackoverflow.com). Members of the community usually answer questions quickly. JavaScript was the first language to reach one million questions asked!

21.3   *What next?*

Get Programming with JavaScript was written as an introduction to programming. Whereas part 1 looked at the building blocks of the JavaScript language, parts 2 and 3 had a greater emphasis on organizing larger projects and getting a taste for things to come. The book was not written as a complete reference but as a practical experience of programming. So where next?

21.3.1   *The companion site*

Articles, tutorials, videos, resources, examples, and links to other support and reference sites will continue to be added to the *Get Programming with JavaScript* website at www.room51.co.uk/books/getProgramming/index.html. Some topics that have been left out of the book, like prototypes, inheritance, working with this, Node.js, and recent additions to JavaScript, will be covered there along with guides to improving the examples from the book, like the quiz app, the fitness app, fitness app news, and My Movie Ratings.

21.3.2   *Books*

There are many, many books on JavaScript. Here are a couple I've read and enjoyed. The first would follow nicely from this one, and the second is a much more in-depth dive into the language:

- *Eloquent JavaScript: A Modern Introduction to Programming* (No Starch Press; 2nd ed., 2014) by Marijn Haverbeke
- *Professional JavaScript for Web Developers* (Wrox; 3rd ed., 2012) by Nicholas C. Zakas

21.3.3   *Sites*

A number of sites mix video tutorials with interactive exercises. One I particularly like is Code School, http://codeschool.com. The folks at Code School have also built a nice introductory JavaScript site at http://javascript.com.

21.3.4   *Practice makes permanent*

Keep practicing. Get on JS Bin and try things out. There are a number of suggestions for projects on the book's website. If you get stuck, feel free to post a question on the book's forum (https://forums.manning.com/forums/get-programming-with-javascript) at Manning.com or join the community at stackoverflow.com.

I hope you've enjoyed working through the book, tinkering with all of the code, making conjectures, and testing out your ideas on JS Bin. Stay curious and *Get Programming with JavaScript!*

21.4 Summary

- Use a text editor to write and save JavaScript and HTML files.
- Organize the files for a project using folders and appropriate filenames.
- Open the HTML files in your browser.
- Find out more and get help at the Mozilla Developer Network and stackover-flow.com.
- Make the most of the resources on the book's website.
- Practice, practice, practice.
- Be curious, adventurous, resilient, and patient. Good luck on your adventures!

index